THE

SHRIVER

REPORT

A Woman's Nation
Pushes Back from the Brink

A Study by Maria Shriver and the Center for American Progress

Edited by Olivia Morgan and Karen Skelton

WITH ROBERTA HOLLANDER, DANIELLA GIBBS LEGER, AND LAUREN VICARY

BECKY BELAND, MELISSA BOTEACH, AND KATIE WRIGHT

 Center for American Progress

 palgrave macmillan

 A Woman's Nation™

THE SHRIVER REPORT: A WOMAN'S NATION PUSHES BACK FROM THE BRINK
Copyright © The Center for American Progress and A Woman's Nation, 2014.

First published in 2014 by PALGRAVE MACMILLAN® in the United States—a division of St. Martin's Press LLC, 175 Fifth Avenue, New York, NY 10010.

Where this book is distributed in the UK, Europe and the rest of the world, this is by Palgrave Macmillan, a division of Macmillan Publishers Limited, registered in England, company number 785998, of Houndmills, Basingstoke, Hampshire RG21 6XS.

Palgrave Macmillan is the global academic imprint of the above companies and has companies and representatives throughout the world.

Palgrave® and Macmillan® are registered trademarks in the United States, the United Kingdom, Europe and other countries.

ISBN: 978-1-137-27974-3

Library of Congress Cataloging-in-Publication Data is available from the Library of Congress.

A catalogue record of the book is available from the British Library.

First edition: February 2014

10 9 8 7 6 5 4 3 2 1

Printed in the United States of America.

JULIE KAAS • Tacoma, Washington

Julie is a preschool teacher who is adjusting to life as a single mother of three teenage boys after her marriage of 25 years ended. Unprepared for her new role as the breadwinner, Julie turned to Washington Women's Employment and Education, or WWEE, for leadership training, "dress for success" courses, technology lessons, and community support. She graduated from the program during the summer of 2013. Julie depends on child support, but she's gaining skills and working toward a job that will give her the financial security and benefits she needs for herself and her sons.

"I dream I will have a job where I can make people feel important and where I will be able to earn enough to keep my home and support myself," she said. "I want to be independent."

Julie's Story

By JULIE KAAS, a 48-year-old part-time preschool teacher and mother of three teenage boys

In August 2012, my marriage ended suddenly after 25 years. It was a shock, but also a relief, because my husband had been angry for years. After he left, it was amazing how there was peace in our house again. But I was scared to death thinking I couldn't make adult decisions, that I wouldn't be able to handle my kids, and that I wouldn't be able to keep a roof over our heads.

Child support covers the payment on our trailer house—but not for too much longer, because my boys are 14, 16, and 18. I can barely pay all the bills. I make $15,000 to $20,000 a year teaching preschool. I know I have to go back to school and change careers. I dream I will get a job where I will be able to earn enough to keep my home and support myself. I want to be independent. My goal is to make $40,000 a year.

I looked up "newly divorced and separated" online and learned about Washington Women's Employment & Education, or WWEE, a nonprofit that helps low-income women learn how to be self-supporting. At first, I was overwhelmed and panicked and bawled the whole way home. But WWEE changed my life.

They taught me computer skills, how to dress professionally, how to interview, and how to write a résumé. They had us examine our strengths, weaknesses, and hang-ups. We looked at lies we had learned to tell ourselves. In my case, I'd told myself I wasn't college material, that I wasn't smart enough, that I was a lovey-dovey nurturing person who would never make it in the work-force. By the end of the course, I had a portfolio, a résumé, and references, as well as the ability and confidence to go on an interview and nail it.

Now I'm going to the WorkSource Center in Tacoma. They're helping me identify what I want to do, where to get training, and how to get financial aid. They treat you like a person, not a number. I'm thinking of going into occupational therapy.

The boys are actually adjusting and doing amazingly well. Right now, my own feelings are pretty good, but in a week or two, I'll have a panic attack. I've never managed my money before, and I've made a few mistakes. But everything's slowly getting better. I'm just getting to the point where I'm confident I'll be fine—that I can go to school, get a decent job, and make it.

Preface

By Neera Tanden

I grew up in a suburb of Boston, the child of two immigrants who had come from India decades earlier. We lived in a house in Bedford, Massachusetts, a quintessential middle-class town. But when I was 5, my parents got divorced and my dad left. My mother was on her own. Having never held a job before, she faced the choice of going back to India or going on welfare to support her two young children. In India, we would have been stigmatized; no one got divorced there in the 1970s. She knew that the children of a divorced woman would have limited life opportunities in India.

So we stayed. We were on welfare. We were on food stamps. And we received Section 8 housing vouchers to help pay the rent. Thanks to a new law in Massachusetts, we were able to use those vouchers to move into an apartment in Bedford and remain in our town's good public schools. My mom eventually got a job as a travel agent and later became a contracts administrator for a defense company. By the time I was 11, she was able to buy her own house in Bedford.

Looking back, I know that whatever success I've achieved in life is thanks to my mother's tenacity and her commitment to giving each of her children a better life. But I also know that she was able to do what she did because of a social safety net that allowed her to get back on her feet. She was lucky to live in a country that says just because you're down, it doesn't mean you're out.

Yet today, our country's commitment to this basic creed is being put to the test. It's harder than ever for many Americans to move up into the middle class and achieve financial security. Too many Americans, particularly women, are struggling to balance their responsibilities at work and at home. And too many women toil away in jobs that don't pay a living wage and don't offer proper benefits. As a result, too many women are living on the brink, unable to achieve their full potential.

These issues are critical to women, but they aren't just "women's issues." By addressing them, we strengthen our families, our economy, and our entire country. That's why as the president of the Center for American Progress, or CAP, I work every day to promote policies that will support women like my mother and ensure that all women are able to give their children the same opportunities my mother gave me.

It's been nearly five years since CAP and *The Shriver Report* first collaborated on *The Shriver Report: A Woman's Nation Changes Everything*, which examined how the rise of women in the workplace is changing the way we work and live. That first report helped spark a national discussion about this profound transformation in American society, and over the past few years, I've been inspired by the growing wave of energy and interest in these issues. In the political sphere, a record number of women were elected to the Senate in 2012, and there is enormous excitement about the prospect of finally electing a woman president. In the media, there's been a vigorous public conversation about women's leadership in the workplace. And in the policy realm, there have been powerful calls for new investments in preschool and child care at the national level.

Now is the time to build on this momentum. We must address the needs of financially vulnerable women to ensure that all women have the stability and security they need to succeed. That's why I'm thrilled that CAP is once again able to collaborate with Maria Shriver on this new report, *A Woman's Nation Pushes Back from the Brink.*

It's true that American women have come a long way. Yet millions are living on the brink, struggling to achieve economic security while also caring for their families. All of the evidence shows that women are much more economically vulnerable than men. For instance, a recent study found that most women probably couldn't come up with $2,000 in 30 days to deal with an emergency. In fact, nearly 70 percent of single mothers and their children are either living in poverty or teetering on the edge. Indeed, women are three times more likely than men to be raising a family on their own, without a partner to pitch in an extra paycheck or parenting time. For women like my mother who struggle as single moms, the safety net often turns out to be a lifeline.

And although most mothers now work outside the home, few jobs provide the paid leave time and flexibility that workers need to be both breadwinners and care-givers. When I was in elementary school, there was no parent at home; luckily, I had an older brother who took care of me after school. But in today's world, par-ents can't even rely on half measures like that. As a result, women and men both face constant conflicts between work and family. These conflicts are especially tough for women, because we still spend more than twice as much time as men caring for children, and more time caring for elderly family members. These care responsibilities force many women to cycle in and out of the workforce, which reduces our pay and makes it harder for us to move up the career ladder.

These care responsibilities force many women to cycle in and out of the workforce, which reduces our pay and makes it harder for us to move up the career ladder.

I learned firsthand about the importance of workplace flexibility when I was rais-ing two young children while working as the policy director on Hillary Clinton's presidential campaign. I have a wonderful husband who truly believes in co-par-enting, but I was able to be successful in my high-pressure job only because I also had an amazing boss who created a culture that respected family responsibilities. That led to some remarkable moments: I remember changing my son's diapers during morning conference calls, but I also remember Hillary reorganizing her schedule so I could go to my daughter's pre-K graduation. Because I worked in a place committed to family-friendly policies, I was able to make it home for dinner most evenings and tuck my children in for bed, before working late into the night. We both knew that what matters is not the exact hours you're at the office, but whether you get the job done. She understood that I wasn't just her employee, but I was also a mother with a family. And she never once gave me less responsibility as a result.

Because of the flexibility I had on the campaign, I was able to grow professionally, and wasn't forced to get off my career track when my children were young. Now

I'm in a leadership position where I can set the workplace policies for my own organization, as well as push for policies to empower more women. But knowing the right policies isn't everything. Tackling the challenges of financial insecurity and work-life conflict will also require kindling a national conversation that places women at the forefront of public debate.

We're the only developed nation that doesn't guarantee mothers paid leave to care for a new child, and we're one of only a few countries that doesn't guarantee workers a right to earn paid sick days.

When it comes to solutions that improve the lives of all women, there is no single silver bullet. Women can use a variety of strategies to better navigate personal and professional challenges. And businesses can provide the flexibility and benefits we need to balance work and care responsibilities, while boosting their own bottom lines.

But as the president of a public policy think tank, I know we also need to put new laws on the books. The United States' workplace and child care policies lag far behind those in other countries. We're the only developed nation that doesn't guarantee mothers paid leave to care for a new child, and we're one of only a few countries that doesn't guarantee workers a right to earn paid sick days. So it shouldn't come as a surprise that most lower-income women don't have access to these benefits. We also lag behind other developed countries when it comes to how much we invest in child care and preschool. As a result, low-income mothers often must choose between paying out of pocket for expensive and often substandard private programs or opting out of work, which can diminish their earning power down the road.

The Center for American Progress has proposed specific ideas to tackle these challenges, including a plan to ensure that every child has access to high-quality preschool. Another plan, called the FAMILY Act, would create a national family and medical leave insurance program that would allow both women and men to take up to 12 weeks of leave with partial wage replacement after the birth or adoption of a child, to provide care for a seriously ill family member, or to recover from their own serious illness. Other promising proposals include the Healthy Families Act, enabling workers to earn up to seven paid sick days a year, and the Working Families Flexibility Act, which would give workers the right to request more flexible work schedules without fear of retaliation. It is our hope that this unique collaboration between CAP and Maria Shriver not only ignites a national conversation, but also spurs real movement on a core set of policy issues.

Policy solutions are critical for progress. But at the end of the day, I know that achieving long-term policy change will also require shifting our culture and attitudes. In order to reform our laws and institutions, women first must recognize that we aren't in this alone; so many of the daily challenges that each of us experiences are also experienced by millions of other women. Today, single mothers face the same struggles my mother faced in the 1970s in Bedford, Massachusetts. As we recognize these connections and commonalities, we will see that these shared challenges aren't inevitable—they are the result of choices that we make as a society.

Once upon a time, people thought illness was purely a personal problem, something we each had to deal with on our own. But now we know better. Now we know that we don't have to accept a world in which you're thrown into bankruptcy by a medical emergency or denied insurance coverage because you're sick. Now we all will have access to health care coverage.

And the same is true for the millions of women living on the brink. Endemic economic insecurity is not inevitable. Work-life conflict is not inevitable. Inadequate and unaffordable child care is not inevitable. These aren't just concerns for each mother or each family. They are national concerns. Because a great country like ours should allow everyone to live to their full potential, and no one should have to sacrifice being a good parent in order to make ends meet.

Americans are now awakening to this realization. We are beginning to understand that things need not be as they have been. And once we are truly roused, our leaders will have to sit up and take notice. I have no doubt that we possess the power to push our way back from the brink.

Contents

How far we've come...

EARNINGS

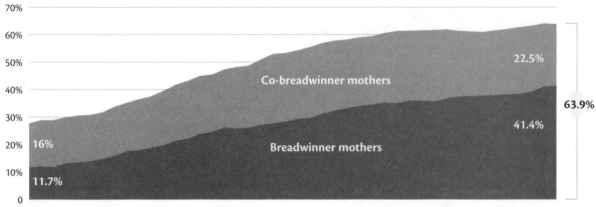

Women are the breadwinners or co-breadwinners in nearly two-thirds of American families

Co-breadwinner mothers

22.5%

16%

11.7%

41.4%

Breadwinner mothers

63.9%

1967 1969 1971 1973 1975 1977 1979 1981 1983 1985 1987 1989 1991 1993 1995 1997 1999 2001 2003 2005 2007 2009

Notes: Breadwinner mothers include single mothers who work and married mothers who earn as much as or more than their husbands. Co-breadwinners are wives who bring home at least 25 percent of the couple's earnings, but less than half. The data only include families with a mother who is between the ages of 18 and 60 and who has children under age 18 living with her.
Source: Heather Boushey and Jeff Chapman's analysis of Miriam King and others, Integrated Public Use Microdata Series, Current Population Survey: Version 2.0 (Minneapolis: Minnesota Population Center, 2009).

CONSUMERS

In recent years, single women accounted for twice as many new home buyers as single men. Women now control more than 20 trillion dollars in global spending.

EDUCATION

Women now outnumber men at every level of the higher education ladder. In 1964, only about 40 percent of women enrolled in any type of college. Today, that figure is 57 percent—there are roughly three million more women currently enrolled in college than men.

EMPLOYMENT

In 1970, fewer than 16 percent of officials and managers in the private sector were women, but by 2007, they made up 40 percent. Women-owned businesses now account for nearly 3 trillion dollars of the gross domestic product in the United States.

...how far we need to go

ON THE BRINK

1 in 3 adult women is living in poverty or on the brink of it.

One-quarter of single mothers spend more than half of their incomes on housing compared to one-tenth of single fathers.

Of all single mothers, nearly two-thirds are working in low-wage retail, service, or administrative jobs that offer little flexibility, benefits, or economic support to both provide for and allow needed family time with children.

MINIMUM-WAGE JOBS

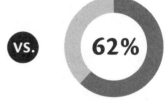

47% vs. **62%**

Percentage of labor force that is female

Percentage of minimum-wage jobs held by women

POOR HEALTH

15% vs. **27%**

Percentage of high-income workforce reporting poor or fair health

Percentage of low-income workforce reporting poor or fair health

HIGH STRESS

22% vs. **42%**

Percentage of low-income men experiencing high levels of stress

Percentage of low-income women experiencing high levels of stress

Definition of 'Living on the Brink'

We call this report *A Woman's Nation Pushes Back from the Brink*. When we refer to "the brink," we are referring to the economic line separating the middle class from the working poor and those people living in absolute poverty. This is the territory in which one in three Americans lives paycheck to paycheck, one incident away from financial crisis. Of these Americans, 70 million are women and the children who depend on them.

The U.S. poverty threshold for a family of four is approximately $23,500 per year.[1] This is an extremely low marker of economic hardship, and over time this threshold has fallen further and further behind what most Americans consider an adequate income to scrape by.

To get a more accurate picture of family economic well-being, researchers have looked into the actual costs to purchase safe housing, food, child care, health care, and other necessary expenses, such as helping an ailing parent or buying appropriate clothes for work or school in communities across the country. What they have found is that across the nation, housing costs eat up between 10 percent and 25 percent of a family's budget.[2] Add to that other necessary expenses and the budget for a family of four in 2013 ranged from $48,144 in Marshall County, Mississippi, to $93,502 in New York City, which averages out to between two and four times the poverty threshold.[3]

Since the U.S. poverty threshold marks the low end of what a family needs, researchers and policymakers often use multiples of the current poverty thresholds, with 200 percent of the poverty line commonly used as the minimum needed for a basic middle-class living standard.

This is consistent with Americans' views on what it costs to make ends meet. In a 2013 Gallup poll, Americans estimated that a family of four would need to earn at least $58,000 per year to get by, which was more than double the U.S. poverty threshold for that family type in 2013.[4] Policymakers have been sensitive to these concerns, and it is because so many families who aren't poor struggle on the brink that the Affordable Care Act provides health insurance subsidies for families with incomes of up to 400 percent of the federal poverty threshold.[5]

Based on this, we define "the brink" as families living below 200 percent of the poverty line—approximately $47,000 per year for a family of four.

ENDNOTES

1   U.S. Department of Health and Human Services, "2013 Poverty Guidelines" (2013), available at http://aspe.hhs.gov/poverty/13poverty.cfm#thresholds.

2   Elise Gould and others, "What Families Need to Get By: The 2013 Update of EPI's Family Budget Calculator" (Washington: Economic Policy Institute, 2013), available at http://www.epi.org/files/2013/ib368-basic-family-budgets.pdf.

3   Ibid.

4   Jeffrey M. Jones, "Public: Family of Four Needs to Earn Average of $52,000 to Get By," Gallup, February 9, 2007, available at http://www.gallup.com/poll/26467/public-family-four-needs-earn-average-52000-get.aspx.

5   Maura Calsyn and Lindsay Rosenthal, "How the Affordable Care Act Helps Young Adults" (Washington: Center for American Progress, 2013), available at http://www.americanprogress.org/wp-content/uploads/2013/05/YoungAdultPremiums1.pdf.

How We Got Here

Why are millions of women doing so well, yet millions more are so financially vulnerable? How could we have evolved so much in the past 50 years, yet at the same time be experiencing historic economic immobility, especially for women? What is it about our nation—our government, businesses, families, and even women themselves—that drives women to the financial brink?

Take a look.

Powerful and Powerless

By Maria Shriver

STUNNING FACT

More than 100 million of us live on or over the brink of poverty or churn in and out of it—and nearly 70 percent of this group are women and the children who depend on them.

Let me state the obvious: I have never lived on the brink. I have never been in foreclosure, never applied for food stamps, never had to choose between feeding my children or paying the rent. I have never feared I'd lose my paycheck when I had to take time off to care for my sick child or parent. I'm not thrown into crisis mode if I have to pay a parking ticket or if the rent or utility bill goes up. If my car breaks down, my life isn't thrown into chaos. I am one of the lucky ones in this country, because I am not stressed about my financial security.

But the fact is, one in three Americans *do* live with this kind of stress, struggle, and anxiety every day. More than 100 million of us live on or over the brink of poverty or churn in and out of it—and nearly 70 percent of this group are women and the children who depend on them. That's almost 42 million women and more than 28 million kids living on the brink.[1]

These are not women who are wondering if they can "have it all." These are women who are already *doing* it all—working hard, providing, parenting, and care-giving. They're doing it all, yet they and their families can't prosper, and that's weighing the U.S. economy down. Finding out why that is and what we as a nation can do about it is the mission of this report. This is a national reality check.

The fact that more than 70 million women and kids live on the brink today in our nation, the most powerful country in the world, is the kind of stark fact that drove my parents into action.

You see, I am the child of two social innovators, two architects of change—a man and a woman who imagined a better America, a more conscious, caring, compassionate America, and then went out and tried to make it a reality. Neither one of them held elective office, but each felt a profound spiritual calling to right what they saw as social injustice.

Fifty years ago, President Lyndon B. Johnson envisioned the Great Society and called for a War on Poverty, naming my father, Sargent Shriver, the architect of that endeavor. My dad and his team at the Office of Economic Opportunity conceived, created, and implemented a suite of powerful public programs such as Head Start, VISTA, Job Corps, Legal Services to the Poor, and Foster Grandparents—all still operating today.

Back then, the phrase "poverty in America" came with images of poor children in Appalachian shacks and inner-city alleys. It was "them" and "us." But President Johnson's War on Poverty shocked Americans into awareness and then national outrage that said: "Not here! Not in America. We can't have this kind of poverty in the greatest country on earth!" And the

As the architect of the War on Poverty, Sargent Shriver helped cut the official poverty rate 42 percent in just one decade. His passion for economic prosperity had a powerful, lasting impact on the United States. {PAUL CONKLIN, PHOTO COURTESY WWW.SARGENTSHRIVER.ORG}

War on Poverty, alongside strong and shared economic growth, cut the official poverty rate a striking 42 percent over the next decade—from 19.5 percent down to 11.1 percent[2]—despite the fact that the nation's attention and resources were eventually diverted to another war, the one in Vietnam.

My mother, Eunice Kennedy Shriver, fought a different war. Although she came from one of the most powerful families in America, she made it her life's work to help the powerless.

In the 1960s, she decided that people with intellectual disabilities like her sister Rosemary, who were treated so unfairly and unjustly, deserved to have full lives. She believed they didn't belong in institutions and could live at home, go to school, and have fun competing on playing fields. To prove her point, she started a summer day camp in our backyard, which eventually grew into the global Special Olympics movement—permanently changing the world for the millions of people with intellectual disabilities and transforming the way the world saw them.

My mother took her campaign to the top, where the power was: from every state capital to every world capital, from the halls of Congress to her brother in the White House. She pushed for the creation of the first President's Council on Mental Retardation. She pressed the National Institutes of Health to create an Institute on Child Health and Human Development, which now bears her name. She changed the world for people with intellectual disabilities and their families with her passion, her drive, her relentless energy—and her understanding of where power resided and how to use it.

Throughout my life, I watched my mother navigate through the nexus of power in politics, sports, philanthropy, business, faith, and her family, and it made me think a lot about power and powerlessness.

About a year before she died, I sat outside with her on a sunny day. I was her only daughter, and she had pushed me to believe I could do anything my four brothers could do. I looked at my mother, frail at the age of 87, and started thinking of all she had accomplished in her life. At the time, my husband was the governor of California and I was first lady—a job that brought a certain amount of acclaim, visibility, and, yes, power to make an impact.

I said to her, "Mummy, you've had so much success in your life. When you look back, aren't you proud of all you've been able to do?"

She was quiet for a moment and then said, "No, not really."

I was shocked. "How you can you say that? You built the world's biggest organization for people with intellectual disabilities. You've changed laws, you've changed attitudes, you've changed lives all over the world. You had a great marriage and raised five kids who've been inspired by you and done well. How could you *not* regard yourself as a success?"

She said, "Of course, I'm proud of my children and my marriage." I'll never forget what she said next: "But I never had any *real* power. I never ran for office, and *that's* where the power is. If I'd run for office, I would have had the power to make the changes I really wanted to make."

Wow. Here was my mother—a woman so smart, so savvy, so accomplished, so honored, and yet somehow she didn't perceive herself as powerful? How could that be?

I believe it was because my mother was raised in a patriarchal family where the message was, "Run for office, and you get the power to change the world." The power was in the office, not in the person, and the power to run for office was in the men. In my mother's time, women almost never ran for office, just like they never became steelworkers. So she never achieved elective office and therefore thought she wasn't powerful enough. This despite the fact that she was the only living woman ever put on the U.S. silver dollar, despite the fact that she was awarded the Presidential Medal of Freedom, and despite the fact that she was a hero and an inspiration to millions around the world.

If *she* felt that way, imagine how women feel who are without her resources, without her opportunities, without her visibility. In my work I have met, talked with, and listened to so many of these women, who have told me they not only feel powerless—they feel invisible.

They say you can't help but feel powerless and invisible when you're working at a job eight or more hours a day and still can't make ends meet. You feel powerless and invisible when you can't get help with child support from the man who fathered your kids. You feel powerless when you can't get any flexibility in your schedule so you can take off a few hours to take your kid to the doctor or care for your parent who has Alzheimer's. You feel invisible when your employer is oblivious and doesn't even understand why you're asking for that flexibility in the first place. They've told me they feel not only powerless and invisible, but also *hopeless* when they don't see their elected officials implementing policies that would help them work and help them make their own lives more manageable.

Washington Women's Employment and Education, or WWEE, offers pre-employment assistance classes in Tacoma, Washington to help women with behaviors and attitudes that keep them from success. Programs like this help participants gain the hope and confidence to make healthy changes in their lives. {BARBARA KINNEY}

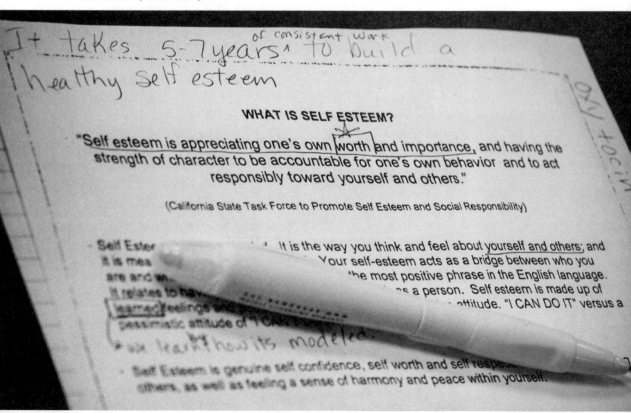

It takes 5-7 years of consistant work to build a healthy self esteem

WHAT IS SELF ESTEEM?

"Self esteem is appreciating one's own worth and importance, and having the strength of character to be accountable for one's own behavior and to act responsibly toward yourself and others."

(California State Task Force to Promote Self Esteem and Social Responsibility)

- Self Ester   • It is the way you think and feel about yourself and others; and
  It is mea   Your self-esteem acts as a bridge between who you
  are and w   the most positive phrase in the English language.
  It relates to hav   s a person. Self esteem is made up of
  learned feelings   attitude. "I CAN DO IT" versus a
  pessimistic attitude of

• we learn how its modeled

• Self Esteem is genuine self confidence, self worth and self respe   others, as well as feeling a sense of harmony and peace within yourself.

For the millions of American women who feel this way, the dream of "having it all" has morphed into "just hanging on." Everywhere they look, every magazine cover and talk show and website tells them women are supposed to be feeling more "empowered" than ever, but the truth is, they don't feel empowered. They feel exhausted.

Which brings me to *The Shriver Report.* For the past several years, these reports have been tracking the status of women in this country. They grew out of my work as first lady of California.

When I became first lady, I decided to use my experience as a reporter to find out how California's families were doing, what they needed, and how I could be of service. I traveled the state and saw firsthand that millions of low-income working families were struggling to combine breadwinning and caregiving. I saw firsthand that so many of them didn't know anything about the public programs designed specifically to help them. I saw firsthand how much good can happen when the private sector worked with the public sector—and how individuals could be powerful agents of support and change.

For instance, while I was first lady, I developed WE Connect, a public-private partnership working with organizations in underserved communities to connect families to resources, including the state's Healthy Families Program, Supplemental Nutrition Assistance Program (formerly food stamps), energy assistance, and the federal Earned Income Tax Credit, which puts money back in their pockets—money they spend on their families, their bills, and out in their communities. It's estimated that to date, WE Connect has helped connect more than 20 million Californians to programs promoting healthier and more financially independent lives.[3] In fact, its success has inspired us to create the Shriver Corps of volunteers that we're presenting in this report.

In 2004, I started producing the California Governor's Conference on Women. The Conference ballooned into an annual gathering of 35,000 women from every walk of life—foster-care graduates, students, teachers, homemakers, public servants, blue-collar workers, businesswomen, and CEOs. These women were hungry for information and inspiration, eager to talk about the obstacles they faced and the experiences they had. They wanted help with managing and succeeding in their various and shifting roles in the family and society. Corporations also came, hungry themselves to learn how they could adapt to a changing America. That's when I decided to dig deeper into the change I was seeing—quantify it, examine it, and find out what it meant for American women and men. The result was *The Shriver Report*.

In 2009, the first *Shriver Report* analyzed the seismic shift in our culture in partnership with the Center for American Progress. We reported that for the first time in U.S. history, women had become fully half the workforce[4] and, even more momentous, mothers were now about two-thirds of the primary and co-breadwinners in American families[5]—truly the engine driving the economy. We called this new state of American affairs *A Woman's Nation Changes Everything,* because the explosion of women becoming breadwinners changed not just the economy, but marriage, families, schools, the workplace, government, health care—everything, including men. As a result, the U.S. House of Representatives called a rare bipartisan subcommittee hearing to discuss *The Shriver Report*'s findings.

Then the following year, *The Shriver Report* focused on women as caregivers. *A Woman's Nation Takes on Alzheimer's* was the largest study ever to examine the cultural, social, and economic impact of the Alzheimer's epidemic—just as the nation's 78 million Baby Boomers were moving into their mid-60s, straight into Alzheimer's territory. We reported that women were not only half the people living with the disease, but also more than half the country's unpaid caregivers.[6] As a result of the report, the Alzheimer's Association experienced a 244 percent increase in people signing up for clinical trials.

It's no longer "us" and "them." The bright lines separating the middle class from the working poor and the working poor from those in absolute poverty have blurred.

Now it's 2014, and we're still A Woman's Nation all right, and tens of millions of women are struggling with their dual roles as breadwinners and caregivers, struggling all the way to the brink. Millions of them are providers without partners, finding themselves invisible to a government that doesn't have policies and practices that can help support and strengthen them in their multiple roles.

So 50 years after the War on Poverty, it's no longer "us" and "them." The bright lines separating the middle class from the working poor and the working poor

MarQuita Jennings, a mother of five, is a long-term employee of the Chambliss Center for Children in Chattanooga, Tennessee. She is married, and although her family has two incomes, she still worries about unexpected financial challenges that may throw her family off track.
{BARBARA KINNEY}

from those in absolute poverty have blurred. The new iconic image of the economically insecure American is a working mother dashing around getting ready in the morning, brushing her kid's hair with one hand and doling out medication to her own aging mother with the other. She's run ragged, and she's running scared. She knows she's just a single incident—one broken bone, one broken-down car, one missed paycheck—away from the brink. And she's not crazy to feel that way:

• Women are nearly two-thirds of minimum-wage workers in this country.[7]

• More than 70 percent of low-wage workers get no paid sick days at all.[8]

• Forty percent of all households with children under the age of 18 include mothers who are either the sole or primary source of income.[9]

• American women are approximately half of all workers in this country, but the average woman earns only 77 percent of what the average man makes, and women of color earn even less.[10]

The American Dream that for decades jet-propelled so many women into the workforce and a hopeful future has disappeared over the horizon and out of sight. It feels like a breach of contract. It feels like the promise of the Dream has been broken.

The promise that a woman could go to work and feel fulfilled and financially independent? Broken. The promise that working would enable her not only to help support her family but also help her to afford a better home and a second car, not to mention pay off the big fat college loan? Broken. The promise that she could provide her kids with a ticket onto the American Dream trajectory, too? For millions of women, that's another promise that's been broken, and they feel powerless to do anything about it.

So in this third *Shriver Report*, we're drilling down for some answers to the questions we women should be asking ourselves now:

What *is* it with us that we've never been in a position where we've had more impact on this society, yet tens of millions of us are living on the brink?

Is it the jobs we choose that keep us insecure? Do we naturally gravitate toward the health care, home care, education, and public-sector jobs that don't pay enough, but may give us some of the flexibility we need to wear all of our hats?

Is it the children we love? Is it our maternal instinct—the desire or need to be caregivers and therefore available at home—that impels us to choose lower-rung jobs that let us take care of our kids? Or is it the "Mommy Penalty"—bosses not hiring women with kids, or if they do, paying them less, because they believe these women can't possibly be totally productive, focused, or committed to their work?

Is it the men we love, whom we think couldn't/wouldn't/shouldn't do the caregiving that has to be done, so we don't even ask them?

Or is it because we don't know how to negotiate for what we need in the workplace? Or because our nation's labor laws are outdated, allowing our employers to stick to pay and benefits policies that keep us from prospering?

Is it because so many of us choose motherhood without marriage, and it's just plain impossible to keep away from the economic brink on one paycheck alone?

Or is it because we automatically go along with that old patriarchal propaganda that a woman doesn't deserve to earn as much as a man for the same job? Do we anesthetize ourselves by thinking, "Men have always had the power, and I can't change it"?

What *does* power mean to women anyway? I've learned that many women feel potent and in control if they can make enough money and at the same time fulfill the multiple roles they love—good parent, good partner, good caregiver, good employee, and good citizen. They feel powerful and fulfilled when they're able to control their schedules and get help when they need it—at home, at work, and in the community.

What has to change so that women who work that hard can make a better life for their families? What has to change so that women can hold their heads up high and stop teetering on the brink?

What has to change? *We* have to change, and we can. We are *A Woman's Nation,* and it's time to *Push Back from the Brink.*

We must recognize that our government programs, business practices, educational system, and media messages don't take into account a fundamental truth: This nation cannot have sustained economic prosperity and well-being until women's new, central role is recognized and women's economic health is used as a measure—perhaps it should be *the* measure—to shape common-sense policies and priorities for the 21st century.

In other words, leave out the women, and you don't have a full and robust economy. Lead with the women, and you do. It's that simple, and Americans know it. In our polling, more than 70 percent of Americans say women's financial contribution to our national economy is essential.[12]

In this third *Shriver Report,* we're not just talking about how we got here. We're also proposing a new social contract built around the reality of the new American family—a social compact based on care, compassion, and consciousness. We need to be conscious that these aren't just women's issues. It's not just women who need child support. It's not just women who need flexible hours. It's not just women who need to take care of elderly parents, not just women who need better wages, sick leave, and health care. It's not just women who need Life Ed, a new program we're proposing in our Personal Solutions chapter. It's not just women who will benefit from updating, restructuring, and redesigning our laws, our business practices, our workplaces, and our culture. Children will. Men will. We all will.

Carmen Rios helped established the "companera" program at the Canal Alliance in San Rafael, California. As a "companera," Carmen provides labor and delivery coaching to low-income, Spanish-speaking clients. Her job, like those at so many small nonprofits, entails long hours with low pay. {BARBARA RIES}

Yes, there's still sexism. Yes, after all these years, there haven't been enough cracks to break the glass ceiling wide open. But neither has there been enough focus on building a firm foundation on which women and their kids can stand. We can help get that foundation built, if we come together.

But the truth is that for so long, America's women have been divided: women who are mothers versus women who are not, women who work at home versus women who work outside the home, those who are married versus those who aren't, pro-life women versus pro-choice, white women versus women of color, Democrat versus Republican, gay versus straight, and young versus old. It feels like the last issue where women came together was fighting for a woman's right to vote!

The Shriver Report offers the blueprint for a new way forward.

We've convened the most innovative and influential thought leaders, academics, and professionals working in the trenches on these issues. We've asked them to propose creative, innovative, and practical ideas for getting the modern American family back on solid financial ground. We are presenting workable **public, private, and personal solutions** to these problems, because it will take all three—government, businesses, and the American people ourselves—to achieve a new way forward.

You'll also hear from women who are living in economic distress right now and women who used to, but got the help they needed and did what they had to do to build economic stability for their families. Their stories are inspirational.

Our groundbreaking, bipartisan poll of 3,500 adults, conducted in partnership with AARP by the firms Greenberg Quinlan Rosner Research and TargetPoint Consulting, provides an often surprising snapshot of how Americans feel about the economy, gender, marriage, education, the future—and what, if anything, we should do when so many American women and their families are living in economic jeopardy.

Here are some highlights from those poll respondents who are women living on or over the brink of poverty or dipping in and out of it:

• Seventy-five percent of them wish they had put a higher priority on their education and career (compared to 58 percent of all those we polled).

• Seventy-three percent of them wish they had made better financial choices (as did 65 percent of all those we polled).

• A whopping 74 percent of these women say their own parents were married—exactly the same percentage as the general population.

• But they themselves are less likely to be married—only 37 percent of them are married (compared to 49 percent of all the men and women we polled).

• Only 18 percent of those low-income women who are divorced *regret* not staying married.

• Thirty percent of those with children wished they had delayed having kids or had fewer of them.

These women also told us that they feel political and business leaders and people in the community don't understand them, so they feel invisible or judged by old stereotypes. They might be surprised to know we found that public opinion is on their side:

Jeannie James of Winslow, Arizona, works hard to provide for her two grown children and three young grandchildren. With no work available in her city, she commutes by both car and bus for four hours each day to get to and from her job. The high cost of transportation means she often has to spend the night away from home. {JAN SONNENMAIR}

• Seventy-three percent of Americans said that, in order to raise the incomes of working women and their families, they strongly favor the government ensuring that women get equal pay for equal work.

- Seventy-nine percent of Americans said the government should expand access to high-quality, affordable child care for working families.

- Almost 60 percent of Americans said women raising children on their own face tremendous challenges and should be helped financially by government, employers, and communities.

Like it or not, the American social landscape has dramatically transformed. The typical American family isn't what it used to be. Only a fifth of our families have a male breadwinner and a female homemaker.[13] Some of us may wish that weren't so, but that's our modern American reality. Businesses haven't adjusted to it, and government hasn't either.

The solutions we need today are also different. We don't need a new New Deal, because the New Deal was an all-government solution and that's not enough anymore. And my father's War on Poverty isn't enough anymore either. As my dad said, the battle should be "fought by those who are not afraid to question, analyze and criticize the relevancy of the programs."[14] I believe now is the time for the kind of questioning and innovation he fought for.

Yes, the country has changed, and we women were the ones who changed it. But let's ask ourselves this: Did we really fight so hard to go out in the world and work, only to be told that the job we fought for doesn't pay us the same as it pays a man? Did we really fight for the right to vote, so Washington could be a men's club that dangles family-friendly promises before us and then yanks them away? Did we really fight for the right to have our own checkbooks, earn our own living, make our own choices, and leave a bad marriage—only to see millions of working single mothers disparaged and scapegoated in public and political discourse for the ills of the nation?

We women can recognize our enormous power, from political power to purchasing power:

- Politicians knock themselves out wooing us, because we're a majority of voters in this country.[15]

- Every corporate marketer and advertiser is after us and our money. We make as much as 70 percent of this country's consumer decisions[16] and more than 80 percent of the health care decisions.[17] We support the multibillion-dollar food, fashion, and beauty industries and buy more than half the cars.[18]

We can exert real pressure on our country and our corporations to change course on many of the issues we care about. For instance, isn't it strange that the United States is the only industrialized nation without a child care policy enabling more women to work more? If America wants the economy firing on all cylinders, it needs women working and earning a living wage. Why aren't we doing everything we can to make that happen?

And while we're at it, how about those of us women who aren't in jeopardy? Do *we* pay the women *we* hire a living wage to help them with child care and elder care— pay it, not because it's the law, but because it's fair? Do *we* give them flexibility when they need to take time for caregiving? If we run businesses, do we educate our workers about public policies and programs that can help them? And can we please stop throwing darts at other women for the choices they've made, the lives they lead, and the struggles they're in? Can we stop judging? As one single mother told me, "You should never judge a woman just from her present circumstance. You never know where that woman is going, and you don't know where she's been."

Which brings me back to my mother. She attributed much of her success to the men in her family, the men she worked with, and the men who held elected office. She didn't realize that those men were in awe of her, even afraid of her. It was her own relentless energy, her intelligence, her drive, creativity, and passion, her prodigious ability to persuade, inspire, and lead that gave her the power. But she didn't truly feel it. She didn't realize that so very often, the most powerful person in the room was, in fact, Eunice Kennedy Shriver. That's a lesson for me—and for all of us women.

Let us realize that *we* are the solution. The real power is in *us*. We are the heart of the families that are the heart of America. We are the caregivers, the collabora- tors and connectors, the consensus-builders and the community-makers. We keep everything going, and we keep it all together. We are the consumer spending engine that makes the economy hum. No group has more unharnessed power. The question is: Are we "man" enough to use it? I believe we are.

I'm so inspired by the optimism and determination of the women on the brink I met and talked to for this *Shriver Report*. They told me they are certain that if we

In 1984, President Ronald Reagan presented Eunice Shriver with the Presidential Medal of Freedom, America's highest civilian award for public service. {COURTESY WWW.EUNICEKENNEDYSHRIVER.ORG}

just saw them, knew how hard they work, and knew their hopes for their children, that we as a nation would *care*. I asked one single mother, what's the most important message she would tell us?

She said, "Please don't count us out!"

We Americans, both women and men, have the power to count them *in*. By pushing back and by putting into practice the solutions we're proposing in *The Shriver Report*, we can re-ignite the American Dream—for ourselves, for our daughters and sons, for our mothers and fathers, and for our nation. We have the power—not just to launch a new War on Poverty but a new campaign for equity, for visibility, for fairness, for worth, and for care.

I believe individuals really can change the world. If we harness our imagination, our innovation, and our optimism, we can do this. And we can do it now.

To that end, I dedicate this report to my parents. Their name is on it, too.

THINK ABOUT THIS

Seventy-four percent of women living on or over the brink say their own parents were married—exactly the same percentage as the general population. But only 37 percent of them are married themselves.

ENDNOTES

1 U.S. Census Bureau, *Current Population Survey: Poverty* (U.S. Department of Commerce, 2012), available at http://www.census.gov/hhes/www/cpstables/032013/pov/pov01_200.htm.

2 http://www.census.gov/hhes/www/poverty/data/historical/hstpov2a.xls

3 WE Connect, "New WE Connect Tool Helps Californians Navigate Health Care Reform and Other Programs," Press release, February 1, 2013, available at http://www.weconnect.net/index.php/newsroom-2/153-february2013/430-february-1-2013.

4 U.S. Bureau of Labor Statistics, *Women in the Labor Force: A Databook*, Report 1026 (U.S. Department of Labor, 2010), available at http://www.bls.gov/cps/wlf-databook2010.htm.

5 Heather Boushey, "The New Breadwinners." In Heather Boushey and Ann O'Leary, ed., *The Shriver Report: A Woman's Nation Changes Everything* (Washington: Center for American Progress and A Woman's Nation, 2009), p. 37, Figure 2.

6 Alzheimer's Association, unpublished data from the National Alliance for Caregiving/AARP 2009 survey of caregiving in the United States, prepared under contract by Matthew Greenwald and Associates, 2010.

7 National Women's Law Center, "Fair Pay for Women Requires Increasing the Minimum Wage and Tipped Minimum Wage" (2013), available at http://www.nwlc.org/resource/fair-pay-women-requires-increasing-minimum-wage-and-tipped-minimum-wage.

8 U.S. Bureau of Labor Statistics, *Employee Benefits in the United States—March 2012*, (U.S. Department of Labor, 2012), Table 5.

9 Wendy Wage, Kim Parker, and Paul Taylor, "Breadwinner Moms," (Washington: Pew Research Center, 2013), available at http://www.pewsocialtrends.org/2013/05/29/breadwinner-moms.

10 Carmen DeNavas-Walt, Bernadette D. Proctor, and Jessica C. Smith, *Income, Poverty, and Health Insurance Coverage in the United States: 2012* (U.S. Department of Commerce, 2013), available at http://www.census.gov/2013pubs/p60-245.pdf, Table 4.

11 National Women's Law Center, "Modest Recovery Largely Leaves Women Behind" (2011), available at http://www.nwlc.org/sites/default/files/pdfs/slowrecoveryfactsheetaug2011.pdf.

12 Greenberg Quinlan Rosner Research, in collaboration with the Center for American Progress and *The Shriver Report*, contacted 3,500 adults by landline and mobile telephone from August 21 through September 11, 2013, for the Open Field Foundation Frequency Questionnaire. Telephone numbers were chosen randomly and in accordance with random-digit-dial, or RDD, methodology. The survey included oversamples of 250 African American (574 in the total sample) and 250 Hispanic adults (501 in the total sample) to allow for more detailed subgroup analysis. The sample was adjusted to census proportions of sex, race or ethnicity, age, and national region. The margin of sampling error for adults is plus or minus 1.7 points. For smaller subgroups, the margin of error may be higher. Survey results may also be affected by factors such as question wording and the order in which questions were asked. The interviews were conducted in English and Spanish.

13 U.S. Bureau of Labor Statistics, "Table 4. Families with own children: Employment status of parents by age of youngest child and family type, 2011–2012 annual averages," available at http://www.bls.gov/news.release/famee.t04.htm. (last accessed month 2013).

14 Sargent Shriver, Address to the National Conference of Catholic Charities Annual Convention, New Orleans, October 12, 1966.

15 U.S. Census Bureau, *Voting and Registration in the Election of November 2012—Detailed Tables* (U.S. Department of Commerce, 2012), available at http://www.census.gov/hhes/www/socdemo/voting/publications/p20/2012/tables.html.

16 Michael Silverstein and Kate Sayre, *Women Want More: How to Capture Your Share of the World's Largest, Fastest-Growing Market* (Boston Consulting Group, 2009).

17 U.S. Department of Labor, "General Facts on Women and Job-Based Health," available at http://www.dol.gov/ebsa/newsroom/fshlth5.html (last accessed October 2013).

18 Ekaterina Walter, "The Top 30 Stats You Need to Know When Marketing to Women," The Next Web, January 24, 2012, available at http://thenextweb.com/socialmedia/2012/01/24/the-top-30-stats-you-need-to-know-when-marketing-to-women.

'When We Were 9, We Were Honest'

By CAROL GILLIGAN, world-renowned psychologist and writer and a current professor at New York University. Her groundbreaking work on women's development, **In a Different Voice,** *was called "the little book that started a revolution." Her research on girls led* **TIME** *magazine to name her one of the 25 most influential Americans. Her most recent book is* **Joining the Resistance,** *where she writes, "The time to act is now."*

I am excited that *A Woman's Nation Pushes Back from the Brink* focuses attention on women's power to create a more just and caring society. The data presented in this report pose a conundrum: At a time when women constitute half the nation's workforce, earn a majority of college and advanced degrees, and are the majority of the country's breadwinners, caregivers, consumers, and voters, why are women and the children who depend on them 70 percent of the more than 100 million Americans living in poverty, near poverty, or going in and out of poverty? On the face of it, it doesn't make sense. Since women are a majority of the voting population, what stands in the way of using our voices and claiming our power to change this situation?

In my book *In a Different Voice,* I write about the power of the word "selfish." I hear women criticize themselves as being selfish for responding to their own desires and perceptions, while considering it good to be "selfless"—responsive to others and seemingly without a voice of their own. I also describe women recognizing that their efforts to render themselves selfless are in fact morally problematic, signifying an abdication of their own voices and an evasion of responsibility and relationship. As more and more women realize, to give up one's voice is to give up on relationship—on the possibility of living in genuine connection with others.[1]

Which brings me to my research with girls, the most illuminating work I have done. I viscerally remember the frank and fearless voices of preadolescent girls. When a newspaper article described the research as helping girls "find their voices," the 9- and 10-year-olds in the project commented: "We have our voices." And they do! Shrewd in their perceptions and discerning about when and to whom they will say what they see, girls are astute readers of the human world around them. In a discussion about whether it is ever good to tell a lie, Elise, 11 years old and a sixth-grader in an urban public school, said, "My house is wallpapered with lies."

What happens to this voice? At the end of a five-year study of girls ages 7 to 18, I asked them how they wanted to be involved, now that we were presenting our findings and preparing to publish them in a book. The 13-year-olds—who were 9 when the study began—responded without hesitation: "We want you to tell them everything we said, and we want our names in the book." But then Tracy, anticipating coming upon her 9-year-old self in a book, said, "When we were 9, we were stupid." I said it would never have occurred to me to use the word "stupid," because what struck me most about them when they were 9 was how much they knew. "I mean," Tracy said, "when we were 9, we were honest." Between 9 and 13, an honest voice came to seem or to sound stupid.[2]

How does this happen? Over and over again, I have heard adolescent girls describe the pressures they have felt and the incentives they were given to dismiss an honest voice as stupid, to hear it as crazy, or to judge it as bad or selfish or wrong. Iris explained, "If I were to say what I was

The startling discovery of my research was many girls' ability to see this. Coming of age, they faced a crisis of connection where having a voice jeopardized relationships and not having a voice meant not being in relationship. My eye was caught by girls' resistance to losing their voices and giving up on relationships and also by the force brought to bear on their resistance—the seeming investment of others and of society at large in their capitulation. To be included and found acceptable in the eyes of the world often hinged on not saying what they saw, not listening to what they heard, and not knowing what they knew.[4]

"The voice that stands up for what I believe in has been buried deep inside me," 16-year-old

> A voice of integrity and conviction resides within us.
> It may have been silenced, but it is not lost. This is the
> voice of love and the voice of democratic citizenship.

feeling and thinking, no one would want to be with me. My voice would be too loud." And then she added, "But you have to have relationships." I agreed and asked, "But if you are not saying what you are feeling and thinking, then where are *you* in these relationships?" Iris saw the paradox: She gave up relationship in order to have relationships, muting her voice so that she could be with other people. The move is adaptive—Iris was the valedictorian of her high school class and was admitted to the competitive college that was her first choice—but it was psychologically incoherent.[3]

Tanya said, and her observation is a reminder to women: A voice of integrity and conviction resides within us. It may have been silenced, but it is not lost. This is the voice of love and the voice of democratic citizenship.[5]

My research on girls' development has now been joined by my studies of boys. Boys also come under pressure to bury parts of themselves—those aspects of themselves gendered as "feminine"—meaning their tenderness, their vulnerability, and their capacity for empathy, cooperation, and care.[6] When adolescent girls

Madie Winans, 10, and her sister Aubrey, 16, wait for their mother Allie to finish cooking dinner. The girls live with both of their parents in Missoula, Montana. {AMI VITALE}

say "I don't know" to cover what they do know and boys say "I don't care" to conceal what they do care about, they are following a path that will lead us over the brink. But as the healthy body resists infection, the healthy psyche resists dissociation. It resists not knowing and not caring.

It is patriarchy, not nature, that characterizes men as the victors and women as the losers, men as independent and women as dependent, men as powerful and women as powerless, calling these qualities "masculine" and "feminine." Within ourselves, we know this is a lie. *A Woman's Nation* will push back from the brink when women do not dismiss an honest voice as stupid or crazy, when women do not disavow truth in the name of goodness, when we do not abandon ourselves or other women, and when we do not dissociate ourselves from our humanity.

REFERENCES

The studies of girls discussed in this essay were part of the Harvard Project on Women's Psychology and Girls' Development from 1981 to 1991. Project researchers interviewed girls from private and public schools and initiated intervention programs, including the Women Teaching Girls/Girls Teaching Women retreats, the Women and Race retreats, and the Strengthening Healthy Resistance and Courage in Girls project.

Brown, Lyn Mikel, and Carol Gilligan. 1992. *Meeting at the Crossroads: Women's Psychology and Girls' Development*. Cambridge, MA: Harvard University Press.

Gilligan, Carol. 2011. *Joining the Resistance*. Cambridge, UK: Polity Press.

Gilligan, Carol, Nona P. Lyons, and Trudy Hanmer, eds. 1990. *Making Connections: The Relational Worlds of Adolescent Girls at Emma Willard School*. Cambridge, MA: Harvard University Press.

Gilligan, Carol, Annie G. Rogers, and Deborah Tolman. 1991. *Women, Girls, and Psychotherapy: Reframing Resistance*. Binghamton, NY: Haworth Press.

Taylor, Jill McLean, Carol Gilligan, and Amy Sullivan. 1995. *Between Voice and Silence: Women and Girls, Race and Relationships*. Cambridge, MA: Harvard University Press.

ENDNOTES

1   Carol Gilligan, *In a Different Voice: Psychological Theory and Women's Development* (Cambridge, MA: Harvard University Press, 1982).

2   Lyn Mikel Brown and Carol Gilligan, *Meeting at the Crossroads: Women's Psychology and Girls' Development* (Cambridge, MA: Harvard University Press, 1992).

3   Carol Gilligan, *The Birth of Pleasure: A New Map of Love, Part II* (New York: Alfred A. Knopf, 2002), chapter "Regions of Lights."

4   Brown and Gilligan, *Meeting at the Crossroads*; Gilligan, *The Birth of Pleasure*; Carol Gilligan, *Joining the Resistance* (Cambridge, UK: Polity Press, 2011).

5   Brown and Gilligan, *Meeting at the Crossroads*; Gilligan, *Joining the Resistance*.

6   Gilligan, *The Birth of Pleasure, Part II*; Judy Chu and Carol Gilligan, *When Boys Become Boys: Development, Masculinity, and Relationships* (New York: New York University Press, 2014); and Niobe Way, *Deep Secrets: Boys' Friendships and the Crisis of Connection* (Cambridge, MA: Harvard University Press, 2013).

NIKKI BROWN • Chattanooga, Tennessee

When she was 20, Nikki dropped out of college to take a high-paying job with General Motors, but she was laid off. She went back and finished school, becoming a registered dental assistant. She earns $13 an hour and works 32 hours a week, putting her and her two children just above the poverty line. With everyday expenses such as rent and electricity growing difficult to afford, Nikki recently moved into her parents' house with her children. She would like to live on her own again, but that would require help with rent and utilities. She is working to pay off her student loans and eventually go back to school to be a dental hygienist, which pays more.

Gender Equality Is a Myth!

By BEYONCÉ KNOWLES-CARTER, multiple GRAMMY Award-winning singer, songwriter, and actress

We need to stop buying into the myth about gender equality. It isn't a reality yet. Today, women make up half of the U.S. workforce, but the average working woman earns only 77 percent of what the average working man makes. But unless women and men both say this is unacceptable, things will not change. Men have to demand that their wives, daughters, mothers, and sisters earn more—commensurate with their qualifications and not their gender. Equality will be achieved when men and women are granted equal pay and equal respect.

Humanity requires both men and women, and we are equally important and need one another. So why are we viewed as less than equal? These old attitudes are drilled into us from the very beginning. We have to teach our boys the rules of equality and respect, so that as they grow up, gender equality becomes a natural way of life. And we have to teach our girls that they can reach as high as humanly possible.

We have a lot of work to do, but we can get there if we work together. Women are more than 50 percent of the population and more than 50 percent of voters. We must demand that we all receive 100 percent of the opportunities.

Time to Wake Up:
Stop Blaming Poverty on the Poor

By BARBARA EHRENREICH, the **New York Times** *best-selling author of 21 books, including* **Nickel and Dimed: On (Not) Getting By in America**, *which chronicled her experience living undercover around the country and working at low-paying, entry-level "women's jobs."*

Fifty years ago, President Lyndon B. Johnson made a move that was unprecedented at the time and remains unmatched by succeeding administrations. He announced a War on Poverty, saying that its "chief weapons" would be "better schools, and better health, and better homes, and better training, and better job opportunities."[1]

So starting in 1964 and for almost a decade, the federal government poured at least some of its resources in the direction they should have been going all along: toward those who were most in need. Long-standing programs like Head Start, Legal Services, and the Job Corps were created. Medicaid was established. Poverty among seniors was significantly reduced by improvements in Social Security. Johnson seemed to have established the principle that it is the responsibility of government to intervene on behalf of the disadvantaged and deprived. But there was never enough money for the fight against poverty, and Johnson found himself increasingly distracted by another and deadlier war—the one in Vietnam.

Although underfunded, the War on Poverty still managed to provoke an intense backlash from conservative intellectuals and politicians. In their view, government programs could do nothing to help the poor because poverty arises from the twisted psychology of the poor themselves. By the Reagan era, it had become a cornerstone of conservative ideology that poverty is caused not by low wages or a lack of jobs and education, but by the bad attitudes and faulty lifestyles of the poor.

Picking up on this theory, pundits and politicians have bemoaned the character failings and bad habits of the poor for at least the past 50 years. In their view, the poor are shiftless, irresponsible, and prone to addiction. They have too many children and fail to get married. So if they suffer from grievous material deprivation, if they run out of money between paychecks, if they do not always have food on their tables—then they have no one to blame but themselves.

In the 1990s, with a bipartisan attack on welfare, this kind of prejudice against the poor took a drastically misogynistic turn. Poor single mothers were identified as a key link in what was called "the cycle of poverty." By staying at home and collecting welfare, they set a toxic example for their children, who—important policymakers came to believe—would be better off being cared for by paid child care workers or even, as Newt Gingrich proposed, in orphanages. Welfare "reform" was the answer, and it was intended not only to end financial support for imperiled families, but also to cure the self-induced "culture of poverty" that was supposedly at the root of their misery. The original welfare reform bill—a bill, it should be recalled, which was signed by President Bill Clinton—included an allocation of $100 million for "chastity training" for low-income women.

The Great Recession should have put the victim-blaming theory of poverty to rest. In the space of only a few months, millions of people entered the ranks of the officially poor—not only laid-off blue-collar workers, but also downsized tech workers, managers, lawyers, and other once-comfortable professionals. No one could accuse these *nouveau* poor" Americans of having made bad choices or bad lifestyle decisions. They were educated, hardworking, and ambitious, and now they were also poor—applying for food stamps, showing up in shelters, lining up for entry-level

Allie Winans in her Missoula, Montana home with the bills she just pulled out of the mailbox. Ninety-five percent of the debt she and her husband have accumulated is from medical bills. Both of their daughters and Allie herself suffer from chronic illnesses. {AMI VITALE}

jobs in retail. This would have been the moment for the pundits to finally admit the truth: *Poverty is not a character failing or a lack of motivation. Poverty is a shortage of money.*

For most women in poverty, in both good times and bad, the shortage of money arises largely from inadequate wages. When I worked on my book, *Nickel and Dimed: On (Not) Getting By in America*, I took jobs as a waitress, nursing-home aide, hotel housekeeper, Wal-Mart associate, and a maid with a house-cleaning service. I did not choose these jobs because they were low-paying. I chose them because these are the entry-level jobs most readily available to women.

residential motel. If you don't have a kitchen or even a refrigerator and microwave, you will find yourself falling back on convenience store food, which—in addition to its nutritional deficits—is also alarmingly overpriced. If you need a loan, as most poor people eventually do, you will end up paying an interest rate many times more than what a more affluent borrower would be charged.

To be poor—especially with children to support and care for—is a perpetual high-wire act. Most private-sector employers offer no sick days, and many will fire a person who misses a day of work, even to stay home with a sick child. A nonfunctioning car can also mean lost pay and sudden

---

Poverty is not a character failing or a lack of motivation. Poverty is a shortage of money.

What I discovered is that in many ways, these jobs are a trap: They pay so little that you cannot accumulate even a couple of hundred dollars to help you make the transition to a better-paying job. They often give you no control over your work schedule, making it impossible to arrange for child care or take a second job. And in many of these jobs, even young women soon begin to experience the physical deterioration—especially knee and back problems—that can bring a painful end to their work life.

I was also dismayed to find that in some ways, *it is actually more expensive to be poor than not poor.* If you can't afford the first month's rent and security deposit you need in order to rent an apartment, you may get stuck in an overpriced

expenses. A broken headlight invites a ticket, plus a fine greater than the cost of a new headlight, and possible court costs. If a creditor decides to get nasty, a court summons may be issued, often leading to an arrest warrant. No amount of training in financial literacy can prepare someone for such exigencies—or make up for an income that is impossibly low to start with.

Instead of treating low-wage mothers as the struggling heroines they are, our political culture still tends to view them as miscreants and contributors to the "cycle of poverty." If anything, the criminalization of poverty has accelerated since the recession, with growing numbers of states drug testing applicants for temporary assistance, imposing steep fines for school truancy, and imprisoning people for debt. Such measures constitute a cruel inversion of the Johnson-era principle that it is the responsibility of government to extend a helping hand to the poor.

Sadly, this has become the means by which the wealthiest country in the world manages to remain complacent in the face of alarmingly high levels of poverty: by continuing to blame poverty not on the economy or inadequate social supports, but on the poor themselves.

It's time to revive the notion of a collective national responsibility to the poorest among us, who are disproportionately women and especially women of color. Until that happens, we need to wake up to the fact that the underpaid women who clean our homes and offices, prepare and serve our meals, and care for our elderly—earning wages that do not provide enough to live on—are the true philanthropists of our society.

ENDNOTE

1   "Speeches and Legislation: LBJ's State of the Union Address January 8th, 1964," available at http://ows.edb.utexas.edu/site/jad2793edc370s/speeches-and-legislation (last accessed June 2013).

Are Women Devalued by Religions?

By SISTER JOAN CHITTISTER, a member and former prioress of the Benedictine Sisters of Erie, Pennsylvania. She is an author, columnist, lecturer, and blogger on issues involving women in the church and society, war and poverty, and religious life and spirituality. She co-chairs the U.N.-supported Global Peace Initiative of Women.

The bad news came in the 2013 "State of the World's Mothers" report. Of the 30 best countries in the world to be a mother, the survey reports that the United States ranks 30th—behind all the countries in Scandinavia, Australia, Canada, and most of the developed world.[1]

How can this situation exist in the United States—one of the world's most religious countries—where so many of us believe that religion is a great force for good? Moreover, what exactly are our religious institutions—our churches, mosques, synagogues, and faith communities—doing to advance the development and status of women?

After all, the Judeo-Christian scriptures, which are the foundation for how so many of us understand the nature and role of women in society, are very clear about women's worth. The Book of Genesis reads, "Let us make them in our own image, male and female let us make them." It is, as the theologian Mary Daly says, "the creative potential in human beings" that is the image and incarnation of God's power in this world—in women as well as men.

This scriptural exaltation of women's equality only makes the actual condition of women in our society more questionable—and the attitudes of many male religious leaders on the subject more suspect. After all, at its best, religion frames our

values and invites each and all us—not just men— to reach for the heights of the human spirit.

Religion, we also know, is a compelling arbiter of personal ethics and public actions. Human behavior is based on assumptions, and where women are concerned, religion has helped define the human community's assumptions about the place and role of women in society. Religion tells us that women are valuable, of course, but also that women are secondary to men.

In fact, religion's power to determine human reality and public morality in every arena has a long and troublesome history.

The astronomer Galileo, for instance, knew that everything to be known about nature and life was not revealed by theology alone. Galileo was silenced and excommunicated for proposing that the Earth traveled around the sun, not the other way around. He responded: "I do not feel obligated to believe that the same God who has endowed us with sense, reason, and intellect has intended us to forgo their use." Galileo, and science with him, paid a high price for staying true to the data when the facts of science and the assumptions of doctrine clashed.

Galileo and science were not the only segments of society attacked by Western theologians for

For the first year of her daughter Azariah's life, Dee Saint Franc of Providence, Rhode Island, relied on government assistance and student loans to get by while working toward her associate's degree. Through night school, she has since received a bachelor's degree and Certified Nursing Assistant, or CNA, license. {BARBARA RIES}

being outside the assumptions of the time. Other debates raged for centuries. Were indigenous peoples fully human? Were American Indians fully human? Were black people fully human? Could these types be baptized, be ordained, or really be as rational and intelligent as whites? Could they be more than slaves, more than property?

It took centuries for the barriers of "otherness" that marked these groups to begin to fade away. It took centuries before we began to speak of humanity as a whole—to see humanness as more than ethnic identity, more than color.

But even as far as we've come, women are still one class of people who are set apart, separated, and given less value and worth by multiple

religious traditions. Religion has defined women by their maternity—just one dimension of a woman's multifaceted humanity. Religion has defined women as "helpmates," as too irrational to lead, too intellectually limited for the public dimensions of life. Though they are endowed with the same degree of sense, reason, and intellect as men, women have been locked out of full humanity and full participation in religious institutions and society at large. This marginalization of women masquerades as "protecting" them and even "exalting" them. Instead, these attitudes serve to deny the human race the fullness of female gifts and a female perspective on life.

As a result, women make up two-thirds of the hungry of this world. Women are two-thirds of

Binita "Bini" Pradhan and her son, Ayush, pray at the start of the day in San Francisco, California. {BARBARA RIES}

the illiterate of this world. And women are two-thirds of the poorest of the poor, because they lack access to the resources and recognition men take for granted. That's not an accident. That is a policy—one supported by religious institutions that call such discrimination "women's place" and "God's will."

What religion has said about women has long been used to justify what society has done to limit their development. Not only does what our churches, mosques, synagogues, and faith communities teach and do about women become the morality of the land. What they do not say or do on behalf of women condones what becomes the *immorality* of the land.

The "State of the World's Mothers" report defines five indicators essential to the well-being of women and their children, and the United States fails on three of them: economic status of women, political opportunities for women, and universal health care. When will religions call for these things to be the moral imperatives of a woman's life?

In our time, a young woman by the name of Malala Yousafzai lives with a bullet wound in her head for wanting to go to school. The Taliban had banned girls' education in her region of Pakistan, and the assassination attempt by a Taliban extremist was meant to intimidate other young women who want to learn how to read.

In our own country, Carie Charlesworth, a mother of four children, was fired from her Catholic school teaching job because her husband violated a court's "protection from abuse" order by stalking her workplace. Apparently, she is the problem, not he.

In our own country, rapes in the military and rapes on college campuses go unpunished because "boys will be boys," and winning wars and football games is more important than protecting the integrity of the women who are the victims of rape.

In our own country, religious people who insist that caring for children is a woman's major responsibility in life have not yet called underpaying single women with children the sin that it is.

It is time for religions to repent the acceptance of assumptions about the social place and roles of women—assumptions that spring from theological definitions of women as less fully rational, less fully human, and less fully essential to the public arena than men.

It is time for religions to repair this distortion of the will of God. Like Galileo, it is time for both women and men to contest such untenable conclusions. For all of our sakes and for the sake of all humanity, it is time.

ENDNOTE

1 Save the Children, "State of the World's Mothers 2013" (2013), available at http://www.savethechildrenweb.org/SOWM-2013/.

Kristy Richardson is her family's breadwinner. She takes her job as a sanitation inspector very seriously and is a stickler for detail, due to her military background. Kristy works 12-hour days, but despite her income, her family still relies on the Supplemental Nutrition Assistance Program, or SNAP, to put food on the table. {MELISSA FARLOW}

A Woman's Place Is in the Middle Class

By Heather Boushey

 STUNNING FACT

Nearly two-thirds of minimum-wage workers
are women, and more than 70 percent of
low-wage workers receive no paid sick days.

When we wrote our first *Shriver* report five years ago, we showed how women were the new breadwinners. We focused on understanding a seismic shift: Between 1967 and 2008, the share of mothers who were breadwinners or co-breadwinners in American families rose from under a third to two-thirds.[1] We told the story of women's progress, a story about how women marched into employment and how millions broke through the glass ceiling. We recognized that women hadn't closed the wage gap with men, but we were optimistic about their overall progress.[2]

But while many women have made gains—with higher employment rates, more college completion, and rising median earnings—too many are living on the brink. Too often, women work at jobs that don't pay enough to secure their place in the middle class, or they lag behind their male colleagues in pay and promotions— even though they have the skills to do their jobs just as well as men. Women continue to bear most of the responsibility for the care of family members, yet they have less access than men to workplace benefits such as family and medical leave insurance, paid sick days, and flexible schedules, creating conflicts that keep them from moving up and out of chronic economic insecurity.

In A Woman's Nation, every woman should have a fair shot at the middle class. Leaving so many women out of our nation's economic progress not only creates hardships for women and their families, but it undermines the strength of our entire economy. According to Heidi Hartmann and Jeffrey Hayes of the Institute for Women's Policy Research, if women received pay equal to their male counterparts, the U.S. economy would produce $447.6 billion in additional income (2.9 percent of 2012 gross domestic product), about equal to the entire economy of the state of Virginia.[3]

If women received pay equal to their male counterparts, the U.S. economy would produce $447.6 billion in additional income.

Recognizing the existence and importance of women workers—especially women with poorly paid jobs—the obstacles they face, and the economic growth potential they represent is critical to our long-term economic vitality. In 2012, one in three adult women lived below 200 percent of the U.S. federal poverty line—that's approximately $47,000 for a family of four[4]—compared to a little more than one in four men.[5] With unionization rates falling, a continuing gender gap at all levels, and high rates of single motherhood, many women struggle on the brink every day.

This chapter will lay out who's been left behind amid so much progress, offer ideas as to why so many are not benefiting from economic growth, and conclude with recommendations for what we can do about it. Investing in women, the middle class, and families will help all of us create a more competitive, thriving economy. We need workers who can focus on their jobs while they work, and we need to make sure that families have the capacity to care for the aging and the sick, while educating and caring for the next generation. We know that a vibrant economy grows a strong middle class. And a strong middle class comes from including all types of workers in all kinds of families.

SOME WOMEN ARE GETTING AHEAD, OTHERS ARE FALLING BEHIND

Women are a critical segment of today's labor force. They work and, by and large, put in full-time hours. The share of working-age women (ages 20 to 64) in the labor force has increased steadily since the 1970s, rising to a peak of 73 percent in 2000, about the same as in 2007, before the financial crash and ensuing Great Recession.[6] On average, in 2011, women worked 35.6 hours per week and only a quarter (26.5 percent) worked part time, about the same share as in 1976.[7] The shift toward paid employment has meant a remarkable transformation in how women spend their days and how they contribute to their family's economic well-being.

Overall, as women moved into employment, they narrowed the gender pay gap, though progress on this front stalled years ago. Between 1967 and 2001, the ratio of earnings of women working full time, year round to those of men working full time, year round increased from 57.8 percent to 76.3 percent, mostly because women's average earnings were rising, while men's earnings were falling or flat.[8] But over the past decade, there has been little progress; the female-to-male earnings ratio—77 percent—is essentially the same as in 2001.[9]

Closing the wage gap would greatly benefit today's families and grow our economy. Hartmann and Hayes find that eliminating the wage gap would increase women's average earnings by 17.3 percent, from $36,129 to $42,380 annually.[10] If married women who are the primary breadwinners in their families were paid the same wages as their male counterparts, for example, it would increase the incomes for married couples by 6 percent.[11] This would increase family incomes on average by $6,776 a year, or $245.3 billion for families nationwide.[12]

As women have moved into jobs outside the home and made progress on the gender pay gap, their earnings have become increasingly important to their family budget, especially within low-income families with children. Due to the sharp rise in mother's employment, there has been an increase in the proportion of mothers who are their family's breadwinners, across all kinds of families. Between 1967 and 2010, the share of mothers who were breadwinners—those bringing home all of the family's earnings or at least as much as their partner—or co-breadwinners—those bringing home at least a quarter of the family's earnings—rose from less than a third (27.7 percent) to two-thirds (63.9 percent).[13]

FIGURE 1

Share of working wives earning as much or more than their husbands, by family income

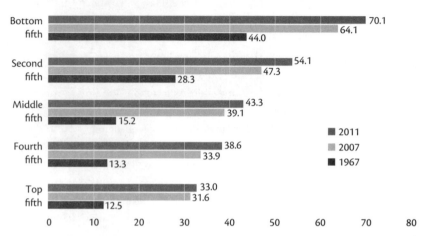

Source: Author and Jeff Chapman's analysis of Miriam King and others, "Integrated Public Use Microdata Series, Current Population Survey: Version 2.0" (Minneapolis, MN: Minnesota Population Center, 2012).

In low-income families, mothers are overwhelmingly their family's breadwinner. In 2011, among working, married-couple families in the bottom fifth of the income distribution, more than two-thirds (70.1 percent) of mothers were their family's primary breadwinner[14] (see Figure 1). Women on the brink with an employed partner rely heavily on both incomes to make ends meet. According to polling conducted by Greenberg Quinlan Rosner Research and TargetPoint Consulting for *The Shriver Report*, 70 percent of women on the brink say they could not get by without both incomes, compared to 47 percent of all participants surveyed. And single-mother households, where women are bringing in all of the income, are disproportionately likely to be low income. The median income for a never-married, breadwinning single mom is only $17,400—which is below the poverty line for a family with two children.[15]

As more women became breadwinners, succeeding generations of girls and women prepared themselves for a lifetime in the workforce. When Congressman Howard W. Smith added "sex" to Title VII of the 1964 Civil Rights Act, many thought it was a joke.[16] But in the years that followed, long-standing employment practices —such as firing women when they married or became pregnant and actively discriminating against women in terms of pay, promotions, and access to higher education—were all challenged in the courts and found to be unlawful.

Kristeen Rogers of Clermont, Florida, is a 23-year-old juggling multiple jobs to provide for her two young daughters. Although she shares custody with the father of her children, she still struggles to ensure that they have all they need. {MELISSA LYTTLE}

At the same time, the introduction of the birth control pill gave women control over the timing of when they had children, providing them with unprecedented freedom to decide when they would make investments in education and careers and when they would start a family.[17]

As doors opened to women professionally, they began to make different choices about what kinds of career paths they would pursue, fanning out into traditionally male occupations, especially management and medical and legal professions. In 1970, about 16 percent of officials and managers in the private sector were women, but by 2007, they made up 40 percent.[18] As a result, the degree of what researchers call "sex segregation" in the labor market fell until the 1990s but has since stalled for all workers, even for those with a college degree.[19]

Many women have *always* worked

Of course, some women have always worked. Much of the increase in employment occurred among women who typically were outside the labor force in the 1950s and 1960s—mothers, married women, and native-born women. Women with less than a college degree, immigrant women, and women of color were always more likely to work outside the home; college-educated women were few and far between, but they were also likely to be employed, especially when they were not married.[20]

African American women have historically been more likely than other racial and ethnic groups to work outside the home. In 1920, African American women's labor force participation rate was 38.9 percent, twice as large as any other racial or ethnic group except Japanese women, of whom 25.9 percent worked.[21] But as the 20th century marched forward, women of all racial groups began working in greater numbers. By 2007, before the Great Recession, labor force participation rates had risen to

nearly 60 percent in all racial groups for women—African Americans the highest at 61.1 percent, white women next at 59 percent, followed by Asians at 58.6 percent and Hispanics at 56.5 percent.[22]

A century ago, a substantial percentage of employed women worked as domestics in other people's homes, and this was fairly consistent across racial and ethnic groups. In 1900, among working women, about a third of Asians and whites and a higher share (43.5 percent) of African Americans held private household service jobs.[23] While many women have fanned out into a much larger array of occupations, recent immigrant women—mostly from Mexico and Central America—are now those most likely to do domestic labor.[24] These jobs tend not only to have low wages, but they are often "under the table" and do not provide workers with the same level of unemployment and Social Security benefits as other kinds of work.

Some women have indeed pulled ahead, breaking down barriers and seeing increases in incomes. For other women, however, the news is not so good. Over the past 40 years, female workers with poorly paid jobs have made only a fraction of the gains in real wages that higher-wage women have made[25] (see Figure 2). The recession only worsened the growing chasm between women: Between 2007 and 2011, women in the bottom 20th percentile saw their real wages drop by nearly 3 percent while those at the very top saw their wages increase by 3.4 percent.[26]

Even as women's investments in acquiring postsecondary education ensure that millions earn more than they would with only a high school diploma, they do not ensure women achieve parity with similarly educated men. According to a recent study by the American Association of University Women, one year after graduation, college-educated women earn an average of about 7 percent less than men, even when both went to the same kind of school, studied the same major, and now work full time, the same number of hours per week, in the same kind of job.[27]

If married women who are the primary breadwinners
in their families were paid the same wages as their male
counterparts, it would increase the incomes for married
couples by 6 percent. This would increase family incomes
on average by $6,776 a year, or $245.3 billion nationwide.

FIGURE 2

Growth in women's inflation-adjusted wages by wage group: 1979–2011

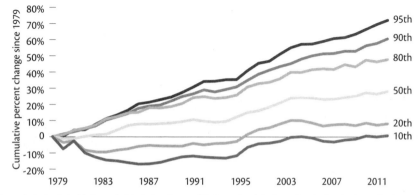

Source: Author's analysis of the Economic Policy Institute Extracts of the Current Population Survey Outgoing Rotation Group microdata.
Available at: http://stateofworkingamerica.org/data/.

But it's not just college-educated women who continue to see a pay gap. At every
level of educational attainment, women earn less than similarly educated men,
though the gap is largest among the highest-educated workers (see Figure 3).

While some women have made enormous progress and gained access to professions
and high-paid jobs, too many continue to work in underpaid, female-dominated
jobs. Even though sex segregation has decreased, women remain clustered in a few
occupations—secretaries, nurses, teachers, and salespersons. In 2012, 43.6 percent
of women worked in just 20 job titles. Men, however, work in a wider array of jobs:
Only 34.2 percent of men worked in the 20 most common male jobs.[28]

Further, even as women have made some progress in professions, they have made
little progress in nontraditional jobs, such as construction or STEM (science, technology, engineering, and math) fields. As we look across the economy, jobs mostly

held by women tend to pay less than those done by mostly men, even when we account for the skill requirements of the job.

It is important to recognize that the kinds of jobs that women hold are the ones projected to grow the most. Every two years, the Bureau of Labor Statistics identifies what are likely to be the fastest-growing occupations over the next 10 years. For more than a decade, it has predicted that most of the new jobs would be in female-dominated occupations.[29] These are jobs such as teachers, nurses, nursing assistants, child care workers, and home health aides. These jobs pay less than average and are held disproportionately by women of color (see Figures 4.1, 4.2).

One reason for the stubborn gender pay gap is that when men enter traditionally female-dominated jobs, they manage to find what University of Texas at Austin sociology professor Christine Williams terms a "glass escalator."[30] Instead of the glass ceiling that women find—seeing their way to the top, but being prevented from getting there—men, especially white men, find that they quickly rise up the ranks and into the higher-paid positions on the "glass escalator." For instance, a recent study found that male nurses are often given preferential treatment over women in hiring and promotion decisions, and they are often cast into leadership roles with enhanced authority and control.[31]

FIGURE 3

Ratio of women's to men's pay, by educational attainment, 2012

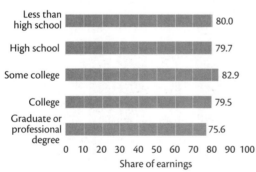

	Share of earnings
Less than high school	80.0
High school	79.7
Some college	82.9
College	79.5
Graduate or professional degree	75.6

Source: Author's analysis of the Center for Economic and Policy Research Extracts of the Current Population Survey Outgoing Rotation Group Files. Notes: Data includes all full-time workers (35+ hours a week), ages 25 to 64. Hourly wages are trimmed to $1–100 and include overtime, tips, and commissions.

The reality is that higher education is one of the only paths into a good job. A half-century ago, many jobs did not require higher education but still paid well because they were unionized. As some jobs become unionized, such as domestic care workers across California, union leaders can begin to negotiate for better wages and benefits.[32] Unionization can increase women's wages by 11.2 percent—relative to nonunion women's wages—and increase the likelihood of having an employer-provided pension and health insurance.[33]

FIGURE 4.1

Top 10 occupations with largest 10-year projected employment growth, by year of projection, 1994–2010

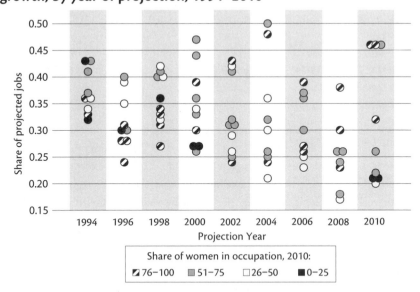

FIGURE 4.2

Wages of female-dominated occupations with largest 10-year projected employment growth, by year of projection

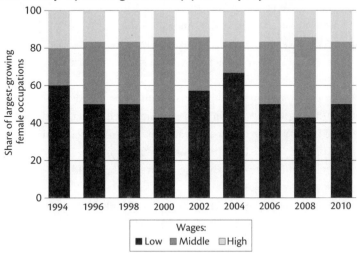

Sources: Bureau of Labor Statistic's Economic and Employment Projections, author uses the top 10 projected largest-growing occupations for each year (1994 to 2010), ranked 1 to 10, available at http://www.bls.gov/schedule/archives/all_nr.htm#ECOPRO; author's analysis of the Center for Economic and Policy Research Extracts of the Current Population Survey Outgoing Rotation Group Files, includes all workers aged 18 to 64; Bureau of Labor Statistic's Current Population Survey Tables, "Table 1: Employment status of the civilian noninstitutional population, 1942 to date," available at http://www.bls.gov/cps/cpsaat01.pdf.

Notes: Select projected occupations are combined into one occupation category in order to match CPS occupation classification codes. For combined occupations, the largest job projection is used in calculations.

For Figure 4.1, the share of projected jobs refers to the number of jobs projected in a particular occupation as a share of the total labor force in the projection year. For Figure 4.2, female-dominated occupations are those with 51 percent or more of women in the occupation.

College-educated women earn on average about 7 percent less than men, even when both went to the same kind of school, studied the same major, and now work full time, the same number of hours per week, in the same kind of job.

And in some cases unions have been able to successfully advocate for legislative change at the state or national level, to create good jobs even for employees who do not have a college degree. In both New York and Hawaii, for example, domestic worker alliances and advocates have helped pass bill of rights legislation for domestic workers, which guarantees the right to be paid a minimum wage, as well as overtime, paid time off, and standardized workweeks.[34]

WORK ISN'T ENOUGH: HIGH EMPLOYMENT HAS NOT MEANT FINANCIAL SECURITY

We can see clearly that more women are in the labor force, have acquired higher education, and have been fanning out into new occupations, even as many continue to work in female-dominated jobs. All women have not progressed at the same pace, however. While some women have moved ahead, too many have been left behind, and continued low pay has left millions living on the brink.

Even as women have made significant gains in education and their earnings are more important than ever to their families' economic well-being, continued low pay has left too many women and their families living on the brink. In 2012, 41.5 million adult women—and 16.8 million adult working women—lived in households with incomes below 200 percent of the federal poverty threshold.[35]

Women are more likely than men to be living on the brink, and single women with and without children are more likely than married women to be living on the brink. Although family structure tells just one slice of the story of why many women live in poverty, a reason for high poverty among women is the prevalence of families headed by single mothers, as Ann O'Leary details in the next chapter. Being the only breadwinner, and still having the responsibilities of care, mothers

Single mother Binita Pradhan is an aspiring entrepreneur in the culinary world, specializing in Nepalese food. She works long hours in the kitchen of La Cocina, a restaurant incubator that is helping her get "Bini's Kitchen" off the ground. She and her 4-year-old son Ayush live in a small apartment in San Francisco, California. {BARBARA RIES}

in single-parent families have a harder time maintaining employment and often have higher expenses because a second parent is not available to provide child care and help with household chores. One-third (33.9 percent) of people in single-mother families in the United States are poor, and 6 in 10 (60.4 percent) live below 200 percent of the poverty threshold.[36]

Living on the brink is more prevalent for African American women and Latinas for three reasons: They experience a larger pay gap; when married to men of color, their spouses earn less than white men; and they are more likely to be heading single-mother families. According to the National Partnership for Women & Families, African American women and Latinas are paid only 64 cents and 55 cents, respectively, for every dollar earned by non-Hispanic white men.[37] Poverty rates are relatively high even for married women of color. One out of five married Hispanic mothers are poor (20.8 percent), for example, compared to 1 out of 20 married white, non-Hispanic mothers (5.6 percent).[38]

And while the majority of single mothers are white, African American and Hispanic women are disproportionately likely to be single mothers, leaving them more likely to have to support a family on their own earnings. In 2012, almost half of single-mother households were white, non-Hispanic; one-third were African American; and one-quarter were Hispanic, even though African Americans and Hispanics make up only about 13 percent and 17 percent of the U.S. population, respectively.[39]

Holding a job doesn't necessarily secure a family's place in the middle class. Figure 5 shows the share of adult men and women (ages 18 to 64) by race and ethnicity living in a family under twice the federal poverty level. Clearly, even if they are breadwinners, women are more likely than men to be poor or on the brink of poverty. This is even more the case for African American women and Latinas.

In 2012, the U.S. Census Bureau reported that a family of three—one parent and two children—would need at least $18,498 to be able to escape poverty.[40] To rise above this threshold, a woman who worked full time, all year (with two weeks off, but unpaid) would have to earn at least $10.57 an hour—not including payroll taxes and basic expenses, such as child care—a $3.32 increase above the minimum wage.[41] Thus, a woman working full time, all year at a minimum-wage job, or a job close to the minimum wage, will not be able to bring her family above the poverty line. Families need an income closer to 200 percent of the federal poverty threshold to escape poverty.

FIGURE 5

Share of women and men at or below 200 percent of poverty, by race, 2011

■ Share of women at or below 200 percent of poverty
■ Share of men at or below 200 percent of poverty

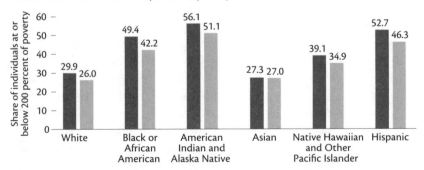

Source: U.S. Census, Current Population Survey, Poverty data, available at http://www.census.gov/cps/data/cpstablecreator.html
Note: Data includes all individuals, ages 18–64.

A woman working full time, all year at a minimum-wage job, or a job close to the minimum wage, will not be able to bring her family above the poverty line. Families need an income closer to 200 percent of the federal poverty threshold to escape the brink.

BENEFITS HELP, BUT THEY'RE NOT ENOUGH

Women living on the brink often rely on public benefits to make ends meet. In tough economic times, these programs can make all the difference. During the Great Recession that followed the financial crash that began in 2007—the worst times for workers and their families in generations—policy went a long way toward keeping families out of poverty. Government policies implemented as part of the American Recovery and Reinvestment Act of 2009 boosted employment and addressed the needs of those hardest hit by the economic downturn by expanding access to food stamps—now known as SNAP, or the Supplemental Nutrition Assistance Program—and unemployment benefits.[42] In 2009 alone, unemployment benefits lifted 3.3 million families out of poverty.[43] Wayne Vroman, economist at the Urban Institute, estimates that the unemployment insurance system closed about one-fifth (18.3 percent) of the shortfall in the nation's gross domestic product during the Great Recession.[44]

Work and income supports help lift many women working in poorly paid jobs above the poverty line or at least near it. But restrictive rules, funding limitations, and barriers to access also limit the extent to which work supports can keep women off the brink.[45]

In particular, income limits on eligibility for work supports are often too low to help low-wage, working women. In many states, income limits produce, among other work-support cliffs, a "child care cliff" for women receiving child care assistance.[46] As a result, a working mother with a poorly paid job who receives a raise may end up worse off in terms of income if it puts her over the income threshold for child care assistance.

FIGURE 6

Employer benefits by wage, 2012

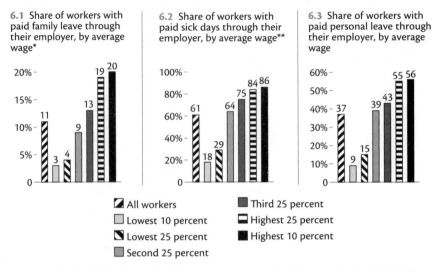

6.1 Share of workers with paid family leave through their employer, by average wage*

6.2 Share of workers with paid sick days through their employer, by average wage**

6.3 Share of workers with paid personal leave through their employer, by average wage

☑ All workers
☐ Lowest 10 percent
◩ Lowest 25 percent
▨ Second 25 percent
■ Third 25 percent
⊟ Highest 25 percent
■ Highest 10 percent

Source: Bureau of Labor Statistics, "Table 32. Leave benefits: Access, private industry workers, National Compensation Survey, March 2012" (U.S. Department of Labor, 2012). Notes: Includes all private industry workers. The categories above are based on the average wage for each occupation surveyed.
* The states of California and New Jersey require paid family leave coverage.
** The state of Connecticut, the District of Columbia, San Francisco, and Seattle require paid sick days coverage.

Another problem is counterproductive restrictions on savings and the value of basic assets, such as a reliable car, that some states apply to such programs as temporary income assistance and food stamps.[47] This can make it impossible to build a nest egg to get out of poverty and forces struggling families to spend down much of their savings before qualifying for temporary help.[48]

Further, when times get tough, states all too often cut back on benefits for working families. While the poverty rate has remained stuck at 15 percent since the end of the Great Recession and the share of "women on the brink" has nudged up, 27 states imposed new restrictions on child care access between 2011 and 2012.[49]

It's not just that public benefits cut off too early. Many poorly paid jobs don't provide the kinds of benefits that well-paying jobs do, and too often they offer only nonstandard work or varying schedules, which are more likely to lead to job churning—or high employee turnover.[50]

Michigan State University economist Peter Berg, CAP sociologist Sarah Jane Glynn, and I have found that workers who are likely to need flexibility the

After a long day waitressing—one of her four jobs—Kristeen Rogers of Clermont, Florida, plays with her daughters in the front yard of their home. Child care costs and bills make day-to-day life tough, but providing stability for Lexi, 4, and Jada, 2, is her top priority. {MELISSA LYTTLE}

most—women workers, single mothers, and low-income workers—are the least likely to have access to paid leave and workplace flexibility offered through their employer.[51] Higher-paid women are more likely than lower-paid women to have access to family-friendly benefits from their employer[52] (see Figure 6). Women of color are also less likely to have access to paid maternity leave, and the odds decrease for all women the younger they are or the less education they have.[53]

Federal laws to help families address work and family often leave out women with poorly paid jobs. As Ann O'Leary and Karen Kornbluh described in the first *Shriver* report, the exemptions to the Family and Medical Leave Act "disproportionately exclude low-wage and younger workers who are less likely to remain employed by the same employer for a year, who are more likely to work for a small business, and who are more likely to work part time."[54] This is in part because of Congress's failure to factor in the relationship between pregnancy and family leave laws with the welfare system during the 1996 welfare reform debates and legislation.[55]

The lack of family-friendly policies that benefit workers across the wage distribution makes it harder for women to stay employed and to move up the job ladder. Those earning the least in our economy—the young, the less educated, and people of color—are also the most likely to have to leave their jobs and to experience a wage drop after changing employers.[56] This is consistent with Census Bureau research that found that new mothers who have access to paid maternity leave are more likely to return to their previous employer, and 97.6 percent of those who return to the same employer do so at their previous pay level or higher. On the other hand, 30.6 percent of women who have to change employers after giving birth experience a drop in pay.[57]

Because of this, many women with poorly paid jobs cycle in and out of work and poverty. The Census Bureau found that between 2009 and 2011, approximately 31.6 percent of the population had at least one spell of poverty lasting 2 or more

Women face increased housing and transportation costs that strain their budgets and limit their opportunities

Julia Gordon and Tracey Ross, Center for American Progress

One of the biggest challenges many families face is finding and securing affordable housing. Over the past few decades, women have gained a more powerful presence in the housing market by making larger contributions to household income and becoming heads of households.[58] In recent years, single women have made up one of the fastest-growing groups of homeowners, accounting for twice as many new buyers as single men.[59]

Since the housing market collapse of 2007, however, millions of families are still dealing with housing insecurity, and trillions of dollars in household wealth have vanished. This loss of wealth will likely hinder progress made in closing the wealth gap between men and women, and it has been particularly hard for women of color, who were among the hardest hit.[60] Further, because women earn less on average than men, they are already more

likely to face housing problems than households headed by married couples or single men.[61] The story is worse for single mothers, with a quarter spending more than half of their incomes on housing compared to one-tenth of single fathers.[62]

As a result of the struggling housing market, more and more families are looking to downsize by entering an already strained rental market. This influx of new tenants is contributing to increased rents for housing that women heavily depend on.[63] Things are worse in the affordable rental housing space, where the number of extremely low-income renters, which are disproportionately women, exceeds the number of affordable units available.[64]

The challenge of finding housing that meets the basic

months. Sustained poverty was comparatively rare, with fewer than 1 in 20 people living in poverty for at least 36 consecutive months.[65]

Other countries do not have so many women, especially working mothers, living on the brink. This is largely because they combine policies aimed at the poor with policies designed to support families. A 2013 study by Cornell University economists Francine Blau and Lawrence Kahn finds that one reason why the United States fell from having the 6th-highest female labor force participation rate in 1990 to the 17th highest in 2010 was because it failed to keep up with other nations and adopt family-friendly policies such as paid parental leave and part-time or flexible work entitlements.[66]

Case in point: The United States is the only developed nation that does not require employers to provide maternity leave.[67] The Project on Global Working Families found that of 173 countries studied, 169 provide some payment for maternity leave; only Liberia, Papua New Guinea, and Swaziland stand with the United States in offering no paid maternity leave.[68]

needs of women is exacerbated by the fact that much of the nation's affordable housing is not linked to the transportation options necessary for families to access employment opportunities, good schools, fresh food, and other amenities. To make matters worse, housing and transportation costs have increased faster than incomes over the past decade. Moderate-income households, for instance, spent nearly three-fifths (59 percent) of income on housing and transportation costs combined.[69]

The housing-transportation disconnect is worse for low-income people, who often live in areas with less reliable and underinvested public transportation. They are less likely to have more convenient options available. Low-income women in particular face difficulties in the transportation system as they are less likely to have access to a car. They are also more likely to navigate public transportation with children, which means purchasing additional transit passes.[70]

As job opportunities continue to spread outside of city limits, moving into more affordable communities with poor transportation is becoming a greater barrier to finding work. This is particularly troubling as studies show that access to good transportation—through owning or having access to a car—is related to better employment outcomes and higher incomes for women, including single mothers with no more than a high school education.[71] But even with the benefits a car can provide, struggling families spend a large percentage of their incomes on gasoline.[72]

As women continue to pursue greater employment and wealth-building opportunities, housing and transportation costs present a real barrier to sustained success. Efforts to address the affordable housing crisis, and to ensure that the public transportation system is more responsive to its core riders, will play a critical role in ensuring that women can lead stable lives with access to greater opportunities.

Family-friendly policies that allow mothers respite from the workplace actually encourage them to stay in the labor force. These policies help women who can only work part time or who have been out of the labor force for a prolonged period, thereby encouraging them to find employment or go back to work.

Yet, in the United States, women with poorly paid jobs too often lack the supports they need to comfortably hold a job. On the one hand, they hold jobs that don't provide them with good benefits such as paid leave, workplace flexibility, predictable hours, employer-provided health insurance, or a retirement plan. On the other hand, they earn "too much" to qualify for work and income supports such as child care and Medicaid.[73]

Very few employers provide workers in low-income families access to work supports, which is a key reason so many women are living on the brink. When it comes to health insurance, the Affordable Care Act has the potential to make a big difference by subsidizing the purchase of health insurance by moderate- and middle-income families and giving states the option to expand Medicaid to more low-income workers.[74] Unfortunately, only about half of the states are currently moving forward on the Medicaid expansion.[75]

Adopting a set of work and income support policies that would benefit all workers would help women—and caregivers more generally—stay in the labor force and reduce lifetime poverty.

So long as caregiving falls mostly on women and they have little support in this important role, their ability to earn family-supporting wages will be limited. This is at the root of why so many women are living on the brink.

PROGRESS MEANS ADDRESSING THE WORK-FAMILY GAP

Because of caregiving responsibilities, women often have to cycle in and out of the labor force, affecting their opportunities for both pay raises and promotions. Yet, even though most workers now have some responsibilities for care, U.S. labor laws and social policies have not been updated to reflect this reality. Instead, they reflect a vision of family life in the 1930s when these policies were first laid out.

Women workers, single mothers, and low-income workers are the least likely to have access to paid leave and workplace flexibility offered through their employer.

Today, women—and caregivers more generally—face serious conflicts between work and family, because they do not have the institutional supports of predictable schedules, paid sick days, family and medical leave insurance, and workplace flexibility. Women are more likely than men to take time off to care for children and for the sick and aging, though this is (slowly) changing.

With so many families depending on women breadwinners, our nation cannot afford to allow women's jobs to be the most poorly paid. Yet these jobs not only pay less than other jobs, they are among those least likely to provide benefits, such as paid sick days or paid family leave. If we truly care about women's economic security, then ensuring that every job creates the potential for an employee to be both breadwinner and caretaker when necessary should be our number one goal.

We get there by:
• A national program for family and medical leave insurance
• The right for every worker to earn paid sick days
• Child care and universal prekindergarten
• New rules that encourage employers to create predictable schedules
• Much-needed flexibility for employees[76]

Until we make it possible to balance care and work, the vast majority of women will not succeed. We know that this agenda will help keep caregivers in the labor force, which is good in the long term for them and for our economy. We also need to recognize that the challenges women face are similar to those faced by all working people. These are tough economic times, and men are also experiencing serious challenges.

NOT JUST A WOMAN'S ISSUE

In fact, the trends we are seeing among women first appeared among male work-ers. While much has been made of whether or not U.S. women were "opting out" of employment, an underexamined issue is that U.S. men's employment rates have fallen over the past 45 years. Between 1960 and 2007—that is, before the Great Recession decimated U.S. labor markets—the employment rate of men age 16 and older fell 9.1 percentage points.[77] The share of U.S. men with a job is lower now than it has ever been since the end of World War II. This is due in part to the Great Recession, but is mostly an ongoing long-term trend.

Housing help: Melissa's story[78]

Melissa has always worked but has struggled to get ahead. "I've been working since I was 13. My first job was doing laundry in the laundromat for a dollar a load. I've always had a job. I've always been doing something. My hardest struggle is competing with somebody who has credentials that I don't have. Because the things I know I learned by doing, not by going to school. I didn't get a degree in it; I lived it, that's the difference."

Subsidized housing has given Melissa the stability she needs to get back on better financial footing and search for a better-paying job.

"For a little while I was living paycheck to paycheck. I'm here until I can dig myself out. I feel like I can't afford to take the risk of leaving and not having any place to really stand firm on my feet," Melissa said.

But she continued, "I'm going to be there soon. I have to get my bills in order, which I did, thank you very much, and build out my credit again, and then from there I'll be in a better position once I get a better job."

As we've seen among women, income inequal-ity has been pulling men apart. Men at the very top have seen strong wage gains, while those in the bottom 80 percent of the earnings distribu-tion saw their wages fall from the late 1970s to the mid-1990s.[79] These men began to recover in the early 2000s, but the Great Recession has wiped out those gains. Like women, only the highest-paid men have seen income growth.

One result of these trends is that for both men and women, eco-nomic mobility has declined, making it harder for low-income families to move into and stay in the middle class.

Dee Saint Franc works as a youth advocate for eight hours a day at Foster Forward in Providence, Rhode Island. Her second job as a care facility nurse keeps her away from her daughter, Azariah, until 11 p.m. every day. {BARBARA RIES}

In a recent paper, University of Ottawa economist Miles Corak showed that the United States is an outlier in terms of economic mobility due to high inequality. Using what he terms the "Great Gatsby Curve," Corak shows that the higher the economic inequality in a nation, the less economic mobility there is.[80] Another way to think of it is that as the rungs on the ladder of economic mobility become farther and farther apart, it becomes harder for people to move up.

CONCLUSION

The continued lack of economic progress for too many women means that in one of the world's richest economies, too many families are living on the brink. We can help women workers by doing more to address the larger challenges in the labor market.

Women's earnings are important for families, and too many are not making enough to lift their families into economic security. While some women have seen strong wage gains, too many have not. As evidenced by our *Shriver Report* research, closing the wage gap is a top priority to increase the average earnings for working women.

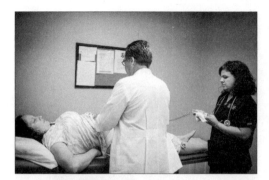

Women working full time in low-wage positions often struggle to keep their families above the poverty line. Family-friendly policies such as paid leave and workplace flexibility would help employees be both breadwinners and caretakers. {BARBARA KINNEY (1,2), BARBARA RIES (3)}

But this is not just a women's story. This is our nation's story. Women's financial insecurity affects our economy: The U.S. economy has seen rising inequality and decreased economic mobility throughout the workforce. Closing the wage gap would strengthen the economy, adding an additional $447.6 billion to GDP and cutting the poverty rate among working women and their families in half, from 8.1 percent to 3.9 percent.[81]

To help women achieve economic security, we need to make sure that the responsibilities of caring for a family do not limit employment and earnings potential. While the lack of family-friendly employment and social policies plays a key role in reducing women's economic security—especially for those not in the highest-paying occupations—there are deeper economic issues that are creating economic insecurity for millions of women and their families. Moving forward, if we want more women to have a secure economic future, we need to make sure that there are good jobs for them and their partners and reconcile the need households have to care for loved ones with the need to hold down the kind of job that pays the rent.

THINK ABOUT THIS

The United States is the only developed nation that does not require employers to provide paid maternity leave.

Unpaid and undervalued care work keeps women on the brink

Riane Eisler and Kimberly Otis, Center for Partnership Studies[82]

Women do most of the care work in families; they care for children, the elderly, the sick, and the disabled. According to the U.S. Census Bureau, women devote more than 110 million hours a year to unpaid interactive child care, more than double men's less than 55 million hours.[83]

This care work is socially and economically essential. But unless we change our current national and state policies, the fact that women do far more of this work than men will continue to be a major reason for women's disproportionate poverty.

According to the U.S. Government Accountability Office, or GAO, women over the age of 65 are twice as likely to live in poverty as men of the same age.[84] This is not only because women tend to live longer, nor is it only because of job discrimination. A major reason is that most of these women were, or are, full- or part-time caregivers.

The failure of U.S. policies to give visibility, value, and support to care work is also one of the reasons why children in female-headed families are so disproportionately poor. This is also a major reason why the United States has the highest child poverty rate of all developed nations except for Romania.[85]

Here are several steps we can take to change these statistics—and the suffering they reflect.

SHOW THE ENORMOUS ECONOMIC VALUE OF UNPAID CARE WORK

A Swiss government survey showed that if the unpaid work performed in households—primarily caring for people—were counted, it would constitute 40 percent of Swiss GDP.[86] A Massachusetts study estimates that adding unpaid care to traditional measures would increase the state's GDP from $352 billion to $504 billion—and that if unpaid care were counted in GDP, it would amount to nearly 30 percent of goods and services produced in the state.[87]

Furthermore, a 2012 report from the Bureau of Economic Analysis at the U.S. Department of Commerce found that household production would have increased U.S. GDP in 2010 by 26 percent.[88] And a recent Australian study—using not only *replacement value* (which is low because care work is so poorly paid in the workplace) but also *opportunity cost* (what caregivers could earn on average if they were earning their potential in the paid economy)—places the value of this work at a whopping 50 percent of that country's GDP.[89]

Mainstream statistical data—the data policymakers use to make decisions—must include the value of this unpaid work, showing the large economic contribution of women through, for example, the new Social Wealth indicators.[90] These indicators identify the attributes of a society that support development of the full capacities of every individual throughout their life span, with special focus on the economic value of caring for and educating children, and hence on the contributions of women. This is essential to reduce women's poverty and economic insecurity, especially in communities of color. In addition, until care work is adequately valued, men may not do more of it, which is critical to enabling women to seek and retain jobs outside of their homes.

SHOW HOW QUALITY EARLY CHILD CARE AND EDUCATION CAN IMPACT ECONOMIC COMPETITIVENESS

Findings from neuroscience show that human capacity development throughout the life span largely hinges on the quality of care children receive early on.[91] This obviously has enormous implications for individuals, but it also has enormous implications for national economic competitiveness. Good education and support for care work in families is essential, especially as we move into the postindustrial service and knowledge economy; economists tell us that the most important capital for a nation's economic success in the global economy is "high-quality human capital."[92]

SHOW HOW OTHER NATIONS ARE SUPPORTING CARE WORK AND THE EMPOWERMENT OF WOMEN, LEADING TO BOTH ECONOMIC SUCCESS AND A HIGHER GENERAL QUALITY OF LIFE

Nations such as Sweden, Finland, and Norway have the lowest gender gaps in the world.[93] These nations were so poor at the beginning of the 20th century that there were famines, but today they are regularly in the highest ranks of the World Economic Forum's Global Competitiveness Reports.[94]

A major factor in this dramatic shift was that these nations invested in developing their "human capital" by empowering women. They provided stipends for child care, generous paid parental leave, high-quality early childhood education, and even social security credit for the first years of caring for a child at home. In addition, most EU countries have adopted caregiver credit programs as part of their social security systems.[95]

We must help U.S. policymakers understand the economic benefits of these policies—for families (especially women and children) and for U.S. economic success. Caregiver credits, not just child tax credits, for example, would help reduce elderly women's unconscionable poverty rates and improve benefits for caregivers.

These kinds of measures are also essential to give more visibility to the work of unpaid care, thereby changing beliefs and attitudes about what is, or is not, economically valuable. And about the best investments a nation can make.

(See Riane Eisler, *The Real Wealth of Nations: Creating a Caring Economics* [San Francisco, CA: Berrett-Koehler, 2007], for a detailed analysis and further proposals.)

ENDNOTES

1 Heather Boushey, "The New Breadwinners." In Heather Boushey and Ann O'Leary, eds., *The Shriver Report: A Woman's Nation Changes Everything* (New York: Simon and Schuster, 2009), available at http://shriverreport.org/special-report/a-womans-nation-changes-everything/.

2 Ibid.

3 Heidi Hartmann and Jeffrey Hayes, "Equal Pay for Working Women and Their Families: National Data on the Pay Gap and Its Costs" (Washington: Institute for Women's Policy Research, forthcoming); Bureau of Economic Analysis, *Widespread Economic Growth in 2012* (Washington: U.S. Department of Commerce, 2013), available at http://bea.gov/newsreleases/regional/gdp_state/2013/pdf/gsp0613.pdf.

4 Carmen DeNavas-Walt, Bernadette D. Proctor, and Jessica C. Smith, "Income, Poverty, and Health Insurance Coverage in the United States: 2012" (Washington: U.S. Census Bureau, 2013), available at http://www.census.gov/prod/2013pubs/p60-245.pdf.

5 Center for American Progress analysis of U.S. Census Bureau, *Current Population Survey, 2012 Annual Social and Economic Supplement* (Washington: U.S. Department of Commerce), available at http://www.census.gov/cps/data/cpstablecreator.html (last accessed September 2013).

6 Center for American Progress analysis of the Center for Economic and Policy Research Extracts of the Current Population Survey Outgoing Rotation Group Files; Bureau of Labor Statistics, *Women in the Labor Force: A Databook* (Washington: U.S. Department of Labor, 2013).

7 Ibid.

8 U.S. Census Bureau, "Historical Income Tables—People," Table P-40, available at http://www.census.gov/hhes/www/income/data/historical/people/ (last accessed September 2013).

9 DeNavas-Walt, Proctor, and Smith, "Income, Poverty, and Health Insurance Coverage in the United States: 2012."

10 Hartmann and Hayes, "Equal Pay for Working Women and Their Families: National Data on the Pay Gap and Its Costs."

11 Ibid.

12 Ibid.

13 Sarah Jane Glynn, "The New Breadwinners: 2010 Update" (Washington: Center for American Progress, 2012). Data limitations prevent us from including same-sex married couples in this analysis at this time.

14 Sarah Jane Glynn, "The New Breadwinners: 2011 Update" (Washington, DC: Center for American Progress, forthcoming).

15 Wendy Wang, Kim Parker, and Paul Taylor, "Breadwinner Moms" (Washington: Pew Research Center, 2013), Chapter 4: Single Mothers, available at http://www.pewsocialtrends.org/files/2013/05/Breadwinner_moms_final.pdf.

16 Robert O. Self, *All in the Family: The Realignment of American Democracy Since the 1960s* (New York: Hill and Wang, 2012).

17 Claudia Goldin and Lawrence Katz, "The Power of the Pill: Oral Contraceptives and Women's Career and Marriage Decisions," *Journal of Political Economy* 110 (4) (2002): 730–770.

18 Catalyst, "Women in Management in the United States, 1960–Present," March 27, 2013, available at http://www.catalyst.org/knowledge/women-management-united-states-1960-present.

19 Ariane Hegewisch and others, "Separate and Not Equal? Gender Segregation in the Labor Market and the Gender Wage Gap" (Washington: Institute for Women's Policy Research, 2010), available at http://www.iwpr.org/publications/pubs/separate-and-not-equal-gender-segregation-in-the-labor-market-and-the-gender-wage-gap.

20 Teresa L. Amott and Julie A. Matthaei, *Race, Gender, and Work: A Multi-Cultural Economic History of Women in the United States* (Cambridge, MA: South End Press, 1996); Chinhui Juhn and Simon Potter, "Changes in Labor Force Participation in the United States," *Journal of Economic Perspectives* 20 (3) (2006): 27–46.

21 Ibid.

22 Center for American Progress analysis of the Center for Economic and Policy Research Extracts of the Current Population Survey Outgoing Rotation Group Files, not seasonally adjusted data.

23 Amott and Matthaei, *Race, Gender, and Work.*

24 Barbara Ehrenreich and Arlie Russell Hochschild, eds., *Global Women: Nannies, Maids, and Sex Workers in the New Economy* (New York, NY: Metropolitan/Holt Paperbacks Book, 2004).

25 Lawrence Mishel and others, *State of Working America, 12th ed.* (Washington: Economic Policy Institute, 2013), Figure 4D—Cumulative Change in Real Hourly Wages of Women, by Wage Percentile, 1979–2011, available at http://stateofworkingamerica.org/chart/swa-wages-figure-4d-change-real-hourly-wages/.

26 Ibid.

27 Christianne Corbett and Catherine Hill, "Graduating to a Pay Gap: The Earnings of Women and Men One Year after College Graduation" (Washington: American Association of University Women, October 2012), available at http://www.aauw.org/files/2013/02/graduating-to-a-pay-gap-the-earnings-of-women-and-men-one-year-after-college-graduation.pdf.

28 Center for American Progress analysis of the Center for Economic and Policy Research Extracts of the Current Population Survey Outgoing Rotation Group Files.

29 Bureau of Labor Statistics, "Archived BLS News Releases—Economic and Employment Projections," available at http://www.bls.gov/schedule/archives/all_nr.htm#ECOPRO (last accessed September 2013).

30 Christine Williams, "The Glass Escalator: Hidden Advantages for Men in the 'Female' Professions," *Social Problems* 39 (3) (1992): 253–267.

31 Timothy B. McMurry, "The Image of Male Nurses and Nursing Leadership Mobility," *Nursing Forum* 46 (1) (2011): 22–28, available at http://onlinelibrary.wiley.com/doi/10.1111/j.1744-6198.2010.00206.x/abstract.

32 Linda Delp and Katie Quan, "Homecare Worker Organizing in California: An Analysis of a Successful Strategy" (Berkeley, CA: UC Berkeley Labor Center, 2001), available at http://laborcenter.berkeley.edu/homecare/DelpQuan.pdf.

33 John Schmitt, "Unions and Upward Mobility for Women Workers" (Washington: Center for Economic and Policy Research, 2008).

34 New York State Department of Labor, "Domestic Workers' Bill of Rights," available at http://www.labor.ny.gov/legal/domestic-workers-bill-of-rights.shtm (last accessed September 2013); Associated Press, "Hawaii Gov Signs Domestic Workers Bill," *The Wall Street Journal*, July 1, 2013, available at http://online.wsj.com/article/AP6c537efafd864377bd2c59b966de8969.html.

35 U.S. Census Bureau, *Current Population Survey, 2013 Annual Social and Economic Supplement, Table POV01: Age and Sex of All People, Family Members and Unrelated Individuals Iterated by Income-to-Poverty Ratio and Race,* available at http://www.census.gov/hhes/www/cpstables/032013/pov/pov01_200.htm, and Table POV22: Work Experience During Year by Age, Sex, Household Relationship and Poverty Status for People 16 Years Old and Over, available at http://www.census.gov/hhes/www/cpstables/032013/pov/pov22_200.htm.

36 U.S. Census Bureau, *Current Population Survey, 2013 Annual Social and Economic Supplement, Table POV18: People in Families by Householder's Work Experience and Family Structure: 2012,* available at http://www.census.gov/hhes/www/cpstables/032013/pov/pov18_000.htm.

37 National Partnership for Women and Families calculation of U.S. Census Bureau, *Current Population Survey, Annual Social and Economic (ASEC) Supplement (2012), Table PINC-05: Work Experience in 2011—People 15 Years Old and Over by Total Money Earnings in 2010, Age, Race, Hispanic Origin, and Sex,* available at http://www.census.gov/hhes/www/cpstables/032011/perinc/new05_000.htm (last accessed November 2012) (unpublished calculation).

38 Shawn Fremstad's calculations of U.S. Census Bureau, *Current Population Survey, 2012 Annual Social and Economic Supplement,* Integrated Public Use Microdata Series (IMPUS), available at: https://cps.ipums.org/cps/.

39 Jonathan Vespa, Jamie M. Lewis, and Rose M. Kreider, *America's Families and Living Arrangements: 2012* (U.S. Census Bureau, August 2013), available at https://www.census.gov/prod/2013pubs/p20-570.pdf; U.S. Census Bureau, "State & County QuickFacts—USA," available at http://quickfacts.census.gov/qfd/states/00000.html (last accessed September 2013).

40 DeNavas-Walt, Proctor, and Smith, "Income, Poverty, and Health Insurance Coverage in the United States: 2012."

41 According to the Bureau of Labor Statistics, full-time workers are those who work 35 hours or more. See Bureau of Labor Statistics, "Glossary," available at http://www.bls.gov/bls/glossary.htm.

42 Heather Boushey, "Accomplishments of the Recovery Act," Center for American Progress, February 16, 2011, available at http://www.americanprogress.org/issues/economy/news/2011/02/16/9078/accomplishments-of-the-recovery-act/; Arloc Sherman, "State-Level Data Show Recovery Act Protecting Millions from Poverty," Center on Budget an Policy Priorities, December 17, 2009, available at http://www.cbpp.org/cms/?fa=view&id=3035.

43 Arloc Sherman, "Looking at Today's Poverty Numbers," Off the Charts Blog: Center on Budget and Policy Priorities, September 16, 2010, available at http://www.offthechartsblog.org/looking-at-today%E2%80%99s-poverty-numbers/.

44 Wayne Vroman, "The Role of Unemployment Insurance as an Automatic Stabilizer During a Recession" (Washington: U.S. Department of Labor, 2010), available at http://wdr.doleta.gov/research/FullText_Documents/ETAOP2010-10.pdf.

45 Randy Albelda and others, "Bridging the Gaps: A Picture of How Work Supports Work in Ten States" (Center for Economic and Policy Research; The Center for Social Policy, 2007), available at http://www.cepr.net/index.php/publications/reports/bridging-the-gaps-a-picture-of-how-work-supports-work-in-ten-states/.

46 National Center for Children in Poverty, "Family Resource Simulator" (2004), available at http://www.nccp.org/tools/frs/.

47 Laura Pereyra, "TANF's Counterproductive Asset Tests," Center for American Progress, May 6, 2010, available at http://www.americanprogress.org/issues/poverty/news/2010/05/06/7846/tanfs-counterproductive-asset-tests/; Corporation for Enterprise Development, "Asset Limit Reform in Public Assistance Programs: Removing Penalties for Savings," available at http://cfed.org/assets/documents/policy/Asset_Test_Reform_Final.pdf.

48 Ibid.

49 National Women's Law Center, "Downward Slide: State Child Care Assistance Policies," October 11, 2012; DeNavas-Walt, Proctor, and Smith, "Income, Poverty, and Health Insurance Coverage in the United States: 2012."

50 See, for example: Susan J. Lambert and Julia R. Henly, "Nonstandard Work and Child-care Needs of Low-Income Parents." In Suzanne M. Bianchi, Lynne M. Casper, and Rosalind B. King, eds., Work, Family, Health, and Well-Being (Mahwah, NJ: Lawrence Erlbaum Associates, Inc., 2005), pp. 473–492.

51 Sarah Jane Glynn, Peter Berg, and Heather Boushey, "Who Gets Time Off? Predicting Access to Paid Leave and Workplace Flexibility" (Washington: Center for American Progress, forthcoming).

52 Heather Boushey and Sarah Jane Glynn, "Comprehensive Paid Family and Medical Leave for Today's Families and Workplaces: Crafting a Paid Leave System That Builds on the Experience of Existing Federal and State Programs" (Washington: Center for American Progress, 2012).

53 U.S. Census Bureau, Maternity Leave and Employment Patterns of First-Time Mothers: 1961–2008 (Washington, DC: U.S. Department of Commerce, 2011), available at http://www.census.gov/prod/2011pubs/p70-128.pdf.

54 Ann O'Leary and Karen Kornbluh, "Family Friendly for All Families." In Heather Boushey and Ann O'Leary, eds., The Shriver Report: A Woman's Nation Changes Everything (Washington: Center for American Progress, 2009), pp. 75–109.

55 Ann O'Leary, "How Family Leave Laws Left Out Low-Income Workers," Berkeley Journal of Employment and Labor Law 28 (2007): 1–62.

56 Julia Lane, "The Role of Job Turnover in the Low-Wage Labor Market," in The Low-Wage Labor Market: Challenges and Opportunities for Economic Self-Sufficiency (Washington: Assistant Secretary for Planning and Evaluation: U.S. Department of Health and Human Services, The Urban Institute, 1999), available at http://aspe.hhs.gov/hsp/lwlm99/lane.htm; Bureau of Labor Statistics, "Employee Tenure Summary," U.S. Department of Labor, September 18, 2012, available at http://www.bls.gov/news.release/tenure.nr0.htm.

57 U.S. Census Bureau, Maternity Leave and Employment Patterns of First-Time Mothers: 1961–2008.

58 "The State of the Nation's Housing 2004" (Cambridge, MA: Joint Center for Housing Studies of Harvard University, 2004), available at http://www.jchs.harvard.edu/sites/jchs.harvard.edu/files/son2004.pdf.

59 National Association of Realtors, "NAR Guide to Women Homebuyers for Realtors," available at http://www.realtor.org/field-guides/field-guide-to-women-homebuyers.

60 Debbie Gruenstein Bocian, Wei Li, and Keith Ernst, "Foreclosures by Race and Ethnicity: The Demographics of a Crisis" (Washington: Center for Responsible Lending, 2010), available at http://www.responsiblelending.org/mortgage-lending/research-analysis/foreclosures-by-race-and-ethnicity.pdf.

61 National Association of Realtors, "NAR Guide to Women Homebuyers for Realtors."

62 Ibid.

63 National Multi Housing Council, "Quick Facts: Resident Demographics," 2013, available at http://www.nmhc.org/Content.cfm?ItemNumber=55508#characteristic_of_apartment_households; Trulia, "Press Release—Trulia Names Las Vegas and Seattle as 2012's Top Turnaround Housing Markets," available at http://info.trulia.com/trulia-price-and-rent-monitor-dec-2012 (last accessed September 24, 2013).

64 Pamela Patenaude and Nikki Rudnick, "Housing America's Future: New Directions for National Policy" (Washington: Bipartisan Policy Center, 2013), available at http://bipartisanpolicy.org/sites/default/files/BPC_Housing%20Report_web_0.pdf; National Multi Housing Council, "Quick Facts: Resident Demographics."

65 DeNavas-Walt, Proctor, and Smith, "Income, Poverty, and Health Insurance Coverage in the United States: 2012."

66 Francine D. Blau and Lawrence M. Kahn, "Female Labor Supply: Why Is the US Falling Behind?" (Bonn, Germany: Institute for the Study of Labor, 2013).

67 Rebecca Ray, Janet C. Gornick, and John Schmitt, "Parental Leave Policies in 21 Countries" (Washington: Center for Economic and Policy Research, September 2008); Australian Government, "Paid Parental Leave," available at http://www.fairwork.gov.au/leave/parental-leave/pages/paid-parental-leave.aspx (last accessed September 2013).

68 Jody Heymann, Alison Earle, and Jeffrey Hayes, "The Work, Family, Equity Index: How Does the U.S. Measure Up?" (Montreal, Canada: Institute for Health and Social Policy, McGill University, 2009), available at http://www.hreonline.com/pdfs/08012009Extra_McGillSurvey.pdf.

69 Robert Hickey and others, "Losing Ground: A Struggle of Moderate-Income Households to Afford the Rising Costs of Housing and Transportation" (Washington: Center for Housing Policy and Center for Neighborhood Technology, 2012), available at http://www.reconnectingamerica.org/assets/Uploads/201210LosingGround.pdf.

70 Susan Herbel and Danena Gaines, "Women's Issues in Transportation," Presented at the 4th International Conference, Irvine, CA, September 27–30 (Transportation Research Board of the National Academies, 2009), available at http://onlinepubs.trb.org/onlinepubs/conf/cp46.pdf.

71 Charles L. Baum, "The Effects of Vehicle Ownership on Employment," *Journal of Urban Economics* 66 (3) (2009): 151–163.

72 "Impact of Rising Gas Prices on Below-Poverty Commuters," Low-Income Working Families Fact Sheets (Washington: Urban Institute, 2008), available at http://www.urban.org/UploadedPDF/411760_rising_gas_prices.pdf.

73 Albelda and others, "Bridging the Gaps: A Picture of How Work Supports Work in Ten States."

74 Calsyn and Rosenthal, "How the Affordable Care Act Helps Young Adults."

75 Center on Budget and Policy Priorities, "Status of the ACA Medicaid Expansion after Supreme Court Ruling," available at http://www.cbpp.org/files/status-of-the-ACA-medicaid-expansion-after-supreme-court-ruling.pdf (last accessed September 20, 2013).

76 For a complete analysis of what policies we need to help working families, see Heather Boushey, Ann O'Leary, and Sarah Jane Glynn, *Our Working Nation in 2013: An Updated National Agenda for Work and Family Policies.*

77 Bureau of Labor Statistics, *Current Population Survey, Labor Force Statistics*, available at http://www.bls.gov/data/.

78 Fair Shot Campaign [Video], "A Plan for Women and Families to Get Ahead," available at http://fairshotcampaign.org/featured/video-a-plan-for-women-and-families-to-get-ahead/.

79 Lawrence Mishel and others, *State of Working America, 12th ed.* (Washington: Economic Policy Institute, 2013), Figure 4C—Cumulative Change in Real Hourly Wages of Men, by Wage Percentile, 1979–2011, available at http://stateofworkingamerica.org/chart/swa-wages-figure-4c-change-real-hourly-wages/.

80 Miles Corak, "How to Slide Down the 'Great Gatsby Curve': Inequality, Life Chances, and Public Policy in the United States" (Washington: Center for American Progress, 2012), available at http://www.americanprogress.org/issues/economy/report/2012/12/05/46851/how-to-slide-down-the-great-gatsby-curve/.

81 Hartmann and Hayes, "Equal Pay for Working Women and Their Families: National Data on the Pay Gap and Its Costs."

82 Founded in 1987, the mission of Center for Partnership, or CPS, is to accelerate movement to partnership systems of human rights and nonviolence, gender and racial equity, economic prosperity, and a sustainable environment through research, education, grassroots empowerment, and policy initiatives. CPS's Caring Economy Campaign, or CEC, focuses on the enormous return on investment in the work of caring for and educating people, starting in early childhood—work still primarily done by women. For more information, visit their website at http://www. caringeconomy.org.

83 Nancy Folbre, *For Love and Money: Care Provision in the United States* (New York: Russell Sage Foundation, 2012).

84 Emma Fidel, "Women Seen Living Retirement in Poverty at Higher Rates Than Men," *Bloomberg News*, July 25, 2012, available at http://www.businessweek.com/news/2012-07-25/women-seen-living-retirement-in-poverty-at-higher-rates-than-men.

85 Max Fisher, "Map: How 35 Countries Compare on Child Poverty (the U.S. is ranked 34th)," *The Washington Post*, April 15, 2013, available at http://www.washingtonpost.com/blogs/worldviews/wp/2013/04/15/map-how-35-countries-compare-on-child-poverty-the-u-s-is-ranked-34th/.

86 Ueli Schiess and Jacqueline Schön-Bühlmann, "Satellitenkonto Haushaltsproduktion: Pilotversuch für die Schweiz (Satellite Account of Household Production for Switzerland)" (Neuchâtel, CH: Statistik der Schweiz, 2004).

87 Mignon Duffy, Randy Albelda, and Clare Hammonds, "Counting Care Work: The Empirical and Policy Applications of Care Theory," *Social Problems* 60 (2) (2013): 145–167.

88 Benjamin Bridgeman and others, "Accounting for Household Production in the National Accounts, 1965–2010" (Washington: U.S. Department of Commerce, Bureau of Economic Analysis, 2012), available at http://www.bea.gov/scb/pdf/2012/05%20May/0512_household.pdf.

89 S.A. Hoenig and A.R.E. Page, "Counting on Care Work in Australia" (Prepared by AECgroup Limited for economic Security4Women, Australia, 2012), available at http://www.security4women.org.au/wp-content/uploads/eS4W-Counting-on-Care-Work-in-Australia-Final-Report.pdf (last accessed September 2013).

90 Caring Economy Campaign, "Public Policy: Social Wealth Indicators Project," available at http://www.caringeconomy.org/content/public-policy-social-wealth-indicators-project (last accessed September 2013).

91 S.P. Walker and others, "Building Human Capacity Through Early Childhood Intervention," *West Indian Medical Journal* 61 (4) (2012): 216–322.

92 David Kirp, ed., *The Sandbox Investment: the Preschool Movement and Kids-First Policies* (Cambridge, MA: Harvard University Press, 2009), pp. 5–10.

93 Ricardo Hausmann, Laura D. Tyson, and Saadia Zahidi, "The Global Gender Gap Report 2012" (Geneva: World Economic Forum, 2012).

94 Xavier Sala-i-Martin and others, "The Global Competitiveness Report 2012-2013" (Geneva: World Economic Forum, 2012), 1.1 Table 3: The Global Competitiveness Index 2012–2013 Rankings and 2011–2012 Comparisons.

95 Riane Eisler, *The Real Wealth of Nations: Creating a Caring Economics* (San Francisco, CA: Berrett-Koehler, 2007), p. 60.

The Gender Wage Gap: A Civil Rights Issue for Our Time

By MAYA L. HARRIS, *a senior fellow at the Center for American Progress, a visiting scholar at Harvard Law School, and a leading voice in civil rights law. She previously served as vice president of the Ford Foundation's global Democracy, Rights and Justice program and was executive director of the American Civil Liberties Union of Northern California, the largest ACLU affiliate in the United States.*

It has been more than 20 years since I arrived at the Stanford Law School campus, a first-year student with dreams of becoming a civil rights lawyer. Like many people of color coming of age in the 1980s, I considered myself a child of the civil rights movement. My mother, a Berkeley activist in the 1960s, raised my sister and me on stories about Medgar, Malcolm, Martin, and Marshall. I was a direct beneficiary of the *Brown v. Board of Education* decision and busing, of voting rights and affirmative action, so I wanted to use the new body of civil rights law to make secure the change the movement had forged—change that I, having grown up black and South Asian, viewed primarily through the lens of race.

So I'm not sure I would have viewed as a civil rights issue the fact that, in all likelihood, the women in my graduating class and I would wind up earning less than our male counterparts for performing the same legal work—even though many of us would graduate at the top of our class, and all of us, male and female, would earn the same prestigious Stanford Law degree.

But years of working as a civil rights lawyer and advocate have reinforced for me this basic fact: Gender pay inequity is undeniably a pressing civil rights issue for our time.

And the reason this is true emanates from our deepest notions of fairness and equality. When we think about the persistent gender pay gap, it raises in us a discomfort and unease similar to the feeling we get when confronting racial injustice today, all these decades after the civil rights movement. We get that unsettling feeling that, as they say, "for all our hopes and all our boasts," we still view and value women as "less than."

Indeed, the core concept of fairness that underlies the pay-inequity discussion animates every equality movement. It is about more than having a comparable paycheck for comparable work, just like the civil rights movement was about more than having racial-equality laws on the books. At its core, pay equity—and the broader idea of women as full participants in the economic life of our country—is about concepts

Jeannie James of Winslow, Arizona, is an administrative assistant at the Department of Social Services. While she loves her job, the long commute makes it difficult to balance work with life at home. {JAN SONNENMAIR}

as old as the republic itself. It is about recognizing that we all deserve basic dignity, respect, equal opportunity, and access to economic security.

To be sure, gender equity in general is more of a reality today than ever before. Women attend college at higher rates than men, earn better grades, and graduate in greater numbers. We now make up almost half of the U.S. workforce and are one-third of the nation's doctors and lawyers—more than triple the number of a generation ago. And more than a quarter of wives outearn their spouses today.

But this progress masks deeper wrinkles of inequity. Most of the progress women have made getting up the pay-equity ladder has come for women in the top 20 percent of earners. And studies have shown the wage gap remains true even when we control for factors such as education level, profession, or position, and it cannot be fully explained by personal choices.

Take, for example, doctors in the same specialty performing similar work. According to a study published in 2012 by the *Journal of the American Medical Association*, "Gender differences in salary exist in this select, homogenous cohort of mid-career academic physicians, even after adjustment for differences in specialty, institutional characteristics, academic productivity, academic rank, work hours, and other factors."[1] In other words, male doctors earn more than female doctors for the same work.

Pay inequity is particularly salient for women of color, for whom the wage gap is more like a wage gulf, and progress toward closing it remains elusive. The expectation that the wage gap could narrow further in the future—with women now earning the majority of advanced degrees and education beginning to outweigh gender as a determinant of wages—is not a panacea for women of color. They continue to face significant barriers to accessing higher education and, in any event, are more likely to work in minimum- and low-wage jobs.

In the 50 years since the passage of the first Equal Pay Act, the gender wage gap has narrowed by only 18 cents—and more than a quarter of this "progress" is due to losses in men's wages as opposed to gains in women's wages. In fact, the reality is that over the past 10 years, the United States has closed its wage gap barely, if at all—by less than one penny—earning the dubious distinction of having one of the largest gender wage gaps among developed nations.

This pay inequity between the sexes carries powerful implications for the health of our economy and the character of our society. It's no mistake that those who gathered on the National Mall 50 years ago regarded their March on Washington as a march for jobs as much as anything else. The architects of the civil rights movement understood that prohibiting access to economic independence through pay inequity, employment discrimination, and job segregation in low-paying, low-skill occupations was an effective way to keep a segment of the population in a perpetually subservient crouch—just as effective a way as denying them their political rights.

I hear echoes of these same patterns of economic disenfranchisement in the experiences of many women today, and pay inequity is the measurable manifestation of that reality.

It's time for action—time to bring equality to working women.

There have been many prescriptions offered to address wage inequality between the sexes:

- The Paycheck Fairness Act, languishing in Congress for nearly a decade, would update our laws for the 21st century and help eliminate discriminatory pay.

- Raising the minimum wage would help close the gap, given that nearly two-thirds of all workers making the minimum wage are women.

- Adopting policies that increase access to quality, affordable child care, paid sick days, and family leave would help reduce wage differences in a workforce where women are the sole or primary source of income for 40 percent of households with children under the age of 18.

Just as the concepts of equality, fairness, and access to economic security amplified the moral force of the civil rights movement, so too should these same ideas spur us to address the pay-equity issue with renewed urgency. We cannot wait another 50 years.

ENDNOTE

1   Reshma Jagsi and others, "Gender Differences in the Salaries of Physician Researchers," *Journal of the American Medical Association* 307 (22) (2012): 2410–2417, available at http://www.med.upenn.edu/focus/user_documents/Gender DifferencesintheSalariesofPhysicianResearchers-JAMA.pdf.

Making the Care Economy a Caring Economy

By AI-JEN POO, director of the National Domestic Workers Alliance, which works to build power, respect, and fair labor standards for the estimated 2 million nannies, housekeepers, and caregivers for the aging in the United States.

Anna is a Filipino live-in nanny in New York. Her workday begins when the children wake up at 6 in the morning and ends around 10 at night, when she puts them to sleep and finishes cleaning up the kitchen. Anna is paid $620 a month. That means she earns about $1.27 an hour.[1]

Domestic workers such as Anna—nannies, housecleaners, and caregivers for the elderly—are the backbone of our "care economy." The work required to care for people in our families across generations is a need and responsibility felt in every American household. As American women increasingly move away from being homemakers and home-based caregivers themselves—instead becoming primary earners or co-breadwinners in most U.S. families—they are increasingly turning to domestic workers to help them at home.

As a result, the domestic work industry grew by 10 percent between 2004 and 2010.[2] There are now an estimated 800,000 to 2 million domestic workers in the United States.[3] The number is bound to grow, with the 78 million Baby Boomers moving into retirement and into a period in their lives when they might require at-home care themselves.

According to the latest U.S. Census, domestic workers are overwhelmingly female—95 percent.[4] Most of their "bosses" are women, too. Domestic workers do the long and hard work of caring for their bosses' children, homes, and aging relatives, taking pride in their ability to perform the duties that enable families to be strong and households to function smoothly. That work, in turn, helps make it possible for women to earn a living, leaving their homes and families in caring, competent hands.

Many a working mom who hires a nanny, housekeeper, or caregiver does not consider herself to be the boss. In her mind, the boss is someone else—someone far outside the sanctuary of her home—and she is the one who is the employee. She is struggling and juggling all of the responsibilities in her own full life, with little support from her employer and little infrastructure to help her navigate all of her various roles. But the truth is, at home she herself is an employer, with the power and responsibilities that go along with that role.

And it is the working mother's own employee— the domestic worker whom she trusts to take care of her home and the most precious people

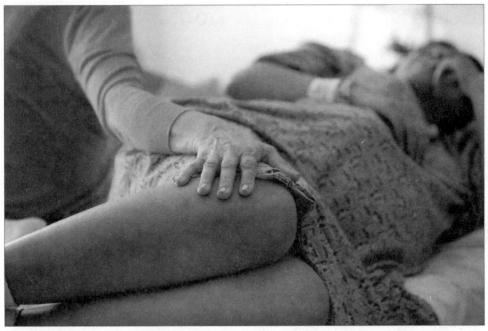

Bringing a child into the world carries with it enormous financial obligations as well as joy. In this picture, Carmen Rios coaches Karina Castaneda through labor in San Rafael, California. Carmen, originally from Puerto Rico, is a "companera" who has been helping Spanish-speaking women deliver babies for nearly two decades. {BARBARA RIES}

in her life—who so often is not paid enough to care for *her* own family and home. Twenty-three percent of domestic workers earn below their state's minimum wage, and 67 percent of domestic workers who live in their employers' homes earn below minimum wage.[5]

This is nothing new. For too long, our society has minimized and undervalued the "invisible" work we take for granted, including childbearing, child rearing, elder care, and home management—the "women's work" that makes other work possible. We have failed to adequately account for the time, work, and energy required to raise families—either by working mothers themselves or by the domestic workers they hire to help them. The

American economic model simply does not take into account the actual value of this work. The cost of that failure cuts across all classes, but low-income women, immigrant women, and women of color are the most vulnerable and have the fewest choices.

These are women such as Marlene Champion, originally from Barbados, who has been a domestic worker all of her working life, raising dozens of children while also raising her own, in addition to caring for the elderly. For most of those years, she earned less than a living wage—sometimes less than minimum wage—and never had health care. This year she will turn 65 years old, and she still needs to work full time to support herself.[6]

In telling the story of our work, I occasionally talk about the harsh light that goes on for many when a domestic worker who is paid less than a living wage sees her employer bring home a $600 pair of shoes. I ask people to imagine what would happen to a place such as Manhattan or Los Angeles if all domestic workers decided not to go to work one day. Again the light bulb goes on: These cities' economies would tremble, or even crumble, without them.

These images grab people's attention. But the truth is, the us-versus-them narrative that worked so well in many campaigns for social change really does not work the same way here. That's because caregiving does not divide us; it unites us and connects us. It's a shared goal and purpose across the infinitely diverse populations in the United States. We need each other. Here in our homes, with the care of our most vulnerable and valuable at stake, what's best for each is best for both.

We need to create a "caring economy" where we acknowledge the true, inherent value of care work. When we reach that place, it will be a moment of great healing that grants long-denied dignity and value to the caregivers in every class of society:

- Those of us who had to figure out how to steal time away from our offices to care for children or elders will no longer feel as if we were stealing at all. Our employers will institute policies such as paid sick leave, paid family leave, and provisions for flexible hours.

- Those of us who employ others to care for our families will celebrate that work, pay fairly, and insist on and provide the best conditions for those workers.

- Those of us who are paid care workers will be able to take pride in providing the best care possible for the families we work for and for our own families—pride in our fundamental contribution to society and the economy.

In such a world, everyone who provides care—paid and unpaid, men as well as women—will be able to acknowledge the immense power, purpose, and value inherent in that role.

We are taking steps toward that goal. In 2000, we founded Domestic Workers United, or DWU, in New York. DWU led the way to the 2010 passage of the nation's first Domestic Workers' Bill of Rights,[7] which extends basic labor protection—such as minimum wage, overtime pay, and paid time off—to more than 200,000 domestic workers in New York. In 2013, Hawaii became the second state to enact domestic workers' legislation,[8] and California passed similar legislation extending overtime pay to some in-home care workers.[9] Today, the National Domestic Workers Alliance brings together more than 44 domestic workers' organizations across the nation,[10] and more than five additional states are considering establishing basic rights.[11] And in 2013, the Department of Labor announced a regulatory change to include nearly 2 million in-home, direct care workers—who care for the disabled and elderly—under the minimum wage and overtime protections of the Fair Labor Standards Act.[12]

These changes represent significant break-throughs for this workforce. Seventy-five years after New Deal labor laws were put into place explicitly excluding domestic workers, we are finally moving toward full inclusion.

It is the beginning of a cultural shift that is necessary for our transformation from just a **care economy** into a **caring economy**. I believe the shift is imperative, both morally and economically. It will entail everything from policy changes that support families who hire caregivers, to training and career ladders for care providers themselves, to tech-based innovations that make care accessible to those who need it.

Becoming a caring economy will release tremendous energy and will help us stem the rising tide of inequality in this country. We can have a robust economy that is based on the ethics of full inclusion and care.

Portions of this essay have appeared in previously published works by the author at http://www.domesticworkers.org/es/news/2013/ building-a-caring-economy and http:// www.huffingtonpost.com/aijen-poo/care-economy_b_3118846.html .

ENDNOTES

1   Author interview with Anna, New York, New York, March 2013.

2   U.S. Census Bureau, "DataFerrett: American Community Survey, 2004–2010," available at http://www.census.gov/ acs/www/data_documentation/data_ferrett_for_pums/ (last accessed August 2013).

3   Linda Burnham and Nik Theodore, "Home Economics: The Invisible and Unregulated World of Domestic Work" (New York: National Domestic Workers Alliance, 2012), available at http://www.domesticworkers.org/pdfs/HomeEconomics English.pdf.

4   Ibid.

5   Ibid.

6   Author interview with Marlene Champion, Brooklyn, New York, September 27, 2012.

7   New York Department of Labor, "Domestic Workers' Bill of Rights," available at http://www.labor.ny.gov/legal/ domestic-workers-bill-of-rights.shtm (last accessed August 2013).

8   Bryce Covert, "Hawaii Becomes Second State to Pass a Domestic Workers Bill of Rights," ThinkProgress, May 2, 2013, available at http://thinkprogress.org/econ omy/2013/05/02/1955901/hawaii-domestic-workers-bill-of-rights/.

9   National Domestic Workers Alliance, "Governor Brown Signs California Domestic Workers Bill of Rights," Press release, September 26, 2013, available at http://www.domesticwork-ers.org/news/2013/governor-brown-signs-california-domes-tic-worker-bill-of-rights.

10 National Domestic Workers Alliance, "Who We Are," avail-able at http://www.domesticworkers.org/who-we-are (last accessed September 2013).

11 Covert, "Hawaii Becomes Second State to Pass a Domestic Workers Bill of Rights."

12 U.S. Department of Labor, "Minimum wage, overtime protec-tions extended to direct care workers by US Labor Depart-ment," Press release, September 17, 2013, available at http:// www.dol.gov/opa/media/press/whd/WHD20131922.htm.

BARBARA RIES

BINITA PRADHAN • San Francisco, California

Binita is a business owner and a single mother to her 4-year-old son, Ayush. After escaping an abusive relationship, Benita depended on various women's shelters before moving into an apartment of her own. She has received enormous assistance from La Cocina, a San Francisco-based restaurant incubator for women, which helped her start Bini's Kitchen, a catering company. Binita works 18-hour days to keep the business afloat and depends on her sister for child care and support.

Although Bini's Kitchen is still in its infancy, Binita feels optimistic about her and Ayush's future. "I am blessed by God, who has given me two hands full of skills, and the knowledge and faith to stand straight up and fight back," she said.

Lesbian, Bisexual, Transgender, and Broke

By DANIELLE MOODIE-MILLS, an advisor on LGBT Policy and Racial Justice at the Center for American Progress. Her political and cultural analysis and commentary have been published in **The Atlantic, Ebony**, **Essence,** *and the* **Huffington Post,** *and she has appeared on MSNBC, Current, and the CBC. She is also the host of* **Politini,** *a politics and pop culture show on blis.fm.*

"You're already black and a woman. How much more do you want to have against you?"

That's what my mother said when I came out to her as a lesbian more than a decade ago. My parents were terrified, because there was no blueprint to help them envision the kind of life I had before me.

Waiting to come out to them until I was 22 and out of college was a strategic move on my part. I wanted to be in a place where I could support and care for myself in case my parents didn't take the news well and put me out. Indeed, this fear of rejection and being cast out is in the hearts of many LGBT youth before they share their sexual orientation or gender identity with their families—fear that the people whose job is to love and protect them will toss them aside, fear that they'll be left alone in a world that doesn't understand or accept them.

My own parents were indeed panicked by the prospect of their youngest daughter being a lesbian, but after the shock subsided a week later, they were where they had always been: in my corner and rooting for my success. I was lucky, unlike so many LGBT youth who are rejected by their families and left to fend for themselves. While these youth make up only 5 to 7 percent of the U.S. population, they comprise a staggering 40 percent of all homeless youth.[1]

Sometimes it's the LGBT teen herself who chooses to leave. Imagine being a 16-year-old gender-nonconforming girl who experiences constant physical and emotional abuse from her peers at school, but at home, her parents tell her the bullying is her own fault, because she's "choosing" to stand out. They believe that all she needs is a "good beating" and berating to teach her how to "act like a lady." End result: The abuse both at home and at school pushes her to the brink, and she feels the streets are her only option.

I'm grateful this was not my story, but it is for 43 percent of LGBT youth living on the streets.[2] For them, family rejection—plus hostile school environments, institutionalized discrimination, and violence—begins what can become a lifetime of economic insecurity and living on the brink.

These stories of LGBT youth being discounted and dismissed are what prompted me to become an advocate. Then my work on the frontlines of the marriage equality movement in the District of Columbia showed me even more evidence that my parents had good reason to be concerned about my coming out. Even as many of us were hailing the Supreme Court decision overturning the Defense of Marriage Act, I came to see that marriage alone isn't the silver bullet of full equality for the thousands of lesbian, bisexual, and transgender women. For them, the basic measure of equality still to be realized is simple economic security.

Contrary to the myth of gay affluence perpetuated in the media, many, many LGBT couples and their families are far from wealthy or even comfortable. Lesbian couples in particular face an economic and cultural double bind. As women, they already earn less than men, and as lesbians—especially those who are gender nonconforming—they are subjected to anti-gay bias in the workplace for not fitting the cultural aesthetics society demands of women.

These women are particularly vulnerable to discrimination at work, given that there are no federal protections to prevent them from being fired from their jobs—or not hired at all—simply because of their sexual orientation or gender identity. Employers in 29 states can legally discriminate against these workers.[3] And the economic consequences are real. Lesbian, bisexual, and transgender women are at the bottom of almost every economic metric.

It's almost unfathomable to believe, in this day and age, that just being a woman in a same-gender relationship immediately qualifies you for a life on or over the brink of poverty, but it does. According to "A Broken Bargain," a joint report by the Center for American Progress, the Movement Advancement Project, and the Human Rights Campaign:

> Two women—even if they individually earn more than comparable heterosexual women—may still have a combined household income that is lower than that of a married different-sex couple, because both earners' wages are affected by the gender wage gap. This "double-gap" multiplier means less money for the entire family every year and fewer resources to save for retirement.[4]

That means that even when both partners are working, they are more likely to be among the "working poor" than their different-sex counterparts.[5]

The economic prospects are even worse for lesbians and transgender women who are black. The CAP report "Jumping Beyond the Broom" revealed that black lesbian couples were five times more likely to be living in poverty than white lesbian couples, at a rate of 21.1 percent compared to 4.3 percent.[6] Transgender women fare worse, with double the rate of unemployment of the general population and higher rates of job discrimination pushing them into extreme poverty. They are four times more likely than the general population to have a household income of less than $10,000 per year.[7]

These numbers make it painfully clear that sexism—coupled with anti-gay bias and then compounded by systemic racism—can result in economic catastrophe for lesbian, bisexual, and transgender women of color. No wonder my parents were terrified.

When you add kids to the picture, it gets worse. Analysis by UCLA's Williams Institute finds that lesbian couples are more likely than different-sex and gay couples to be raising children, and 37.7 percent of those children are living in poverty. It's not surprising then that these families are also more than twice as likely to receive government assistance—14.1 percent compared to just 6.5 percent of different-sex couples.[8] Antiquated family policies[9] that ignore LGBT family structures, limit parental rights, and deny these children legal ties to their families further perpetuate the cycle of poverty. These are the women and families I advocate for every day.

We are seeing in this *Shriver Report* that when we invest in women, we invest in entire communities and our economy as a whole. Similarly, ensuring that our public policies work for lesbian, bisexual, and transgender women and their families is essential to boosting the economic outcomes for the gay community overall. This is why we need to pass the federal Employment Non-Discrimination Act and update our family and anti-poverty policies, so that children of lesbian parents do not fall through the safety net.

Despite the progress toward LGBT equality we've seen since I came out more than a decade ago, the economic condition of lesbians in particular remains virtually the same. Kids are coming out at younger ages, but more LGBT youth are living on the streets. Women make up half of the workforce, but two women working to provide for one household still fall short, because of pay inequity and workplace discrimination. The Defense of Marriage Act has been dismantled, but family policies have not been updated to reflect all varieties of the modern American family.

These are the facts, but we also know this to be true: Not too long ago, there were no examples of openly LGBT couples. Today, there are. There were no models of thriving lesbian-headed households. Today, there are. Despite the obstacles we still have to overcome and the myths we still have to dispel, today there is a blueprint for LGBT youth to follow. Now it's up to us to ensure that public policy evolves in pace with our culture.

ENDNOTES

1 Laura E. Durso and Gary J. Gates, "Serving Our Youth: Findings from a National Survey of Services Providers Working with Lesbian, Gay, Bisexual and Transgender Youth Who Are Homeless or at Risk of Becoming Homeless" (The Palette Fund, The True Colors Fund, and the Williams Institute, 2012), available at http://williamsinstitute.law.ucla.edu/wp-content/uploads/Durso-Gates-LGBT-Homeless-Youth-Survey-July-2012.pdf

2 Andrew Phifer and Jeff Krehely, "Gay and Transgender Homeless Youth Face Huge Obstacles" (Washington: Center for American Progress, 2012), available at http://www.americanprogress.org/issues/lgbt/report/2012/07/12/11954/gay-and-transgender-homeless-youth-face-huge-obstacles/.

3 Movement Advancement Project, Human Rights Campaign, and Center for American Progress, "A Broken Bargain: Discrimination, Fewer Benefits and More Taxes for LGBT Workers" (2013), available at http://www.americanprogress.org/issues/lgbt/report/2013/06/04/65133/a-broken-bargain/.

4 Ibid.

5 M.V. Lee Badgett, Laura E. Durso, and Alyssa Schneebaum, "New Patterns of Poverty in the Lesbian, Gay, and Bisexual Community" (Los Angeles: The Williams Institute, 2013), available at http://williamsinstitute.law.ucla.edu/research/census-lgbt-demographics-studies/lgbt-poverty-update-june-2013/.

6 Aisha C. Moodie-Mills, "Jumping Beyond the Broom: Why Black Gay and Transgender Americans Need More Than Marriage Equality" (Washington: Center for American Progress, 2012), available at http://www.americanprogress.org/wp-content/uploads/issues/2012/01/pdf/black_lgbt.pdf.

7 Jaime M. Grant, Lisa A. Mottet, and Justin Tanis, "Injustice at Every Turn: A Report of the National Transgender Discrimination Survey" (National Center for Transgender Equality and the National Gay and Lesbian Task Force, 2011), available at http://www.thetaskforce.org/downloads/reports/reports/ntds_full.pdf.

8 Badgett, Durso, and Schneebaum, "New Patterns of Poverty in the Lesbian, Gay, and Bisexual Community."

9 Jennifer Chrisler, Ineke Mushovic, and Jeff Krehely, "Making Public Policy Work for All Households: How Current Laws Fail to Address the Changing Reality of American Families" (Washington: Center for American Progress, 2011), available at http://www.americanprogress.org/issues/lgbt/report/2011/10/25/10474/making-public-policy-work-for-all-households/.

The Changing Face of American Women

By ANGELA GLOVER BLACKWELL, *one of America's leading authorities on race and poverty issues and founder and CEO of PolicyLink, a national research and action institute advancing economic and social equity. She served as senior vice president of the Rockefeller Foundation and as a partner at Public Advocates, a nationally recognized public interest law firm.*

The story of the mid-21st century is this: The face of America is changing. Whether that turns out to be a story of triumph or disaster will depend on how the nation deals with the centuries-old conundrums of race and gender. By 2045, the majority of women—and most women in the workforce—will be women of color.[1]

This shift has already occurred in California, Texas, New Mexico, and a growing list of metropolitan regions around the country. In 2012, for the first time, the majority of newborn girls in the United States—51 percent—were girls of color.[2] An astonishing 92 percent of the nation's population growth over the past decade has come from people of color—primarily Latinos, Asian Americans, and people who identify as mixed race.[3] If we want to secure the economic future for women, children, and the nation as a whole, we must embrace and invest in these demographic changes.

Race and ethnicity lie at the root of the contradiction that this *Shriver Report* explores, which is why women have come so far yet are more vulnerable than ever. Long-standing racial inequities have resulted in significant gaps in education, health,

and wealth among the very groups our nation will rely upon to provide the innovators and leaders of tomorrow. These gaps leave women of color lagging far behind their white counterparts on just about every measure of well-being.

For every dollar in wealth owned by white women, women of color have only a fraction of a penny.[4] Women of color are twice as likely to work in low-wage sectors such as the service industry.[5] Yet they must succeed if we are to put women and their children on a more secure economic footing. In short, alleviating poverty and eliminating gender disparities requires racial equity: just and fair inclusion in a society in which all can participate and prosper.

To make the progress that women need, the women's movement must learn to see through a racial lens. The idea that women can have the same fair shot at success as men has always been a pipe dream for the millions of girls and women of color saddled with going to failing schools, living in underinvested communities, and watching their men struggle with high unemployment and other barriers to opportunity. Now that women of color are becoming the majority, the degree to which they are disadvantaged limits the progress women have made in this country.

Broad measures of gender inequality mask the depth of distress in communities of color. As we highlight throughout this report, women working full time earn only 77 cents for every dollar earned by their male counterparts. But African American women earn only 70 cents on that dollar,[6] and Latina women earn less than 60 cents.[7] In 2011, 14.6 percent of all American women were poor, the highest rate in 18 years. But African American and Latina women had even higher poverty rates—26 percent and 24 percent, respectively.[8]

And more than one-fifth of the nation's children live in poverty, the worst rate in the developed world. The numbers are even higher for children of color: 38 percent of African American children and 35 percent of Latino children are poor.[9]

No nation can afford to squander the contributions of such a large segment of its population. But America is only beginning to recognize that racial and cultural diversity is a tremendous asset in an increasingly competitive global economy. Diversity can inspire knowledge-driven innovations that arise from a mix of ideas, perspectives, and backgrounds. It can provide the broad skills, flexibility, and openness to others that we need

Dee Saint Franc, left, was raised in Rhode Island's foster care system. She worked her way through school while raising her daughter, Azariah, and now works two jobs. She relies on foster family members for help with child care. {BARBARA RIES}

La Cocina, a restaurant incubator in San Francisco, California, helps women start their own businesses. Rosa Flores is one of the many entrepreneurial Latina women working in its kitchen. {BARBARA RIES}

to succeed in an ever-changing, interconnected world. If we adopt a growth model grounded in the American ideals of fairness, inclusion, and opportunity for all, we can ensure that our economy will remain preeminent.

This means advancing three broad policy goals:

1. GROW GOOD JOBS. We can start with two areas of major importance to women. First, entrepreneurship: Before the recession effectively halted lending, women of color were launching businesses at a faster pace than any other group. For instance, the number of African American female-owned firms increased by 67 percent from 2002 to 2007. Businesses owned by women of color employed 1.2 million workers and generated $186.2 billion in gross receipts.[10] Federal programs that make capital available must target women entrepreneurs of color to foster growth and development of a broad range of business ventures, especially ones that create jobs.

Second, we must improve the pay and quality of low-wage jobs, the fastest-growing segment of employment. Women held 62 percent of

minimum-wage jobs in 2011, though they represented only 47 percent of the labor force.[11] Strong union protections and increases in the federal minimum wage would benefit all women.

2. BUILD CAPABILITIES. By 2018, 45 percent of jobs will require at least an associate's degree, but among today's workers, only 27 percent of African Americans, 26 percent of U.S.-born Latinos, and 14 percent of Latino immigrants have achieved this level of education.[12] If we do not raise education levels among our fastest-growing communities, we will lose our edge in the global economy. There are a few good places to begin to close the gap: strengthening the community college system, expanding universal pre-K, ensuring equitable school financing in all neighborhoods, and increasing science and technology education for girls and children of color.

3. ELIMINATE BARRIERS TO SUCCESS AND EXPAND OPPORTUNITIES. Targeting gender barriers is important but insufficient. Deep, sustained progress also requires the dismantling of the racial barriers to economic inclusion and civic participation.

Sadly, in America, one's address has become a proxy for opportunity. While federal and state laws prohibit many overtly discriminatory policies, the nation's map remains carved into separate, shamefully unequal communities. Unaddressed racial discrimination in housing has concentrated poor and low-wage families of color in communities with failing schools, few jobs, inadequate transportation that can connect to jobs, and unsafe neighborhoods. More than half of Latinos and nearly 65 percent of African Americans live in neighborhoods of color[13]—generally low-income ones. Two-thirds of black children live in high-poverty communities, compared to 6 percent of white children—a percentage that has not changed in 30 years.[14] To level the playing field, investments and policies must be aimed at rebuilding distressed communities, turning them into communities of opportunity that can provide access to strong schools, good jobs, reliable transportation, and other vital services.

As the nation's economic challenges converge with changing demographics, we have a golden opportunity. It's time to link women's advocacy with advocacy for racial equity. That is how we can build a just, fair, and prosperous society for everyone.

ENDNOTES

1   Vanessa Cárdenas and Sarah Treuhaft, eds., *All-In Nation: An America that Works for All* (Washington: Center for American Progress, 2013), p. 32, available at http://www.allin nation.org.

2   Author's calculations based on U.S. Census Bureau, "2012 National Population Projections: Downloadable Files," available at http://www.census.gov/population/projections/ data/national/2012/downloadablefiles.html (last accessed September 2013).

3   Sabrina Tavernise, "Whites Account for Under Half of Births in U.S.," *New York Times,* May 17, 2013, available at http://www. nytimes.com/2012/05/17/us/whites-account-for-under- half-of-births-in-us.html?pagewanted=all.

4   Insight Center for Community Economic Development, "Lifting as We Climb: Women of Color, Wealth, and America's Future" (2010), available at http://www.cunapfi.org/ download/198_Women_of_Color_Wealth_Future_ Spring_2010.pdf.

5   Sophia Kerby, "The State of Women of Color in the United States" (Washington: Center for American Progress, 2012), available at http://www.americanprogress.org/issues/race/ report/2012/07/17/11923/the-state-of-women-of-color-in- the-united-states/.

6   National Partnership for Women & Families, "African American Women and the Wage Gap" (2013), available at http://go.nationalpartnership.org/site/DocServer/ Wage_Gap_for_African_American_Women_in_20_States. pdf?docID=11702.

7   National Partnership for Women & Families, "Latinas and the Wage Gap" (2013), available at http://go.national partnership.org/site/DocServer/Wage_Gap_for_Latinas_ in_20_States.pdf?docID=11701.

8   National Women's Law Center, "Women's Poverty Rate Stabilizes, Remains Historically High," available at http:// www.nwlc.org/womens-poverty-rate-stabilizes-remains- historically-high (last accessed September 2013).

9   University of Michigan National Poverty Center, "Poverty in the United States: Frequently Asked Questions," available at http://www.npc.umich.edu/poverty/ (last accessed September 2013).

10   U.S. Department of Commerce, "Minority Women-Owned Firms Are the Fastest Growing," available at http://www. mbda.gov/node/1201 (last accessed September 2013).

11   Shetal Vohra-Gupta, "Women of Color and Minimum Wage: A Policy of Racial, Gender, and Economic Discrimination" (Austin, TX: The University of Texas at Austin Institute for Urban Policy Research & Analysis, 2012), available at http:// www.utexas.edu/cola/insts/iupra/_files/pdf/IUPRA%20 brief%20Minimum%20Wage.pdf.

12   Cárdenas and Treuhaft, *All-In Nation.*

13   National Fair Housing Alliance, "Summer 2008 Lott Leadership Exchange: Race, Religion and Reconciliation in a Comparative Dialogue," PowerPoint presentation, July 3, 2008, available at http://www.nationalfairhousing.org/LinkClick.aspx?fi leticket=mkUgz4m5QGE%3D&tabid=3917&mid=5418.

14   Patrick Sharkey, "Neighborhoods and the Black-White Mobility Gap" (Washington: Pew Charitable Trusts, 2009), available at http://www.pewtrusts.org/uploadedFiles/ wwwpewtrustsorg/Reports/Economic_Mobility/PEW_ SHARKEY_v12.pdf.

Empowering Latinas

By EVA LONGORIA, actress, producer, and activist. The Eva Longoria Foundation supports programs helping Latinas excel in school, attend college, and succeed as entrepreneurs.

I am impressed by the women I meet who have achieved great success and improved the world. From Maria Shriver to Supreme Court Justice Sonia Sotomayor, I feel honored to know them. But for every empowered woman I meet, I see many more with tremendous potential who don't have the opportunity to realize their dreams. As a ninth-generation Texan and proud Mexican American, I'm especially committed to improving outcomes for my fellow Latinas.

Latinas are incredibly entrepreneurial. The number of Latina-owned businesses has increased at eight times the rate of men-owned businesses in recent years.[1] Yet in spite of their ambition and drive, many Latinas are not achieving the American Dream. One in three of us drops out of high school,[2] and 25 percent of Latinas live in poverty.[3] Latina unemployment is high at 9 percent,[4] and when they are in the workforce, Latinas earn less than 60 cents for every dollar a white man earns for the same job.[5]

With more than 25 million Latinas in the United States[6] and projections putting us at 15 percent of the total population by 2050, we must all pay attention to the fate of Latinas[7] because the economic future of our country depends on it.[8]

The good news is that we know what works. Education is the single most powerful tool to help people pull themselves out of poverty and change their life trajectory. I founded the Eva Longoria Foundation to help more Latinas do just that.

When I learned that 80 percent of Latina high school students aspire to attend college, but only 15 percent hold college degrees, I wanted to understand why. My foundation partnered with UCLA's Civil Rights Project on a study to identify factors that would increase high school graduation and college enrollment rates for Latinas. The results were interesting but not surprising.[9]

We found that interventions such as involvement in extracurricular activities, exposure to Latino teachers and counselors, high-quality math instruction from a young age, and parent engagement all significantly impact Latinas' ultimate success, even against strong odds. Knowing that a complete overhaul of our struggling education system is not imminent, it's heartening to learn that feasible interventions like these can make a life-changing difference. I'm working on it, and I'm not alone.

To give just one example of this kind of doable change: Research shows that parent involvement plays a major role in helping kids graduate high school and attend college. So my foundation supports a nine-week parent-engagement program, which teaches parents the basics of what their kids need to make it to college. It educates them about class requirements, how and why to set up meetings with teachers and counselors, how to assist with homework, and how and when to file college applications and financial aid forms.

The results: Students whose parents complete the program have a 90 percent graduation rate,

The Eva Longoria Foundation was founded by the actress and activist to help Latinas succeed in school, attend college, and prosper as entrepreneurs.
{COURTESY EVA LONGORIA}

compared to the 62 percent rate of Los Angeles–area students overall. A nine-week course like this one can open up a lifetime of possibilities for these Latino families.

The good news is there are many programs like this, but they need our help. By giving our time, financial resources, and advocacy, we can contribute in some way to improving educational outcomes for Latinas.

No matter how large or small our contribution, we must do our part to help these students succeed. Together, we can create a world that doesn't need a *Shriver* report about "women on the brink" because women—all of our women—will have the opportunities they need to gain access to the American Dream.

ENDNOTES

1 U.S. Census Bureau, "American FactFinder," available at http://factfinder2.census.gov/faces/tableservices/jsf/pages/productview.xhtml?pid=SBO_2007_00CSA01&prodType=table (last accessed September 2013).

2 Education Week, "Trailing Behind, Moving Forward: Latino Students in U.S. Schools," June 7, 2012, available at http://www.edweek.org/ew/toc/2012/06/07/.

3 National Women's Law Center, "Poverty Among Women and Families, 2000-2010: Extreme Poverty Reaches Record Levels as Congress Faces Critical Choices" (2011), available at http://www.nwlc.org/sites/default/files/pdfs/povertyamongwomenandfamilies2010final.pdf.

4 U.S. Bureau of Labor Statistics, "Table A-3. Employment status of the Hispanic or Latino population by sex and age," available at http://www.bls.gov/news.release/empsit.t03.htm (last accessed September 2013).

5 U.S. Bureau of Labor Statistics, "Table 7. Median usual weekly earnings of full-time wage and salary workers by selected characteristics, annual averages," available at http://www.bls.gov/news.release/wkyeng.t07.htm (last accessed September 2013).

6 U.S. Census Bureau, "National Characteristics: Vintage 2011," available at http://www.census.gov/popest/data/national/asrh/2011/tables/NC-EST2011-03.xls (last accessed September 2013).

7 U.S. Census Bureau, "Facts for Features: Hispanic Heritage Month 2012: Sept. 15–Oct. 15," Press release, August 6, 2012, available at http://www.census.gov/newsroom/releases/archives/facts_for_features_special_editions/cb12-ff19.html.

8 U.S. Census Bureau, "An Older and More Diverse Nation by Midcentury," Press release, August 14, 2008, available at http://www.census.gov/newsroom/releases/archives/population/cb08-123.html.

9 Patricia Gándara and others, "Making Education Work for Latinas in the U.S." (Los Angeles: Eva Longoria Foundation, 2013), available at http://www.evalongoriafoundation.org/wp-content/uploads/2012/05/Making-Education-Work-for-Latinas-in-the-US-by-the-Eva-Longoria-Foundation1.pdf.

The shape of the traditional American family has evolved over the past 50 years. {BARBARA KINNEY}

Marriage, Motherhood, and Men

By Ann O'Leary

 STUNNING FACT

More than half of babies born to women under age 30 are born to unmarried mothers.

Fifty years ago, the pioneers of the War on Poverty saw no need to call for a strengthening of the American family as a critical component to combating poverty. At the time, marriage—centered around motherhood and the man of the family—was still the prevailing norm for raising children and staving off poverty.

The goal of the War on Poverty was to assist families in poverty with greater access to basic food, education, housing, and job training to increase their economic prospects[1] and to enable nuclear families to thrive. Families were the first line of defense against poverty.[2]

But one year after President Lyndon B. Johnson officially launched the War on Poverty, a young government official at the U.S. Department of Labor, Daniel Patrick Moynihan, began to look at trends in the African American community. He worried that the rise in the number of children born to unmarried mothers and the increasing number of households headed by single mothers would lead to persistent, generational poverty.[3] The report was rightly met with severe criticism for the tone and the blame it placed on the African American community.

Julie Kaas eats lunch at home in Graham, Washington, with sons Danny, Joey, and Jesse, and Danny's girlfriend, Jessica Bailey. Julie is divorced and takes classes she hopes will give her the skills and confidence to land a higher-paying job. {BARBARA KINNEY}

Yet 50 years later, we must confront the reality that the trend that Moynihan first noticed in the African American community—the decline in the proportion of nuclear families—has since extended across all racial and ethnic groups.[4] Of course, there have been many positive trends in the past 50 years that have allowed our society to move beyond the constraints of the so-called traditional family and for families to diversify, flourish, and form in ways that strengthen the fabric of America. No-fault divorce has allowed women to exit abusive and unhealthy marriages. The opening of the labor market, the evolving economy, and the civil rights movement made marriage more egalitarian, with men and women more likely to share fluid roles as both breadwinners and caregivers. Marriage is now open to same-sex couples in a growing number of states. Single parents are no longer shunned by society. And women are no longer pressed into marriage by necessity or to gain access to economic resources and benefits.

But in spite of these positive shifts, the trend Moynihan identified has only gotten worse—unplanned births to unmarried mothers who are living in poverty or on the brink continue to rise. And while not accepted as a national crisis then, it should be today. In too many cases, parents who had not intended to get pregnant are unprepared for the responsibilities associated with raising a child alone, and society thus far has been unwilling or unable either to curb the rise in unplanned pregnancies or to accommodate fully this change in family makeup.

> In too many cases, parents who had not intended to get pregnant are unprepared for the responsibilities associated with raising a child alone, and society thus far has been unwilling or unable either to curb the rise in unplanned pregnancies or to accommodate fully this change in family makeup.

What has happened? Why have so many women begun the journey of motherhood without marriage? And where are the men in this equation? This chapter focuses on the fact that many women are not "deciding" to have babies before marriage—in fact, women living on the brink of poverty are the most likely to have babies as a result of unplanned and unintended pregnancies. And when they do so outside of marriage, they discover the support they need is missing: Men are largely absent from providing economic support to raise the child, and society offers little support to help these women gain the education they need or to help them balance their work with their family obligations.

Rather than indulging in the moral handwringing and judgment that often accompany investigations into changes in the marriage rate, this chapter argues that our country will be better served by doing the following:

• Concretely tackling the rise in unplanned pregnancies to unmarried mothers. We can do so by encouraging women to plan their pregnancies through the responsible use of more fail-safe contraceptive methods and to choose to parent at the time that is the most stable and sensible for them. The public, philanthropic, and nonprofit sectors can play a critical role in increasing the awareness about and access to the most effective contraceptive methods, including long-acting reversible contraception, or LARC.

• Rather than promoting marriage as a silver bullet for women's economic troubles, the government should instead promote policies that allow women to complete their educations, to find stable and well-paying jobs, and to have the work supports necessary to meet their family needs, including child care and family-friendly workplace policies.

If we do not take these steps, the United States will soon have a generation of children who were raised without the full support of our society and who are not fully prepared to have jobs that will allow them to compete in the 21st-century global economy.

THE REALITY OF MARRIAGE, MOTHERHOOD, AND MEN IN AMERICA

The roles of marriage, motherhood, and men in America have changed dramatically in the past several decades. The short narrative is that a rising number of women (and men) are increasingly having children before they get married. Everyone—across race, education, and class—is marrying later than they did 50 years ago. Women are more likely to be working in the paid labor force while caring for their children, often juggling both on their own without the support of a husband or a stable partner. And more men are living apart from their children than ever before. At the same time, those men who are living with their children are more active and involved in their children's lives than ever before. However, there are serious class divisions in family structures, with women in poverty or on the brink of it much more likely to give birth before they marry and to be raising children outside of marriage.

MARRIAGE AND MOTHERHOOD BY THE NUMBERS

Americans have not given up on marriage, but women of all educational and income levels are marrying later in life. And although most will marry at some point in their lives, for some groups of women, child rearing is more likely to come first.

College-educated women are much more likely to have their first babies later in life, after completing their education. But for women with only a high school diploma or a little college—those most likely to be living on the brink—marriage often comes after children. In fact, although single motherhood has

Snapshot: The trend in unplanned births to unmarried mothers

In 1964, less than 10 percent of all births were to unmarried mothers.[5] Today, that number is more than 40 percent, and more than 50 percent for women under 30 years old.[6] In fact, for women as a whole, the median age at which women give birth to their first child (25.7) is now, on average, lower than the median age at which women marry (26.5).[7]

Accompanying the decline in marital births is the rise of unmarried mothers in cohabiting relationships. For many couples, cohabitation has become a replacement (or lengthy prerequisite) for marriage. In fact, most nonmarital births occur to cohabiting couples—almost three in five nonmarital births from 2006 to 2010 were to cohabiting couples.[8] But cohabiting couples often have less stable and lasting relationships than married couples,[9] and on the whole, the shift away from the traditional family structure has left more women and children in a state of vulnerability and financial insecurity. In fact, sociologist Andrew Cherlin has documented that the nature of cohabiting relationships in the United States is less stable than in Europe, and that Americans are much more likely to change partners several times over their lifetimes, leaving both the adults and the children in the relationship in more financially and emotionally precarious situations.[10]

risen substantially in the population as a whole, different patterns emerge among women by education levels, class, age, and race.

It is still quite rare for a woman with a college degree to have a child outside of marriage. Ninety-one percent of all births to women who have completed college occur within marriage.[11] Yet only 39 percent of births to women with less than a high school education occur within marriage.[12] This maps neatly along the age divide as well: 83 percent of older moms (ages 35 to 39) are married when they first give birth, whereas only 38 percent of younger moms (ages 20 to 24) are married upon giving birth.[13] The educational divide also closely tracks the class divide: Of women in households making more than $200,000, 91 percent were married when they gave birth, but for women in households making less than $10,000, only 31 percent were married upon giving birth.[14]

The race divide is not as clear as it is often portrayed in the media. It is true that white children are most likely to be born to married parents (71 percent), black children are least likely to be born to married parents (28 percent), and Hispanic children fall somewhere in the middle (47 percent are born to married parents).[15] But in terms of sheer numbers, most children in the United States born to

FIGURE 1
Demographics of unmarried mothers

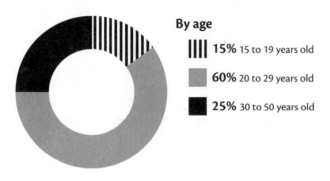

By age

15% 15 to 19 years old

60% 20 to 29 years old

25% 30 to 50 years old

By educational attainment

26% Less than high school graduate

32% High school graduate (includes equivalency)

35% Some college or associate's degree

7% Bachelor's degree or higher

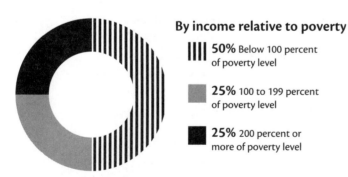

By income relative to poverty

50% Below 100 percent of poverty level

25% 100 to 199 percent of poverty level

25% 200 percent or more of poverty level

Source: American Community Survey, 2011

unmarried parents are white, non-Hispanic children, followed by Hispanic children of any race, and finally by black children.[16] This shows, importantly, that large swaths of our society are bearing children outside of marriage and that the trend persists across all racial and ethnic groups.

What about women on the brink—those who are on the edge of poverty, just one paycheck away from falling in, or constantly churning in and out? Women who are living in poverty or just above the poverty line are about evenly divided—half are having babies within marriage and half are not.[17] But again, the trend falls along lines of educational attainment. It is the less-educated and younger women living in poverty or on the brink of poverty who are more likely to have children outside of marriage.[18]

Currently, only 7 percent of women with a college degree have a child outside of marriage.
{BARBARA KINNEY}

Consider these statistics that show the breakdown of who is having children outside of marriage:

• Ninety-three percent of unmarried births are to women who have less than a college degree.

• Nearly three-quarters of unmarried births are to women who are living in poverty or on the brink of poverty.

• More than 60 percent of unmarried births are to women in their 20s, with the largest share, at 37 percent, to women ages 20 to 24.

As these statistics show, a mother's education level is by far the most significant predictor of whether she will have children within marriage or not, with income levels and age also playing important roles. However, it is difficult to disentangle

A mother's education level is by far the most significant predictor of whether she will have children within marriage or not.

which comes first. Are women with less than a college degree more likely to have a child before marriage, or does having a child prevent women from completing their education? There is evidence to support both arguments.[19] It is clear that encouraging women's educational attainment and supporting their ability to attend and complete college are in the best interests of individual mothers and their families, as well as the economy as a whole.

These early patterns of mothering and marriage—those established at the birth of a child—do not paint the complete picture of the trends of marriage, motherhood, and men in America.

Among babies born in 2002, more than half of births to unmarried women who were cohabiting at the time of birth and more than two-thirds of births to women who were not married and not cohabiting were a result of unintended pregnancies.

First, women who are unmarried when they give birth are not necessarily without a partner. Fifty-eight percent of the births to unmarried women were to women who were cohabiting at the time of birth.[20] Taking a step back, this means that roughly 60 percent of all births are to married mothers, 23 percent are to unmarried women who are living with the father of their child, and only 17 percent are to mothers who are unmarried and not living with a partner.

Despite the fact that around 80 percent of new mothers are either married or cohabiting, we know that these cohabiting relationships are often less stable and economically secure than marriages, leaving many women to start motherhood with a live-in partner and then find themselves single after a few years.[21] For unmarried women who had their first baby in their 20s while living with the father of their child, nearly 40 percent had split up by the child's fifth birthday, compared to only 13 percent of married mothers divorcing the father of their child by the child's fifth birthday.[22]

This is not to say that marriage is a guaranteed pathway to stability. Most mothers will be married at some point in their lives, but marriage is not necessarily a permanent relationship. After 10 years, about one-third of all first marriages

Dolliethea Sandridge, a single mother, walks her son, Josiah, through the halls of the Chambliss Center for Children in Chattanooga, Tennessee. Before she got pregnant and dropped out of school, Dolliethea was studying sociology at Tennessee State University. {BARBARA KINNEY}

end in divorce,[23] with divorce even more common among women who marry early in life or who have less than a college degree.[24] Still, the fate of couples who live together without marrying is by contrast much worse, with 62 percent of such relationships having ended after 10 years.[25] Marriage is no guarantee, but it is much more stable than cohabitation.

Single mothers and cohabiting mothers are at the heart of women living on the brink with low incomes and few safety nets. Of all single mothers, nearly two-thirds are working in low-wage retail, service, or administrative jobs that offer little flexibility, benefits, or economic support that would provide and allow for needed family time with children.[26] Similarly, cohabiting mothers experience a great degree of financial insecurity: More than half of cohabiting mothers live in poverty, in spite of the fact that the majority—about two-thirds—are employed.[27] Because single mothers so often rely on only one income and may not have a partner to help shoulder the responsibilities of child rearing, the lack of policies around paid sick days, paid family and medical leave, workplace flexibility, and affordable and

In all American households with children under the age of 18, more than one-quarter are supported primarily or solely by the income of a single mother.

accessible child care solutions have a disproportionately negative effect on unmarried parents. In fact, in polling conducted by Greenberg Quinlan Rosner Research and TargetPoint Consulting for *The Shriver Report*, 96 percent of working single mothers identified the ability to take up to 10 paid sick leave days to care for themselves or an ill family member as the workplace policy that would help them most.

Finally, and perhaps most important, the number of women having children outside of marriage does not fully shine a light on one variable that, more than any other, is almost entirely within the parents' control: the intention to conceive a child. Most unmarried mothers report that their pregnancies were unintended, which is in stark contrast to married mothers. According to the Centers for Disease Control and Prevention, in 2002, less than one-quarter of the births to married women were a result of unintended pregnancies, whereas more than half of births to unmarried women who were cohabiting at the time of birth and more than two-thirds of births to women who were neither married nor cohabiting were a result of unintended pregnancies.[28]

MEN, MARRIAGE, AND FATHERHOOD BY THE NUMBERS

Single parenting is not just a women's issue. Clearly, more men are also having children outside of marriage, and their profiles are similar to the women's: Less-educated and lower-income men are much more likely to have a child out of wedlock.[29]

In 1960, only 11 percent of fathers did not live with their children. Today, 27 percent do not. And for low-income and the least-educated fathers, about 40 percent do not live with their children.[30]

Fathers across the income spectrum who do not live with their children have a varying degree of involvement in their children's lives in terms of time and connectedness,[31] but for fathers who do live with their children, involvement with their daily lives has more than doubled since 1960.[32] Kathryn Edin describes in her essay in this report how noncustodial fathers in low-income communities are placing increasing importance on their relationships with their children, even if they are unable to provide for them financially.[33]

The breadwinning necessary to support children in families where the father is absent is left largely to the mother—the very woman who is in poverty or on the brink of it. In all American households with children under the age of 18, more than one-quarter are supported primarily or solely by the income of a single mother.[34] Oftentimes, women are left with no economic support from the absent father. Only half of custodial mothers have a formal court agreement for child support, and of those with a formal agreement, only 41 percent receive the full amount of payment.[35]

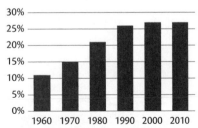

FIGURE 2

Fathers living apart from their children, 1960–2010

Sources: Census Bureau, *Current Population Survey* (U.S. Department of Commerce, 2013); Census Bureau, (U.S. Department of Commerce, 1960).

THE 'WHY' AND 'SO WHAT' OF TRENDS IN MARRIAGE, MOTHERHOOD, AND MEN

There is widespread agreement that some combination of shifts in culture have led to the surge of women having babies outside of marriage and raising children on their own.[36] These societal changes include an evolution in attitude (regarding sex outside of marriage); advances in technology (the birth control pill contributing further to the acceptance of sex outside of marriage); and the transformation of the economy (with a decrease in the ability of men to be the sole breadwinner in a family and an increase of women in the workforce).

The overwhelming evidence regarding women having children outside of marriage, however, points us back to two trends. First, these births are overwhelmingly the result of unplanned and unintended pregnancies. And second, the United States stands out distinctly in its failure to provide information about and access to fail-safe contraception that can stop unintended pregnancies. Women in the United States have much lower rates of contraceptive use in their teens and 20s and are half as likely as their European counterparts to use more effective contraceptive methods, such as IUDs. [37]

Unmarried women with children are at the heart of
women living on the brink, pushing themselves to
the max to earn family income and provide care for
their kids. {BARBARA RIES (LEFT X2), BARBARA KINNEY (RIGHT)}

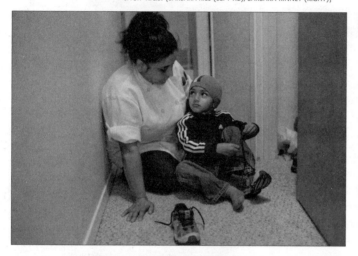

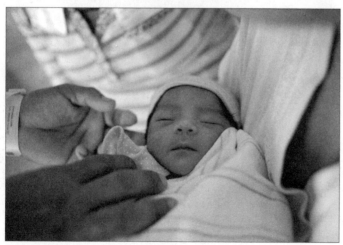

In addition to the failure of our society to address unplanned and unintended pregnancies through greater access to contraception, there remains widespread disagreement over the extent to which cultural shifts impact our society. Can or should the government intervene to try to reverse this trend? And, if so, at what axis point could the government most impact this problem either to reverse the trend or ameliorate its effects?

A comparison of the United States and other developed nations shows that on nearly every support measure meant to benefit children and families, from child care to income support to family-friendly workplace policies, the United States lags far behind.

Indeed, in the polling conducted for *The Shriver Report*, a solid majority—64 percent—of the public believes that the government should set a goal of helping society adapt to the reality of single-parent families and use its resources to help children and mothers succeed regardless of their family status. Also, a majority—51 percent—believe that the government should set a goal of reducing the number of children born to single parents and use its resources to encourage marriage and two-parent families.

The social science literature is quite clear that children of single-parent families, particularly those living in low-income households, do not fare as well as their peers living in two-parent families, and that these poorer outcomes persist, even when you control for socioeconomic differences.[38] The United States also appears to be unique in comparison to other countries, where researchers have found that the poor outcomes for children from single-parent families are almost entirely correlated with income.[39] International measures also note stark differences. On international tests of reading, for example, American children in single-parent households score 23 points lower than their peers from two-parent families—far worse than the average differential of five points in other developed countries—even after accounting for socioeconomic background.[40]

Of course, marriage is not the panacea for improving child outcomes. A comparison of the United States and other developed nations shows that on nearly every support measure meant to benefit children and families, from child care to income support to family-friendly workplace policies, the United States lags far behind.[41] The importance of this finding cannot be overstated. While the popular narrative often implies that American single mothers are somehow "worse" than married mothers or single mothers in other countries, the truth is that they are often simply without any support. Moreover, this outcome does not reflect public policy

What can we learn from the marriage equality debate?

The country has been engaged in an important national conversation about marriage, spurred in part by the debate surrounding same-sex marriage equality and the two cases decided by the U.S. Supreme Court in June 2013. Those for and against marriage equality disagreed strongly over who should be able to marry and have the legal rights and benefits that go along with marriage. But in the course of this tense and heated debate, both sides agreed that marriage offered the greatest stability for children because legal recognition of a relationship grants stability and resources to its partners, which can have particularly strong benefits for children.[45]

In their opening brief, the opponents of marriage equality argued that "Government from time immemorial has had an interest in having . . . unintended and unplanned offspring raised in a stable structure that improves their chances of success in life and avoids having them become a burden on society."[46] At the same time, the proponents of marriage equality also placed primacy on the benefits that a stable marriage imparts to children, regardless of how children enter a family.

Many medical and psychological associations also agreed on the positive effects. The American Medical Association, American Psychological Association, and American Academy of Pediatrics, among others, submitted a joint brief saying that "family instability and parental divorce

are often associated with poor adjustment and problems that can last into adulthood." They described the medical community's view that "in order to further enhance child outcomes and well-being, we should encourage stable and financially secure family units."[47] The American Sociological Association also weighed in, arguing that:

> . . . in order to further enhance child outcomes and well-being, we should encourage stable and financially secure family units—including same-sex parented families—rather than exclude the hundreds of thousands of children living with same-sex couples from the stability and economic security that marriage provides.[48]

Although the two sides fundamentally disagreed on federal recognition of marriages, the debate served to bring to light key areas of agreement on the importance of stable family structures and parental resources to the well-being and future prospects of our children. Certainly not all marriages are stable, and in abusive or dysfunctional families, children are often markedly better off along a variety of dimensions in the wake of a divorce.[49] But marriage can provide structures and benefits to help families gain stability and economic security to better support their children.

choices. In the poll conducted for this report, there was strong public support for policies designed explicitly to increase support for nontraditional families, including increasing access to child care—79 percent in favor—and increasing the number of low-income single mothers who go to college by providing them financial assistance and child care—77 percent in favor.

It is also clear that financial insecurity negatively impacts the health and well-being of women who are pushing themselves to the max to earn the family income and care for their children on their own.[42] Never-married single mothers are also more likely than not to rely on some form of public assistance.[43] The poll showed that a majority of women living on the brink report feeling elevated levels of stress. High levels of interpersonal stress and financial strain have been shown to have negative impacts on mothers—effects that transfer to their children.[44]

In short, we have compelling reasons to figure out how to reduce the number of unintended pregnancies to unmarried women and how to better support single parents and their children. If we do not, this underperformance of children raised by single parents will become an economic problem and the educational achievement gap will lead to an unprepared workforce. To avoid this future, we must consider how best to educate tomorrow's children, including children born to unmarried parents, so that we have the human capital we need to compete in the 21st-century global economy.

THE GOVERNMENT'S ROLE IN PROMOTING STABLE FAMILIES

MARRIED FAMILIES AS THE FIRST SAFETY NET

Fifty years ago, when marriage was more prevalent across all socioeconomic classes and levels of education, it was widely accepted—both through government policy and social norms—that both adults and children were best supported economically within a stable family structure. It was also recognized as the first line of defense against economic catastrophe.

Social policy—from the Social Security Act to tax laws—was constructed on the assumption that married families would support children and that the government would step in only if there were a catastrophe, such as unemployment, long-term disability, or death, and the breadwinner could no longer earn an income. When less catastrophic events occurred—a temporary job loss for the

Caitlin Bell of Chattanooga, Tennessee, drives daughters Zoey and Kessler McCarver to the Chambliss Center for Children. Caitlin planned to attend college, but dropped out of high school during her senior year after she met the father of her children. {BARBARA KINNEY}

breadwinner husband, for example—the stay-at-home wife often entered the labor market to make up for lost wages.[50]

SUPPORT FOR WOMEN AND CHILDREN OUTSIDE OF MARRIAGE

As the norms of marriage, divorce, and childbearing outside of marriage began to change, the laws—originally constructed to provide for women who lost the income of their husbands through death or disability—soon had to accommodate a growing group of women who had never married or who became single through divorce or separation.

Our social welfare policy at first discouraged cohabitation and marriage—economically punishing women on welfare for getting married or having a man in the house by reducing or even taking away their benefits. This was unsurprising given prevailing norms around women's sexuality and the notion of men as the usual breadwinners within families. But in 1996, welfare was reformed. It was no longer an entitlement—in which all economically disadvantaged single parents received cash assistance to provide support for their young children—but rather a time-limited program requiring single parents to work in order to receive benefits. At the same time, many lawmakers also shifted their stance on marriage promotion. Recognizing that the government's prior policies may have discouraged marriage, some members of Congress made strong statements about the importance of marriage, kicking off a trend of altering social policy not to penalize marriage.[51]

Welfare reform was the first major attempt by the government to address the growing number of children born to unmarried parents. It promoted marriage as the ideal family structure in which to raise children, harkening back to previous social policy programs that took for granted the family as the first social safety net. In fact, the findings of the welfare-reform legislation start by stating that "Marriage is the foundation of a successful society" and "Marriage is an essential institution of a successful society which promotes the interest of children."[52] The findings also pointed out the concern over the increase in "out-of-wedlock births" and the negative consequences of such births on the mother, the child, the family, and society.

Yet this course shift was also a drastic move away from ensuring a safety net for single mothers—and, in the eyes of many, an unrealistic assumption that public policy could effectively shift responsibility to the family by encouraging marriage. Peter Edelman, in his essay for this report, provides an eloquent description of the fallout from these assumptions and course shifts resulting in a serious hole in our country's safety net.[53]

Welfare reform is now widely accepted as successful in increasing single mothers' participation in the labor force, while simultaneously being widely accepted as having failed at reducing either childhood poverty or the overall rate of births to unmarried mothers.

PROMOTING MARRIAGE FOR LOW-INCOME WOMEN

Recognizing that the changes in welfare were not affecting the overall trend in births to unmarried mothers or the marriage rate, in 2005, President George W. Bush advocated for Congress to enact the Healthy Marriage Initiative and fund $150 million worth of programs to support marriage as a poverty alleviation policy.[54] The initiative was aimed at promoting the stability of existing marriages and increasing the rate of marriages. But rigorous evaluations of the funded programs have found them to be unsuccessful in meeting either of these goals.[55]

Those who criticized the initiative as Congress was considering it now seem prescient. Stephanie Coontz, contributor to this report and professor of history and family studies at Evergreen State College, and Nancy Folbre, professor of economics at the University of Massachusetts Amherst, both argued strongly that government efforts to encourage lower-income women to marry were out of touch with the reality faced by many of these women. The men in their prospective marriage pools are unlikely to find or hold on to steady work, incarcerated, using drugs or alcohol, or abusive, leaving low-income women unable to find partners who can provide economic stability.[56]

Strikingly, very few divorced, now-single moms in the poll conducted for *The Shriver Report* regret leaving their marriages (15 percent). A 63 percent majority, with the clarity of hindsight, tell us they would have delayed getting married, and 47 percent would have delayed having children. Among lower-income women, just 19 percent regret leaving their marriages. In contrast, 53 percent of lower-income men said they regret leaving their marriages.

Further research has shown that they were right. Low-income women state that they would like to marry but that economic stability for both partners is an important prerequisite to marriage.[57] And research on financially secure men shows they are much more likely to choose to marry women who are similarly economically stable, as opposed to "rescuing" a woman from poverty.[58] Indeed, it is telling that cohabiting families with children are more likely to be living in poverty than single-mother families.[59] A partner with little to no income can quickly become just another mouth to feed, rather than an equally contributing member of the household. Our poll shows that 53 percent of women on the brink are not satisfied with the level of financial support they receive from their child's other parent, and 58 percent are unsatisfied with the level of caretaking by the other parent.

WHERE DO WE GO FROM HERE?

We must confront the fact that our public policies to curb unintended and unplanned pregnancies and those aimed at ameliorating the economic precariousness of single-parent households have largely failed to affect demographic trends in the timing of marriage and motherhood. While access to and use of contraception have increased, use and access rates for young American women are still much lower than those for young women in other developed nations. Welfare reform has not alleviated the burdens on low-income women and children, and the Healthy Marriage Initiative did nothing to reverse the trend.

We must also re-enter the marriage debate with a shared understanding that legally recognized relationships are granted social and economic benefits that tend to make them, as a whole, more stable and financially secure. This stability and financial security, which is often correlated with marriage, can have a deep impact on parents' ability to raise healthy children with bright futures, as well as promoting women's economic security and prosperity.

In addition to economic incentives to promote marriage among low-income communities, the government should focus its efforts on reducing unplanned births to unmarried women and increasing the educational and economic prospects of single moms. Specifically:

• **Stable relationships matter.** Those on the left and right should acknowledge their shared agreement that a stable relationship is the preferable family form for raising children and that married relationships tend to be more stable than other relationships as a whole. Our public policies should encourage marriage or stable cohabiting relationships.

• **Curbing unintended and unplanned pregnancies must be a public priority.** In addition to economic incentives to increase marriage rates, the government should tackle the problem at its root by aiming to reduce unintended and unplanned pregnancies among unmarried mothers in the same way that Congress and the nonprofit sector have tried to tackle teen pregnancy through increased public education and awareness and better information about and access to contraception. The teen pregnancy rate has been reduced by 42 percent since the 1990s, and the National Campaign to Reduce Teen Pregnancy has recently turned its efforts to addressing unplanned pregnancy among unmarried young adults. This effort should be supported and expanded.

- **Increasing access to highly effective contraception is critical to the effort to curb unintended pregnancies.** Efforts to reduce unintended and unplanned pregnancies should be tied to increasing awareness about and access to new technologies for long-acting reversible contraception, or LARC, which has a much higher rate of effectiveness (99 percent) than other methods. Through the expansion of access to health care offered by the Affordable Care Act, many women will have greater access to contraception. This access, however, will need to be tied to increased education and awareness about the effectiveness of LARC, particularly for young women most at risk of unintended pregnancies.

- **Single parents need education and good jobs to help their children thrive.** Both sides should acknowledge that marriage, as an institution for raising children, is not always possible. Accepting that even a reversal in the trend of unmarried births will not end the need to support single-parent families, the government should provide greater educational opportunities and work supports to help single parents gain access to better jobs with more stable incomes and supports such as child care, paid family leave, and equal pay, as outlined in great detail in the Public Solutions chapter. Single mothers in our survey were more likely to regret leaving school (70 percent) than regret the timing or number of their children (47 percent).

By working to reduce the number of unplanned pregnancies to unmarried parents, policymakers must also acknowledge the lack of economic and educational opportunities afforded to low-income young adults. While we should encourage young women to get an education before having a baby and encourage both parents to be economically secure before entering into parenthood, this suggestion must come with real policies to support these efforts, as outlined in the Education chapter.

CONCLUSION

Over the past 50 years, there have been key moments—from the Moynihan Report to the 1996 welfare reform law to the Healthy Marriage Initiative—in which the government recognized and responded to the challenges faced by women living in poverty or on the brink of it and women faced with raising and supporting children on their own. None of these efforts, however, has resulted in a reversal of the trend of more and more women having children outside of marriage with limited support for raising and caring for their children.

Kristeen Rogers, 23, puts her daughters to bed in Clermont, Florida. She works multiple jobs, so time with her girls is limited. On this night, she read them a book, sang them each a song of their choice, and helped say prayers before kissing them goodnight. {MELISSA LYTTLE}

THINK ABOUT THIS

Low-income single mothers are more likely to wish for more caregiving help than more money from their children's fathers.

ENDNOTES

1 American Rhetoric, "Lyndon Baines Johnson: First State of the Union Address," available at http://www.american rhetoric.com/speeches/lbj1964stateoftheunion.htm (last accessed October 2013).

2 Stephen D. Sugarman, "What Is a 'Family'? Conflicting Messages from Our Public Programs," *Family Law Quarterly* 42 (2) (2008): 231–261, available at http://www.law.berkeley.edu/files/What_is_a_Family-Conflicting_Messages(1).

3 U.S. Department of Labor, "The Negro Family: The Case for National Action," available at http://www.dol.gov/oasam/programs/history/webid-meynihan.htm (last accessed October 2013).

4 For a thoughtful look at the Moynihan Report nearly 50 years later, see Gregory Arcs and others, "The Moynihan Report Revisited" (Washington: Urban Institute, 2013), available at http://www.urban.org/UploadedPDF/412839-The-Moynihan-Report-Revisited.pdf.

5 Data for births in 1964 were derived from U.S. Department of Health, Education, and Welfare, "Vital Statistics of the United States: 1964" (1964), available at http://www.nber.org/vital-stats-books/nat64_1.CV.pdf. The number of total births in 1964 was 4,027,490 (Table 1-1 [1-3], p. 12), and the number of total unmarried births—or illegitimate births—was 275,700 (Table 1-26 [1-30], p. 39) for a rate of 6.8 percent.

6 Joyce Martin and others, "Births: Final Data for 2011" (Washington: Centers for Disease Control and Prevention, 2013), available at http://www.cdc.gov/nchs/data/nvsr/nvsr62/nvsr62_01.pdf.

7 National Marriage Project at the University of Virginia, National Campaign to Prevent Teen and Unplanned Pregnancy, and Relate Institute, "Knot Yet: The Benefits and Costs of Delayed Marriage in America," available at http://twentysomethingmarriage.org/ (last accessed October 2013).

8 Martin and others, "Births."

9 Kristin Anderson Moore, Susan M. Jekielek, and Carol Emig, "Marriage from a Child's Perspective: How Does Family Structure Affect Children, and What Can We Do About It?" (Washington: Child Trends, 2002), available at http://www.childtrends.org/wp-content/uploads/2013/03/MarriageRB602.pdf.

10 Andrew Cherlin, *The Marriage-Go-Round* (New York: Vintage Books, 2009).

11 Gretchen Livingston and D'Vera Cohn, "Record Share of New Mothers are College Educated" (Washington: Pew Research Center, 2013), available at http://www.pewsocialtrends.org/2013/05/10/record-share-of-new-mothers-are-college-educated/.

12 Ibid.

13 Ibid.

14 Rachel M. Shattuck and Rose M. Kreider, "Social and Economic Characteristics of Currently Unmarried Women with a Recent Birth: 2011" (Washington: Census Bureau, 2013), available at http://www.census.gov/prod/2013pubs/acs-21.pdf.

15 Martin and others, "Births."

16 Ibid.

17 Shattuck and Kreider, "Social and Economic Characteristics of Currently Unmarried Women with a Recent Birth." In households with incomes between $15,000 and $24,999, 53 percent of births were to unmarried mothers; in households with incomes between $25,000 and $34,999, 46.5 percent of births were to unmarried mothers. The federal poverty level in 2013 for a family of two—one adult and one child—is $15,510; the federal poverty level for a family of three—one adult and two children—is $19,530. See Office of the Assistant Secretary for Planning and Evaluation, "2013 Poverty Guidelines," available at http://aspe.hhs.gov/poverty/13poverty.cfm.

18 U.S. Census Bureau, "American Community Survey 2011 1-Year Estimates," tables B13014, B13002, B13010, available at http://www.dof.ca.gov/research/demographic/state_census_data_center/american_community_survey/#ACS2011x1.

19 Sandra L. Hofferth, Lori Reid, and Frank L. Mott, "The Effects of Early Childbearing on Schooling over Time," *Family Planning Perspectives* 33 (6) (2001): 259–267; Margaret Mooney Marini, "Women's Educational Attainment and the Timing of Entry into Parenthood," *American Sociological Review* 49 (4) (1984): 491–511.

20 Martin and others, "Births."

21 Mark Mather, "U.S. Children in Single-Mother Families" (Washington: Population Reference Bureau, 2010); Centers for Disease Control and Prevention, "New Report Sheds Light on Trends and Patterns in Marriage, Divorce, and Cohabitation," Press release, July 24, 2002, available at http://www.cdc.gov/nchs/pressroom/02news/div_mar_cohab.htm.

22 National Marriage Project at the University of Virginia, National Campaign to Prevent Teen and Unplanned Pregnancy, and Relate Institute, "Knot Yet."

23 Matthew Bramlett and William Mosher, "Cohabitation, Marriage, Divorce, and Remarriage in the United States" (Washington: Centers for Disease Control and Prevention, 2002), available at http://www.cdc.gov/nchs/data/series/sr_23/sr23_022.pdf.

24 Adam Isen and Betsey Stevenson, "Women's Education and Family Behavior: Trends in Marriage, Divorce and Fertility," Working Paper 15725 (University of Pennsylvania, 2010).

25 Bramlett and Mosher, "Cohabitation, Marriage, Divorce, and Remarriage in the United States."

26 Mather, "U.S. Children in Single-Mother Families."

27 Julissa Cruz, "Single, Cohabiting, and Married Mothers in the U.S., 2011" (Bowling Green, OH: National Center for Family & Marriage Research, 2011), available at http://ncfmr.bgsu.edu/pdf/family_profiles/file119797.pdf.

28 William D. Mosher, Jo Jones, and Joyce C. Abma, "Intended and Unintended Births in the United States: 1982–2010" (Washington: Centers for Disease Control and Prevention, 2012), available at http://www.cdc.gov/nchs/data/nhsr/nhsr055.pdf. Also see Elizabeth Wildsmith, Nicole R. Steward-Streng, and Jennifer Manlove, "Childbearing Outside of Marriage: Estimates and Trends in the United States" (Washington: Child Trends, 2011), available at http://www.childtrends.org/wp-content/uploads/2013/02/Child_Trends-2011_11_01_RB_NonmaritalCB.pdf.

29 Gretchen Livingston and Kim Parker, "A Tale of Two Fathers: More Are Active, But More Are Absent" (Washington: Pew Research Center, 2011), available at http://www.pewsocialtrends.org/files/2011/06/fathers-FINAL-report.pdf.

30 Ibid.

31 Kathryn Edin ,"What About the Fathers?," in this report.

32 Ibid.

33 Ibid.

34 Wendy Wang, Kim Parker, and Paul Taylor, "Breadwinning Moms" (Washington: Pew Research, 2013), available at http://www.pewsocialtrends.org/files/2013/05/Breadwinner_moms_final.pdf.

35 Timothy Grall, "Custodial Mothers and Fathers and Their Child Support: 2009" (Washington: U.S. Census Bureau, 2011), available at http://www.census.gov/prod/2011pubs/p60-240.pdf.

36 See Charles Murray, *Coming Apart: The State of White America, 1960–2010* (New York: Crown Forum, 2012); Naomi Cahn and June Carbone, *Red Families v. Blue Families* (New York: Oxford University Press, 2010); Cherlin, *The Marriage-Go-Round.*

37 Christine Bachrach and others, "Unplanned Pregnancy and Abortion in the United States and Europe: Why So Different?" (Washington: The National Campaign to Prevent Teen and Unplanned Pregnancy, 2012), available at http://www.thenationalcampaign.org/resources/pdf/pubs/international-comparisons.pdf.

38 Mather, "U.S. Children in Single-Mother Families." Also see Fragile Families and Child Wellbeing Study, "Fragile Families and Child Wellbeing Study Fact Sheet," available at http://www.fragilefamilies.princeton.edu/documents/FragileFamiliesandChildWellbeingStudyFactSheet.pdf (last accessed October 2013).

39 Sheila B. Kamerman and others, "Social Policies, Family Types and Child Outcomes in Selected OECD Countries" (Paris: Organisation for Economic Co-operation and Development, 2003), available at http://www.oecd.org/social/family/2955844.pdf; Paul R. Amato, "The Impact of Family Formation Change on the Cognitive, Social, and Emotional Well-Being of the Next Generation," *The Future of Children* 15 (2) (2005): 75–96; Simon Chapple, "Child Well-Being and Sole-Parent Family Structure in the OECD: An Analysis" (Paris: Organisation for Economic Co-operation and Development, 2003), available at http://search.oecd.org/officialdocuments/displaydocumentpdf/?doclanguage=en&cote=delsa/elsa/wd/sem(2009)10. This suggests that earlier research summaries may overstate the conclusiveness of the effect.

40 Organisation for Economic Co-operation and Development, "PISA 2009 Results: Executive Summary" (2010), available at http://www.oecd.org/pisa/pisaproducts/46619703.pdf.

41   Timothy Casey and Laurie Maldonado, "Worst Off—Single-Parent Families in the United States: A Cross-National Comparison of Single Parenthood in the U.S. and Sixteen Other High-Income Countries" (Washington: Legal Momentum, 2012), available at http://www.legalmomentum.org/sites/default/files/reports/worst-off-single-parent.pdf.

42   Jane Waldfogel, Terry-Ann Craigie, and Jeanne Brooks-Gunn, "Fragile Families and Child Wellbeing," *Future Child* 20 (2) (2010): 87–112, available at http://www.ncbi.nlm.nih.gov/pmc/articles/PMC3074431/. Also see Bendheim-Thoman Center for Research on Child Wellbeing, "Maternal Stress and Mother Behaviors in Stable and Unstable Families" (2004), available at http://www.fragilefamilies.princeton.edu/briefs/ResearchBrief27.pdf.

43   Isabel Sawhill, Adam Thomas, and Emily Monea, "An Ounce of Prevention: Policy Prescriptions to Reduce the Prevalence of Fragile Families," *Future Child* 20 (2) (2010): 133–155, available at http://futureofchildren.org/futureofchildren/publications/docs/20_02_07.pdf.

44   Robert Pianta and Byron Egeland, "Life Stress and Parenting Outcomes in a Disadvantaged Sample: Results of the Mother-Child Interaction Project," *Journal of Clinical Child Psychology* 19 (4) (1990): 329–336; Aurora P. Jackson and others, "Single Mothers in Low-Wage Jobs: Financial Strain, Parenting, and Preschoolers' Outcomes," *Child Development* 71 (5) (2003): 1409–1423.

45   Professor Melissa Murray recognized this agreement and has written a thought-provoking piece about what the agreement may mean for "illegitimate" children. See Melissa Murray, "What's So New about the New Illegitimacy?" *American University Journal of Gender, Social Policy & the Law* 20 (2012): 387.

46   *United States of America v. Edith Schlain Windsor and Bipartisan Legal Advisory Group of the United States House of Representatives*, Supreme Court of the United States (January 22, 2013) (No. 12-307), available at http://sblog.s3.amazonaws.com/wp-content/uploads/2013/01/BLAG-merits-brief-1-22-131.pdf.

47   *United States of America v. Edith Schlain Windsor, in Her Capacity as Executor of the Estate of Thea Clara Spyer, et al.*, Supreme Court of the United States (March 1, 2013) (No. 12-307), available at http://www.scribd.com/doc/128173263/12-307-Brief-for-the-American-Psychological-Association.

48   *Dennis Hollingsworth, et al. v. Kristin M. Perry, et al., & United States, Petitioner, v. Edith Schlain Windsor in her Capacity as Executor of the Estate of Thea Clara Spyer, and Bipartisan Legal Advisory Group of the United States House of Representatives, Respondents*, Supreme Court of the United States (February 28, 2013) (No. 12-144), available at http://www.scribd.com/doc/127819899/12-144-307-American-Sociological-Association-Amicus.

49   Joan Kelly, "Children's Adjustment in Conflicted Marriage and Divorce: A Decade Review of Research," *Journal of the American Academy of Child & Adolescent Psychiatry* 39 (8) (2000): 963–973; Paul R. Amato, "The Consequences of Divorce for Adults and Children," *Journal of Marriage and Family* 62 (4) (2000): 1269–1287.

50   Melvin Stephens Jr., "Worker Displacement and the Added Worker Effect." Working Paper 8260 (National Bureau of Economic Research, 2011), available at http://www.nber.org/papers/w8260.pdf?new_window=1.

51   Dorit Geva, "Not Just Maternalism: Marriage and Fatherhood in American Welfare Policy," *Social Politics* 18 (1) (2011): 24–51; Sean Brotherson and William Duncan, "Rebinding the Ties that Bind: Government Efforts to Preserve and Promote Marriage," *Family Relations* 53 (5) (2004): 459–468.

52   *Personal Responsibility and Work Opportunity Reconciliation Act of 1996*, Public Law 193, 104th Cong. (August 22, 1996).

53   Peter Edelman, "Beyond Welfare Reform: Economic Justice in the 21st Century," *Berkeley Journal of Employment and Labor Law* 24 (1) (2003): 475–486.

54   *Deficit Reduction Act of 2005*, Public Law 171, 109th Cong. (February 8, 2006).

55   Joy Moses, "Strengthening Families and Communities: Strategies to Promote Better Economic and Social Outcomes for All Families." In Half in Ten Annual Report 2013 (Washington: Center for American Progress, 2013).

56   Stephanie Coontz, "Marriage, Poverty, and Public Policy," *The American Prospect*, March 21, 2002, available at http://prospect.org/article/marriage-poverty-and-public-policy.

57   Kathryn Edin and Maria Kefalas, *Promises I Can Keep: Why Poor Women Put Motherhood before Marriage* (Los Angeles: University of California Press, 2005).

58   Valerie Oppenheimer and Vivian Lew, "American Marriage Formation in the 1980s." In Karen Mason and An-Magritt Jensen, eds., *Gender and Family Change in Industrialized Countries* (Oxford: Oxford University Press, 1994), pp. 105–138; Sharon Sassler and Robert Schoen, "The Effects of Attitudes and Economic Activity on Marriage," *Journal of Marriage and the Family* 61 (1) (1999): 148–149.

59   Cruz, "Single, Cohabiting, and Married Mothers in the U.S., 2011."

America's Working Single Mothers: An Appreciation

By LEBRON JAMES, the NBA Championship-winning forward for the Miami Heat.

I am honored to participate in a project that is trying to help single mothers who are struggling to make a living and raise their kids, because that perfectly describes my mother when I was growing up. You think LeBron James is a champion? Gloria James is a champion too. She's my champion.

My mother really struggled. She had me, her only child, when she was just 16 years old. She was on her own, so we lived in her mom's great big house in Akron, Ohio. But on Christmas Day when I was 3 years old, my grandmother suddenly died of a heart attack, and everything changed. With my mom being so young and lacking any support and the skills and education necessary to get ahead, it was really hard for us.

We lost the house. We moved around from place to place—a dozen times in three years. It was scary. It was catch as catch can, scraping to get by. My mom worked anywhere and everywhere, trying to make ends meet. But through all of that, I knew one thing for sure: I had my mother to blanket me and to give me security. She was my mother, my father, my everything. She put me first. I knew that no matter what happened, nothing and nobody was more important to her than I was. I went without a lot of things, but never for one second did I feel unimportant or unloved.

Finally, when I was 9 years old, my mother made a supreme sacrifice. She decided that while she was figuring out how to get on her feet, I needed some stability in my life. I needed to stay in one place and experience the support and security that she had felt growing up in a big family. So she sent me to live with my pee-wee football team coach, "Big Frankie" Walker, and his family. She later said to me, "It was hard, but I knew it was not about me. It was about you. I had to put you first."

I stayed with the Walkers for a year, and what a gift that was! I was in the same school all year, slept in the same bed all year, played on the same football team all year, and Big Frankie put me on my first basketball team. I saw my mom every weekend.

When my mother was able to rent a two-bedroom apartment with the help of a government-assistance program, I moved back in with her. We stayed together until I finished high school. The rest is history.

People always say I am devoted to my mother. That's true, but only because for every minute of my life, she has been devoted to me. My mother taught me what devotion truly means. I have tried to pass along her example by helping kids who are growing up in single-parent homes through the LeBron James Family Foundation and the Boys & Girls Clubs of America.

Gloria James raised her only child and future NBA phenom alone after becoming pregnant at age 16. LeBron says that it is her love and devotion that made it possible for him to pursue his dreams. {COURTESY LEBRON JAMES}

After the Heat won the 2012 NBA Championship, the team was invited to the White House. Speaking about me, Dwyane Wade, and Chris Bosh, President Barack Obama said, "For all the young men out there who are looking up to them all the time, for them to see somebody who cares about their kids and is there for them day in and day out, that's a good message to send. It's a positive message to send, and we're very proud of them for that."[1]

The truth is that everything I've learned about being a parent to my boys—9-year-old LeBron Jr. and 6-year-old Bryce—I learned from my mother. Everything I know about being loving and caring, and sacrificing and showing up and being present in my children's lives—I learned all of that from her example.

Gloria James was a working single mother who struggled and got the job done.

And for that, I say, "I love you, Mom. Thank you."

ENDNOTE

1   The White House, "Remarks by the President in Welcoming the Miami Heat," Press release, January 28, 2013, available at http://www.whitehouse.gov/the-press-office/2013/01/28/remarks-president-welcoming-miami-heat.

To the Brink and Back

By CATHERINE EMMANUELLE, who went from living as a single mother on public assistance to being an elected member of the Eau Claire, Wisconsin, City Council. She is also a family living educator at the University of Wisconsin-Extension, partnering with local and state organizations and agencies to help families dealing with poverty, incarceration, and immigration.

One spring morning about seven years ago, my husband gave me his usual kiss goodbye as he left to go to work. Hours later, he came home and—out of the blue—told me he wanted a divorce. I was blindsided, shocked, and devastated. I know that people get divorced every day, but I never thought that would be my reality.

Just 120 days after he filed the paperwork, I was magically transformed from being a wife, a middle-class stay-at-home mom of a toddler, and an active community member into a struggling single mother. Even after factoring in the child support and alimony received, and an ex-husband who remained a loving father, I was now living well below the poverty level. In those new moments, I was not earning a steady income, had no vehicle, a sparse pantry, and no hope.

In my newfound poverty, I was desperate for help. I went to the county Health and Human Services office, telling my story through buckets of tears. The caseworker looked up and said, "Oh, you're a displaced homemaker."

That stopped the tears. "You think I'm a *what*?"

"I am not saying what I *think* you are. I am telling you that you *are* what we call 'a displaced home-maker.'"

I had never heard that term, so you'd better believe that this newly minted displaced home-maker looked it up. Guess what I found out? "Displaced homemaker" refers to a person whose primary job has been homemaking and who has lost her main source of income through separa-tion, divorce, disability, or death. Yep, that was me.

I was awarded child care assistance, food assis-tance, and Medicaid insurance. While I was grateful for the help, I found the experience to be humbling, embarrassing, and eye-opening. When I shared my embarrassment with friends and fam-ily, they commonly replied, "That's what the help is for. It's for when you need it!" That didn't make me feel better.

So now I had to consider what to do. Like thou-sands of my sister "displaced homemakers" who have had the emotional and financial rug pulled out from under them, I knew I had to rebuild my life. I didn't want to live out that unfair ste-reotype of the single mother living on public assistance, mooching as much as she could for as long as she could. I considered my options for creating a sustainable life for my daughter and me. I could: 1) go it alone, working several jobs to make ends meet and probably be broke, or 2) go to school with the help of public assistance and education grants, picking up part-time jobs as I could on the side. Yes, I'd still be broke, but I'd be educating myself for the future.

I had a few college credits, so I opted for the latter. I signed up at the University of Wisconsin-Eau Claire, getting my degree in women's studies and economics. I wanted to learn about women like me, so I studied displaced homemakers and other marginalized groups.

My research led me to the organization Women Work! The National Network for Women's Employment. I read their eye-opening report on all of us displaced homemakers entering the workforce:

> ... often staggeringly unprepared to compete for the kinds of jobs that support a family in today's economy. Instead of confidently stepping onto career ladders, they may lose their footing as they take those tentative next steps, sending them down the slippery chutes of low-wage jobs, limited access to education and training, and unstable economic futures.[1]

That was my "aha" moment. Walking through my heartbreak, through economic jeopardy, through humiliating need—all of it had shaped me into the resilient woman I'd become, and I would use my journey into and out of poverty to help others like me. I would go into public service.

Today, I am a 33-year-old politician and policy-maker and the youngest female and first Latino person elected to office in my community. I've initiated a weekly community resource day for marginalized people, led civic-engagement initiatives, and presented at conferences of organizations working to alleviate poverty. I am also Mom to a thriving 9-year-old, and, yes, I am in love again, with a committed partner who empowers people through education.

My daughter and I are two of the millions of Americans affected by public assistance and the policy governing it. The assistance we received provided a win-win situation for us and for our community. It gave us access to healthy food and good medical care, and I got a good education. Because of that support, I now am able to contribute to my community as both a taxpayer and a public servant.

May my story serve as a reminder that our sisters and brothers who are in poverty are not just people taking from the public treasury. People living on the brink are part of our community. When we help them achieve economic security and stability, we strengthen society at large.

ENDNOTE

1 Women Work! The National Network for Women's Employment, "Chutes and Ladders: The Search for Solid Ground for Women in the Workforce" (2005), available at http://s3.amazonaws.com/zanran_storage/www.womenwork.org/ContentPages/52424749.pdf.

Marriage and Children: Another View

By RON HASKINS, co-director of the Center on Children and Families at the Brookings Institution and senior consultant at the Annie E. Casey Foundation. He was the welfare counsel to Republicans on the House Ways and Means Committee for more than a decade and a senior advisor for welfare policy to the President George W. Bush White House.

There is a lot to like in Ann O'Leary's chapter on marriage, motherhood, and men. In this essay, I want to emphasize one or two of her major points, but also offer a few arguments that differ somewhat from her perspective.

The most basic facts from U.S. Census data since 1970 conspire to paint a gloomy picture of the future of the married-couple family.[1]

With the exception of college-educated women, marriage rates for women have been declining for all age, ethnic, and education groups for at least four decades. The share of married 20- to 24-year-olds plummeted from 61 percent in 1970 to 16 percent in 2010, while the share of married black women ages 40 to 44 fell from 61 percent to 37 percent. The share of married women with a high school degree fell from about 86 percent to 59 percent.

Although their marriage rates are way down, unmarried 20-somethings have not stopped having sex, which of course means nonmarital birth rates are way up, increasing from 5 percent to more than 40 percent since 1960.

The upshot of falling marriage rates and rapidly increasing nonmarital births is that the landscape of family households has changed dramatically. Since 1970, the percentage of women who are married with children has fallen by 34 percent, while all other family forms have increased—especially single mothers with children, up by an amazing 122 percent.

How do we account for these dramatic changes? Many of the cultural barriers to divorce and nonmarital births have gone the way of the horse and carriage, thereby greatly increasing the acceptable choices regarding childbearing, marriage, and living arrangements from which young adults can choose, without having much social pressure to make a different choice. But the result is that more and more of the nation's kids—around 50 percent during the course of their childhoods—live in single-parent families.[2]

So what? Well, there is now near-universal agreement that the best rearing environment for children is a married-couple family, a view with which O'Leary agrees. Since the publication of *Growing Up with a Single Parent* by Sara McLanahan and Gary Sandefur in 1994,[3] research has shown that children from female-headed families demonstrate a range of problematic developmental outcomes, including mental-health issues, lower school achievement, higher delinquency

Air Force veteran Kristy Richardson and her husband, Shawn, are working together to raise their two sons, Elijah (shown here) and Kristian. The family lives together in Pittsburgh, Pennsylvania. {MELISSA FARLOW}

and idleness (no job, no school), more teen pregnancy, and many others.[4]

Several important conclusions follow from this litany of developmental impacts. First, we are a nation greatly concerned about both poverty and economic opportunity. But the rise of single-parent families is a major factor in the nation's high poverty rates, because children in

female-headed families are four to five times as likely to be poor as children in married-couple families.[5] Add to that the fact that poor and minority children are much more likely to live in single-parent households and therefore to have suboptimal development, and it must be concluded that nonmarital births and divorce are contributing to lower economic opportunity for millions of children. If more poor parents got and stayed married, poverty rates would fall, and fewer children would live in poverty.[6]

Moreover, keeping in mind that single parents are four to five times as likely to be poor as married-couple families, abundant research shows that low-income parents invest less in their children than middle-class parents do.[7] Income may play a role here, but critical parenting inputs, such as talking with and reading to the child, avoiding physical punishment, and going on outings, are not expensive. Rather, they reflect parents' willingness to invest time in their children.

Two lines of response by public policy are warranted. First, we should continue our current commitment to helping poor single parents have enough money to get by, especially if they work. The federal government and states have created cash-earnings supplements, universal health insurance coverage for low-income children, plus other benefits for the children of working, low-income parents, especially single mothers. All these programs should be protected from cuts—and further investments in quality preschool programs also seem justified in cost-benefit terms. Unfortunately, the continuing federal budget deficit makes it likely that it will take serious fights in Congress just to protect the current programs.

We should also continue our efforts to encourage marriage. Most of this work must be done through churches and community-based organizations, but there are a few public actions that might help. For instance, a number of recent changes in the tax code have reduced the marriage penalty. In fact, a majority of low-income cohabiting couples would probably be financially better off if they married, because on average, their work-based tax credits would increase.[8]

The Building Strong Families program, a central part of the marriage initiative conducted by President George W. Bush, was arguably the most important federal attempt to improve the relationships of poor couples who had a baby together. The goal was to help them stay together, cooperate in rearing their children, and perhaps get married. Building Strong Families randomly assigned about 5,000 couples in eight sites around the country to either a program group or a control group. Program couples participated in up to 42 hours of marriage-education curriculums especially adapted for use with low-income couples. The program couples also worked with a family support coordinator who met with them regularly and attempted to broker community-based services such as child care, mental-health services, and job-search advice.

The study found that marriage rates did not increase and that couples' relationships did not improve on average. One site, however, did show positive impacts on the couples' relationships, and the couples stayed together longer. Forty-nine percent of the couples enrolled in the Oklahoma City program were still together after three years, as compared with 41 percent of control couples. On the other hand, the Florida program had negative impacts on the couples' relationship quality, the fathers' involvement, and family stability. It would be useful to find out why the

Oklahoma program had positive impacts and then try to replicate that program.

As a nation, we have moved a long way from the day when nearly all our children had two married parents. Despite numerous efforts in the private and public sectors, it seems unlikely that the dissolution of the traditional family will be reversed any time soon, if ever. Meanwhile, our programs for single parents become more important every year. But given the benefits, we should not give up on private and public efforts to restore marriage to its previous status as the gold standard for rearing children.

ENDNOTES

1 Unless otherwise indicated, all references to Census Bureau data are taken from a Brookings Institution analysis of the past five decennial Census Bureau reports (1970, 1980, 1990, 2000, and 2010).

2 Sheela Kennedy and Larry Bumpass, "Cohabitation and Children's Living Arrangements: New Estimates from the United States," *Demographic Research* 19 (47) (2008).

3 Sara McLanahan and Gary Sandefur, *Growing Up with a Single Parent: What Hurts, What Helps* (Cambridge, MA: Harvard University Press, 1997).

4 For reviews of this literature, see Sara McLanahan, Elisabeth Donahue, and Ron Haskins, "Introducing the Issue," *The Future of Children: Marriage and Child Wellbeing* 15 (2) (2005); David Autor and Melanie Wasserman, "Wayward Sons: The Emerging Gender Gap in Labor Markets and Education" (Washington: Third Way, 2013).

5 Carmen DeNavas-Walt, Bernadette D. Proctor, and Jessica C. Smith, "Income, Poverty, and Health Insurance Coverage in the United States: 2012, Current Population Reports" (Washington: U.S. Census Bureau, 2013).

6 Isabel V. Sawhill and Ron Haskins, "Work and Marriage: The Way to End Poverty and Welfare" (Washington: The Brookings Institution, 2003).

7 Jane Waldfogel and Elizabeth Washbrook, "Early Years Policy," *Child Development Research* (2011): 1–12; Ariel Kalil, "Inequality Begins at Home: The Role of Parenting in the Diverging Destinies of Rich and Poor Children," Paper prepared for the 21st Annual Symposium on Family Issues, Pennsylvania State University, October 7–8, 2013.

8 Gregory Acs and Elaine Maag, "Irreconcilable Differences? The Conflict between Marriage Promotion Initiatives for Cohabiting Couples with Children and Marriage Penalties in Tax and Transfer Programs" (Washington: Urban Institute, 2005).

What About the Fathers?

By KATHRYN EDIN, *professor of public policy and management at the Harvard Kennedy School and a leading researcher on women and poverty. She is the co-author of* **Promises I Can Keep: Why Poor Women Put Motherhood before Marriage** *with Maria Kefalas and* **Doing the Best I Can: Fatherhood in the Inner City** *with Timothy Nelson.*

As the author of two books about low-income single mothers, I often give talks or appear on call-in shows. Audiences always want to know about the men single mothers have children with. They ask me, "Why don't you talk to the dads? What about the fathers?"

I used to brush the question aside. After all, I had spent years living and talking with black, white, and Hispanic single mothers in some of the nation's toughest urban neighborhoods in Philadelphia, Chicago, the deep South, and the West Coast—10 cities in all. I thought I had learned everything there was to know about these men from the moms. Besides, didn't everyone know the guys were irresponsible? That they really didn't care about the kids they conceived? In 2008, even presidential candidate Barack Obama was calling them out, saying they had better stop acting like boys and have the courage to raise a child, not just create one.

Finally, fellow researcher Tim Nelson and I began actually talking to these men—more than 100 low-income noncustodial dads living in poor neighborhoods in the Philadelphia area. As it turns out, "everyone" wasn't right. We were all dead wrong—me, the country, and even Barack Obama.

After several years of interviewing, observing, and living among these fathers, I've learned that not caring about their children is not the problem. Our 2013 book, *Doing the Best I Can: Fatherhood in the Inner City*, reveals that these men desperately want to be good fathers, and they are often quite intensively involved in the early years of their children's lives. Yet they usually fail to stay closely connected as their kids grow older.

If lack of caring isn't the problem, then what is? To answer that question, we have to start with how their relationships form.

Romance in the inner city typically proceeds quickly. Just six or seven months after they first begin "kicking it," most of these couples "come up pregnant." Usually neither he nor she explicitly plans to have a baby, but neither of them does much to avoid pregnancy, at least not for long. Inner-city youth often view condoms as a method of disease prevention, not contraception. They believe that ongoing condom use says you don't trust your partner to be faithful, so as soon as there is a kernel of trust, the condom stays in the drawer—a ritual marking the transition to a more serious relationship.

Pretty soon, the women are skipping doses of the pill or letting the patch or other forms of contraception lapse. Why? In these communities, motherhood often exerts a strong pull on young women's hearts and minds and weakens their motivation to avoid pregnancy. Being a mom serves as the chief source of meaning and identity in neighborhoods where significant upward mobility is rare. She realizes that her circumstances aren't ideal, so she doesn't explicitly "plan" to get pregnant. But she'll readily admit that it wasn't exactly an accident either. She'll say she knew full well where unprotected sex would lead.

For their part, the men typically say they "just weren't thinking" about the possibility of pregnancy when conception occurs. Yet contrary to the hit-and-run stereotype of the deadbeat dad, 7 times out of 10, men's reaction to the news of a pregnancy is happiness—even downright joy. In fact, we found they are more likely to be happy than the mothers are! Andre Green, still in high school, told us he shouted "Thank you, Jesus!" when he heard the news, even though he and the would-be mother were no longer together.

What accounts for this strong, latent desire for kids among young people who can ill afford to support them? Here, context is key. Andre Green

and his peers are coming of age in some of the most violent and poverty-stricken neighborhoods in America. Their lives are marked by trauma. Just months before Andre learned that he was about to become a dad, his brother was murdered, and his mother turned to drugs as a salve. Like Andre, many men we spoke with described their lives up to that moment with a single word: "Negativity."

In this context, a baby—fresh and innocent—is pure potential, a chance to move away from the mistakes of the past and turn to activities that are wholly good. Celebrating those precious first words and first steps. Spending the night soothing a fussy teether. Carefully fixing a little girl's hair. For middle-class teens coming of age on Philadelphia's affluent Main Line, early pregnancy ruins lives—a bright future snuffed out, or at least diminished. But if you're already at the bottom, a baby means something else entirely.

As I've said, poor women find meaning in motherhood when sources of meaning are in short supply. But what we often fail to appreciate is how large the rewards of fatherhood also can be for men in extraordinarily challenging circumstances. Seven White, who conceived his first child at 17, told us, "I couldn't imagine being without them, because when I am spending time with my kids it is like, now *that* is love! That is unconditional love. . . . It is like a drug that you got to have. I would never want to be without them."

Some argue that the "deadbeat dad" stereotype is mostly a myth, claiming that young disadvantaged men want to be involved in their children's lives and that they want to redefine fatherhood to fit their circumstances. {BARBARA KINNEY}

These young people know that the right time to have a child is when you are economically ready, but many are afraid that the right time may never arrive. And they're right. Because of deindustrialization, automation, and outsourcing, there are precious few well-paying or even steady jobs for those without skills these days. Byron Jones, an inner-city dad who is now in his mid-30s, told us that he advised younger men in his neighborhood to hold off on having kids until "you are financially able to take care of the children." Then he paused and added, "And that's when nowadays? I have no idea, because—when is it? I mean, shoot, for the average guy, stable employment don't last long. You might work this week and be out the next week, you know?" So, with little confidence that the right moment to have a child will ever arrive, they allow fate to dictate the timing.

In this corner of America, pregnancy is often the impetus for a relationship, not the outgrowth of one. He and she usually become a "couple" only after a baby is on the way. Shotgun relationships have replaced the shotgun marriage. Yet as the time bomb of pregnancy ticks, men rarely flee. Instead, they try mightily to "get it together for the baby"—the "it" being the relationship with the woman who is about to become their child's mother. In fact, when the baby enters the world, more than 8 in 10 men are still together with the mother. Yet due to their laissez-faire route to conception, they may not really know their kid's mom very well when the child is born.

Those first, very tough months of being new parents put these fragile relationships under tremendous strain, made worse by a lack of money. With hardly any shared history to draw on, is it any wonder that half of these couples break up before their child's first birthday? Even the relationships of middle-class married couples are often tested when a baby comes into the picture. Usually, though, they can draw on the trust generated by the years they've already shared when those hard times hit.

Some readers might wonder, "Why don't they get married?" The young couples we interviewed certainly aspire to marriage. In fact, they revere it. But they strongly reject the idea that a hasty wedding is a good idea. Isn't it better, they reason, to wait until they can get their finances in order and be sure the relationship is strong? Why get married if you're just going to get a divorce? For them, this would merely make a mockery of a sacred institution. For reasons I've outlined above, most of these relationships soon fail their own test.

After the breakup, inner-city dads firmly believe that a shattered couple bond should not get in the way of a father's relationship with his most precious resource: his kid. They're not just out to claim status with their peers by getting women pregnant. They long to engage in the father role. But the young men we spoke to have tried to redefine fatherhood to fit their circumstances.

All fathers across America, rich and poor alike, have avidly embraced fatherhood's softer side. Imparting love, maintaining a clear channel of communication, and spending quality time together are seen as the keys to being a good dad. This "new father" model, which spurred middle-class men to begin changing diapers several decades ago, has gained amazing traction with disadvantaged dads in the inner city, perhaps because it's the kind of fatherhood they can most easily afford. But while middle-class men now combine these new tasks with being breadwinners, low-income fathers who face growing economic adversity are trying to substitute one role for the other.

Here is the problem: Neither society nor their children's mothers are willing to go along with this trade-off. Love and affection are all fine and good, but who's going to pay the light bill? What about keeping the heat on? If a child's father can't provide money, the attitude goes that he's more trouble than he's worth. Why strive to make sure he stays involved with the kids?

But we're wrong about that too. From the kid's point of view, it is hard to make up for the loss of a parent. When a single mom in the inner city feels her kid's father has failed to provide, there is an enormous temptation to "swap daddies," pushing the child's dad aside while allowing a new man—perhaps one with a little more going for him economically—to claim the title of father. These moms are often desperate to find a man who can help with the bills so they can keep a roof over their kid's head. The problem is that these new relationships may be no more stable than the old ones.

When a mom moves from one relationship to another—playing gatekeeper with the biological father while putting her new boyfriend into the dad's role—she puts her kids on a "father-go-round." In the end, will any of these men have the long-term commitment it takes to put these kids through college?

Meanwhile, the biological fathers themselves end up on a family-go-round, having kids by other women in a quest to try to get what they long for—the whole father experience. Each new child with a different mom offers another chance—a clean slate. With eagerness, they once again invest every resource they can muster in service of that new fragile family. But while succeeding with

a new child, they often leave others behind. So, while they are good dads to some of their children, they end up being bad dads to others.

As is so often the case, these men often have good intentions. They want to heal their own fatherless childhoods by embracing the father's role. But good intentions aren't enough. All of their children—not just some—need them.

If they want to stop the father-go-round, moms will have to do what they can to keep the biological dad involved with his child and not push him aside. It's up to them, because currently, mothers have most of the power de facto, if not de jure. Almost always, an unmarried mother has presumed custody, even if the dad willingly signs documents to establish legal paternity. When an unmarried dad gets a child support order, there is no corresponding automatic process that grants visitation. Therefore, there is seldom any guarantee that the father will even be able to see his child, regardless of whether he pays child support.

So here is my message to the single moms I've come to know and admire over the years, the ones who do so much of the nurturing and caring—those who often struggle mightily just to keep a roof over their kids' heads: You can't easily substitute someone else for your kid's dad. If the two of you don't manage to stay together, find a way to keep him involved with his kids.

Here is my message to young disadvantaged men: If you really want to be a good dad, wait until you are financially ready to have a child, preferably your mid-to-late 20s, if not beyond. Make sure your relationship with the child's mother is on a solid footing first.

But the dads aren't going to listen to my advice unless the rest of America hears what I have to say too: You've got to give these men hope, which would mean a real shot at a stable future. Stop locking them up for nonviolent offenses. Make sure they have decent schools to attend, not the broken disgraces that litter our inner cities. Promote programs that instruct them on how to navigate the rocky shoals of their relationships. Increase the supply of decent jobs and, for those who can't find work, provide jobs of last resort. Make good on the promise upon which America was founded: that here, if you are willing to work hard, you can make it, no matter who you are.

But the most important thing I need you to do—all of you, even Barack Obama—is to change your attitude about these fathers. They care deeply about their kids. They are not lacking the will. Let's join together to help them find the way.

All names in this essay have been changed in the interest of confidentiality.

BARBARA KINNEY

BRITANI HOOD-MONGAR • Chattanooga, Tennessee

Britani is a single mom raising two-year-old twin girls, Parker and Presley. Their father left after Britani told him she was pregnant, despite their engagement.

She and the twins live in an apartment with her mother. Britani works as a cafeteria worker at a local elementary school as a contract worker, and she receives no benefits and no summer salary. She recently went to a food pantry for the first time.

Despite her daily struggles, she tries to stay upbeat for her daughters. "I'm not going to let my kids know that we are struggling every day. I just want to make sure that they are happy and to be able to give them the love [that I can], because I can't give the love that a father can give," she said.

A Call to Men: Ending Men's Violence Against Women

By TONY PORTER, nationally recognized speaker, educator, activist, and co-founder and co-director of A Call to Men: The Next Generation of Manhood. (www.acalltomen.org)

Men's violence against women is the leading cause of women's injuries in this country.[1] The Centers for Disease Control and Prevention reports that almost a quarter of heterosexual American women have experienced some form of severe physical violence at the hands of their male intimate partners.[2] To me, statistics such as these indicate that men's violence against women is an epidemic and should be addressed as such.

Of course, the overwhelming majority of men in this country don't perpetrate violence against women. The majority of men are good, and a good man would not assault a woman. A good man believes women should be respected. A good man honors the women and girls in his life. A good man believes in equality for women.

Even so, it's time for good men to acknowledge that while we would never physically hurt women, our collective socialization is the foundation on which violence against women is built. We have to acknowledge that our society's rigid definitions of manhood—definitions we adopt for ourselves and pass along to our sons and other young men in our lives—provide fertile ground for violence to take root and flourish. We have to acknowledge that far too often we define ourselves as men by devaluing women and girls.

I once asked a 12-year-old boy, a football player, "What would happen if the coach said to you, in front of all your teammates, that you were playing like a girl?" I expected him to say he'd be mad, sad, or angry. Instead, he said, "It would *destroy* me!" I thought, "Oh my God. If it would *destroy* him to be told he was playing like a girl, then what are we teaching him about girls?"

Here is what I believe we are teaching him: In defining manhood, our society has created what I call "the Man Box." As our collective socialization of manhood, the Man Box contains many rigid definitions of manhood that limit who we are, what we're expected to think and feel, and how we should regard and behave toward women.

We have been taught—and we teach our boys—to be tough, strong, and courageous. We have been taught—and we teach our boys—to feel no fear and no pain or any other emotion, except for anger. In order for men to feel strong, someone else must be weak, and far too often, that falls on the women and girls in our lives. In the Man Box, men are taught to be dominating, so women must be submissive. Men are strong and women are vulnerable and weak. Men are superior and women are inferior. Men are in charge, which means women are not.

Unfortunately, this need for power—physical, emotional, or financial—is central to the collective socialization of men. When a man is without power, he is viewed as being less than a man. When his female partner has more power than he does in these areas, it can be very challenging.

A young man once told me a story about meeting the girl of his dreams while they were waiting to sign up for karate school. They began taking classes together, and eventually they fell in love and moved in together. After a while, he stopped taking karate, but she continued on, becoming a highly skilled, master-level karate expert. His friends began to tease him on a regular basis, saying that if it ever came down to it, his girlfriend could "kick his butt." He shared with me that her greater physical power negatively impacted his self-esteem. He felt so insecure in the relationship that he ended it.

I have heard it said that most female law enforcement officers wind up in relationships with other law enforcement officers, but not just because of the work they share. It's because men who aren't in law enforcement feel insecure about their manhood when they are in relationships with female cops.

From generation to generation, this male need for power is passed on as a legacy. It's time for men to move with purpose to address, challenge, and re-educate ourselves, our sons, and other boys.

As men, we teach our boys—as we were taught—to be held hostage to the norms of the Man Box, including hypermasculinity and homophobia.

I actually believe that homophobia is the glue that keeps the Man Box together. We fear not conforming to these definitions, and the fear paralyzes and holds us hostage to the Man Box. Outside the box are women and men who are seen as less than "fully male."

Most good men don't see themselves as part of the problem of domestic and sexual violence, which is why we don't focus on being part of the solution. The truth of the matter is we are part of the problem, consciously or subconsciously. Let me tell you why.

The Man Box supports three key aspects of our traditional male socialization that create, foster, and even justify men's abuse and violence against women. We good men must begin to unpack and deconstruct these deeply ingrained beliefs:

Men are taught to view women as "less than." Far too many aspects of manhood and masculinity are defined by devaluing women. Men are taught to have higher expectations of our sons and lower expectations of our daughters. That's because the men before us taught us to minimize and trivialize the experience of women and girls—even the women and girls in our own lives. We pass that teaching on to our sons and other boys. I'm not saying this is true for every man, but I am saying that it happens far too often, with far too many of us.

Men are taught to treat women as property. Knowingly or not, men continue to perpetuate and support the myth that women are the property and possession of the men in their lives. One of the principal justifications men give for

Traditional socialization may trap boys and men in society's rigid definitions of "manhood." Sociologists argue that teaching men that it is okay to have feelings and emotions can open the door to more respect for and less oppression of the opposite sex. {JAN SONNENMAIR (1,3), MELISSA FARLOW (2)}

perpetrating domestic violence is the belief that "she's mine, so I get to punish her if I don't like her actions or attitudes." While most men know and agree that this belief is out of line, inappropriate, and just not true, the myth of ownership that underlies such thinking is deeply embedded in our collective socialization.

Men are taught to view women as objects. Devaluing women and regarding them as property creates an environment that supports objectifying them. Throughout every stratum of society—whether it's the entertainment industry, advertising, corporate America, or even on a street corner—men see and treat women as objects, particularly sex objects. If society at large dehumanizes and objectifies women, it's much easier for violent men to justify and minimize what they do to them.

All of this must change. This is the work that men must do. It is definitely true that over the past 40 years, we have made significant gains in holding men accountable for violence against women, and we have increased services to those who have been victimized. But violence has still not declined. If women could end the violence by themselves, they would have. In order for the violence to end, men—good men—must be part of the solution.

Good men must begin to acknowledge and own their responsibility, and we must be part of the solution to end violence against women and girls. Good men and boys must play a critical role. I'm talking about new attitudes, new training, and new language. I'm talking about partnering with women and respecting their voices, experience, and wisdom about what it would take for us to promote and actualize an equitable society.

Every time we are about to tell a boy to "stop playing like a girl" or "stop acting like a girl," we need to ask ourselves: "What am I teaching him about girls?" Instead, let's teach boys that it's okay not to dominate. Teach them it's okay to have feelings and emotions. It's okay to promote equality. It's okay to have women who are just friends, no more. We don't have to conquer. We don't have to possess.

It's time that we let women and girls know that we don't have to run them down in order to feel like men. Let's treat them as the equals that they are, whether they're our life partners or colleagues. Our liberation as men is tied to the liberation of women. Acknowledging our own humanity will come only when we appreciate theirs.

ENDNOTES

1   U.S. Senate Committee on the Judiciary, "Violence Against Women: A Week In the Life of America" (1992).

2   Centers for Disease Control and Prevention, "NISVS: An Overview of 2010 Summary Report Findings" (2010), available at http://www.cdc.gov/violenceprevention/pdf/cdc_nisvs_overview_insert_final-a.pdf.

Women and Poverty: The Role of Lawyers and Family Law

By JOHN BOUMAN, president of the Sargent Shriver National Center on Poverty Law, and WENDY POLLACK, founder and director of the Women's Law and Policy Project at the Shriver Center

During the Shriver Center's many years of representing women in poverty, we have learned that these women often have family and relationship pressures and crises that threaten their basic economic survival. Those problems underlie or even cause other legal problems, such as job loss, eviction, lack of child support, and personal safety issues.

Dealing with all of these underlying family and relationship issues is often at the heart of sorting out other legal concerns. Successfully addressing the problems would allow these women to get on a path to stability, upward mobility, and a decent quality of life, but doing so heavily depends on whether they have competent lawyers to assist them. Yet that isn't as simple as it sounds.

Lawyers representing women in poverty come from underfunded legal-aid programs or from volunteer programs that provide pro bono private attorneys. The largest source of federal legal-aid funding is from the Legal Services Corporation, or LSC. The LSC wisely allows local program boards to set priorities among the many competing legal needs in their communities, but the distribution of scarce resources often leaves women's family-law issues short staffed.

LSC and state bar groups have conducted "legal needs" studies[1] to discover the issues for which low-income people need lawyers. These studies show that attorneys handle less than half of the family-law matters presented by low-income clients in which an attorney is required. Often the clients represent themselves, sometimes using so-called self-help articles or brochures. LSC's report presents further evidence of what common sense tells us: Self-represented clients are at a distinct disadvantage, especially when they are up against an adversary with an attorney. They fail to assert their own rights and defenses, they fail to effectively present their side, and they lose.

An even sadder truth is that women often do not even know that they have any rights in the first place or what those rights are, let alone how to access legal information or representation. Justice in those cases is accidental or absent altogether.

Today, there are nowhere near enough lawyers to meet the needs of the low-income population, and that is a genuine crisis in our justice system. Congress and state legislatures must step up their efforts to fund and staff poverty-law programs adequately. At the same time, bar associations, law firms, law schools, and court systems must continue to develop and expand successful programs for new volunteer attorneys.

One example of such a program is the Harriett Buhai Center for Family Law in Los Angeles, which not only offers legal representation on family-law matters, but also educates women on marriage, divorce, child-custody, and child-support law. It operates on a volunteer-lawyer model that can and should be replicated around the country.

In addition to beefing up the poverty-attorney corps, there are policy and systemic solutions that would prevent, ameliorate, or solve many family and relationship issues if they became law or established practice in our states. We have seen proof of this around the country already:

- Lawyers representing women have been responsible for important systemic changes, such as no-fault divorce,[2] child-support collection systems,[3] and the Violence Against Women Act.[4]

- More than 20 states have passed laws protecting the workplace rights of domestic and sexual violence survivors.[5]

- A number of states have beefed up tenants' rights already on the books, with additional rights for tenants who have survived domestic or sexual violence.[6]

- Illinois has passed a law promoting the educational rights of students who are pregnant or parenting or are survivors of domestic violence.[7]

- Some states have changed their child-support collection systems to foster cooperative parenting and to help well-intentioned low-income fathers succeed, rather than just punishing them by default.[8]

But much more is needed in many more states.

Developing such family-friendly, women-friendly

policies and practices is as important as representing low-income women in individual cases. But many states do not have legal organizations with the capacity for policy advocacy on behalf of women in poverty.[9] Building that capacity is an important part of helping low-income women—indeed, all women—deal with family and relationship matters.

The message is clear. The legal system itself and access to it is an important way for a caring society to help women climb their way out of the poverty trap—or avoid it in the first place.

ENDNOTES

1   Legal Services Corporation, "Documenting the Justice Gap In America: The Current Unmet Civil Legal Needs of Low-Income Americans" (2009), available at http://www.lsc.gov/sites/default/files/LSC/pdfs/documenting_the_justice_gap_in_america_2009.pdf.

2   See Stephanie Coontz, "Divorce, No-Fault Style," *The New York Times*, June 16, 2010, available at http://www.nytimes.com/2010/06/17/opinion/17coontz.html?_r=0.

3   Child support collection systems have developed in all states under Title IV-D of the Social Security Act, 42 U.S.C. 651 et seq.

4   *Violence Against Women Reauthorization Act of 2013*, Public Law 113-4, 113th Cong. (March 7, 2013), available at http://www.gpo.gov/fdsys/pkg/PLAW-113publ4/pdf/PLAW-113publ4.pdf.

5   Legal Momentum, "State Law Guide: Employment Rights for Victims of Domestic or Sexual Violence" (2013), available at http://www.scribd.com/doc/160011402/State-Law-Guide-Employment-Rights-for-Victims-of-Domestic-or-Sexual-Violence.

6   *Safe Homes Act*, 765 ILCS 750 (January 1, 2007), available at http://www.ilga.gov/legislation/ilcs/ilcs3.asp?ActID=2817&ChapterID=62

7   Ensuring Success in School Task Force, Public Act 95-0558 (August 30, 2007), available at http://www.ilga.gov/legislation/publicacts/fulltext.asp?Name=095-0558.

8   See, for example, Illinois Child Support, "Child Support Services," available at http://childsupportillinois.com (last accessed October 2013).

9   The shortage of attorneys engaging in policy-type activity on behalf of women in poverty is due in part to the fact that, since 1996, Congress has forbidden attorneys in legal-services programs to engage in legislative advocacy and related activities. See 45 CFR Part 1612.

Evolution of the Modern American Family

By STEPHANIE COONTZ, *professor of history and family studies at The Evergreen State College in Olympia, Washington, and co-chair of the Council on Contemporary Families, a nonprofit, nonpartisan association of family researchers and practitioners. She is a frequent op-ed contributor to* The New York Times *and other newspapers.*

Many people believe that the problems facing women today are due to the breakdown of the "traditional" male breadwinner family. But the real problem facing women today—and increasingly, the problem facing men as well—is that the male breadwinner family was a short-lived historical anomaly that does not work as a model for 21st-century gender norms and social policy. In the mid-20th century, the United States codified its notions of what can be expected of a "normal" workforce on the basis of a family form that rested on an exceptional and temporary conjuncture of economic trends and gender arrangements.

For thousands of years and all across the world, families were productive units in which every single member—husbands, wives, and children alike—labored to produce the material necessities of life. Colonial Americans, for example, did not expect men to be the primary providers for their families. They recognized that families were equally dependent on the labor of men's "yoke-mates," as wives were called in those days. These co-provider families were by no means egalitarian, but one reason patriarchy was so strict was because men needed the authority to organize and discipline the household labor force, including overseeing the personal lives of all its members.[1]

Only in the 19th century did Americans begin to think that men should devote themselves almost exclusively to paid work outside the home, while wives should handle domestic matters and kinship obligations. Yet even after this new ideal took hold, most families still required the earnings of the wife or the children to get by. It wasn't until the 1920s that a bare majority of children grew up in families where the father's labor purchased the family's provisions, while their mother did unpaid child care, elder care, and housework.

The Great Depression and World War II disrupted this family form, but it roared back in the 1950s, when the percentage of wives and mothers who were supported entirely by their husbands' wages reached a high that has never been equaled, before or since.

The male breadwinner family of the postwar era was based on two distinctive developments. One was positive: an unprecedented increase in real wages for men. From 1950 to 1970, the average real earnings of American men from ages 25 to 64 increased by 50 percent, with the increases earned by less-educated and more-educated workers alike. In that era, unlike today, wages grew hand in hand with productivity.[2] This favorable economic climate enabled more men than ever before to support their families without a second income.

But the heyday of the male breadwinner family was also due to a negative feature of that era: the exclusion of women from this economic expansion, their subordination within marriage, and the growth of a new ideology that Betty Friedan famously labeled "The Feminine Mystique."[3]

"Experts" insisted that it was abnormal for women to have any personal aspirations beyond becoming wives and mothers. When women did work, they were relegated to low-wage jobs and treated as a supplementary, part-time labor force who filled low-skill jobs before childbirth or after their children were in school. It was assumed they did not deserve or even desire raises, promotions, or job security, because first and foremost, they were homemakers, and that was all they really wanted out of life.[4]

The combination of men's burgeoning job opportunities and women's immersion in the feminine mystique meant that most men in that era received a substantial "patriarchal dividend," according them preference over women at work and deference from women at home. In many cases, the material benefits of this male dividend did trickle down to men's "dependents," providing their wives with better homes and

more comfortable lives than they had previously experienced—a luxury that was especially appreciated after the hardships of the Great Depression and World War II. But women's economic dependence on men also drove many women to enter or remain in unhappy marriages, and it frustrated the growing number of women who resented their exclusion from the unprecedented economic, educational, and technological progress they saw around them.

The male breadwinner/female homemaker family, whatever its good and bad features, reigned supreme for only about 25 years and now is gone for good. In part, this is because during the late '60s and '70s, so many women successfully struggled to gain access to new educational and occupational opportunities. And it is also because business reneged on its side of the postwar wage bargain that had linked wages to productivity—instead demanding full-time or more hours and commitment from the male workforce while cutting wages and reducing job security.

As women became more educated, they married later and worked for longer portions of their lives. More wives entered the labor market—some by choice, some from necessity as their husbands' wages stagnated. At the same time, men's decreasing ability to earn a family wage, combined with women's increasing freedom to leave relationships that were unequal or unfair, created growing numbers of single-mother families. The workforce lost its predominantly male character. Family caregiving obligations became more widely distributed, increasingly shared by both partners in two-earner families, but in

A household headed by a single mother is twice as likely to be poor as a household headed by a single father.

single-parent families they were shouldered by the same person who was the primary earner.

Today, 70 percent of American children live in families where every adult in the household is in the labor force.[5] Yet employers and government cling to work practices and policies designed for a labor force composed of full-time male workers who have someone else back at home taking care of family obligations.

Organizing business and government policies around this illusory norm is particularly hard on women and is one of the main reasons why the gender revolution has stalled. Women have made immense strides in upgrading their skills and entering new occupations. But women are still expected—and most women still expect—to make most of the adjustments needed to raise children or care for elderly parents. So, in the absence of family-friendly work policies and affordable quality child care that would allow couples to share work and family responsibilities equally, women are more likely than their male partners to quit or cut back on work to handle family obligations.

This has created what sociologists call a "motherhood penalty." Economist Sylvia Ann Hewlett reports that on average, a woman loses almost 20 percent of her lifetime earning power when she leaves the workforce for just a year to have and

care for a child. If she spends three to four years away from work to raise her child, she loses a full 40 percent of her potential earnings.[6]

Combining motherhood with work is especially difficult for lower-income, poorly educated women, who are much more likely than college-educated women to have an out-of-wedlock birth and are more likely to divorce if they do marry, as Ann O'Leary details in her chapter. When a relationship ends and children are involved, the woman generally ends up as the residential parent, usually without adequate child support or affordable child care.

These mothers and their children are among the most disadvantaged Americans. A household headed by a single mother is twice as likely to be poor as a household headed by a single father.[7] Despite the gains that other women in America have made, things have been getting worse for these women. From 1990 to 2004, families with incomes less than 50 percent of the federal poverty line—most of which are headed by unmarried mothers—experienced a 20 percent reduction in the total resources available to them.[8]

Some people claim that the solution to this problem is to promote a return to the male breadwinner marriages of the 1950s. But there is considerable evidence that unwed births and unstable relationships are more of a result than a cause of the impoverished conditions in which these women and their pool of potential partners live, as Kathryn Edin points out in her essay.[9]

For many working-class men, becoming the family breadwinner is now impossible. The median earnings of male high school graduates who work full time have declined by more than 25 percent since 1968, and the wages of full-time male workers who did not complete high school have dropped by almost 40 percent.[10]

Trying to shoehorn women whose expectations of equal treatment have been rising into marriages with men whose economic prospects have been falling is no solution to contemporary work and family dilemmas. Women are far less likely than in the past to put up with the kind of behavior that so often accompanies economic loss and chronic employment stress—such as drug or alcohol abuse and domestic violence—and we should not encourage or incentivize them to do so.[11]

The bad news is that the punishing economic climate of the past 30 years has led to increased economic insecurity for the majority of men *and* women in America. Despite their gains relative to men, women—along with children—remain the most economically vulnerable members of society. The good news is that these trends create a convergence of interests between men and women. The same measures that will reduce the pay gap between women and men will provide more economic benefits for low-income men as well as low-income women, and a more balanced life for all workers.

The first step toward achieving social and gender justice is to abandon the assumption that the ideal worker is a male breadwinner with a wife at home to take care of family obligations. Instead, we must design family-friendly work policies and social programs that put front and center all workers' interests as caregivers as well as food providers—which has been the double-sided role of women in the past. This will help both women and men meet their work and family obligations without sacrificing either.

In reality, the motherhood penalty is actually a caregiving penalty. The major gender difference today is that employers assume all mothers will engage in caregiving and penalize them in advance, whether they ask for work-family accommodations or not. By contrast, they assume that all fathers will delegate caregiving to their wives and do not penalize them unless they violate those expectations and directly ask for work-family accommodations.

Just knowing that a woman is a mother leads employers to discriminate against her in hiring decisions. When researchers sent out fake job applications for women with identical qualifications, but included information in some résumés indicating the woman was a mother, employers were half as likely to call her back as they were the presumably childless woman.[12] Mothers with the same level of education, the same experience, and the same job type as their childless female counterparts are paid lower wages per hour, whether they work full or part time.[13]

Men are not automatically penalized when they become parents. In fact, they often get a de facto fatherhood bonus. But men who actually request family leave face a greater risk of being demoted or downsized than their male co-workers who do not ask. And, like their female counterparts, men whose résumés show they have ever quit work for family reasons incur a financial penalty compared to other employees.[14]

Nevertheless, whether out of desire or necessity, growing numbers of men are taking on significant child care and elder care responsibilities. This explains why today men report equal or higher levels of work-family conflict than women.[15] Family-friendly work policies would reduce not only the gender gap but also the stress levels of all workers, male and female, who have caregiving obligations.

Similarly, comprehensive and affordable child care would increase gender equity by enabling mothers, married or unmarried, to work more regularly and earn more. In countries with minimal public child care for infants and toddlers, the motherhood penalty subtracts about 10 percent from a woman's paycheck per child. That penalty falls to just 4.3 percent in countries with more expansive public child care programs.[16] But again, reliable, affordable child care would be a boon to all parents, married or single, male or female.

It is time to discard the outdated assumption that only women are "real" parents and only men are "real" workers. This assumption once conferred economic privileges on men. But now it burdens more men than it benefits, disadvantages the majority of mothers who work for pay, makes family life more stressful, and drags down the whole economy. Between 1990 and 2010, the United States fell from 6th to 17th place in female labor participation among 22 affluent countries, with almost a third of the decline resulting from our failure to keep pace with other countries in initiating family-friendly work policies.[17]

In developing policies for the American worker, male or female, we should start not with the outmoded male breadwinner model but with the model of today's woman—someone who has extensive responsibilities to children, parents, and community, as well as to work. By designing family leave policies and child care systems and social programs to accommodate her needs—as the rest of the industrialized world already does[18]—we will help women and their families rise, and we will pull men up in the process.

ENDNOTES

1 For this and the next two paragraphs, see Stephanie Coontz, *The Way We Never Were: American Families and the Nostalgia Trap* (New York: Basic Books, 1992); Stephanie Coontz, *Marriage, a History: How Love Conquered Marriage* (New York: Penguin Books, 2005).

2 Michael Greenstone and Adam Looney, "Trends: Men in Trouble," *Milken Institute Review* (2011), available at http://www.milkeninstitute.org/publications/review/2011_7/08-16mr51.pdf; Lawrence Mishel and Heidi Shierholz, "A Decade of Flat Wages: The Key Barrier to Shared Prosperity and a Rising Middle Class" (Washington: Economic Policy Institute, 2013), available at http://www.epi.org/publication/a-decade-of-flat-wages-the-key-barrier-to-shared-prosperity-and-a-rising-middle-class/.

3 Betty Friedan, *The Feminine Mystique* (New York: W.W. Norton & Company, 1963).

4 Stephanie Coontz, *A Strange Stirring: The Feminine Mystique and American Women at the Dawn of the 1960s* (New York: Basic Books, 2011).

5 Joan C. Williams and Heather Boushey, "The Three Faces of Work-Family Conflict" (Washington: Center for American Progress, 2010), available at http://www.americanprogress.org/issues/labor/report/2010/01/25/7194/the-three-faces-of-work-family-conflict/.

6 Sylvia Ann Hewlett, *Off Ramps and On Ramps* (Boston: Harvard Business School Press, 2007), p. 45; Ann Crittendon, *The Price of Motherhood* (New York: Metropolitan Books, 2001), p. 89.

7 Carmen DeNavas-Walt, Bernadette D. Proctor, and Jessica C. Smith, "Income, Poverty, and Health Insurance Coverage in the United States: 2011" (Washington: U.S. Department of Commerce, 2012), available at http://www.census.gov/prod/2012pubs/p60-243.pdf.

8 Eva Bertram, "NET Gains and Losses: A Modern Labor Market and a New Deal Welfare State" (Washington: Third Way, 2013), available at http://content.thirdway.org/publications/648/third_way_report_-_net_gains_and_losses_a_modern_labor_market_and_a_new_deal_welfare_state_.pdf.

9 Stephanie Coontz and Nancy Folbre, "Marriage, Poverty, and Public Policy" (Coral Gables, FL: Council on Contemporary Families, 2002), available at http://www.contemporary-families.org/Marriage-Partnership-Divorce/marriage-poverty-and-public-policy.html; Gabrielle Raley, "Avenue to Adulthood." In Stephanie Coontz, ed., *American Families* (New York: Routledge, 2008); *The Economist*, "Economist Debates: Marriage: Opening statements," December 11, 2012, available at http://www.economist.com/debate/days/view/908; *The Economist*, "Economist Debates: Marriage: Rebuttal Statements," December 14, 2012, available at http://www.economist.com/debate/days/view/913; *The Economist*, "Economist Debates: Marriage: Closing Statements," December 19, 2012, available at http://www.economist.com/debate/days/view/914.

10 Greenstone and Looney, "Trends: Men in Trouble."

11 Although domestic-violence rates have been falling in the United States, Duke University researcher Linda Burton and her team of Fragile Families researchers discovered that two-thirds of the impoverished single mothers they interviewed had experienced serious abuse at the hands of their partners. Council on Contemporary Families, "Is That a Fact? Council on Contemporary Family Researchers Offer Guidance on Making Sense of Competing Factoids and Claims about What Causes What," Press release, August 18, 2009, available at http://www.contemporaryfamilies.org/all/is-that-a-fact.html.

12 Shelley J. Correll, "Equal Pay? Not Yet for Mothers," Council on Contemporary Families, available at http://www.contemporaryfamilies.org/Economic-Issues/equal-pay-not-yet-for-mothers.html.

13 Ibid.

14 Scott Coltrane and others, "Fathers and the Flexibility Stigma," *Journal of Social Issues* 69 (2) (2013).

15 Kerstin Aumann, Ellen Galinsky, and Kenneth Matos, "The New Male Mystique" (New York: Families and Work Institute, 2011), available at http://familiesandwork.org/site/research/reports/newmalemystique.pdf; Ellen Galinsky, Kerstin Aumann, and James T. Bond, "Times Are Changing: Gender and Generation at Work and at Home" (New York: Families and Work Institute, 2011), available at http://familiesandwork.org/site/research/reports/Times_Are_Changing.pdf.

16 Joy Misra, "Which Policies Promote Gender Pay Equality?" Council on Contemporary Families, available at http://contemporaryfamilies.org/Economic-Issues/which-policies-promote-gender-pay-equality.html.

17 Janet Gornick and Markus Jantti, eds., *Income Inequality: Economic Disparities and the Middle Class in Affluent Countries* (Stanford, CA: Stanford University Press, 2013), p. 29; Female Labor Supply: Francine D. Blau and Lawrence M. Kahn, "Why is the US Falling Behind?" Working Paper 18702 (National Bureau of Economic Research, 2013).

18 Jody Heymann and Kristin McNeil, *Children's Chances: How Countries Can Move from Surviving to Thriving* (Cambridge, MA: Harvard University Press, 2013).

Education is what can help low-wage women push back from the brink. It can be their ticket into the middle class. {BARBARA RIES}

Get Smart: A 21st-Century Education for All Women

By Dr. Anthony P. Carnevale and Dr. Nicole Smith

STUNNING FACT

The greatest regret of women living on the brink is
not staying in school longer or investing more in their education.

I n the 50 years since President Lyndon Johnson launched the War on Poverty, women have made unprecedented strides in education. They now outnumber men on every rung of the higher education ladder. In 1964, only about 40 percent of women enrolled in any type of college. Today, that figure is 57 percent.[1]

There are roughly 3 million more women currently enrolled in college than men.[2] About 62 percent of all associate's and master's degrees now go to female candidates, and the ratio is almost the same for bachelor's degrees.[3] In the 2005-06 academic year, women surpassed men in earning doctoral degrees as well.[4]

FIGURE 1

Total fall enrollment of first-time degree/certificate-seeking students in degree-granting institutions, 1955–2010

By gender, in thousands

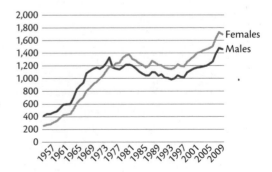

Source: Center on Education and the Workforce, or CEW, analysis of National Center for Education Statistics, Biennial Survey of Education in the United States; Opening Fall Enrollment in Higher Education, 1963 through 1965; Higher Education General Information Survey (HEGIS), "Fall Enrollment in Colleges and Universities" surveys, 1966 through 1985; Integrated Postsecondary Education Data System (IPEDS), "Fall Enrollment Survey" (IPEDS-EF: 86-99); and IPEDS spring 2001 through spring 2011, enrollment component. Original table was prepared in November 2011.

All in all, the story of women's access to higher education, as well as their graduation rates in recent decades, is one of remarkable success.

For far too many women living on the economic brink, however, their education story is one of continued struggle and stagnation. For millions of women, college remains a distant dream at best.[5]

According to polling conducted for *The Shriver Report* by Greenberg Quinlan Rosner Research and TargetPoint Consulting, among the biggest regrets of women living on the brink is not staying in school longer or investing more in their education. For instance, 80 percent of Latina high school students aspire to go to college, but only 15 percent hold college degrees.[6]

In our knowledge- and service-based economy, a postsecondary degree is the closest thing to a golden ticket to the middle class.

Even those women who make it into a postsecondary program aren't guaranteed upward mobility. The strains of work, family care obligations, and enormous debt—in conjunction with their studies—may prove overwhelming, especially at educational institutions not fully accommodating students who need to work and/or raise children at the same time. The women who manage to complete their programs are often saddled with significant and lingering debt. And not all degrees are created equal. Women often need to choose degrees that lead to "family-supporting" work. But while some certificates and degrees pay lifelong dividends, others have little value.[7]

The barrier to higher education for women who can't afford it or have competing family obligations is especially harmful to our economy. We know that educational attainment is the surest predictor of future financial stability.[8] But attaining a postsecondary degree is not a guarantee of financial security. And decisions about education—what to study and how to pay for it—continue to impact women's lifelong earnings potential. Still, in our knowledge- and service-based economy, a postsecondary degree is the closest thing to a golden ticket to the middle class.

Today, when women are increasingly the financial backbone of their families, we know investing in their education yields returns across generations. Low-wage working women understand the value of an education and recognize college as the path to financial success for themselves and their children. But it is estimated that in 2013, 460,000 girls graduating from high school did not go on to college in the fall immediately following high school completion.[9]

Disproportionately, these girls will come from families that have fewer resources, less direct experience with college, and greater financial insecurity. Students from high-income families are 50 percent more likely to enroll in college than students from low-income families.[10]

So why do some women forgo postsecondary education, while others make education their on-ramp to the American Dream? What are the factors that influence girls in high school to make education a priority? How can we ensure that girls are savvy about college, so when they do enroll in postsecondary programs, they understand the financial implications of a variety of career paths, as well as the impact of student loans?

This chapter will try to answer these questions and identify the barriers that limit women's educational success. We begin by explaining why education is such a critical component to help struggling women pull back from the brink. Then we track the educational path from preschool through high school. We then look at the reasons low-income women struggle to complete a college degree and subsequently fall into the cycle of low-wage work. We look at the life choices women make in school to prepare for the workplace and how these choices influence wage outcomes. Finally, we examine the deep-seated biases and social pressures that may explain why so many women gravitate to occupations, programs of study, and college majors that offer relatively low pay and an insufficient income to support a family.

A NEW SOCIAL COMPACT: WHY EDUCATION MATTERS MORE THAN EVER FOR GETTING WOMEN OFF THE BRINK

Perhaps no single factor has influenced women's economic well-being more in the last 50 years than the dramatic increase in the number and types of jobs requiring a higher education.

In the 1960s, working-class men with high school diplomas could often support families on a single income, even without a college degree, because they belonged to unions or worked in booming manufacturing sectors such as the auto industry, aerospace, or construction. Today, that social contract has dissolved. The fully government-funded public high school diploma has been replaced by the much more costly college degree as the passport to the middle class. That trend will only become more pronounced. By 2020, almost two-thirds of U.S. jobs are projected to require some form of postsecondary education.[11]

This new reality demands a level of awareness and planning on the part of all Americans. Today's young people have to make significant financial decisions about their future even before beginning their careers, in a way that previous generations did not. This is especially true for women, who, regardless of their education level, still find their earnings eclipsed by the persistent gender wage gap.

As this report explains, the reasons for this are complex and by no means limited to the educational and occupational choices women make for themselves. But the wage gap does mean that even when a low-income woman completes a postsecondary degree, her wages are unlikely to match those of her male counterparts. Men continue to outearn women at every level of educational attainment. Women with a bachelor's degree earn what a man with an associate's degree makes, and women with an associate's degree earn what men who only have some college credits make. Even a woman with a Ph.D. earns what a man with a bachelor's degree makes.[12]

Even with the gender wage gap, however, the lifetime value of higher education is beyond dispute. In 2012, the median weekly earnings of a person with a high school diploma were $652 a week. That's $33,904 a year, far below the nearly $47,000-per-year income that's needed to escape the financial brink for a family of four. A person with an associate's degree earns 20 percent more annually than someone with a high school diploma, and someone with a bachelor's degree earns 63 percent more.[13] Over a lifetime, a worker with an advanced degree can earn up to $2.1 million more than someone who drops out of college.[14]

FIGURE 2

Real wages for men are higher than those for women at every level of educational attainment

Men: Wages by education level, in 2011 dollars   *Women: Wages by education level, in 2011 dollars*

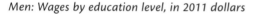

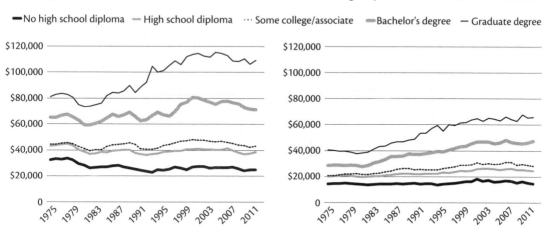

Source: Bureau of Labor Statistics and U.S. Census Bureau, Current Population Survey, various years.

Higher education also plays a significant role in breaking the intergenerational cycle of poverty within a family. Studies show that parents' educational attainment strongly correlates to their children's educational outcomes, and thus their economic success.[15] In fact, parental educational attainment is now more important than family income in predicting a child's future opportunity. Among children whose parents have a Ph.D. or professional degree, 73 percent obtain a bachelor's degree or higher. Among those whose parents are high school dropouts, that figure is only 6 percent.[16]

FIGURE 3

Workers with advanced degrees earn up to $2.1 million more than college dropouts over a lifetime

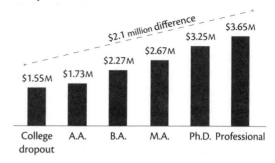

Source: Anthony P. Carnevale, Stephen J. Rose, and Ban Cheah, "The College Payoff: Education, Occupation, Lifetime Earnings" (Washington: Georgetown University Center on Education and the Workforce, 2011).

FIGURE 4

Child educational attainment is highly correlated with that of the parent

Seventy-three percent of students whose parents earned a Ph.D. or professional degree obtained a B.A. or better

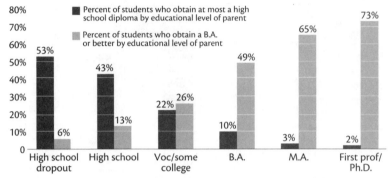

Source: Georgetown University Center on Education and the Workforce calculations using Table 341, *Digest of Education Statistics*, 2011.

MAPPING THE EDUCATIONAL PATH: HURDLES, INEQUITIES, AND DECISION POINTS

There are forks at every stage of a girl's or woman's education that determine how likely she is to attend a two- or four-year college and how successful she will be in her studies, and subsequently in the job market. By mapping these decision points, we can see the path most likely to lead to college and its promise of financial security and upward mobility—and help women and girls head down that path.

THE FIRST FORK: EARLY CHILDHOOD EDUCATION

In the United States, about half the inequality in the present value of lifetime earnings is due to factors determined by age 18.[17] Formal education doesn't typically begin until age 5 in the United States, but we know that children begin learning at birth. The early years, particularly the first three, are critical

---

Among children whose parents have a Ph.D. or professional degree, 73 percent obtain a bachelor's degree or higher. Among those whose parents are high school dropouts, that figure is only 6 percent.

Kessler McCarver, 4, spends her days in early childhood education at the Chambliss Center for Children in Chattanooga, Tennessee, while her mother, Caitlin Bell, works at a doctor's office. {BARBARA KINNEY }

for brain development and later success.[18] Access to high-quality preschool is important not only because it ensures that low-income children enter school ready to learn, but also because it provides a work support for low-income parents who cannot afford child care.

The Head Start program, one of the successful programs started by Sargent Shriver 50 years ago, serves about 1 million low-income children with high-quality early education and comprehensive services such as medical screenings and referrals to social services. But due to budget restraints, Head Start serves only half of eligible 4-year-olds and about 5 percent of eligible infants and toddlers.

Forty states now have publicly funded preschool programs, but they serve only a quarter of 4-year-olds nationwide. Many 4-year-olds and most younger children don't have access to affordable high-quality preschool. This is particularly problematic for low-income single parents, who must work. They often don't have access to reliable and stable preschool or child care that both meets their children's developmental needs and conforms to their work schedule.

There is a well-established link between high-quality early childhood programs and later positive outcomes. Without high-quality early childhood intervention, an at-risk child is 25 percent more likely to drop out of school, 40 percent more likely to become a teen parent, and 60 percent more likely never to attend college.[19] Preschool must, therefore, be part of any discussion on improving long-term employment and earnings, for both the parent and the child.

THE SECOND FORK: QUALITY KINDERGARTEN TEACHERS

The effectiveness of a kindergarten teacher appears to have a lifelong effect on children, according to a study led by Harvard economist Raj Chetty. He and his team re-examined 20-year-old data from the Tennessee STAR study that randomly assigned students to classrooms—the gold standard in experimental design.

The STAR study was designed to look mainly at the effect of smaller class size. However, Chetty and his team followed the life paths of nearly 12,000 children in the study to see if kindergarten students who had been in classrooms with teachers who had increased children's achievement scores—regardless of class size—had different life outcomes. Although the smaller-class-size effects had long faded by high school, the researchers found that children who had higher scores in kindergarten were more likely to be earning significantly more than their counterparts with lower kindergarten scores. They were also more likely to go to college, own a home, and save for retirement.

THE NEXT FORK: ELEMENTARY AND SECONDARY EDUCATION

Girls and boys perform differently in elementary and secondary education—the substantive 13 years between kindergarten and graduation from high school. For low-income girls, lower academic achievement in school during this phase is much more significant than for boys. While the gender gap by test score has narrowed over time, no doubt due in part to the passage of Title IX in 1972, gender gaps do emerge that are especially influential for low-income girls. When these girls don't complete high school, their prospects are far worse than those for boys. The labor force participation rate for high school dropouts is 73 percent for young men but only 50 percent for young women.[20]

In truth, low-income girls face more than just academic challenges or barriers. As Ann O'Leary details in her chapter, pregnancy is one nonacademic factor likely to drive a girl from high school.[21] The good news is that this problem is decreasing nationwide. In 2012, the teen birth rate declined by 6 percent to a historic low

Innovative programs can help teen moms clear the high school hurdle

Despite the challenges they face, there is hope for teen moms. Intervention can help—and innovative help for students with complex lives can make a difference.

Here is just one example: After searching for a location that was easily accessible by public transportation and with job opportunities nearby, school administrators in Alexandria, Virginia, opened a satellite high school campus at the local mall. This unique campus location offers a modern alternative and flexible scheduling for students struggling to balance schoolwork, class attendance, child care, and part-time work.

The Alexandria City Public School District blended virtual learning and an online curriculum with face-to-face instruction from certified teachers. Through weekly reports, school staff can track their students' progress with the online coursework and immediately intervene if they see a student start to disengage. Teachers partner with counselors, social workers, an on-call school psychologist, and a school nurse to support the students in all aspects of their lives. Although students have the opportunity to complete much of their coursework outside of the physical campus, school staff stay in touch with students and their families through the online portal and more traditional means such as phone calls, email, and home visits.[22]

As a result of these intense interventions, out of 51 seniors enrolled at the mall campus in the 2012–13 school year, two moved away from Alexandria, and all of the remaining 49 were on track to graduate.[23]

Even if girls stay in school, the economic class into which they are born can have an enormous impact on the quality of their elementary and secondary education. {JAN SONNEMAIR, MELISSA LYTTLE}

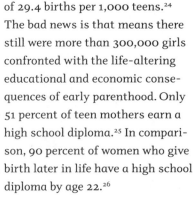

of 29.4 births per 1,000 teens.[24] The bad news is that means there still were more than 300,000 girls confronted with the life-altering educational and economic consequences of early parenthood. Only 51 percent of teen mothers earn a high school diploma.[25] In comparison, 90 percent of women who give birth later in life have a high school diploma by age 22.[26]

THE GED IS NOT ALWAYS THE ANSWER

Many educators believe that the General Education Diploma (GED) is interchangeable with a "regular" high school diploma, and thus an answer for students who may drop out due to early parenthood. But the existing evidence suggests that obtaining a GED is not always the answer.

The GED was envisioned as a way to allow World War II veterans to quickly complete high school and use the G.I. Bill to attend college. But data from the Beginning Postsecondary Education study suggest that the GED is not working as originally intended, and in fact, preparing for the GED does not always prepare someone for success in postsecondary education.

Rather, it is a single, high-stakes test. Only 34 percent of students (and 38 percent of women) who had a GED and enrolled in postsecondary education completed a degree or certificate within six years of enrolling, compared to 51 percent for students (and 53 percent of women) who had a regular high school diploma.[27]

The GED is being completely revised by the GED Testing Service, a joint venture of Pearson Education Services and the American Council on Education, which created the GED. The goal of this revision is to ensure that the GED can effectively play its intended role of indicating that someone earning it is ready for postsecondary work.[28]

Of course, teen mothers and their children can be as successful as anyone else—President Barack Obama is famously the son of a teen who became a single mother. But their path is much narrower. Teen parenthood—though nationally on the decline—can be a nonstop ticket to life on the brink, not only for the young mother, but for her child as well. The children of teenage mothers are more likely to have health problems, be incarcerated during adolescence, and face unemployment as young adults. They are also more likely to become pregnant and drop out of high school themselves.

ECONOMIC STATUS AFFECTS QUALITY ELEMENTARY AND SECONDARY EDUCATION

Even if girls stay in school, economic status at birth can have a lasting impact on the quality of elementary and secondary education. Low-income, elementary-school-age children face barriers to future success regardless of gender, including: poor neighborhoods and communities, lack of access to quality early learning and kindergarten, and lower-quality primary and secondary education.[30]

Schools serving low-income students are allocated federal, state, and local dollars by funding formulas that either mask inequities or allocate resources without applying the appropriate weights to per-pupil funding based on the needs of students in a particular school.[31] School funding inequities are most widely reflected in the disparities among state and local property tax rolls, which mean school districts serving high numbers of low-income students have limited resources.

The allocation of effective teachers is another area of concern for schools serving low-income students. Several studies have found that on average, low-income students are taught by teachers who are less experienced, less effective, and teach classes out of their field of study.[32]

Low expectations for students in low-income areas also contribute to differences in achievement. One recent study found a strong association between teachers' low expectations for students—especially those teaching low-income students in the early grades—and student performance on standardized tests.[33] At the same time, when teachers had high expectations for students, it disproportionately helped low-income students on tests.[34]

While low-income kids often are saddled with low-quality educational infra-structure, they are further disadvantaged by entering the classroom less prepared than their peers. What parents earn affects the nature of their children's lives. For example, a large body of research shows that compared to higher-income parents, low-income parents typically talk less with their children.[35] They use fewer number words (e.g., "two dogs," or counting "one, two, three, four, five," etc.),[36] and they spend less time on literacy-related activities, such as reading them stories.[37]

All of this means that children of low-income parents generally have substan-tially fewer intellectually rich experiences in early childhood. As a result, they enter formal schooling with drastically fewer skills and less knowledge than their higher-income peers. In particular, when they begin kindergarten, low-income children have significantly fewer math skills than their higher-income peers, according to the Early Childhood Longitudinal Study, Kindergarten Cohort, a nationally representative study of schools offering kindergarten.[38]

FIGURE 5.1

NAEP Mathematics 2009, grades 4, 8, and 12; percent at or above proficient

FIGURE 5.2

NAEP Science 2009, grades 4, 8, and 12; percent at or above proficient

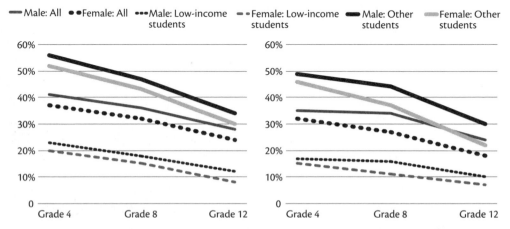

Legend: ━━ Male: All ● ● Female: All ●●● Male: Low-income students ＝ ＝ Female: Low-income students ━━ Male: Other students ━━ Female: Other students

Source: CAP analysis using student achievement data available from the U.S. Department of Education, National Center for Education Statistics. Here, NAEP refers to the National Assessment of Educational Progress, Main Assessment. All of this data is publicly available through the NAEP Data Explorer at http://nces.ed.gov/nationsreportcard/naepdata/.

According to polling conducted for The Shriver Report, when prompted, women on the brink listed having children as the biggest reason for why they are not doing today what they thought they would be doing when they were younger.

As these students continue into elementary grades and high school, the gaps increase. In fourth grade, only 20 percent of low-income girls are proficient in math, compared to around 50 percent of their higher-income peers, according to a recent administration of the National Assessment of Educational Progress. Results are similar in science. At the end of high school, even fewer students are proficient in 12th-grade math or science. Only 7 percent of low-income female students are proficient in science, compared to 22 percent of their higher-income peers. [39]

ANOTHER FORK: GIRLS OPT OUT OF STEM EVEN WHEN THEY'RE GOOD AT IT

To more fully understand why some women, particularly women on the brink, end up in lower-paying jobs, we must also focus on the areas of study that arguably lead to the highest-paying fields in the 21st century: science, technology, engineering, and math, or STEM. Gender gaps in STEM-related skills do not arise until after children enter the first grade, and even then they are relatively small.

Data show that boys only slightly outperform girls in math and science on standardized tests in K-12, and in some instances girls earn higher grades in math and science than boys. Girls and boys appear to be roughly equally prepared to pursue STEM majors in college.

So why don't they?

Implicit cultural biases and stereotypes play a significant role. A recent report, for example, looked at the extent to which societal beliefs and learning

The quality of girls' education in elementary and high school can help shape the course of the rest of their lives. {BARBARA RIES}

Influencing smart decisions

Girls Who Code is part of a growing national movement to engage young girls in computer science. Alongside similar groups such as the Hackbright Academy, Girls Teaching Girls to Code, Girl Develop It, and Black Girls Code, Girls Who Code aims to increase the number of women in technology careers by teaching girls basic computer code-writing skills at a young age.

In 2012, Girls Who Code launched its eight-week summer immersion program in New York City, where top industry engineers and entrepreneurs taught 20 high school girls—many from underserved communities—about computer science, robotics, algorithms, web design, and mobile development. One year later, the program expanded to Detroit; San Jose, California; Davis, California; and San Francisco, and plans to continue are growing nationwide.[43]

environments impact girls' interest and achievement in science and math.[40] Relying on the work of Stanford psychology professor Carol Dweck, the authors found that when teachers and parents tell girls that their intelligence is not "static" and can grow with experience and learning, girls do better on math tests and are more likely to say they want to continue to study math in the future.[41] While this was true for all students, it was particularly helpful for girls' performance in math—an area where girls have internalized negative stereotypes.[42]

The study also found that girls' self-assessments about their abilities lowered their math achievement. Girls, on average, had lower assessments of their ability to solve math problems than boys who had similar math achievements. At the same time, girls held themselves to higher standards than boys, believing that they had to be exceptional in order to succeed in what were perceived as "male" fields.[44] Even when girls had good grades and test scores, their lower self-assessments combined with their higher standards for performance meant that fewer aspired to STEM careers.[45]

THE LEAP TO POSTSECONDARY: DECISIONS, DECISIONS . . . AND DEBT

Even when low-income students attend college, they remain at a disadvantage. Children from low-income families have only a 10 percent chance of graduating with a four-year college degree by the age of 24, a significantly lower chance than their peers from middle-income families (25 percent) or high-income families (50 percent).[46] For low-income students, this number has remained stagnant over the past several decades, despite a 12 percentage point increase since 1975 in the share of Americans ages 25 to 29 with a bachelor's degree.[47]

Binita "Bini" Pradhan reads to her 4-year-old son, Ayush. After she left a difficult marriage, Bini moved into an apartment with Ayush. He will soon start kindergarten. {BARBARA RIES}

The costs of attending a two- or four-year public university have increased far faster than the rate of inflation, and families are taking on a larger share of financing higher education.[48] For public universities, net tuition per student was $5,189 in academic year 2012, an all-time high.[49]

Women who invest in higher education do so at a higher cost than men, limiting the potential for lower-income women to access education. Compared to men, women are more likely to take on student debt and to take on larger amounts. Among students graduating in the 2007-08 school year, for example, 63.2 percent of women took on student debt, compared to 57.4 percent of men. While 49.3 percent of

Children from low-income families have
only a 10 percent chance of graduating with
a four-year college degree by the age of 24.

Two-thirds of college seniors who graduated in 2011 had student loan debt that averaged $23,300 for all borrowers.

women took out more than $19,000 to finance a college degree, only 44.7 percent of men took on that much debt.[50] Two-thirds of college seniors who graduated in 2011 had student loan debt[51] that averaged $23,300 for all borrowers.[52]

The outstanding overall student loan balance in this country now stands at an astounding $1.2 trillion, surpassing both the total credit card balance and the total auto loan balance. And this number is only expected to grow as college enrollments increase and tuition costs rise. For a young woman earning $19,000 a year and considering whether to go to college, adding to her debt load is inconceivable when she has to decide whether to spend money on a book or bread, milk, and utilities. While women are more likely than men to receive federal aid such as Pell Grants (45 percent versus 37 percent), they are also more likely than men to need to borrow from the federal student loan programs (42 percent versus 37 percent). This may be because some institutions attempt to maintain gender balance by awarding merit-based aid to men. At these institutions, women may indeed be victims of their own success.[53]

On average, college tuition has risen in real inflation-adjusted terms by 134 percent since 1980. This represents an annual nominal growth rate of about 7 percent per year.[54] The costs of four-year institutions—both private and public—have risen at much faster rates than those of two-year institutions. The cost of attending a four-year public college or university, after adjusting for inflation, has increased by 257 percent over the last 30 years.[55] Private for-profits have come under special scrutiny for their rising tuition and high default rates among recent college grads.

But even though college costs have risen, the wage premium for those with college degrees has risen faster. The average value of a college degree over one's lifetime compared to a high school diploma is about $960,000 in additional earnings.

GETTING TRULY SMART IN COLLEGE: KNOWING WHAT TO STUDY AND WHERE

In most instances, incurring debt to go to college is a smart bet, if done wisely. Today, when girls and women can expect to be the primary or co-provider for themselves and their families, developing their knowledge and skills is their smartest investment. The loans that cripple are the ones that cannot be repaid. So which classes, certificates, and majors result in earnings high enough to avoid incurring crippling debt that drives women to a life on the brink?

In today's complicated higher education system, there is very little information about which courses of study lead to middle-income careers. But we do know that overwhelmingly, the majors with the lowest post-graduation earnings potential are dominated by women.[56] There is every reason to believe that if women were provided with more information about the long-term earnings implications of where and what they study, their college decisions would be smarter.

CHOOSING A PATH: POTENTIAL SOURCES OF KNOWLEDGE

The basic elements of a college and career information system already exist. At the federal level, the U.S. Department of Education's College Navigator system and the U.S. Department of Labor Statistics' *Occupational Outlook Handbook* are available. At the state level, the State Longitudinal Data Systems provide access to longitudinal databases and wage record data that already link education programs to workforce outcomes on a student-by-student basis.

Coordinating these data would make it possible to show the earnings capacity of former students, linked all the way down to specific college courses. Better access to that information would allow everyone involved to make a better cost-benefit analysis of particular degrees and programs of study.

The federal government has begun to address this issue by making a College Scorecard available and encouraging

FIGURE 6

Percent B.A. attainment by sex and aggregated major

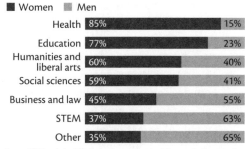

■ Women ■ Men

	Women	Men
Health	85%	15%
Education	77%	23%
Humanities and liberal arts	60%	40%
Social sciences	59%	41%
Business and law	45%	55%
STEM	37%	63%
Other	35%	65%

Source: CEW analysis of U.S. Census Bureau, American Community Survey, various years, and Survey of Income and Program Participants, various years.

The rising cost of tuition at two- and four-year public universities has forced families to rely heavily on student loans with high interest rates. {BARBARA KINNEY}

institutions to use a standardized Financial Aid Shopping Sheet. But the scorecard and the shopping sheet still lack actionable information about student debt and earnings by major, field of study, and institution.

In 2011, the Obama administration enacted the "gainful employment" rule, which held for-profit colleges and certificate and vocational programs to a new federal standard on employability and student debt. For the first time, these programs could lose eligibility for federal financial aid programs if the debt students take on outweighs labor market benefits for their students. The Obama administration is currently reworking the gainful employment rule to address problems identified in the federal courts, but the one element that remains in effect are consumer disclosures critical to students choosing among postsecondary programs.

Noting what he called the "crisis" in college affordability and student debt, in 2013 President Obama proposed tying federal financial aid to factors such as an institution's student debt and default rates, how many students graduate and whether they do so on time, what kind of salaries those students earn, and the number of low-income students who graduate with the benefit of Pell Grants. Under this new Obama plan, much of which must be approved by Congress, students attending colleges that provide better value would see more federal aid. Congressional action on this plan is expected in 2014 with improved consumer tools, including a rating system, by 2015.

In May 2013, Senators Ron Wyden (D-OR), Marco Rubio (R-FL), and Mark Warner (D-VA), and Representatives Duncan Hunter (R-CA) and Robert Andrews (D-NJ) introduced bipartisan legislation aiming to provide students and families with the information they need to make more informed decisions about higher education. Specifically, the Know Before You Go Act would streamline existing institutional reporting requirements to enable students, families, institutions, and policymakers to assess schools and programs based on a wide range of key data—including graduation rates for nontraditional students, transfer rates, frequency with which graduates go on to pursue higher levels of education, student debt, and post-graduation earnings and employment outcomes.

Regardless of the vehicle, it is critically important that women on the brink be armed with the information they need so that they will think twice before incurring $30,000 in student debt to qualify for a cosmetology job that pays less than $23,000 a year.

Programs such as REACH Plus at Washington Women's Employment & Education (WWEE) in Tacoma, Washington, help teach women how to use computers and craft a résumé, among other skills. {BARBARA KINNEY}

VOCATIONAL CERTIFICATES: IT PAYS TO CHOOSE LIKE A MAN

Despite recent efforts by the Obama administration to increase accountability through transparency, so far there is little information available for students to make sound decisions about certificate degrees and for-profit colleges—two avenues that may sound like good options, but in reality do not provide economic security for women living on the brink.[57]

Certification can be pursued after high school or can be a steppingstone on a somewhat circuitous education pathway. Many students with an associate's

Policy Prescription: Knowledge is Power

Ultimately, if we are to tackle the inequalities that exist today, we will need policies that address the biases and social pressures that affect the choices women make on courses of study and occupations. This will likely require, among other things, substantial changes to several factors, such as classroom culture and gender stereotypes.

Though it is unclear what actual effect it will have on the labor market decisions of students, it is important for colleges to provide greater transparency regarding the real-life financial value of different majors and courses of study. The value, expected payoff, and long-term costs of specific college majors and programs of study should be available to every potential and current college student.

degree or better who have trouble finding jobs may decide to earn a certificate in some related field—for example, office management or health care—in an effort to make themselves more marketable.

Of the 15 different certificate fields of study identified at postsecondary institutions qualifying for U.S. federal student aid, 13 are extremely "sex segregated"—meaning that one gender makes up at least 75 percent of enrollment.[58] That may in part be due to the types of certificates women earn—for instance, cosmetology, health care, or food service—while men gravitate more often to higher-paying fields, such as welding and air conditioner repair.

Overall, the wage premium conferred by earning a certificate, as compared to a high school diploma, is 27 percent for men, but only 16 percent for women. The disparity is so great that it's often better for women to forgo earning certificates and instead choose at least a two-year associate's degree—though there are caveats. Women in certain high-earning certificate fields—for example, business/office management and computer and information sciences—do well compared to their male counterparts. Certificates may also be a good option for women who are interested in a credential that will give them the flexibility to accommodate family responsibilities.

FIGURE 7.1

Distribution of certificates by field of study, women

FIGURE 7.2

Distribution of certificates by field of study, men

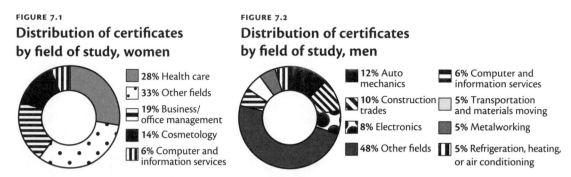

28% Health care
33% Other fields
19% Business/office management
14% Cosmetology
6% Computer and information services

12% Auto mechanics
10% Construction trades
8% Electronics
48% Other fields
6% Computer and information services
5% Transportation and materials moving
5% Metalworking
5% Refrigeration, heating, or air conditioning

Source: CEW analysis of U.S. Census Bureau, American Community Survey, various years, and Survey of Income and Program Participants, various years.

TABLE 1

Female certificate holders' earnings are low, especially in food service and cosmetology

Certificate field	Distribution	Median earnings	Relative earnings to all female certificate holders
All		$27,191	
Business/office management	19.4%	$32,690	20.2%
Computer and information services	6.1%	$29,986	10.3%
Police/protective services	0.5%	$27,761	2.1%
Other fields, not specified	29.9%	$26,938	-0.9%
Health care	27.5%	$25,753	-5.3%
Transportation and materials moving	0.7%	$25,686	-5.5%
Cosmetology	14.3%	$22,711	-16.5%
Food service	1.4%	$20,974	-22.9%

Source: Anthony P. Carnevale, Stephen J. Rose, and Andrew R. Hanson, "Certificates: Gateway to Gainful Employment and College Degrees" (Washington: Georgetown University Center on Education and the Workforce, 2012).

The opportunity cost of obtaining a postsecondary vocational certificate is even greater for women if they do not find a job directly related to their certification. In fact, women with just a high school diploma outearn women who hold certificates when the latter work in jobs not directly related to their educational credential.

FIGURE 8

Entry-level bachelor's degrees earnings by major and sex

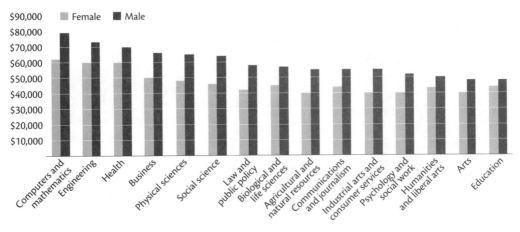

Source: CEW analysis of American Community Survey data—2010–2012 (pooled data)

WOMEN AND BACHELOR'S DEGREES: CHOICE OF MAJOR MATTERS

Ideally women would strive to attain bachelor's degrees. Here too, though, their earnings may be stifled by what they choose to study. There are two key issues: One is the pernicious wage gap in certain fields, so that women are paid less than men even when they have the same degree. The other is that women choose and dominate low-paying fields.

Among bachelor's degree holders, the entry-level salary range for women is $40,000 to $62,000, and for men it's $48,000 to $79,000. The highest median earnings are found in engineering, where there are relatively few women, while the lowest are in education, psychology, and social work, where women outnumber men. Women make up 97 percent of all early childhood education majors, followed by medical assisting services (96 percent women) and communication disorders sciences and services (94 percent women). Men, on the other hand, concentrate in majors such as naval architecture and marine engineering (97 percent men) and mechanical engineering and related technologies (94 percent men). And even though many occupations in the female-dominated social sciences and humanities require a graduate-level education, wages earned by those graduate degree holders still never quite reach the wage levels of higher-paying, male-dominated majors.[59]

By the time bachelor's degree holders are in their peak earning years of 45 to 49, women are earning $37,000 less than men. By retirement age, this can result in a lifetime wage differential of as much as $795,000—or in real (inflation-adjusted) dollars, almost $1 million. This may work for women who are partners in two-earner families, but in today's reality, when women must be prepared to be primary providers, that's a million dollars their families can't afford to lose.

The promise and perils of online learning

The advent and growth of online learning opportunities offers great promise. Whether from institutions that offer entire degree programs online or the newer providers, such as massive open online courses, that offer only courses, online learning provides unique educational opportunities for people who are tied down with family and work obligations or are place-bound. Today, two-thirds of the students enrolled in institutions exclusively online are women—a total of 200,000. This has doubled in just five years.

There are, however, significant perils: The retention rate for students enrolled at exclusively online institutions is half that of other four-year institutions.[60]

Jessica McGowan and her classmates study at the Virginia College of Business and Health in Chattanooga, Tennessee. Jessica is studying to become a pharmaceutical technician. {BARBARA KINNEY}

IF WOMEN ARE SO SMART, WHY ARE THEY CHOOSING SO POORLY?

Women's lifetime earnings are clearly directly related to their choice of fields of study—and that conscious choice is heavily influenced by a host of unconsciously absorbed cultural and social pressures. Disparities in pay are only symptoms of more deep-seated biases and social pressures that affect why women gravitate to the occupations, courses of study, and majors that they do. These disparities in turn have a powerful effect on their economic bargaining power and lifelong earning potential.

Even when women select college majors with more economic promise, they choose occupations related to those majors that offer relatively lower pay, and they are less likely to change occupations once those choices have been made. A woman who earns a mathematics degree, for example, may go to work as a high school math teacher, while a man with the same degree might pursue a more lucrative career in aerospace.

Occupational Information Network

The so-called female occupations are defined by a cluster of distinct characteristics—a generalization we can make based on an analysis of a detailed database called the Occupational Information Network, or O*NET.

O*NET has limitations: It describes the characteristics of occupations, not workers themselves, and it does not show us which competencies are more important than others. Even so, O*NET offers the most comprehensive and rigorous description by workers themselves of some 1,100 occupations, broken down by cognitive measures, such as knowledge, skills, and abilities, as well as by noncognitive measures, such as interests, values, work context, and personality traits. Values include such intangibles as recognition, achievement, autonomy, advancement, and social service. Interests generally fall into one of six categories: realistic, investigative, artistic, social, enterprising, and conventional.

Since job performance and job satisfaction are so dependent on the extent to which the job matches an individual's interests and values, noncognitive measures are just as important as cognitive measures in determining a worker's choice of occupation and success in any given field. Someone interested in working with others, for example, might find being a desk-bound mathematician unsatisfying, even if he or she is highly skilled at math. At the same time, a skilled teacher who highly values her own personal autonomy might chafe at working under a principal who micromanages her lesson plans.

While there is some overlap, distinctly different sets of values and interests emerge when we look at those in female-dominated occupations, such as nurses, health care workers, teachers, and food service workers, versus those in traditional male-dominated occupations, such as assembly line workers, engineers and scientists, surgeons, and lawyers.

Data from the Occupational Information Network, or O*NET, show that in male-dominated occupations, values linked to job satisfaction are *achievement*, *independence*, *work conditions*, and *support*. In female-dominated occupations, the most important values determining job satisfaction are *relationships, achievement*, and, to a lesser degree, *independence*.

Achievement and *independence* are hallmarks of jobs that allow a worker to use the best of his or her abilities and to stand out from the crowd. Not surprisingly, these are values common to both male- and female-dominated occupations. The big difference comes in *relationships,* a value accorded a high importance by workers in 75 percent of all female-dominated occupations.

Realistic, enterprising, conventional, and *investigative* work interests are most highly associated with success in male-dominated occupations, which tend to involve hands-on problem solving and factual research. In female-dominated occupations, the traditional work interests linked to jobs are *social, enterprising,* and *conventional*. These interests usually describe jobs involving communicating with and teaching people, often in professions that provide service to others.

FIGURE 9

Dominant work interests in sex-segregated occupations

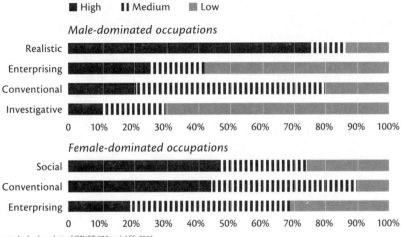

Source: Author's analysis of O*NET 17.0 and ACS, 2012

Dee Saint Franc, 23, was already a single mother when she started working her way through higher education. She has received her associate's degree in business management and her bachelor's degree in social work. {BARBARA RIES}

What is immediately apparent is that male-dominated fields tend to pay higher wages, even for those with relatively lower levels of attainment, such as production workers. Indeed, 30 percent of high-school-educated males in production occupations can earn upward of $35,000 per year. In comparison, only 5 percent of similarly qualified women earn that much.

Why male-dominated fields pay higher wages is less clear. It may be simply a societal history and habit of valuing production over relationships, or men's work over women's work. Whether this evolves with the job market of the 21st century remains to be seen. What is clear, though, is that for now, women will be better able to achieve financial stability if they follow typically male paths of study and work.

GETTING MOTHERS A COLLEGE DEGREE

Even if a young woman with a child beats the odds and reaches college, she will face significant barriers to completing her degree. According to polling conducted for *The Shriver Report*, when prompted, women on the brink listed having children as the biggest reason for why they are not doing today what they thought they would be doing when they were younger.

For many of these young women, juggling multiple roles as student, breadwinner, and caregiver are enough to drive them to quit school. According to the U.S. Department of Education, nearly half of student parents (49.7 percent) are more likely to have abandoned their college education without their degree after six years of study, compared to less than a third of nonparents (31.1 percent).[61]

The lack of accessible, affordable child care looms as a primary barrier to a postsecondary education. According to one study, only 5 percent of the child care needed by student parents is provided at on-campus child care centers, pointing to an enormous gap in the support system for low-income women attempting to further their educations.[62] This problem overwhelmingly affects women, who make up 81 percent of the 1.5 million students who are low-income single parents.[63]

Expanding child care access, therefore, would offer enormous support for student mothers trying to achieve a college degree. But the need for child care goes beyond the hours in the classroom. Student parents often work full time during the school year and need child care in the evenings and on weekends as well. But according to the National Coalition for Campus Children's Centers survey, only 13 percent of these centers provided evening care and only 3 percent provided weekend care.[64]

On-campus care centers offering flexible, accessible hours would help mothers trying to balance both school and caregiving responsibilities. Further, studies show that campus children's centers improve economic outcomes for low-income families by offering both short- and long-term benefits. Parents can focus on their studies, greatly improving their chances of completing a postsecondary degree, while their children gain exposure to learning environments at a young age, allowing them to reap the enormous benefits of early childhood education.[65] This two-generation approach is discussed in further detail in Anne Mosle's chapter, "Personal Action, Collective Impact."

Hurdle helper

Some child care centers on college campuses offer a range of comprehensive services to parents, including academic, financial, parenting, and personal counseling. In 2005, the University of Michigan launched an initiative to increase child care capacity, enlarge enrollment for infants and toddlers, and improve their care facilities.

The university met all three of these goals by 2011, after joining all of their care centers under one administrative umbrella and establishing a coordinated system offering an array of shared services, including child care referral specialists, summer camps, child care subsidies, and loans to cover child care expenses.

CONCLUSION

Our nation needs to recognize women and girls as the assets they are and invest in them. Education has historically been the ladder to upward mobility and the surest way to bring succeeding generations out of poverty. Today's girls are tomorrow's family providers and the economic drivers of this nation. We have to invest in their education but also foster the mind-set that they must invest in themselves.

Starting with the early years, low-income students face hurdles to a quality education in the form of poorly resourced neighborhoods, inequitable education funding, and lower-performing teachers, to name a few. Girls on the brink also face another layer of hurdles, such as teen pregnancy or the lack of encouragement to pursue STEM careers, creating a mountain of obstacles that sometimes even the brightest and most resourceful young women cannot overcome.

It is a testament to the resourcefulness and tenacity of young women that despite these obstacles, they continue climbing and striving for higher education. Imagine what they could accomplish if we paved the pathway to the middle class with robust investments in early education or public school reform. Or encouraged young women to pursue higher-paying STEM fields.

Once they get past the high school hurdles, choosing a postsecondary institution and program is the first big investment decision made by young people, the majority of whom will finance their education with student loans. It isn't a decision they should be making in a vacuum. They need to understand the risks and rewards associated with their choices of colleges and fields of study, especially as the costs of particular certificates and degrees rise and job markets shift.

Aligning education more closely with careers is also the best way to encourage student success. People who are given some navigational tools are more likely to get where they want to go.

 THINK ABOUT THIS

The labor force participation rate for high school dropouts is 73 percent for young men and only 50 percent for young women. And only 51 percent of teen mothers earn a high school diploma.

ENDNOTES

1   Thomas D. Snyder and Sally A. Dillow, "Digest of Education Statistics 2012" (Washington: National Center for Education Statistics, 2013), Table 221.

2   Ibid.

3   Ibid., Table 310.

4   Ibid.

5   National Center for Education Statistics, "Digest of Education Statistics 2012—Table 10. Number of persons age 18 and over, by highest level of educational attainment, sex, race/ethnicity, and age: 2012," available at http://nces. ed.gov/programs/digest/d12/tables/dt12_010.asp.

6   Patricia Gándara and others, "Making Education Work for Latinas in the U.S." (Los Angeles: Eva Longoria Foundation, 2013), available at http://www.evalongoriafoundation.org/wp-content/uploads/2012/05/Making-Education-Work-for-Latinas-in-the-US-by-the-Eva-Longoria-Foundation1.pdf.

7   Anthony P. Carnevale, Stephen J. Rose, and Andrew R. Hanson, "Certificates: Gateway to Gainful Employment and College Degrees" (Washington: Georgetown University Center on Education and the Workforce, 2012), available at http://cew.georgetown.edu/certificates/.

8   Ibid.; Anthony P. Carnevale, Stephen J. Rose, and Ban Cheah, "The College Payoff: Education, Occupations, Lifetime Earnings" (Washington: Georgetown University, Center for Education and the Workforce, 2011), available at http://cew.georgetown.edu/collegepayoff/.

9   582,000 boys won't go either. Authors' estimate based on analysis of previous year's continuation rate and current enrollment levels. See Bureau of Labor Statistics, "College Enrollment and Work Activity of 2012 High School Graduates," News release, April 17, 2013, available at http://www.bls.gov/news.release/hsgec.nr0.htm.

10 National Center for Education Statistics, "Digest of Education Statistics 2012."

11 Lumina Foundation, "A Stronger Nation through Higher Education: Visualizing data to help us achieve a big goal for college attainment" (2013), available at http://www.luminafoundation.org/publications/A_stronger_nation_through_higher_education-2013.pdf.

12 Carnevale, Rose, and Cheah, "The College Payoff: Education, Occupations, Lifetime Earnings."

13 Bureau of Labor Statistics, "Employment Projections: Earnings and unemployment rates by educational attainment," available at http://www.bls.gov/emp/ep_chart_001.htm.

14 Carnevale, Rose, and Cheah, "The College Payoff: Education, Occupations, and Lifetime Earnings."

15 Kevin Miller and Barbara Gault, "Improving Child Care Access to Promote Postsecondary Success Among Low-Income Parents" (Washington: Institute for Women's Policy Research, 2011).

16 Georgetown University Center on Education and the Workforce calculations using National Center for Education Statistics, *Digest of Education Statistics* 2011—Table 341, "Percentage distribution of 1990 high school sophomores, by highest level of education completed through 2000 and selected student characteristics: 2000," available at http://nces.ed.gov/programs/digest/d11/tables/dt11_341.asp (last accessed June 2013).

17 See James J. Heckman, "The Case for Investing in Disadvantaged Young Children." In First Focus, ed., *Big Ideas for Children: Investing in Our Nation's Future* (Washington: First Focus, 2009), p. 49, available at http://www.heckman equation.org/content/resource/case-investing-disadvantaged-young-children.

18 See, for example, Peter R. Huttenlocher, "Morphometric Study of Human Cerebral Cortex Development," *Neuropsychologia* 28 (6) (1990): 517–527; Betty Hart and Todd R. Risley, *Meaningful Differences in the Everyday Experience of Young American Children* (Baltimore: Paul H. Brookes Publishing, 1995).

19 The Ounce of Prevention Fund, "Why Investments in Early Childhood Work," available at http://www.ounceof prevention.org/about/why-early-childhood-investments-work.php.

20 Bureau of Labor Statistics, "Table 2. Labor force status of persons 16 to 24 years old by school enrollment, educational attainment, sex, race, and Hispanic or Latino ethnicity, October 2012," available at http://www.bls.gov/news.release/hsgec.t02.htm.

21 Lisa Shuger, "Teen Pregnancy and High School Dropout: What Communities Can Do to Address These Issues" (Washington: National Campaign to Prevent Teen and Unplanned Pregnancy and America's Promise Alliance, 2012),

available at http://www.thenationalcampaign.org/resources/pdf/teen-preg-hs-dropout.pdf.

22 See Alexandria City Public Schools, "Report of TC Satellite Student Progress" (2013), available at http://www.acps. k12.va.us/satellite/update.pdf.

23 See Michael Alison Chandler, "Virtual School in Shopping Mall Helps Alexandria Students Graduate," *The Washington Post*, June 14, 2013, available at http://articles.washingtonpost.com/2013-06-14/local/39976865_1_shopping-mall-t-c-williams-high-school-virtual-school.

24 Centers for Disease Control and Prevention, "About Teen Pregnancy," available at http://www.cdc.gov/teen pregnancy/aboutteenpreg.htm.

25 Kate Perper, Kristen Peterson, and Jennifer Manlove, "Diploma Attainment Among Teen Mothers" (Washington: Child Trends, 2010), available at http://www.childtrends.org/wp-content/uploads/2010/01/child_trends-2010_01_22_FS_diplomaattainment.pdf.

26 Ibid.

27 Center for American Progress analysis of National Center for Education Statistics, 2003–04 Beginning Postsecondary Students Longitudinal Study, Second Follow-up, available at http://nces.ed.gov/surveys/bps/ (last accessed September 2013).

28 For some "at-risk" students, however, completion of the GED may present better options than the alternative of not completing it at all. A study of the impact of a GED on wages and earnings of young adults by cognitive ability showed that 27-year-old male dropouts with weak cognitive skills as 10th graders were able to earn higher wages with a GED than not having one at all. Richard J. Murnane, John B. Willett, and John H. Tyler, "Who Benefits from Obtaining a GED? Evidence from High School and Beyond," *Review of Economics and Statistics*, 82 (1) (2000): 23–37, available at http://www.mitpressjournals.org/doi/abs/10.1162/003465300558605?journalCode=rest.

29 CDC, "About Teen Pregnancy."

30 Bruce D. Baker and Sean P. Corcoran, "The Stealth Inequities of School Funding: How State and Local Finance Systems Perpetuate Inequitable Student Spending" (Washington: Center for American Progress, 2012); Greg J. Duncan and Richard J. Murnane, "Introduction: The American Dream, Then and Now." In Greg J. Duncan and Richard J. Murnane, eds., *Whither Opportunity? Rising Inequality, Schools, and Children's Life Chances* (New York: Russell Sage Foundation, 2011).

31 Cynthia G. Brown, "Toward a Coherent and Fair Funding System." In Paul Manna and Patrick McGuinn, eds., *Education Governance for the Twenty-First Century: Overcoming the Structural Barriers to School Reform* (Washington: Brookings Institution Press, Thomas B. Fordham Institute, and Center for American Progress, 2013).

32 National Center for Education Statistics, "Monitoring Quality: An Indicators Report" (2000), available at http://nces. ed.gov/pubs2001/2001030.pdf; Heather G. Peske, and Kati Haycock, "Teaching Inequality: How Poor and Minority Students are Shortchanged on Teacher Quality" (Washington: The Education Trust, 2006); Tennessee Department of Education, "Tennessee's Most Effective Teachers: Are They Assigned to the Schools That Need Them Most?" (2007), available at http://www.state.tn.us/education/nclb/doc/TeacherEffectiveness2007_03.pdf.

33 Nicole S. Sorhagen, "Early Teacher Expectations Disproportionately Affect Poor Children's High School Performance," *Journal of Educational Psychology* 105 (2) (2013): 465–477.

34 Ibid.

35 Hart and Risley, *Meaningful Differences in the Everyday Experience of Young American Children*.

36 Susan C. Levine and others, "What Counts in the Development of Young Children's Number Knowledge?" *Developmental Psychology* 46 (5) (2010): 1309–1319.

37 Meredith Philips, "Parenting, Time Use, and Disparities in Academic Outcomes." In Duncan and Murnane, eds., *Whither Opportunity?*

38 Data from the Early Childhood Longitudinal Study, Kindergarten Cohort, is analyzed by Lee and Burkam in Valerie E. Lee and David T. Burkam, *Inequality at the Starting Gate: Social Background Differences in Achievement as Children Begin School* (Washington: Economic Policy Institute, 2002).

39 Richard J. Murnane and Jennifer L. Steele, "What Is the Problem? The Challenge of Providing Effective Teachers for All Children," *The Future of Children* 17 (1) (2007): 15–43; Hamilton Lankford, Susanna Loeb, and James Wyckoff, "Teacher Sorting and the Plight of Urban Schools: A Descriptive Analysis," *Educational Evaluation and Policy Analysis* 24 (1) (2002): 37–62.

40 Catherine Hill, Christianne Corbett, and Andresse St. Rose, "Why So Few? Women in Science, Technology,

Engineering, and Mathematics" (Washington: American Association of University Women, 2010), available at http://www.aauw.org/files/2013/02/Why-So-Few-Women-in-Science-Technology-Engineering-and-Mathematics.pdf.

41 In Ibid., Hill and others above cite the following among other works by Carol Dweck on beliefs about intelligence: Carol S. Dweck and Ellen Leggett, "A Social-Cognitive Approach to Motivation and Personality," *Psychological Review* 95 (2) (2010): 256–273.

42 Catherine Good, Aneeta Rattan, and Carol S. Dweck, "Why Do Women Opt Out? Sense of Belonging and Women's Representation in Mathematics," *Journal of Personality and Social Psychology* 102 (4) (2012): 700–717.

43 Keith Wagstaff, "'Girls Who Code' Looks to Close the Tech Gender Gap," *Time*, June 28, 2012, available at http://techland.time.com/2012/06/28/girls-who-code-looks-to-close-the-tech-gender-gap/.

44 Good et al., "Why Do Women Opt Out?"; Shelley J. Correll, "Gender and the Career Choice Process: The Role of Biased Self-Assessments," *American Journal of Sociology* 106 (6) (2004): 1691–1730; Shelley J. Correll, "Constraints into Preferences: Gender, Status, and Emerging Career Aspirations," *American Sociological Review* 69 (1) (2004): 93–113.

45 Ibid.

46 Miller and Gault, "Improving Child Care Access."

47 National Center for Education Statistics, "Digest of Education Statistics—Table 9. Percentage of persons 25 to 29 years old with selected levels of educational attainment, by race/ethnicity and sex: Selected years, 1920 through 2012," available at http://nces.ed.gov/programs/digest/d12/tables/dt12_009.asp.

48 Phil Oliff and others, "Recent Deep State Higher Education Cuts May Harm Students and the Economy for Years to Come" (Washington: Center on Budget and Policy Priorities, 2013), available at http://www.cbpp.org/cms/?fa=view&id=3927.

49 State Higher Education Executive Officers Association, "State Higher Education Finance (SHEF) Report for FY2012 Released," Press release, March 6, 2013, available at http://www.sheeo.org/news/state-higher-education-finance-shef-report-fy2012-released.

50 John Schmitt and Heather Boushey, "The College Conundrum: Why the Benefits of a College Education May Not Be So Clear, Especially to Men" (Washington: Center for American Progress, 2010), available at http://www.americanprogress.org/wp-content/uploads/issues/2010/12/pdf/college_conundrum.pdf.

51 The Project on Student Debt, "Student Debt and the Class of 2011" (2012), available at http://projectonstudentdebt.org/files/pub/classof2011.pdf.

52 Meta Brown and others, "Grading Student Loans," Liberty Street Economics Blog, comment posted March 5, 2012, available at http://libertystreeteconomics.newyorkfed.org/2012/03/grading-student-loans.html.

53 Tracey Hunt-White, "2011–2012 National Postsecondary Student Aid Study (NPSAS:12)" (Washington: National Center for Education Statistics, 2013).

54 National Center for Education Statistics, "Fast Facts: Tuition Costs of Colleges and Universities," available at http://nces.ed.gov/fastfacts/display.asp?id=76.

55 The College Board Advocacy and Policy Center, "Trends in College Pricing 2012" (2012), available at http://trends.collegeboard.org/sites/default/files/college-pricing-2012-full-report-121203.pdf.

56 Anthony P. Carnevale, Jeff Strohl, and Michelle Melton, "What's It Worth: The Economic Value of College Majors" (Washington: Georgetown University, Center on Education and the Workforce, 2011) available at http://cew.georgetown.edu/whatsitworth/.

57 Department of Education, "Proposed Rule Links Federal Student Aid to Loan Repayment Rates and Debt-to-Earnings Levels for Career College Graduates," Press release, July 23, 2010, available at http://www.ed.gov/news/press-releases/proposed-rule-links-federal-student-aid-loan-repayment-rates-and-debt-earnings-l.

58 Carnevale, Rose, and Hanson, "Certificates: Gateway to Gainful Employment and College Degrees."

59 Ibid.

60 Unpublished CAP analysis of data from the Integrated Postsecondary Education Data System, or IPEDS. Data available at National Center for Education Statistics, "IPEDS Data Center," available at http://nces.ed.gov/ipeds/datacenter/.

61 Miller and Gault, "Improving Child Care Access."

62 Ibid.

63 Ibid.

64 Ibid.

65 Ibid.

Turning Poverty Around: Training Parents to Help Their Kids

By JENNIFER GARNER, award-winning actress, producer, and mother. She is an advocate for early childhood education and for Save the Children, a nongovernmental organization providing education, health, and protection programs to children in need in the United States and around the world.

For many people, it's easier to comprehend and try to address poverty in the slums of India or in drought-scorched Africa than here in the United States. But one in four children in this country is growing up poor.

Growing up in West Virginia, I saw this kind of poverty around me in the forgotten mountain communities—kids growing up resigned to their own helplessness. But I always wanted to do something to help, inspired by my own mother's story.

My mom grew up in Oklahoma during the Great Depression. Her family of 11 lived on a farm that produced almost nothing during those Dust Bowl years. Still, the few photos from her childhood show her as a girl with a neat braid, smiling. She remembers her family playing games, singing songs, reciting poetry, and having fun. Only one generation later, my mother raised her own kids with ballet and piano lessons, solidly in the middle class.

How did my mom turn poverty around? Education. She had a teacher who sparked her interest in learning, and she went on to put herself through college.

Inspired by my mom's experience, five years ago I went looking for people who help educate kids like the ones I knew growing up in West Virginia. My search led me to Mark Shriver and a wonderful organization called Save the Children.

Here is the eye-opening lesson Save the Children taught me: Children who are born into poverty are already behind when they start kindergarten. In fact, by the time they turn 4, poor children are typically 18 months behind their middle-class counterparts.[1] And most children who start behind never catch up.

But I've also learned that we can help kids living in poverty start school on an equal footing with other kids by helping their mothers teach them during those crucial first five years, when 90 percent of brain growth occurs.[2] This is one of the ways Save the Children helps, and this is where I get excited. I can't tell you how many times I have been privileged to watch the lights turn on for these kids and their young mothers.

Think about it: Raising kids can be difficult in the best of circumstances. In isolated, resource-poor communities across America, moms face additional risk factors such as unemployment, teenage pregnancy, preterm births, and poor health care. All of these can negatively impact their children's development.

Actress, producer, and mother Jennifer Garner works as an advocate for early childhood education with Save the Children. {COURTESY JENNIFER GARNER}

Save the Children hires people from within the communities in which they'll work and trains them to be early childhood coordinators. Through pediatricians, hospitals, and local schools, the coordinators connect with pregnant women and young mothers in their own homes.

They talk to expectant moms about their babies' developmental progress, the importance of a well-balanced diet, and the necessity for prenatal counseling and health care. Once the baby arrives and through its first five years, the coordinator plays a hundred different roles: mother hen, friendly neighbor, fount of information, parenting trainer, all of it at once. She assesses the developmental health of the child and the well-being of the parents, teaches parents how to care for and play with their babies, and provides age-appropriate activities. She offers a shoulder to lean on and, above all, education and encouragement.

During a recent visit to one of Save the Children's sites in my native West Virginia, I met a young mom bubbling over with enthusiasm and pride for her new baby. She told me her girlfriends believe that the best thing to do for infants is to lay them in front of the TV, so they'll be quiet and "learn." But thanks to Save the Children, *she* is the one who has learned—to sing to her baby, to read to him, and to look at him when she speaks to him. I watched as she "narrated" to her son what she was doing, talking sweetly to him as she changed his diaper, got him dressed, and fed him. This baby was obviously connected to his mama, following her everywhere with his eyes. She glowed in the encouragement and praise she received from her coordinator.

What a difference this kind of stimulation, engagement, communication, and teaching makes for a child's future. It is within such warm,

Nikki Brown and her daughter, Kristian, read a book together while waiting for Sunday church services to start in Chattanooga, Tennessee. {BARBARA KINNEY}

supportive relationships with parents, caregivers, and teachers that children come to know their world and how to operate within it.

The young mother told me that all of this felt "silly" at first. Many women similar to her live far from family or other community and, even more importantly, have grown up without seeing anyone model good parenting. It isn't natural for them to play "This Little Piggy" or sing "Itsy Bitsy Spider" to a newborn. But they learn. She learned. This home visitation model can be a critical lifeline.

I went on a site visit to San Bernardino, east of Los Angeles, last year. The young parents I visited had a two-week-old infant and an 11-month-old. They looked as tired and overwhelmed as you might imagine. As is so often the case with the homes I visit, this household had no toys or books. I saw their older boy sitting in front of the TV without paying attention to it, without moving, and without making a sound. It was as if he had turned himself off.

Then the Save the Children coordinator showed up with a bag of tricks—developmentally appropriate toys and activities to engage the child's curiosity. I was thrilled and lucky to witness the 11-month-old boy play with a ball for the very first time. In an hour, this child went from listless and eerily quiet, to curious, to animated, to babbling. Now that I have a son, I finally understand the crazy magnetism between boys and balls! The coordinator coaxed the parents into rolling the ball back and forth with their son, encouraging and teaching them to watch for his cues and gently prodding them to respond. Their son smiled

and babbled at their attention, and the parents smiled back. By the end of our visit, the room had an entirely different energy. Everybody learned. Everybody was communicating. The light was turned on for this family.

With every site visit I make, I focus less on what the families don't have and more on what Save the Children helps bring out in them: love, support, attention, words, and connection. These days, brain scientists will tell you that this connectedness actually causes the growth of the very nerve pathways that enable children to develop and understand and learn. But I know that from what I've seen with my own eyes: The quality of relationships within families can powerfully affect children's motivation and confidence to learn. In fact, it teaches them that they *can* learn. It gets children up to speed so that when they get to kindergarten, they are ready to go with the rest of the kids.

I am so grateful to everyone who interacted with my mother as a child, giving her a leg up in this world. She certainly has proven herself worthy of their efforts. I hope Save the Children reaches every child living in poverty in our nation because all of our children deserve to have their lights shine. They're worth it, too.

ENDNOTES

1 Save the Children, "Jennifer Garner Calls for Early Education Investment at Senate Hearing," Press release, November 18, 2010, available at http://www.savethechildren.org/site/apps/nlnet/content2.aspx?c=8rKLIXMGIpI4E&b=6196021&ct=8884603&notoc=1.

2 Ibid.

Living the Head Start Dream

By ALMETA KEYS, executive director and CEO of the Edward C. Mazique Parent Child Center in Washington, D.C.

In 2015, we will celebrate the 50th anniversary of Head Start, the hallmark War on Poverty program for low-income children that Sargent Shriver and his team began. So far, Head Start has provided education, health, and social services to nearly 30 million children up to age 5. The genius of the program was its recognition that breaking the cycle of poverty meant preparing kids for kindergarten and simultaneously engaging, training, and educating their parents. In 1965, they called it "parent involvement." Today, we call it "parental engagement." Either way, it works.

I know this because I was one of those parents, and Head Start changed my life.

I was born in Louisiana's impoverished St. Mary Parish, the 11th of 13 children. I was a curious kid, and one day I dug up my father's paycheck stub: $27 for two weeks' work as a sharecropper in the nearby sugarcane fields. That's poverty. I asked him why it was so little, and he said, "Girl, that's a lot of money for the kind of work I do." He was a proud man.

I always knew I wanted to go to college, but I kept taking detours. After a shotgun wedding to Gabriel, an Army veteran, I had my first child at 17 and had four more after that. My husband had dreamed of going to college on the G.I. Bill, but with a wife and kids to support, he worked at the local shipyard instead. Then one day, the shipyard shut down. He started his own business as an auto mechanic but made less than minimum wage. We were in trouble.

For the longest time, we tried to make it without public assistance—"Not us!"—until one day, I found myself standing at the stove trying to stretch a little pasta with a little tomato sauce, already wondering where our next meal would come from. I realized I had to do something, so I swallowed my pride and applied for food stamps.

Right around that time, someone told us about Head Start. My first reaction was, "Head Start? That's for poor people!" I am my father's daughter and refused to admit that the P-word applied to me. But we knew it was the worst economic time we had ever faced, so we went to Head Start for help, broken and ashamed. Little did we know that Head Start would literally transform our lives.

We enrolled our son Fabian in the program. Teachers and social workers took our whole family under their wings, nurturing us and helping us get much-needed medical and dental care, nutrition counseling, job-readiness training, and giving us the family-strengthening tools we would use for the rest of our lives. They kept us engaged in parental leadership activities and training. They taught us how to parent our children while we pulled ourselves out of poverty. They taught us how to beat the odds, live our dreams, and be self-sufficient and successful. They taught us how to transfer our new life skills to our children so that they could succeed in school and one day live out their own dreams, too.

Our family experienced a paradigm shift, and education became the key focus of our lives. With the support and encouragement of the Head Start staff, I enrolled in college on a federal Pell Grant and a Head Start scholarship. I was 35 years old and had been out of school for 17 years. I remember the first essay I wrote in college: "Woman Comes Alive at 35!" Getting my degree seemed to take forever, but I went to work at Head Start and kept on going to school year after year—while my children were also in school, year after year.

Here's how it went. My first Head Start child, Fabian, eventually received his master's degree in engineering. On the same day, I graduated with my bachelor's degree. College dream #1 was accomplished. Around the same time that my second Head Starter, Julian, got his bachelor's degree in business, I got my master's degree in education— dream #2. When my third Head Start child, Elizabeth, got her medical assistant associate's degree, I achieved my second master's degree, this one in divinity—dream #3. Joycelyn, my fourth and last Head Start child, works in Head Start. When she expects to get her bachelor's degree in education, I hope to be fulfilling dream #4—receiving my doctorate in counseling. Our oldest son, Gabriel, served in the Air Force during Operation Desert Storm, and today he is a deep-sea diver working offshore in Louisiana. All of our children are high achievers.

As for my husband, Gabriel, he sacrificed his own college dreams so that I could go, but Head Start showed him that he had leadership and organizational skills and empowered him to use them. He got a job as a school bus driver and became president of our school bus drivers association. He moved on to become a St. Mary Parish sheriff and rose to the rank of sergeant. While serving as Mr. Mom during my studies, he became a prominent figure in community affairs. I am sad to tell you that after we moved to Washington, D.C., several years ago, Gabriel died of a massive heart attack at the age of 62. He was a giant in our family and our community.

Ever since I was introduced to Head Start in 1979, I have continued my involvement with it—and I'm not alone. As Sarge laid out in the original plan, many of the workers at Head Start are former parents who have come up through the ranks. Like me, they feel vested in the program and want to give back. Since 1989, I have run and expanded Head Start programs in Louisiana and Washington, D.C. I've had the honor of advocating for disadvantaged families and representing Head Start on Capitol Hill.

And who would have thought that this poor little girl from rural Louisiana—who might once have been considered the least likely to succeed— would end up standing in front of the president of the United States at the White House saying, "Mr. President, my name is Almeta Richards Keys from St. Mary Parish, Louisiana, and I am an empowered former Head Start parent, now serving as the executive director of the Edward C. Mazique Parent Child Center, here in the District of Columbia."

I owe it all to Sargent Shriver's brainchild, Head Start!

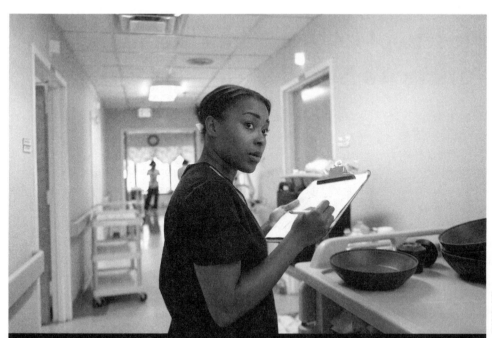

BARBARA RIES

DEE SAINT FRANC • Providence, Rhode Island

Dee is a 23-year-old, single mother to her 5-year-old daughter, Azariah. After leaving foster care at age 18, Dee worked two jobs and depended on government assistance for the first year of her daughter's life.

Dee has earned associate's degree from Johnson & Wales University; her bachelor's degree in social work from Rhode Island College; and her certified nursing assistant, or CNA, license while working two jobs, and she struggles to find time to spend with her daughter. "Being a single mother can be tough," she said. "Often, I feel lonely in more ways than one when it comes to parenting alone. But I refuse to settle for less because my daughter deserves a happy and healthy family."

Preschool for All: The Path to America's Middle-Class Promise

By ARNE DUNCAN, U.S. Secretary of Education, and KATHLEEN SEBELIUS, U.S. Secretary of Health and Human Services

In his January 8, 1964, State of the Union address announcing the War on Poverty, President Lyndon B. Johnson pledged that his administration would bring opportunity to Americans living on what he called "the outskirts of hope."

Head Start was one of the many efforts President Johnson spearheaded as a result of this pledge. Since its creation, Head Start has helped to change the lives of more than 30 million children and their families. By helping children build a strong foundation for school and providing parents with valuable tools and resources, Head Start can help set the stage for success.

Yet we must do more to ensure that all Americans have an equal chance at success. In his 2013 State of the Union address, President Barack Obama spoke forcefully about America's basic bargain. "People who work hard and shoulder their responsibilities should be able to join a thriving middle class," the president said. "Restoring that bargain is the unfinished work of our generation."[1]

Imagine striving to do your best, day after day, shadowed by the fear that your child is missing out on the fundamentals needed to succeed in life. Imagine the sacrifices and soul-searching involved in making trade-offs and compromises in the care of your child—whether that means leaving your job to provide home care yourself or seeking care that may carry a steep cost or dubious quality. How would these decisions affect your monthly budget, your ability to perform well at work, and your efforts to keep your family afloat and secure?

These concerns are all too real for many American families—including millions of working mothers.

Study after study confirms that young children who experience secure, stimulating environments with rich learning opportunities from an early age are better prepared to thrive in school. Indeed, both of us have watched our own children expand their worlds and minds in the years before they entered school, both at home and in quality early learning settings.

But we are lucky. Fewer than 3 in 10 American 4-year-olds attend high-quality preschool programs.[2] And the availability of high-quality care and educational services for infants and toddlers is even lower.

The gap is especially pronounced in low-income communities, and it carries a high cost. Children from disadvantaged families start kindergarten an average of 12 to 14 months behind their peers in both language development and prereading.[3] The first rung on the ladder to success is missing for millions of children, because they miss out on the early learning opportunities that would prepare them to do well in school.

The Obama administration is committed to closing this costly, unfair opportunity gap through a plan that, in partnership with the states, will expand high-quality early learning services for children from birth through age 5, including high-quality preschool for every 4-year-old in America.

Strong early learning can translate into more school success, which in turn can lead to college, good employment, and ultimately a robust economy. Nobel Prize–winning economist James Heckman found that every public dollar spent on high-quality early childhood education returns $7 through increased productivity and savings on public assistance and criminal justice programs.[4]

The benefits of high-quality early learning for children are clear. But their mothers and families can benefit, too.

Child care expenses for families with working mothers can range from 20 percent to nearly 50 percent of that mother's monthly salary.[5] The costs are especially high for single mothers. The prohibitively high cost of child care can lead many women to put off pursuing their own educational and career goals—goals that would be critical to supporting their families.

International studies show that free or subsidized child care can increase women's participation in the workforce.[6] In the United States, single mothers are nearly 50 percent more likely to still be employed after three years if they receive at least some child care subsidy.[7]

President Obama understands what it's like for families with parents who struggle to care for young children, make a living, and pursue their own education. He has spoken about how hard his single mother and grandparents worked to raise him. He also understands that when we give children a strong start in high-quality free or subsidized early learning programs, we help parents balance their many responsibilities in ways that promote stability in their homes, careers, and finances.

As a nation, we can't afford *not* to make this investment.

The president's plan will:

- Make voluntary, universal, high-quality preschool available to 4-year-olds from low- and moderate-income families through a partnership with states, territories, and the Bureau of Indian Education, while creating incentives to expand these preschool programs for additional children from middle-class families and to provide full-day kindergarten. This new partnership would encourage states to cover all families who want to send their children to high-quality preschools with small class sizes, qualified teachers, and stimulating learning experiences.

- Launch a new Early Head Start–Child Care partnership to significantly expand the availability of high-quality early learning opportunities for children from birth to age 3.

- Expand highly effective, voluntary home-visiting programs where nurses, family educators, and social workers connect low-income families to health, social, and educational support through the Maternal, Infant, and Early Childhood Home Visiting Program created under the Affordable Care Act.

These actions build on steps the administration has already taken to boost early learning for our most vulnerable children. Our efforts have ranged from improving the accountability and quality of Head Start services, to nearly $1 billion in total funding for the Race to the Top Early Learning Challenge grant program, which aims at improving the quality and effectiveness of early learning and development programs around the country.

As we move forward with this vital effort, we can look to states that have shown the way. In Michigan and Massachusetts, Govs. Rick Snyder (R-MI) and Deval Patrick (D-MA) have made expanding access to preschool programs a priority. In Alabama, Gov. Robert Bentley (R) has proposed new resources to rapidly expand early education.[8] These leaders represent a bipartisan consensus that America can't win the race for the future by holding back children at the starting line.

And it's not only state officials who are investing in high-quality preschool. Voters from both political parties in cities such as Denver, San Antonio, and St. Paul are approving tax increases to support preschool initiatives.[9]

In the decades since President Johnson's call to action, the evidence that high-quality early learning works has multiplied many times over.

Other high-performing countries recognize the value of early learning and have rapidly expanded their early childhood education programs. The Organisation for Economic Co-operation and Development reports that the United States now ranks 28th among developed countries in its enrollment of 4-year-olds in early learning programs.[10] By contrast, Japan—which has outperformed the United States in recent international assessments—enrolls nearly 100 percent of its 4-year-olds in preschool. Other countries have made early education available at even younger ages.

If we don't act, we risk falling even further behind the rest of the world in preparing our children for school. We risk failing to support the parents who need this help to give their children a strong start in life.

Early childhood education is one of the best investments we can make in America's future. Now is the time to redouble our efforts and complete our unfinished work. It's time to answer the call that President Johnson sounded half a century ago to help families move from the outskirts of hope into the heart of a thriving middle class.

Doing right by our youngest children and our hardworking families—including our nation's heroic working moms—is essential to fulfilling the promise of the American Dream. We are proud to be working together to make this happen.

Portions of this essay have appeared in previously published works by the authors.

ENDNOTES

1 Office of the Press Secretary, "Remarks by the President in the State of the Union Address," Press release, February 12, 2013, available at http://www.whitehouse.gov/the-press-office/2013/02/12/remarks-president-state-union-address.

2 T.D. Snyder and S.A. Dillow, *Digest of Education Statistics 2011* (U.S. Department of Education, 2012).

3 Jack P. Shonkoff and Deborah A. Phillips, *From Neurons to Neighborhoods: The Science of Early Childhood Development* (Washington: National Academy Press, 2000).

4 James J. Heckman and others, "The Rate of Return to the High/Scope Perry Preschool Program." Working Paper 15471 (National Bureau of Economic Research, 2009), available at http://www.nber.org/papers/w15471.

5 U.S. Census Bureau, "Table 6: Average Weekly Child Care Expenditures of Families with Employed Mothers that Make Payments by Age Groups and Selected Characteristics: Spring 2011," available at http://www.census.gov/hhes/childcare/data/sipp/2011/tables.html (last accessed September 2013).

6 Tarja K. Viitanen, "Cost of Childcare and Female Employment in the UK," *Labour* 19 (1) (2005): 149–170, available at http://onlinelibrary.wiley.com/doi/10.1111/j.1467-9914.2005.00325.x/abstract.

7 Heather Boushey, "Staying Employed After Welfare: Work Supports and Job Quality Vital to Employment Tenure and Wage Growth" (Washington: Economic Policy Institute, 2002), available at http://www.epi.org/page/-/old/briefing-papers/128/bp128.pdf.

8 U.S. Department of Education, "Early Learning: America's Middle Class Promise Begins Early," available at http://www.ed.gov/early-learning (last accessed September 2013).

9 Association of School Business Officials International, "Archive of Past 100 Announcements," available at http://network.asbointl.org/Home/Announcements/ (last accessed September 2013).

10 Organisation for Economic Co-operation and Development, "Education at a Glance 2012: OECD Indicators" (2012), available at http://www.oecd.org/edu/EAG%202012_e-book_EN_200912.pdf.

Afterschool Programs: Investing in Our Cities by Investing in Our Kids

By MAYOR BETSY PRICE (R) of Fort Worth, Texas. She is also a member of the board of the Afterschool Alliance, a national nonprofit advocacy organization.

As the mother of three children, I have always been passionate about education. I've always recognized the importance and impact of a quality education on a young person's life—not just education in the classroom, but also opportunities for kids to learn and be engaged outside of school. That's critical, too, and it requires family and community support.

My husband Tom and I were fortunate to be able to be involved in our children's afterschool activities. Whether it was dancing, football, baseball, swimming lessons, or reading programs, we made sure our kids' minds and bodies were engaged. But afterschool programs are not accessible for some—particularly families on or over the brink of poverty.

The citizens of Fort Worth have learned that we have the power to change that by helping more folks understand the importance of what children miss when they're not in school. The evidence is clear: Kids in afterschool programs are more engaged and interested in their education; have better school attendance; rate their school experience more positively; score higher on state education accountability tests; and are less likely to commit or be victims of crimes.

So what can local government do to help struggling families help their kids? We in Fort Worth believe we have some of the best afterschool programs in the country, and we have used two high-impact strategies to make the most of taxpayer dollars.

Our first strategy is collaboration on funding. Fort Worth After School is a collaborative partnership between the city and the Fort Worth Independent School District. By combining the financial resources of these public entities with available federal funding, we provide financial security for our afterschool programs, which now serve more than 12,000 elementary and middle school students at more than 80 sites around the city.

The second strategy is convening elected officials, civic leaders, educators, pastors, nonprofit agencies, and service providers to coordinate and support afterschool programs at a citywide level. Our newest initiative is called Fort Worth Strengthening Programs Through Advocacy, Resources and Collaboration, or SPARC! Among other things, SPARC! will be a resource center for parents looking for afterschool programs and for providers looking to set up those programs.

Preschool and afterschool programs like this one in Chattanooga, Tennessee, are invaluable rungs on the education ladder. {BARBARA KINNEY}

Subsidizing and expanding access to afterschool programs simply makes good sense. These programs allow working parents to stay at work and keep their jobs and provide their kids with a safe place to learn and grow.

Investing in our future starts with giving all of our children the opportunities and tools they need to be successful in the classroom, which translates into success in life. Fort Worth's afterschool programs are paving a clear pathway to achieving these goals and creating a better society.

Higher Education:
Interrupting the Cycle of Poverty

By DR. EDUARDO J. PADRÓN, president of Miami Dade College, the nation's largest and most diverse institution of higher education, with more than 175,000 students on eight campuses and in many outreach centers. He has been appointed to national education posts by six U.S. presidents—most recently by President Barack Obama to head the White House Initiative on Educational Excellence for Hispanic Americans. He is a past chair of the American Council on Education and the Association of American Colleges and Universities.

Despite the months and years by which we chart our lives, the quiet reality is that our lives unfold in far-smaller increments—in moments. Along the way, there are moments that seem to stop time, leaving a lasting imprint.

For Fabienne Joseph, one of those moments arrived with a massive jolt—the 2010 earthquake that hit her homeland of Haiti and took the life of her son's father. For Ashley Cooks, it was the moment she heard that her husband had been incarcerated. Two months later, another time-stopping moment brought her son into the world. For Natasha Delisme, the stop-cold moment came with questions: Would there be enough money for college? Could she go? Who would care for her two children?

These three women are among more than 106 million people in our country with incomes below 200 percent of the federal poverty level. About 42 million of them are the women and 28 million are the children we are reading about in this report.[1] In the United States, more than one in three women lives in poverty or on the brink

of it, and just over 4 out of every 10 children living in poverty or on the brink are in families headed by women.[2] Too many of these women face terrible choices: rent or utilities, child care or health care, groceries or graduation.

One casualty women face when confronting moment-to-moment crises and challenges that too often trap them in an endless cycle of poverty: their aspirations. Dreams are put on hold— sometimes permanently—and human potential is too often wasted. That means incalculable losses reverberating across families, communities, and a nation that can ill afford to lose its most valuable resource: the dreams of its people, the American Dream.

But Fabienne, Ashley, and Natasha share another bond. All three go to Miami Dade College, or MDC, where most of our students are women and where the challenges they confront are met and solved in an environment of support that extends beyond the classroom. With 70 percent of our students low-income (including the 46 percent of the student body that lives below the poverty line); we at MDC understand that their success in college is more than an academic pursuit. More than half of our students are the very first members of their families to go to college.[3] They need real support to help them attend in the first place and even more support to help them stick with it and finish.

That is why we go beyond teaching and training. We have helped thousands of students such as Fabienne, Ashley, and Natasha gain access to federal and state programs that give women who are both breadwinners and caregivers the support and breathing space they need to be students too. These are programs such as Medicaid for children and other family members, the Supplemental Nutrition Assistance Program, or SNAP (formerly known as food stamps), energy assistance, Head Start, and pregnancy support. Access to these benefits, as well as financial and legal counseling, are made available through our partnership with Single Stop USA, a national nonprofit organization that helps low-income individuals and families become economically secure.[4]

We also help them through other MDC partnerships with national leaders, such as the Ascend Fellowship at the Aspen Institute, which is introducing creative two-generation support models. Support for mothers who want to go to college, for example, does not mean much if they do not also have access to effective child care. Additional partnerships with great organizations such as iMentor and Year Up provide our students with access to invaluable internship opportunities, career planning, peer-engagement programs, and connections to experienced mentors out in the workplace.[5]

All of these life supports are integrated into their ongoing college lives, from orientation to graduation, with the goal of helping them get into careers that produce economic security and stability.

We provide onramps to the current job market with short-term industry certification programs that provide well-paying entry-level jobs in high-demand areas of the regional economy. MDC engages nearly 500 business leaders on advisory teams, helping us design curricula and programs in areas such as nursing, information technology, public safety, biological sciences, film, TV and digital technology, and much more. MDC has developed more than 80 new certificate, associate, and baccalaureate degrees that directly feed the emerging economy of South Florida.[6]

As the two-generation projects suggest, all of this is not just about the students themselves. Some years ago, a study of college-going mothers from poor, working-class backgrounds demonstrated the intergenerational impact of attending college. The educational expectations for their children immediately went up.[7] These women became more involved in their children's schools, as well as community and religious groups. They took their children to museums, theaters, and other forms of cultural enrichment, and the children's school performance improved.[8] In effect, these college-educated mothers interrupted the cycle of poverty.

We watch the promise unfold every day at Miami Dade College. In the not-too-distant future, Fabienne and Ashley will become nurses, and Natasha will become a radiologist. Their fellow

Investing in the education of our
nation's girls would benefit not
only them, but also the economy
and society as a whole.

{BARBARA RIES}

students at MDC will fulfill every imaginable role in the nation's workforce. They will get themselves out of poverty and ensure that their children never rejoin those ranks.

Which makes me wonder: Why are we still having the conversation about equity and opportunity for women in our society? That is a question without a good answer. But if we are having the conversation, then we should talk about and celebrate solutions that we know are working, as we are doing in this report.

Higher education is one of those solutions that can help fulfill the potential of the women on the brink in our country—their potential for productivity and self-sufficiency. Combined with a safety net of support, higher education can produce not only those shining life moments filled with hope and inspiration, but also moments of real confidence and pride in accomplishment.

But it's not just moments. Higher education generates the *momentum* that wipes out inequity for generations to come.

ENDNOTES

1 Center for American Progress tabulation of data from Current Population Survey, 2013 Annual Social and Economic Supplement using Census Bureau CPS Table Creator.

2 Ibid.

3 Miami Dade College and Single Stop USA, "2-year Report" (2013), p. 1, available at http://www.singlestopusa.org/wp-content/uploads/2013/01/FINAL_MDC_2_YR.pdf.

4 Single Stop USA, "Programs," available at http://www.singlestopusa.org/program/ (last accessed September 2013).

5 iMentor, "Mission and Work," available at http://www.imentor.org/mission-and-work (last accessed September 2013); Year Up, "About Year Up," available at http://www.yearup.org/about/main.php?page=aboutus (last accessed September 2013).

6 Miami Dade College, "General Information," available at https://www.mdc.edu/hr/employeehandbook/general information.asp (last accessed September 2013).

7 Paul A. Attewell and David E. Lavin, "Passing the Torch: Does Higher Education for the Disadvantaged Pay Off Across Generations?" (New York: Russell Sage Foundation, 2007), p. 103.

8 Ibid., p. 82.

Nikki's Story

By NIKKI BROWN, a dental assistant and single mother of two. She was struggling to pay rent, student loans, car payments, and child care fees, so she and her kids moved in with her parents. She is going back to school to be a dental hygienist, which will pay more. She also sells Mary Kay cosmetics to supplement her income.

I come from a household where my mother and father were married—and are still married. I guess being a pastor's daughter with two children from two different fathers, I sometimes get looked down upon.

I've only seen my daughter's father in child-support court, and it's "Can I sign my rights away?" My son hasn't seen his father in years because he's locked up now, though he calls sometimes. Before I even conceived my son, my mom told me, "He doesn't love you. You're so smart. You could go so much further." I didn't listen. I don't want my kids to make the same choices I made. I want them to make better choices and have better opportunities.

Different girls at the church think I'm doing so well because I keep it all together. I tell them, "Honey, you have no clue." Struggling every day and with things being so hard, I don't want anybody to see that. But there can be nights when I'll be in the shower, and that's where I cry.

I feel like I'm on my way. I'm not going to let my circumstances keep me in a box. I work at the dentist's office Monday through Thursday. Not working that one day allows me to qualify for food stamps so I can feed my kids. The last thing I want the government to think is that I want to continue to stay on benefits or that I want to extend my benefits or qualify for an extended period of time. It's like, help me out so I can go to school, and while I am in class, I can know that there is child care.

I want to educate myself and I want to go further. I want my kids, when they get older, to be like, "Yeah, my mom's that awesome hygienist. Go get your teeth done by her!" I want them to know that your mom did it, so you can do it. There's no excuse. You can do anything. "Can't" is not in your vocabulary.

That's why I don't consider myself poor, because I know if I continue to do what I'm doing, then I'm eventually going to get to be where I want to be. It's just taking me longer. And that's okay.

Why We Must
Push Back

The Consequences of
Living on the Brink

We have just outlined the cultural and economic forces and complicated factors that can push women to the brink. We have documented the radically changed circumstances of women over the past half century and what these changes mean for American women today.

What would happen if we did nothing? If some women are doing better than ever before, what is so wrong with the status quo? Why do we argue in this report that the nation must push back from the brink?

If we remain passive, if we do not force an evolution in policies to adapt to today's reality, not only will the nation fail to realize the full economic potential of half its population, but also women's and families' costs will escalate. And financial insecurity has mental, physical, and economic consequences that span generations.

Take a look.

The Chronic Stress of Poverty: Toxic to Children

By DR. NADINE BURKE HARRIS, M.D., M.P.H., a pediatrician and founding physician of San Francisco's Bayview Child Health Center and the Center for Youth Wellness and an advisor to the Clinton Foundation and Next Generation's "Too Small to Fail" initiative, aimed at improving the health of children ages 0 to 5 years old. She was the subject of a 2011 profile in **The New Yorker** *of her groundbreaking work on the relationship between chronic childhood stress and long-term health.*

The first time I met Anthony,[1] it felt like a kick in the stomach—literally. He was sitting on an exam table in my clinic, and as I leaned in close to examine him, he got scared, lost control, and wham! He got me. Anthony's mother brought him in not just for his rash, but also because she had heard that we had a different way of doing things at the California Pacific Medical Center's Bayview Child Health Center.

I founded the clinic in 2007 to address health disparities in the Bayview-Hunters Point neighborhood of San Francisco. Bayview is home to thousands of families struggling every day to make ends meet. Many San Franciscans are not even aware that Bayview exists, let alone that it is home to the highest density of children in the city, many of them in women-led households.

Over and over again, I heard stories in the clinic such as the one from Anthony's mom. Her child had a rash and she was worried about it, but what she was really worried about was his behavior. At age 6, he was struggling to sit still in class and frequently interrupting the teacher. Sometimes he lost control and would hit, kick, or run out of the classroom. She was worried about having to

leave work so often to talk to school officials. Her son was a sweet kid, but he had been through a lot. His dad had struggled with sobriety, there had been domestic violence, and his dad was now out of the picture. While his mom was grateful that the drama had ended, she missed having someone to help with Anthony, and every month it was a challenge to make ends meet.

As a physician, I could see that the stress of poverty was affecting my patients in a very direct way. The question was, how? I immersed myself in research on how stress and trauma affect the developing brains and bodies of children. What I found validated the clinical picture that presented itself to me daily, and it transformed my frustration into hope.

The first big insight came when I found the Adverse Childhood Experiences, or ACEs, Study.[2] It turned out that I was not the only one making connections between childhood stress and bad health outcomes. Dr. Vincent Felitti at Kaiser San Diego and Dr. Robert Anda at the Centers for Disease Control and Prevention conducted the ACEs study. Together, they completed a survey of more than 17,000 adult patients for what are called "adverse childhood experiences," including abuse, neglect, exposure to domestic violence, and household dysfunction such as parental substance use, mental illness, incarceration, or divorce. Using the study data, they correlated the number of ACEs against health outcomes. What they found was striking.

First, ACEs are incredibly common. Sixty-seven percent of the study population had experienced at least one ACE, and 12.6 percent had experienced four or more. Second, there was a dose-response relationship between ACEs and health problems later on. That means that the higher the ACE score, the worse the health outcomes are later in life. A person with four or more ACEs has a relative risk of chronic obstructive pulmonary disease (COPD) that is an astonishing 260 percent of the risk for someone with no ACEs—more than two and a half times the risk. For hepatitis, it was 250 percent of the risk; for depression, it was 460 percent. If a patient had seven or more ACEs, their relative risk of ischemic heart disease, the number one killer in the United States, was 360 percent—more than three and a half times the risk of someone who had never undergone adverse childhood experiences.

Since the publication of the original ACE study in 1998, dozens of studies have corroborated the dose-response effect. Most important, the studies have started to point to a mechanism for how it works, which is where the hope lies. Understanding the mechanism of a biological problem is critical to targeting effective interventions.

Here's what we know so far. The principal actor in the link between ACEs and disease is the hypothalamic-pituitary-adrenal, or HPA, axis governing the

Young children raised in poverty are often exposed to trauma and chronic stress, putting them at a higher risk for behavioral and health problems that continue into adulthood.
{BARBARA RIES (1), BARBARA KINNEY (2)}

body's "fight-or-flight" response. That's the familiar heart-pounding feeling we get when we experience what we perceive to be a sudden threat to our survival. The HPA axis releases a surge of stress hormones, including adrenaline and cortisol, which creates a cascade of chemical reactions in the brain and body. When activated occasionally—say, when someone in the next car suddenly slams on the brakes, or a dog comes from out of nowhere and growls and snaps—this system bypasses our thinking brain, the prefrontal cortex, and activates the primitive reactions that can get us out of the way of a mortal threat.

The problem comes when the system is overtaxed by repeated, intense, or chronic stress. That cascade of chemicals and reactions goes from saving one's life to damaging one's health. As it turns out, children are particularly vulnerable to the harmful effects of chronic stress and trauma and the resulting bath of stress hormones, because their young brains, nervous systems, and organs are just developing.

Anthony's behavior put him at higher likelihood of failure in school and all of the associated social risks. But his high ACEs score told me that he was also at higher risk of COPD, heart disease, hepatitis, autoimmune disease, and cancer. Science points to two reasons for this.

First, the effect of trauma on the ventral tegmental area, or VTA, of the brain's nucleus accumbens—the reward and addiction center—dramatically increases the chance he will engage in high-risk behaviors such as smoking, substance use, and early sexual activity. These behaviors can result in poor health.

But second, and more surprisingly, even if Anthony somehow manages to avoid all of those negative outcomes in his life, the data show that he is still at an increased risk for chronic disease. Why? It turns out that the HPA axis—that brain system squirting out all the fight-or-flight stress chemicals—is also closely involved with the immune system. That means that people exposed to chronic stress in childhood show increased signs of chronic inflammation in adulthood. Chronic inflammation is a driver of such ailments as heart disease and COPD.

So if biology is destiny, what could I do about that in my clinic? As it turns out, quite a bit.

The first step for healing young children exposed to trauma and chronic stress is what we call dyadic or two-generation work. That means looking at the parent and child as a single unit to be treated, then engaging, educating, and empowering caregivers to be buffers between their kids and the stressors they face. Therefore, at our clinic, we provide many single mothers with the appropriate counseling, social connections, and community resources to help them overcome their own challenges for the sake of their kids' health.

One of the most effective ways of doing this is something called Child-Parent Psychotherapy, or CPP, developed by Dr. Alicia Lieberman at the University of California, San Francisco.[3] CPP helps parents address their own often-traumatic histories so that they can establish healthy attachments to their children and break the intergenerational cycle of trauma. Other promising interventions include teaching both mothers and kids practices such as mindfulness—meditation—and biofeedback, which help them with self-regulation so that they can calm the overactive fight-or-flight response. In addition, a healthy diet and regular exercise are key to giving the brain the good hormones necessary to regulate mood and behavior.

I referred Anthony to my colleague at California Pacific Medical Center, Dr. Ruby Ng, who is trained in biofeedback. She hooked him up to electrodes that measured things such as heart rate, breathing, and the hair that stands up on the back of his arms, and then she stressed him out! She gave him tasks that frustrated him, and at the same time, he got the chance to see a screen that showed how his body was reacting to the stress. Then she showed him how to bring the reactions back under control with breathing techniques and other tricks, and he watched his heart rate and other markers calm down on the screen. It was a cool game for a 6-year-old boy. It was HPA axis rehab!

I have continued to follow Anthony over the years, and he is doing so much better that it makes my heart ache for all of my patients who don't have access to these therapies. Ninety percent of our patients are covered by Medicaid, which doesn't pay for biofeedback. But seeing such improvement in Anthony and other kids like him has transformed my clinical practice.

Today, I work with the hopeful urgency of a doctor on the frontier of medicine. We recently created the Center for Youth Wellness in San Francisco to pilot and evaluate multidisciplinary interventions that heal the impacts of Adverse Childhood Experiences. One of our goals is to share best practices in ACE treatment with others around the country. We are also working on the policy level to get these therapies reimbursed so that all kids who need them have access to resources that go to the heart of their problems.

All in all, this convergence of basic science, clinical research, and public health is reframing a problem so common that it was hidden in plain sight: Chronic stress and trauma are toxic to our children. We now know the targets to go after—early childhood brain development, HPA axis regulation, and chronic inflammation—and that creates opportunities for intervention. We have an obligation to our kids, to their caregivers, and to our society to advance the standard of practice to meet the state of the science.

ENDNOTES

1   The patient's name and identifying details have been changed in the interest of confidentiality.

2   The Adverse Childhood Experiences Study, "What Is the ACE Study?", available at http://acestudy.org (last accessed September 2013).

3   University of California, San Francisco, "Alicia F. Lieberman, PhD," available at http://psych.ucsf.edu/faculty.aspx?id=322 (last accessed September 2013).

The Trap: Mental Illness and Women in Poverty

By RON MANDERSCHEID, Ph.D., executive director of the National Association of County Behavioral Health and Developmental Disability Directors and adjunct professor at Johns Hopkins Bloomberg School of Public Health. He has also served at the National Institute of Mental Health and the Substance Abuse and Mental Health Services Administration, both at the U.S. Department of Health and Human Services.

Poverty exacts a vicious toll on people—including oppressive social inequality, exploitation, social isolation, abuse and trauma, danger, and fear. These life experiences actually lead to poor health—more illness, early onset of chronic disease, and even early death. But poverty does not just take a toll on physical health. It contributes to poor mental health, too.

Women in poverty are subjected to very difficult life circumstances. For more than 50 years, research has documented that the adverse social and psychological experiences of poverty cause mental illness and substance use disorders.[1] Almost half of women living in poverty may suffer from some form of debilitating mental illness. Once a poor woman experiences mental illness, that illness is very likely to trap her in poverty. This happens for two reasons: First, mental illness is likely to sap her energy, direction, and purpose. Second, the appropriate care to help her recover is not likely to be available.

Part of the solution to this difficult dilemma lies with the 2014 implementation of the Affordable Care Act, or ACA—the national health reform initiative that is changing the landscape of health insurance. Under the ACA, virtually all poor women are eligible for health insurance through Medicaid if their states adopt the ACA's optional provision to expand Medicaid eligibility. Once these women are covered, they can get health care through their local public health, mental health, and substance use programs. Furthermore, they will be eligible for disease prevention and wellness programs that promote good physical and mental health.

But health care isn't enough. We also need to develop more fundamental solutions for the millions of women trapped by poverty and mental illness. We can do this by helping prevent the adverse effects of financial struggles on mental health before they occur, which would involve directly supporting these women and developing what we sociologists call "opportunity structures" to provide them with the steps leading out of financial insecurity. Here are some thoughts on the potential shape such interventions could take:

- To prevent the adverse effects of living paycheck to paycheck, women need several different types of support. These include building friendship groups in their local communities that would provide opportunities for social support

Chrystal Thompson, left, was living on the streets of Chicago, Illinois, before she was able to regain steady employment and stability. Here, she gives her phone number to a woman who she knows from the homeless shelter where they both spent time. {BARBARA KINNEY}

and inclusion; mentors who would identify needed training and reasonable job choices; support for and information about basic life tasks, such as child-rearing, housing, and food choices; and help with decisions about risky behaviors.

- To initiate this support, we need more not-for-profit organizations working with women on the brink to serve as hubs fostering local friendship and social support groups. Positive "sister" role models are very important to guide women to make healthy choices and to encourage actions that move them up the economic ladder.

- More opportunity structures need to be created for work. That way, lower-income women can access entry-level jobs that offer training and career trajectories to help them advance to more complex roles. If developed carefully and intelligently, such programs will make it possible for all women to participate in the emerging global economy.

The future global competitiveness of the United States is likely to depend on our success in empowering these women. We must develop approaches that work to help low-wage women escape from the traps of poverty and mental illness. If America is to compete and ascend, we must strive to bring these women along now.

ENDNOTE

1 Christopher G. Hudson, "Socioeconomic Status and Mental Illness: Tests of the Social Causation and Selection Hypotheses," *American Journal of Orthopsychiatry* 75 (1) (2005): 3–18, available at http://onlinelibrary.wiley.com/doi/10.1037/0002-9432.75.1.3/abstract; Jack Carney, "Poverty & Mental Illness: You Can't Have One Without the Other," Mad in America, March 7, 2012, available at http://www.madinamerica.com/2012/03/poverty-mental-illness-you-cant-have-one-without-the-other/.

CHRYSTAL THOMPSON • Chicago, Illinois

Chrystal is a 35-year-old single mother to her 16-year-old son. Chrystal struggled to regain her footing after the economy turned and her health began to deteriorate, and she has been in and out of homelessness over the past few years. Recently, Chrystal started a new job at the Field Museum in Chicago through LIFT's support, but she still relies on government-assistance programs to make ends meet. Despite these hardships, she looks to the future with an open heart and still gives back to those in need. Her goal is simple: stability for herself and her son. She knows they both are worth it.

Armed and Vulnerable: Women in the U.S. Military

By DR. SONYA BORRERO, assistant professor and researcher at the University of Pittsburgh School of Medicine and the Veterans Health Administration Center for Health Equity Research and Promotion Development, or CHERP. Her research focuses on gender and racial disparities in health care.

Women have been signing up for military service in unprecedented numbers, currently comprising a record 14 percent of the active-duty force and 18 percent of the National Guard and Reserves.[1] They enter the military for reasons ranging from a desire to serve and protect their country to wanting access to its education benefits and loan-repayment programs. Many also see service as a way to escape abusive or socioeconomically oppressive circumstances.

For many of the 2 million female veterans, military service has been empowering—an avenue to career, personal, and educational advancement. But for many others in this newest, post-9/11 generation, reintegration back into civilian life is a painful struggle.

This is especially tragic because at the same time that the scope of women's roles in the military is expanding, so are their sacrifices. Since 9/11, women have served in combat support roles in Iraq and Afghanistan, which put them in hostile battle zones, where many of them sustain debilitating injuries or die in the line of fire, just like their male counterparts engaged in direct combat.

Now that the Pentagon has formally recognized women's valor on the battlefield by ending its ban on direct combat for women, women's sacrifices will undoubtedly increase.

The issue that disproportionately affects servicewomen compared to civilian women and that has garnered the most attention and outrage is military sexual trauma, or MST. Sexual violence is an endemic problem in our society, but women in the military face a much higher risk of sexual assault than civilian women. Across various studies, between 9.5 percent and 33 percent of women have reported experiencing an attempted or completed rape while serving in the military.[2]

MST is associated with adverse psychological, physical, and economic consequences. Studies show that veterans who have experienced MST have more mental-health diagnoses (such as PTSD, depression, and substance abuse disorders), more physical health symptoms (such as chronic pain and insomnia), greater difficulty with seeking and maintaining employment, and a higher likelihood of experiencing homelessness.[3]

There is also the issue of justice—or the lack thereof—that likely contributes to victims' mental anguish. The Department of Defense estimates there are about 26,000 sexual assaults in the military each year, but only a fraction of cases are reported and processed.[4] Many women do not report sexual assault largely because they fear retaliation from the historically male-centric power hierarchy in the military. Victims often say that the perpetrator not only outranked them but also was the same official to whom they would have to report the crime. Advocates for servicewomen inside and outside of government are calling for an overhaul of the military justice system, recommending that the reporting and investigation of sexual assault charges be removed from the chain of command and put entirely in the hands of third-party prosecutors.

The effects of MST are at an extreme end of the spectrum of problems for women veterans coming back home. Women face many other readjustment and re-entry issues that mirror those of their male counterparts. But women can face additional impediments to their ability to reintegrate back into society.

Similar to men, women veterans are finding it hard to find jobs in a tough economy, but the difficulties appear to be greater for women. The unemployment rate for women veterans of the conflicts in Iraq and Afghanistan is approaching 13 percent, higher than the 10 percent rate for male veterans and much higher than the 8 percent rate for female nonveterans.[5] Furthermore, women veterans are now the fastest-growing segment of the homeless population in the United States. They are at a much higher risk for homelessness than their male counterparts and are almost three times more likely to be homeless compared to female nonveterans.[6]

Both men and women veterans experience stress when reconnecting with their families, but women may experience higher distress resulting from the guilt, social stigma, and other repercussions of leaving husbands and children behind. Divorce rates are significantly higher among female veterans and service members than among men,[7] and some women report that their service caused them to lose child custody battles.

Both men and women veterans must cope with service-related medical disabilities and psychiatric conditions, but women veterans have a greater physical and mental-health disease burden. Recent research indicates that 31 percent of women veterans carry both medical and mental-health diagnoses, compared to 24 percent of male veterans.[8] While the Veterans Health Administration has made tremendous progress in providing health care for women, it remains underequipped to provide comprehensive care for the surge of women veterans coming to Veterans Affairs clinics and hospitals with their unique health care needs.[9]

The bottom line is that while women are playing increasingly substantial roles in today's military, some women's trajectories toward career and

Kristy Richardson, an Air Force veteran living in Pittsburgh, Pennsylvania, is transitioning back into civilian life. She suffers from PTSD from her experiences in the military. {MELISSA FARLOW}

life success are being thwarted by the stressors of military service and by sexual victimization. Great strides have been made toward ending homelessness and providing high-quality health care for women vets. But given the pervasiveness of sexual violence in the military and society at large, eradicating it—and the systemic and cultural factors that perpetuate it—will be no easy task. Leaders in the Departments of Defense and Veterans Affairs have launched initiatives to mitigate the staggering rate of military sexual trauma. They are committed to ensuring that military service is a path to empowerment and economic stability for our nation's veterans, regardless of gender.

ENDNOTES

1   Women Veterans Task Force, *Strategies for Serving Our Women Veterans* (U.S. Department of Veterans Affairs, 2012), available at http://webcache.googleusercontent.com/search?q=cache:ffVPbiefkdYJ:www.va.gov/opa/publications/draft_2012_women-veterans_strategicplan.pdf+&cd=1&hl=en&ct=clnk&gl=us&client=firefox-a.

2   Jessica A. Turchik and Susan M. Wilson, "Sexual Assault in the U.S. Military: A Review of the Literature and Recommendations for the Future," *United States Aggression and Violent Behavior* 15 (1) (2010): 267–277, available at http://www.researchgate.net/publication/222606398_Sexual_assault_in_the_U.S._military_A_review_of_the_literature_and_recommendations_for_the_future.

3   Donna L. Washington and others, "Risk Factors for Homelessness among Women Veterans," *Journal of Health Care for the Poor and Underserved* 21 (1) (2010): 82–91, available at http://bpwfoundation.org/documents/uploads/Washington_JHCPU_2010_corrected.pdf; Katherine M. Skinner and others, "The Prevalence of Military Sexual Assault among

Female Veterans' Administration Outpatients," *Journal of Interpersonal Violence* 15 (3) (2000): 291–310, available at http://jiv.sagepub.com/content/15/3/291.short; A.G. Sadler and others, "Health-Related Consequences of Physical and Sexual Violence: Women in the Military," *Obstetrics and Gynecology* 96 (3) (2000): 473–480, available at http://www.ncbi.nlm.nih.gov/pubmed/10960645; S.M. Frayne and others, "Medical Profile of Women Veterans Administration Outpatients Who Report a History of Sexual Assault Occurring While in the Military," *Journal of Women's Health & Gender-Based Medicine* 8 (6) (1999): 835–845, available at http://www.ncbi.nlm.nih.gov/pubmed/10495264; S.G. Haskell and others, "The Association of Sexual Trauma with Persistent Pain in a Sample of Women Veterans Receiving Primary Care," *Pain Medicine* 9 (6) (2008): 710–717, available at http://www.ncbi.nlm.nih.gov/pubmed/18565005; U.A. Kelly and others, "More than Military Sexual Trauma: Interpersonal Violence, PTSD, and Mental Health in Women Veterans," *Research in Nursing and Health* 34 (6) (2011): 457–467, available at http://www.ncbi.nlm.nih.gov/pubmed/21898452; Alina Suris and Lisa Lind, "Military Sexual Trauma: A Review of Prevalence and Associated Health Consequences in Veterans," *Trauma Violence and Abuse* 9 (4) (2008): 250–269, available at http://tva.sagepub.com/content/9/4/250.

4   Sexual Assault Prevention and Response Office, *Department of Defense Annual Report on Sexual Assault in the Military: Fiscal Year 2012* (U.S. Department of Defense, 2013), available at http://www.sapr.mil/index.php/annual-reports.

5   U.S. Bureau of Labor Statistics, *Employment Situation of Veterans—2012* (U.S. Department of Labor, 2013).

6   Stacy Vasquez, "Homelessness among Women Veterans" (U.S. Department of Veterans Affairs, 2011), available at http://www.va.gov/WOMENVET/2011Summit/VasquezFINAL.pdf.

7   Kathryn E. Kanzler, Amanda C. McCorkindale, and Laura J. Kanzler, "U.S. Military Women and Divorce: Separating the Issues," *Journal of Feminist Family Therapy* 23 (1) (2011): 250–262, available at http://www.tandfonline.com/doi/abs/10.1080/08952833.2011.604866#preview; A.E. Street, D. Vogt, and L. Dutra, "A New Generation of Women Veterans: Stressors Faced by Women Deployed to Iraq and Afghanistan," *Clinical Psychology Review* 29 (8) (2009): 685–694, available at www.ncbi.nlm.nih.gov/pubmed/19766368.

8   Women Veterans Task Force, *Strategies for Serving Our Women Veterans*.

9   Ibid.

Human Trafficking and Slavery in the United States: 'You Don't See the Chains'

By JADA PINKETT SMITH, *actress, director, producer, businesswoman, and founder of Don't Sell Bodies, an organization dedicated to ending human trafficking*

When my daughter Willow was just 11 years old, she came to me very disturbed. She had learned about children in Africa who were systematically stolen from their families and forced into military and sexual slavery. She did some research of her own, and what she discovered about trafficking shocked us both.

"Mommy! Did you know there are girls my age who are sex slaves here in our own country?"

No, I did not know—not then. But my child's concern spurred me into education, action, and advocacy.

Human trafficking has always seemed like a foreign issue, an issue that happens "over there." I know I wasn't alone in thinking that the problem existed only in impoverished areas of the developing world. But this is not a foreign issue. This is a global issue. And my daughter was right: More than 150 years after President Abraham Lincoln signed the Emancipation Proclamation abolishing slavery in this country, it is still a plague in poor and powerless communities within our borders.

Accurate statistics are hard to come by, but it's estimated that 40,000 people—most of them women and children—are enslaved in our country at any one time. They are victims of sex trafficking, child sex trafficking, forced labor, child labor trafficking, and other forms of involuntary servitude.[1] Human bodies can be sold over and over again to multiple buyers a day. This is one of the reasons why the selling of human beings surpassed the selling of firearms to become the second-largest global criminal enterprise after drugs.[2] According to our Department of State, "The United States is a source, transit, and destination country for men, women, and children—both U.S. citizens and foreign nationals—subjected to forced labor, debt bondage, involuntary servitude, and sex trafficking."[3]

Although no class or race is immune, growing poverty in the United States plays a role in creating the vulnerability that feeds human trafficking here. Pressures and stresses on poor families can lead children to settings such as the foster care system, where they often fall through the cracks. Research consistently shows that girls who "run from their homes, group homes, foster homes, or treatment centers, are at great risk of being targeted by a [trafficker] and becoming exploited."[4]

Today, victims of sex slavery, labor trafficking, and other forms of involuntary servitude are held in the shadows of American towns and cities. Instead of being seen as victims, they often face indifference or hostility from a legal system that treats them as willing perpetrators of prostitution or illegal immigration. They often are not regarded as slaves, because you don't see the chains. These days, steel chains and shackles have been replaced by psychological manipulation and exploitation. Most traffickers bind their slaves using fear, intimidation, violence, and false promises of love, hope, or opportunity to keep their victims cooperative, dependent, and fearful.

does not belong. . . . Many times there were no walls, no doors, no locks holding me back from running, but a child at someone else's mercy, whether that someone is a man, a woman, a relative or a stranger, is in a prison.[5]

We are horrified when we hear these kinds of stories, but we have to ask ourselves: What is it that allows such slavery to take root and flourish in our society?

Look at our history. Ingrained racism dehumanized blacks, thereby legitimizing and justifying

---

Most traffickers bind their slaves using fear, intimidation, violence, and false promises of love, hope, or opportunity to keep their victims cooperative, dependent, and fearful.

My advocacy has introduced me to survivors with experiences as diverse as their backgrounds. These survivors have lived the terrors of modern-day slavery. I call them "survivor soldiers," and they are the heartbeat of the anti-trafficking movement. Their individual experiences of battle and victory provide a window into the tenacity of the human spirit.

Carissa Phelps was 12 years old when she was recruited into trafficking. After she ran away from juvenile hall, she lived on the streets. She says:

When we call sexual exploitation of youth "prostitution" we put all the blame where it

African slavery in the United States for 250 years. During World War II, Japanese Americans were rounded up and thrown into internment camps just because of their ethnicity. Mexican farm workers toiled under slave-labor conditions until the late 1970s. Native Americans have been marginalized and stigmatized throughout our history.

And today? Today, the "chains" still bind the disenfranchised in our nation. The objectification of individuals allows them to be used and thrown away. They do not matter, so *it* does not matter. I am here today to tell you that they *do indeed matter*.

Activists around the world join Jada Pinkett-Smith in speaking out against human trafficking. Somaly Mam, seen here speaking at the 2009 Women's Conference, is a survivor and a champion for those affected by sex slavery.
{COURTESY A WOMAN'S NATION}

Is it a reach to say that a culture where the haves are seen as "better" than the have-nots—where the poor are not just unfortunate, but blamed for it—is a culture that can turn a blind eye when people are abused? I don't believe that it is a stretch to say that a culture that tolerates the objectification of women and girls for sexual gratification is a culture that can give rise to the dehumanization, exploitation, and enslavement of girls and women. If we want to break this vicious cycle, it is our duty to re-examine the ways that we love, value, and care for one another. If we don't teach our children that they are worth more, even if they are in families struggling financially, then they will certainly never expect more.

I am proud to say that as a country, we have made significant progress. The Trafficking Victims Protection Act has been reauthorized, and the Violence Against Women Act has passed. President Barack Obama signed an executive order making U.S. government contractors operating overseas responsible for any subcontractors that use forced labor and abuse to get their work done cheaply. These are magnificent strides on the road to change and improvement, but we have a long way to go.

ENDNOTES

1 Kevin Bales, Zoe Trodd, and Alex Kent Williamson, *Modern Slavery: The Secret World of 27 Million People* (Oxford: Oneworld Publications, 2009).

2 The United Nations Office on Drugs and Crime, "Transnational Organized Crime: The Globalized Illegal Economy," available at http://www.unodc.org/toc/en/crimes/organized-crime.html (last accessed September 2013).

3 Office to Monitor and Combat Trafficking in Persons, *Trafficking in Persons Report 2012* (U.S. Department of State, 2012), p. 359, available at http://www.state.gov/documents/organization/192598.pdf.

4 Heather J. Clawson and others, "Human Trafficking Into and Within the United States: A Review of the Literature" (Washington: U.S. Department of Health and Human Services, 2009), available at http://aspe.hhs.gov/hsp/07/humantrafficking/litrev/.

5 Carissa Phelps, "How I Came to Talk About My Abuse," The Huffington Post Blog, July 19, 2012, available at http://www.huffingtonpost.com/carissa-phelps/child-abuse-runaway-girl_b_1686791.html.

Britani's Story

By BRITANI HOOD-MONGAR, a single mother of 2-year-old twins. Her job as a school cafeteria worker runs only through the school year, and she must find other work during the offseason. She shares an apartment with her kids and her mother.

I'm a mother of 2-year-old twin girls. I was 15 when I started dating their dad. Having not grown up with a dad, it was the only love from a man that I knew. We were together for almost six years, got engaged, and as soon as we found out that I was pregnant, he left.

He actually called the girls yesterday to wish them happy birthday. He doesn't pay me child support—nothing. I've told him "As long as you have a relationship with the girls, you don't have to. I'll make sure the girls are okay." I don't want my girls growing up thinking it's their fault that their dad's not in their life, because they had nothing to do with it.

I'm not going to let my kids know that we are struggling every day. I just want to make sure they are happy and be able to give them love. I can't give the love that a father can give, because I don't know it.

The kids feed off of it. When you feel like you're struggling and you have all this baggage, just to smile in front of your kids makes a big difference. Because when I'm down, I can definitely see their attitude change. You know, they might be 2 years old, but they can definitely feel: "Is mommy okay?" When I feel like "Am I going to make rent?" they get anxious. You can definitely tell, because those nights, they don't sleep.

I get government assistance. I get food stamps. At first I didn't want to because of the stereotypes people have and because of my pride and because my ego was too big. But I had to put that aside to take care of my girls. I make $8.75 an hour, and I'm lucky to get 30 hours a week. I'm a hardworking woman, but assistance is something that I need. I definitely won't be on it for the rest of my life. I don't want my girls to grow up and believe you have to have help in order to do it.

The Nation
Reimagined

In the previous chapters we looked at why 42 million women are struggling to make ends meet even though they are working hard as breadwinners and caregivers. Three major cultural and economic changes over the past 50 years—in the workforce, in our family structure, and in the necessity for higher education—have steadily pushed women to the brink.

Is this our vision of America—where one in three women struggles financially? We think it is not. We argue for a Woman's Nation Reimagined, a nation with a modern social architecture designed to make individuals, businesses, and government stronger, more innovative, and better adapted to the realities of America's working and caregiving women.

Take a look.

BARBARA KINNEY

A New America that Cares

By Anne-Marie Slaughter

STUNNING FACT

Women do most of the care work in families; they care for children, the elderly, the sick, and the disabled. According to the U.S. Census Bureau, women devote more than 110 million hours a year to unpaid interactive child care, more than double the hours men spend on child care.

Throughout its history, America has continued to reinvent itself, each time producing a better society for more of us than the one that preceded it. Reconstruction improved on the pre–Civil War republic. The New Deal created a "new America" that was a great improvement on the Gilded Age America. The civil rights movement generated legislation guaranteeing the equality promised in the Constitution and the Declaration of Independence.

This constant reinvention is fueled by what I call "the idea that is America"—the principles of liberty, democracy, equality, justice, tolerance, humility, and faith on which our country was founded. As I've written, our history is a continual "process of trying to live up to our ideals, falling short, succeeding in some places, and trying again in others."[1]

The next period of American renewal cannot come fast enough. The gap between the richest and poorest Americans is growing wider. In fact, the top 10 percent took in more than half of all income in 2012, the highest share since the data series started.[2] Yet the United States has among the highest child poverty rates of any developed economy. We spend more but get less for our health care and education dollars than Canada, the United Kingdom, South Korea, and other peer nations. We are falling behind on these important measures of human progress in the world—but even more important, we are falling behind in terms of our ability to live up to our own values.

My personal vision is of a renewed America that cares—both about and for its people.

This will require a shift. Right now, we are a nation that embraces and thrives on competition, from sports teams to small businesses to Silicon Valley. But in the competition paradigm, success is defined in terms of *who wins,* typically through a combination of talent, luck, and working harder and longer than anyone else. In this paradigm, if everyone is pursuing self-interest and striving to beat out competitors to get to the top, society as a whole will benefit.

I'm all for competition—in its place. But we have lost sight of the care paradigm, which is the necessary complement to competition. As the great capitalist and philanthropist Bill Gates put it, "the two great forces of human nature are self-interest and caring for others."

The care paradigm starts from the premise that human beings cannot survive alone. Our progress as a species flows from our identity as social animals, connected to one another through ties of love, kinship, and clanship. Success is defined not as individual victory but as group progress, whether the group is family, clan, community, company, or any particular subdivision of society. In the care paradigm, the individual does not disappear; the progress of the group advances the individual as well. All members of the group also have the security of knowing that whether they are young or old, ill or weak, they will be cared for in their turn. So caring is part and parcel of building community.

An America that puts an equal emphasis on care and competition would be a very different place. We would invest in a national infrastructure of care in the same way that we invest in the infrastructure of capitalism. We would institute:

• High-quality and affordable child care and elder care facilities
• Higher wages and training for paid caregivers
• Support structures to allow elders to live at home longer
• Paid family and medical leave for women and men

• Flexible work arrangements and career life cycles to give breadwinners who are also caregivers equal opportunity to advance over the course of their careers
• Financial and social support for single parents
• Far greater social esteem for the "caring" professions

In short, we would build a social infrastructure that allows people to care for one another, in the same way we provide the basic physical infrastructure that allows them to compete.

All this talk of an America that cares is not pining for Neverland, but rather a call to recommit to a communal strand that runs through our history and our civic mythology. Frontier stories of barn-raisings and quilting bees are just as celebrated as Wild West shoot-outs between the sheriff and the outlaw. Nineteenth-century French historian Alexis de Tocqueville focused less on America's rugged individualism than on our remarkable social capital—the civic associations we created for every purpose imaginable, or what he called our "habits of the heart."

Coming together to advance a common purpose creates the bonds of trust and empathy that make us not just statistics and stereotypes, but *visible* to each other as individual human beings. It is then far harder *not* to care. This is the same social capital and cohesion that is the foundation of successful democracy and the indispensable precondition for achieving America's founding credo of equality.

We are wired for it. Thirty years ago, psychologist Carol Gilligan (see her essay in this report) studied adolescent girls and identified in them an "ethic of care"— a dimension of human nature every bit as elemental as an "ethic of justice." It turns out that "You don't care!" is just as much a part of who we are as "That's not fair!" Gilligan says that "given that children are less powerful than adults and rely on [adult] care for survival, concerns about justice and care are built into the human life cycle. The potential for oppression (using power unfairly) and for abandonment (acting carelessly) inheres in relationships."[3]

This means that not being cared for is just as much a marker of inequality as being discriminated against. *Both* conditions are ways that those with power can enforce inequality against those without power—the young, the old, the sick, the disabled, the different, the structurally disadvantaged. "You don't care" can mean

"You don't see me or hear me; you don't give me equal regard." But it can also mean "You don't give me what I need to survive and thrive on an equal basis with my fellow citizens."

I imagine a new America in which citizens recognize that providers of physical, intellectual, emotional, and spiritual care are as indispensable to our society and our economy as providers of income. If we truly valued breadwinning and caregiving equally—as equal components of the American promise of equal opportunity—then we would value male caregivers as much as we value female breadwinners and every permutation and combination in between. But we would also recognize that single parents—who must be sole breadwinners *and* caregivers in families that often include elder relatives, as well as children—need special help and support. We would embrace marriage for everyone and support policies that would strengthen long-term commitments among family members, however these families might be constructed.

Even as we strive for equality in this next era of American renewal, we must also redefine and reprioritize the pursuit of happiness, the most personal of America's founding values. Happiness can certainly be achieved through individual achievement, through winning the competition. But it is equally reached through a web of strong and fulfilling relationships—the warp and woof of connectedness and care. When we use solitary confinement as one of our most severe forms of punishment, we recognize the equation between isolation and *unhappiness*.

The biggest questions in 21st century America will be: "Who cares?" and then, "If we do not care for others, who will care for us?" Let us answer those questions by reinventing ourselves yet again—competing fiercely, but caring deeply, too.

THINK ABOUT THIS

Not being cared for is just as much a marker of inequality as being discriminated against. Both conditions are ways that those with power can enforce inequality against those without power—the young, the old, the sick, the disabled, the different, the structurally disadvantaged.

Sabrina Jenkins visits her 95-year-old great aunt, Carolia Gilliard, at her home in Awendaw, South Carolina. Sabrina cares for her aging relatives as much as possible. {CALLIE SHELL}

ENDNOTES

1   Anne-Marie Slaughter, *The Idea that Is America: Keeping Faith with Our Values in a Dangerous World* (New York: Basic Books, 2007).

2   Emmanuel Saez, "Report Striking It Richer: The Evolution of Top Incomes in the United States" (Berkeley: University of California, 2013).

3   Carol Gilligan, *Joining the Resistance* (Cambridge, MA: Policy Press, 2011).

America's Promise, One Woman at a Time

By MARIANNE COOPER, Ph.D., Sociologist at Clayman Institute for Gender Research, Stanford

The Shriver Report challenged a leading center for women's studies, Stanford University's Clayman Institute for Gender Research, to look 20 years into the future and present us with a real-life rendering of the potential results of the recommendations proposed in this report.

Could our society be so thoroughly reimagined?

Fundamental change is possible. Women have shown that they can dramatically transform our society in a very short period of time.

There is no question that we can harness our power together to achieve what Anne-Marie Slaughter describes as "a new America"—where we truly value breadwinning and caregiving equally and we provide help and support where families, and especially single parents, need it.

The following is one positive vision of a nation reimagined.

June 17, 2034
Graduation ceremony

Antonia Jarvis has been looking forward to this day for a long time. At 26 years old, she is older than most of the other students in the packed auditorium, but that doesn't bother her. She knew with everything on her plate—her part-time job, her now 6-year-old son, and her coursework—that it would take her a bit longer to finish college. But her day is finally here. Not only is she receiving her degree today, but she is also embarking on a promising career in software security.

There was a time in Antonia's life when this day seemed out of reach. At the age of 20, she gave birth to her son, Jimmy. She never thought she would become a single mother. But when her relationship with her boyfriend fell apart a few months after she learned she was pregnant, Antonia was left to face early parenthood alone. Antonia worried about her ability to be the sole provider for her child. Her own mother, Dolores, had given birth to Antonia when she was just 19 years old. After watching Dolores struggle with the difficulties of being a single parent, Antonia was fearful about what she was up against.

Today, on her graduation day, Antonia is reflecting back on the past several years, and how her life has turned out so differently than that of her mother. She is grateful for the choices she has been able to make and that it has been possible for her to finish school and keep working, unlike her mom. Back in 2008, Dolores was fired from her job for missing too much work when Antonia was born. Subsequently, Dolores struggled to find jobs with enough flexibility to care for her daughter and adequate pay to afford good day care. As a result, Dolores moved from one low-paying job to the next, having to leave or getting fired when the need to care for Antonia came into conflict with her ability to work. With her time and energy devoted to raising her child amid such great economic insecurity, pursuing her own educational goals became impossible.

Fortunately, Antonia was spared from facing the same set of insurmountable hurdles her mother faced. And today she has many people to thank for this—people looking on from the audience, smiling proudly at her. There is Kelly, her community college advisor; Kevin, her boss; Professor Clark, her mentor; and, of course, Antonia's mom, Dolores, holding Jimmy on her lap.

Kelly, Antonia's advisor at Glenwood Community College, was instrumental in keeping Antonia on track to achieve her dreams. Despite Antonia's concern that having a child would prevent her from continuing on with her studies, Kelly assured her that she would be able to complete her education. Kelly provided Antonia with information about all of the benefits, programs, and services she was eligible for, including 12 weeks of paid family leave; paid sick days; affordable, 24-hour child care; and subsidized, high-quality preschool. Kelly helped Antonia begin to see that she could continue with her education while making sure Jimmy had quality care and proper early education as well. Armed with all of this information, Antonia's worries subsided. Her stress level declined, she began to sleep easier, and, importantly, she began to see a path forward—she started to see how she could hold onto her dream of attending college and be a single parent.

With Kelly's help, Antonia found Capital Day Care—an affordable and flexible facility within walking distance from campus. Antonia was impressed the first time she visited the center. Her tour revealed competent and enthusiastic teachers, stimulating and fun games for the children, and an accommodating schedule that proved Capital Day Care understood the difficult balancing act of being a working—and studying—mom. And, most important, Jimmy soon loved it there and began to thrive under the center's care.

Antonia's optimism about her future was also fueled by her boss, Kevin, who is now sitting alongside some of Antonia's co-workers at her ceremony. Since high school, Antonia has worked for Kevin at a local retail outlet of a national clothing chain; she always loved the company and knew it was supportive. In fact, when she was in high school, the company addressed its high turnover rate by creating a more effective and efficient scheduling system. All employees were guaranteed a minimum number of work hours per week with days and times agreed upon a month in advance. The company also used a tracking system that allowed employees to enter in their extra availability, making it easier for managers to call in additional help, or for employees to swap shifts.

Although Antonia had always appreciated her company's efforts to work with employees' scheduling needs, she was anxious about how she would combine her job and her studies with her new role as a mom. But when Antonia explained her situation to Kevin, they worked together to find a solution; Kevin created a set weekly schedule with a minimum of 25 hours a week for when she returned from maternity leave. Antonia can now look back and smile, recalling the relief she felt knowing she would continue to have a stable job with a predictable schedule so she could plan for her child care needs in advance.

Kevin also assured Antonia that she had health care options available that would ensure a healthy pregnancy and delivery. He put Antonia in touch with a representative from a health care company, who provided her with information about her coverage options and doctors in her area.

After Jimmy was born, Antonia's set work hours allowed her to sign up for college classes around her work schedule in the late afternoons and evenings, keeping her on track for graduation. On weeks where she was able to work more, she picked up extra shifts to earn more money. On nights when she needed extra hours to study, or days when she wanted to spend more time with Jimmy, she could often find someone to cover her shift.

While money was tight, and the many demands on her made her feel a bit overwhelmed at times, Antonia knew she was moving forward with her goals. After three years at Glenwood Community College, Antonia transferred to an in-state university with a significant scholarship for the excellent grades she had achieved. At work, her responsibilities increased, as did her pay. Kevin noticed Antonia had a knack for improving the design of the software systems the company used for tracking merchandise and coordinating schedules, and suggested Antonia consider a career in software design. It had never occurred to her to pursue something technical, but she took some classes, loved the work—and was good at it—and eventually declared a major in computer systems analysis.

Soon after choosing her new path, Antonia met Professor Clark, who taught COMP 300: Information and Software Security. Professor Clark was impressed by Antonia's quick wit, ability to see problems and come up with novel solutions, and her obvious passion for the subject. Professor Clark recommended Antonia for a government fellowship providing students with a valuable apprenticeship experience. Antonia loved the idea of on-the-job training, which would enable her to apply her skills in a real-world setting. She applied and received the fellowship, set to begin one month from today.

As Antonia is listening to the graduation speakers, she is thinking about all of the things that enabled her to get to this day: the support of her employer; the day care that served as a second home for her son; the policies and benefits that enabled her to provide her son with the care and education he deserves; her love for Jimmy, which inspired her to create a better life for him; and her own persistence in the face of challenges. After the speeches come to an end, the dean pauses before handing out the diplomas; this is the precise moment Antonia has been waiting for. "Stand up," he says, "if you are the first person in your family to graduate from college." As these words hang in the air, Antonia Jarvis plants her feet firmly on the floor and stands up. With arms outstretched as if to take in all 30 students who stood up, the dean exclaims, "Congratulations! You are the American Dream. You are America's promise."

This is a fictional rendering of what life could be like 20 years from now for one woman in America. All characters appearing in this work are fictitious. Any resemblance to real persons, living or dead, is purely coincidental. The names of businesses and institutions are also fictitious.

HOW WE PUSH BACK

We can reinvent our nation, producing a better society for more of us and greatly improving the quality of life for millions of American families.

Some change will require government involvement, some of it does not. Some of our solutions involve collective actions, and some of them require individuals to act.

There is no silver bullet to bring about a Nation Reimagined. It will take public, private, and personal solutions.

Take a look.

BARBARA KINNEY

Kristy Richardson leaves the Veterans Leadership Program of Western Pennsylvania, an organization helping her return to life at home after multiple tours abroad. The leadership role she held in the military is one of her proudest achievements. {MELISSA FARLOW}

Putting Women at the Center of Policymaking

By Melissa Boteach and Shawn Fremstad

STUNNING FACT

If women working full time, year round, were paid the same for their work as comparable men, we would cut the poverty rate for working women and their families in half.

In the 50 years since President Lyndon Johnson issued his War on Poverty declaration, much has changed for women and families. The share of young women in college has doubled, with women's attendance rates surpassing men's since the late 1980s. The share of women who are both breadwinners and caregivers has steadily increased. The gender wage gap has narrowed considerably, though a substantial gap still remains. And the value of the minimum wage, both in inflation-adjusted terms and as a percentage of the average wage, has declined.

Public policies have played an important role in all of these trends, along with cultural, technological, and social changes. Still, our public policies haven't adjusted to a world in which nearly two-thirds of mothers are primary or co-breadwinners. The consequences have been particularly troubling for low-income mothers, who are much less likely to receive decent wages and family-friendly benefits from their employers than other working moms.

Britani Hood-Mongar works in the cafeteria at an elementary school in Chattanooga, Tennessee. Because she is considered a contractor, she is not eligible for benefits like paid sick leave or family leave. {BARBARA KINNEY}

We need new policy prescriptions for a new time—ones that will benefit these women and strengthen our economy as well.

To enact these new policies, we must first ask a game-changing question: How do we put women and their families at the center of our public policymaking? In a woman's nation, every woman who wants to work should be able to join the labor force, and women should earn equal pay to their male counterparts. Unfortunately, we are still far from achieving these goals.

Currently, 70.5 percent of working-age women participate in the labor force compared to 83.1 percent of working-age men.[1] While some women may choose not to work, the lack of policies to help families manage conflicts between work and family takes the choice of working away from too many women. In fact, between 1990 and 2010, the United States dropped from 6th to 17th in female labor force participation among 22 developed countries. More than a quarter of our relative drop was attributable to the fact that other developed countries expanded "family-friendly" policies such as parental leave, while the United States largely stagnated in enacting policies to help women balance the demands of work and care.[2]

As we outline throughout our report, women in the labor force face a persistent wage gap that undermines their economic security, earning 77 cents for every dollar earned by men. As economists Heidi Hartmann and Jeffrey Hayes of the Institute for Women's Policy Research have found, if women working full time, year round were paid the same for their work as comparable men, they would earn $6,250 more a year on average. This increased income would cut the poverty rate for working women and their families in half. Of the 5.8 million working women living below the poverty line, just over 3 million would be raised above it. And the U.S. gross domestic product would increase by 2.9 percent, or $450 billion, an amount roughly equal in size to Virginia's economy. The economic benefits could not be clearer.

With so much at stake, how do we remove barriers for women and unleash their economic potential?

Some key public solutions could help millions of women and their families join the middle class and strengthen the nation's economy. It is essential to remember that today's women are increasingly both caregivers and breadwinners, and they face serious trade-offs in both of these roles. To help women manage their care responsibilities in a way that bolsters their potential as breadwinners, we need to ensure that workers at all income levels have access to paid time off as well as access to affordable and high-quality child care and preschool—like nearly all other developed nations. We also need to ensure that women get fair and equal pay, and that they have access to the public supports and educational opportunities they need to put themselves on a stable path to middle-class economic security.

RECOGNIZING CARE

Women have long performed, without pay, the central human work of caring for children, the sick, and the elderly. And as Riane Eisler and Kimberly Otis note in Heather Boushey's chapter, to this day, the economic value of this work largely goes unrecognized. Care work, for example, is only counted toward GDP when it is provided for pay.[3]

As women have joined the workforce in increasing numbers, they have turned to both formal and informal care providers, often at considerable expense. At the same time, only so much of parents' care responsibilities can be—or should be—outsourced. Even with affordable child care, a working parent still needs to take time off to care for a sick child. And taking family leave to care for a new infant should be encouraged and supported. Yet, for the most part, our public policies don't recognize the impact these care responsibilities have on workers.

OFFERING PAID FAMILY LEAVE INSURANCE

Fifty years ago, about half of all married mothers were "stay-at-home" moms who weren't in the labor force at all.[4] Today, only one-fifth of married moms stay at home, and a greater share of all mothers are unmarried and in the labor force. As a result, most mothers today have to balance their caregiving roles with their breadwinning ones.

Nationwide only about 12 percent of American workers have access to paid family leave through their employers to care for a new child or seriously ill family member.

Many well-paid professionals and managers have paid family leave benefits that allow them to take time off to meet these family responsibilities, while still meeting their breadwinning responsibilities. And three states—California, New Jersey, and Rhode Island—operate paid family leave insurance programs.

California's program, for example, effectively provides up to six weeks of partial wage replacement per year for covered workers to care for a new child or a seriously ill family member. For mothers, these benefits are in addition to the 10 to 12 weeks of partial wage replacement for covered pregnant and postpartum workers under California's temporary disability insurance program.[5]

But nationwide, only about 12 percent of American workers have access to paid family leave through their employers to care for a new child or seriously ill family member.[6] Workers without paid family leave cobble together paid sick days or vacation days—which are typically inadequate, if available at all—or they take unpaid leave if they can afford it, or leave their jobs altogether. Either caregiving comes at the expense of breadwinning or the other way around.

Paid family leave for the price of a cup of coffee

Legislation recently introduced in the U.S. Congress, and modeled on the existing state family leave programs, would enable more breadwinners to accrue paid family leave to help balance their work and care responsibilities. The Family and Medical Insurance Leave Act, or FAMILY Act, is a proposed social insurance program that would give all workers the ability to earn up to 12 weeks of paid leave to care for a new child, a seriously ill family member, or the worker's own serious illness. Benefits would equal two-thirds of a worker's typical wages up to a capped amount.

The program would be funded by a small increase in the payroll tax that would be shared by employers and employees. The cost for the average full-time worker earning the median hourly wage would be about $1.50 per week, less than a small cup of coffee at Starbucks.[7]

Under the proposed legislation, a worker's eligibility for leave would depend on whether he or she has sufficient past work history, with the amount of past work required increasing with age. For instance, a new parent under age 24 would need to have worked in at least six calendar quarters in the past three years to be eligible, while one between the ages of 24 and 30 would need to have worked in at least half of the calendar quarters between age 21 and their leave date.

Workers in poorly compensated jobs, who are disproportionately women on the financial brink, bear the greatest financial burdens and are the least likely to have paid time off of any sort. Additionally, the lack of paid leave likely contributes to the gender gaps in both pay and employment.

A growing body of research suggests that allowing all workers to earn paid family leave would have long-term benefits, beyond the partial replacement of earnings it provides for workers, their families, and the overall economy. Most important, research suggests that paid family leave will increase the employment of women on the brink who are caregivers, mostly by increasing the share of women who will return to the same employer after taking leave.[8]

Case in point: Comparing outcomes for working women who took paid leave after a child's birth with those of new mothers who did not, Rutgers University researchers have found that the women taking paid leave were more likely to be working 9 to 12 months after a child's birth, more likely to report wage increases in the year following a child's birth, and less likely to receive public assistance.[9]

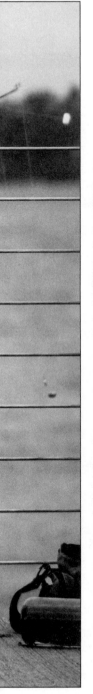

All forms of the modern American family could benefit from paid family leave. Providing paid sick days would also have broad public health benefits. {BARBARA KINNEY (L), JAN SONNEMAIR (R1), BARBARA RIES (R2)}

By making the workplace more family friendly, a national paid family leave program will help close the gender gaps in employment and wages, while bolstering women's long-term economic security. New mothers and family caregivers who return to work after their leave, instead of dropping out of the labor force for longer periods of time, will boost their lifetime earnings, be more likely to earn further raises and promotions, and accumulate greater retirement savings through Social Security.

In today's world, where more mothers work than stay home, paid family leave's time has come. It is one of the most effective ways the government can adapt to the realities of today's families and one of the surest ways to increase the economic stability of women on the brink.

PROVIDING PAID SICK DAYS

Paid family leave is designed to help workers meet caregiving responsibilities that typically last weeks. But, of course, workers also need time to address short-term health and medical issues: a child home from school with the flu, an elderly parent's medical emergency, or their own illness.

Unfortunately, 39 percent of private-sector workers do not have a single paid sick day.[10] Even worse, 71 percent of private-sector workers in low-wage jobs—which are disproportionately held by women—go without any paid sick days.[11] Working caregivers without paid sick days often have to make lose-lose choices: send a child to day care with the flu or sacrifice a day's wages that were going to pay for this week's groceries? Go into work with a contagious cold, or risk losing the job altogether in this tough economy?

A whopping 87 percent of women on the brink—and 96 percent of single mothers —said paid sick days would be "very useful" to them; our poll found it to be the number one policy they thought would help them—even more than an increase in wages or benefits.

The solution is simple: a basic national standard that enables workers to earn paid, job-protected sick days. One national proposal, the Healthy Families Act introduced in Congress in 2013, would ensure that workers in businesses with 15 or more employees are able to earn one hour of paid sick leave for every 30 hours worked, up to seven days annually.[13]

There is growing momentum for this type of change. In 2012, Connecticut became the first state to adopt a law that allows a substantial share of workers to earn paid sick days. And in 2013, Portland, Oregon, and New York City became the fourth and fifth major cities to adopt paid sick days laws, joining San Francisco, Seattle, and Washington, D.C.

Typically, these laws allow workers to earn five or more days of paid sick leave annually. In San Francisco, for example, workers earn one hour of paid sick leave for every 30 hours worked, up to nine days annually, or five days if they work for employers with 10 or fewer employees.

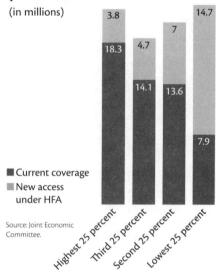

FIGURE 1

Number of workers who would gain paid sick days under Healthy Families Act, by wage percentile

(in millions)

■ Current coverage
■ New access under HFA

Source: Joint Economic Committee.

Sick and fired: Elose's story

Elose worked as a dishwasher in a Miami restaurant to support her teenage son and relatives living back in her home country of Haiti. One day, Elose's boss told her to hurry and do the job as fast as she possibly could. In her rush around the kitchen, she slammed her hand in the dishwasher door, injuring herself badly.

She went to the clinic to get treated, but as Elose notes, when she returned, "Without even asking me how I was and without explanation, my boss told me that I no longer had my job at the restaurant. I was in shock. I went home sick for getting hurt on the job, and was

fired when I returned with a doctor's note. . . . Getting fired was devastating."

Elose says this wasn't just her problem. At the restaurant where she worked, "I noticed many people would come to work sick because when calling in sick the boss would say they'd need to come in anyway."

Elose and her colleagues were vulnerable because they, like 71 percent of private-sector workers in low-wage jobs, had no job-protected paid sick days.[12]

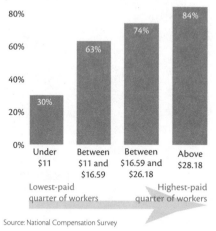

FIGURE 2

Share of workers with access to paid sick leave, by wage percentile

Source: National Compensation Survey

As with paid family leave, a national standard for paid sick leave would increase the financial security of the millions of workers currently unable to take paid time off to care for a sick child or themselves when ill. Low-income, working women, who are constantly juggling their caregiving and breadwinning roles, would be among those helped the most. According to the Joint Economic Committee of Congress, of the roughly 30 million additional workers who would have access to paid sick leave under the Healthy Families Act, nearly half are working in jobs that pay less than $11.50 an hour.[14]

In addition, providing paid sick days would have broad public health benefits. Nobody wants a cook with a bad case of the flu preparing his or her lunch, or a child care worker with a contagious illness taking care of his or her child. But millions of workers in these and similar industries involving direct interpersonal contact go without paid sick days, including the workers in the Miami restaurant where Elose worked[15] (see text box). And low pay in these same jobs likely limits the extent to which many sick workers can take unpaid time off.

A national standard, like the one in the Healthy Families Act, would ensure that the vast majority of these workers are able to earn paid sick leave, allowing them to stay home when it's the best thing for their health and yours.

ENSURING ACCESS TO QUALITY PRESCHOOL AND CHILD CARE

There are 7.6 million U.S. families with children under age 6 living on the financial brink.[16] If more of the mothers in these families were able to work steadily in a decent job, many of them would be able to move away from the brink and toward the middle class.

Low-income mothers are especially in need: quality child care assistance is associated with increased employment and earnings. {BARBARA KINNEY}

Let's look at single mothers. Four out of every five single mothers with young children had incomes that put them on the economic brink in 2012. But when these mothers are able to work full time, year round, they're twice as likely to have incomes that lift them off the brink. While far too many of these working mothers are still struggling to make ends meet, having earnings from a full-time job can make a big difference.[17]

However, to work full time, year round, mothers of young children need child care and preschool options that they can trust and afford. Not surprisingly, considerable economic research shows that receiving child care assistance is associated with increased employment and earnings among low-income mothers.[18] Further, high-quality preschool delivers considerable long-term economic benefits. Jennifer's story (see text box) shows the power of affordable, quality preschool to help mothers work, as well as to improve outcomes for their children, delivering long-term economic benefits.

FIGURE 3

Average yearly costs for center-based care for a 4-year-old in 2011

Mississippi	$3,911
Arkansas	$4,695
Idaho	$5,059
Louisiana	$5,364
Oklahoma	$5,397
South Carolina	$5,455
South Dakota	$5,665
Alabama	$5,668
Kentucky	$5,766
West Virginia	$5,806
Missouri	$5,928
Utah	$5,988
Georgia	$6,062
New Mexico	$6,145
Florida	$6,368
Ohio	$6,376
Nebraska	$6,386
Texas	$6,414
Tennessee	$6,578
North Dakota	$6,807
Arizona	$7,263
Montana	$7,285
Wyoming	$7,316
Nevada	$7,532
Iowa	$7,551
Delaware	$7,592
Hawaii	$7,752
North Carolina	$7,774
Maine	$7,904
Michigan	$7,930
Indiana	$7,975
California	$8,237
Virginia	$8,296
Kansas	$8,305
Washington	$8,320
Oregon	$8,542
Pennsylvania	$8,588
Vermont	$8,758
Alaska	$8,856
Illinois	$8,996
New Jersey	$9,098
Colorado	$9,239
Maryland	$9,278
New Hampshire	$9,541
Wisconsin	$9,588
Rhode Island	$9,932
Minnesota	$10,470
Connecticut	$10,530
New York	$11,585
Massachusetts	$11,669
District of Columbia	$15,437

Source: Child Care Aware of America January 2012 Survey of State Child Care Resource and Referral Networks.

Rigorous studies have found that for every $1 invested in high-quality preschool, we save an average of $7 in future public costs due to reductions in crime and the need for remedial education, and increases in workers' productivity.[19] In our poll, 88 percent of women on the brink said that providing affordable child care to working families would improve the nation's economic security, and 64 percent of them strongly favored it as a government economic policy.

Yet the average market cost of a full-time spot in a child care center for a 4-year-old ranges from $3,911 a year (in Mississippi) to $15,437 a year (in Washington, D.C.).[20] With the majority of working women earning less than $30,000 a year, many families are priced out of quality care, or pay an amount disproportionate to their earnings. Of the 3.13 million working mothers with preschoolers and a family income below 200 percent of the poverty line, just over 1 million make payments for child care. On average, the amount these mothers spend on child care each week is equal to more than one-third of their personal income.[21]

What about the low-income, working mothers of preschoolers who can't afford child care? Most rely on family members and friends to help. After fathers, grandparents play the biggest role, serving as the primary child care providers to nearly 900,000 preschool children of low-income, working moms.[22]

A head start for families: Jennifer's story

When Jennifer's husband lost his welding job during the Great Recession, she started working to help support the family. Unfortunately, the couple, residing in southeast Arkansas, couldn't afford daycare.

Thankfully, the family found the Hamburg Arkansas Better Chance, or ABC, program which received federal funding from several sources, including Head Start. With daycare taken care of, Jennifer's husband was able to take the time to find other employment, and Jennifer could hold down two jobs to help keep the family afloat.

Jennifer writes, "If this ABC program wasn't available, over half of that [income] would've been spent on daycare." The ABC program also helped two of her children with developmental disabilities and emotional and social problems reach critical milestones and make important progress.

Jennifer was one of the lucky ones. Today, only about 18 percent of eligible children receive federally funded child care assistance, and while nationwide preschool enrollment has increased in recent years, the lowest-income children are the least likely to participate in preschool programs.[23]

Existing child care assistance and preschool programs help, but they remain underfunded and a patchwork. Because of insufficient funding, only about 18 percent of eligible children actually receive federally funded child care assistance.[24] Similarly, the Head Start program, which provides early learning opportunities for low-income children, serves just 8 percent of all 3-year-olds and 11 percent of all 4-year-olds, and state preschool programs serve just 28 percent of 4-year-olds and 4 percent of 3-year-olds.[25]

We need to build on these existing systems to enable every child to attend two years of high-quality, full-day preschool. We must ensure that working mothers have affordable, quality child care options for their young children.

In his most recent budget, President Barack Obama took a historic step toward these goals. His Preschool for All initiative would create a new federal-state partnership to substantially expand the availability of high-quality preschool.[26] States would be able to receive federal funding to extend preschool to all 4-year-olds from low- and moderate-income families, and they would have financial incentives to expand access to middle-class families.

In our poll, 88 percent of women on the brink said that providing high-quality, affordable child care to working families would improve the nation's economic security.

We also need to address the "child care cliff" in many states for parents who receive child care assistance; when a parent's earnings increase, even a bit, she may find herself over an income threshold and no longer eligible for child care assistance. This income limit or cliff can mean that to pay for child care, a working parent ends up with considerably less take-home pay despite getting a raise or working more hours. Some struggling single parents turn down raises or promotions, and even ask for pay cuts, to avoid going off the cliff.[27]

To address these problems, we need to increase our investment in the Child Care and Development Fund, the primary source of federal funding for child care assistance for low- and moderate-income families. We need to turn the cliff into a gradual off ramp for parents working their way into the middle class.

Finally, we need to improve the quality of care by improving the required qualifications of the early childhood workforce, as well as their compensation. Under the president's Preschool for All proposal, states would need to meet quality standards to receive federal funds, including requiring preschool teachers to have a bachelor's degree and ongoing professional development, as well as requiring preschool staff salaries to be comparable to K-12 salaries. Similar reforms should be made to improve the quality of child care provided with federal dollars under the Child Care and Development Fund.[28]

GIVING CAREGIVERS A RIGHT TO REQUEST FLEXIBLE WORK ARRANGEMENTS

For many working women, including those in well-compensated professional jobs, the hours and lack of flexibility interfere with their family obligations. Women in low-paying fields such as health care, retail, and the restaurant industry often work too few hours to financially support their families and are more likely to face unpredictable and unstable schedules.

Kristy Richardson talks with Robert Davis, a housing case manager at the Veterans Leadership Program of Western Pennsylvania. Much of her life is spent waiting to meet with someone who may be able to help her family get by. {MELISSA FARLOW}

We can do much more to encourage employers to allow flexible work arrangements for employees who want them, as well as more predictable, stable scheduling practices in poorly compensated service jobs. Flexible work arrangements include nontraditional start and end times for work, compressed workweeks, the ability to reduce hours worked, and the ability to work from home.

Less than half of employers currently offer flexible work arrangements to their employees. But the business case for allowing flexible work arrangements is strong. Researchers have found that employees with access to flexible work arrangements tend to be more satisfied and engaged with their jobs.[29] These factors have been found to increase productivity and employee retention, both of which improve a business's bottom line.[30] Examples of companies implementing flexible work arrangements—and what practices are working best for each organization—are highlighted in detail by Ellen Galinsky, James T. Bond, and Eve Tahmincioglu in the Private Solutions chapter.

As we pointed out in our first report, in the United Kingdom and several other countries, parents and caregivers have a "right to request" flexible work arrangements to accommodate caregiving responsibilities. Under U.K. law, an employer must meet with an employee requesting flexible work and make a decision about whether to accommodate the employee's request within two weeks of the meeting.[31] Employers can reject the request, but only for business-related reasons specified in the law. Vermont became the first U.S. state to adopt a right-to-request law last year; employers can generally refuse an employee's request, but they have to discuss the request with the employee in good faith.[32]

In June 2013, Rep. Carolyn Maloney (D-NY) and Sen. Bob Casey (D-PA) introduced legislation that would give all U.S. employees the right to request flexible work arrangements from their employers.[33] Employers would be required to respond to applications made by employees. If an employer were to reject an application, he or she would be required to provide the reasons to the employee in writing.

Although employees wouldn't be able to challenge an employer who denies a request, simply formalizing the right to request may have a positive effect on employers' responsiveness to flexible work. According to the Confederation of British Industries, the largest employers' organization in the United Kingdom, the right to request flexible work "has made huge strides in promoting different ways of working—with nine out of 10 requests accepted by employers."[34]

BOOSTING INCOMES FOR WOMEN BREADWINNERS

Seventy percent of Americans believe the financial contribution women make to our national economy is essential. Yet as Heather Boushey's chapter explores, women are disproportionately consigned to low-wage work, with incomes that leave them unable to support a family, including in critical care professions set to grow over the next decade.

In trying to access the work and income supports women need to care for their families, they face a daunting web of bureaucracy. And when trying to access educational opportunities to move off the brink, women face a lack of information and support in moving into higher-paying fields.

To help millions of women push back from the brink, we must boost the incomes of female breadwinners by improving the quality of low-wage jobs, streamlining access to work and income supports, paving the path toward higher education, and ensuring equal pay.

Minimum wage fails to keep pace

$7.25

**Current federal
minimum wage**

About
$10

**How much minimum
wage would be today**

if it had remained equal
to half of average wage
for production and
nonsupervisory workers

About
$16.50

**How much minimum
wage would be today**

if it had kept pace
with productivity growth
since 1968

Source: Janelle Jones and John Schmitt, "The Minimum Wage Is Not What It Used to Be," CEPR Blog, July 17, 2013, available at http://www.cepr.net/index.php/blogs/cepr-blog/the-minimum-wage-is-not-what-it-used-to-be.

INCREASING THE MINIMUM WAGE

Our economy and our families are stronger when we reward an honest day's work with honest wages and benefits, regardless of a worker's gender. Increasing the minimum wage would help us reach this goal. As President Obama noted in his 2013 State of the Union address, an increase in the minimum wage "would mean customers with more money in their pockets. And a whole lot of folks out there would probably need less help from government."

For nearly 25 years following World War II, the minimum wage provided an adequate floor, one that was regularly adjusted to keep pace with increases in productivity. In 1964, the minimum wage was equal to half of the average wage for production workers.[35] But not long after that, federal policymakers let the value of the minimum wage decline. If the minimum wage today were at the same level relative to the average production worker 50 years ago, it would be just over $10 per hour. If it had been adjusted over roughly the same period to keep pace with gains in productivity, it would be about $16.50 an hour.[36]

The minimum wage should put a floor under wages, one that ensures employers pay enough for their workers to afford the basics. If employers don't pay their workers enough to maintain spending on necessities such as food, housing, clothing, transportation, and other items, families and our economy suffer. Increasing the minimum wage to $10.10 over the next two years would mean as much as $51 billion in additional earnings for poorly compensated workers during this period.[37]

Fulfilling the Affordable Care Act's promise for women on the brink

Access to affordable health care is essential to women's economic security and well-being. Without insurance, a broken bone or a child's asthma attack can quickly drain a family's savings and lead to bankruptcy. Without access to routine checkups, a preventable illness can quickly escalate.

Yet about 18.9 million nonelderly women were uninsured in 2012.[38] Just over half of them will be eligible for Medicaid starting in 2014, as long as they live in states that take the Affordable Care Act's option to extend coverage to them.[39] While roughly half of states have approved or are moving toward the Medicaid expansion, in the other states, debate about whether to expand Medicaid is ongoing or not under consideration at this time.

The holdout states should go forward with the expansion, which is in the best interest of the people they represent. From 2014 through 2016, the federal government will cover all of the costs of expanding Medicaid. After that, states will need to pay only a modest share of the costs (5 percent in 2017, increasing by 1 percent up to a maximum of 10 percent in 2020 and beyond).

As a practical matter, states that adopt the expansion will improve their balance sheets and their economies because the expansion will create jobs and allow states to draw down federal funding for certain health care services they're already providing. In Ohio, for example, projections show that implementing the expansion is expected to result in $1.9 billion in savings and increased revenues by 2022.[40] In contrast, states that fail to take up the expansion will deny health insurance to tens of thousands of low-income workers and harm their states' balance sheets.

Low-income workers are more likely than other workers to spend any pay increases on necessities that they couldn't afford before. Grocery stores, clothing stores, and other retailers would all benefit from the increased spending power of these workers. In fact, in a recent nationally representative poll, two out of every three small business owners supported the increase.[41]

There is growing momentum for raising the minimum wage, as more than 20 states already have minimum wages higher than the federal level.[42] In September 2013, California became the latest state to raise the minimum wage, hiking it to $10 an hour by 2016.[43]

At the federal level, we should follow California's example and gradually raise the nation's minimum wage from $7.25 to at least $10.10 per hour and then update it annually, as Sen. Tom Harkin (D-IA) and Rep. George Miller (D-CA) have

Allie Winans and her two daughters rely on multiple prescriptions and numerous doctors' visits every week. These health care costs have driven their family to the financial brink. {AMI VITALE}

proposed.[44] We should also increase the minimum wage for employees who receive tips, from $2.13 to at least $7 per hour. These increases would be particularly helpful for low-income women. According to the Bureau of Labor Statistics, women are twice as likely as men to be paid wages at or below the minimum wage.[45]

STREAMLINING AND MODERNIZING PUBLIC WORK SUPPORTS

For women on the brink and other poorly compensated breadwinners, one of the most important developments over the past several decades has been the establishment and gradual expansion of public work supports. These include Medicaid; the Supplemental Nutrition Assistance Program, or SNAP (formerly food stamps); the earned income tax credit and child tax credit; and child care assistance. These programs acknowledge that many jobs in our economy don't pay adequate wages or provide essential benefits for families.

Work supports are incredibly effective. In 2011, for example, the earned income tax credit and child tax credit made it possible for 9.4 million people in working families with children to live above the poverty line.[46]

Unfortunately, obtaining these supports is too often a time-consuming and byzantine process, especially for low-wage workers juggling work and caregiving responsibilities with little time to wait in line at a government office. This is especially the case for low-wage workers seeking more than a single work support. A working mother with low earnings, for example, may be eligible for Medicaid, SNAP benefits, and child care assistance. But in many states, in order to access and maintain benefits, she has to navigate two or three different and largely uncoordinated processes. If you haven't been through a typical application process yourself, imagine a tedious trip to your DMV office, multiply that by two or more, and you start to get the picture.

States need to streamline and coordinate the delivery of work supports in ways that reduce burdens on both the families seeking benefits and the agencies providing them. Many states are already well on the way. As California's first lady, Maria Shriver developed WE Connect, a public-private partnership established in 2005. WE Connect works with organizations in underserved communities to connect families to resources such as the earned income tax credit, California's Healthy Families Program, and CalFresh. The program continues to help millions of Californians through its community events, web-based tools, public-private partnerships, and collateral materials. Through her leadership, Shriver has connected more than 20 million Californians with programs and services in an effort to promote healthier and more financially independent lives. [47]

Florida is also on its way, having completely modernized the way it delivers SNAP and other benefits over the past decade through its Automated Community Connection to Economic Self Sufficiency, or ACCESS, Florida initiative. The state changed eligibility rules to better align programs, shifted largely to an online application process, reduced other paperwork required from applicants, and made a number of other changes to streamline the process. Today, about 95 percent of applications for benefits in Florida are made online, rather than through a paper application process, and the state has reduced the costs of taking and processing applications by hundreds of millions of dollars.[48]

The Work Support Strategies Initiative, a multiyear demonstration project funded by the Ford Foundation and several other major foundations, is currently working with a select group of states to design, test, and implement "21st century" approaches that will make it easier for families to get the work supports for which they are eligible. As noted in Gov. C.L. "Butch" Otter's (R-ID) essay following this chapter, these modern approaches aim to deliver work supports more effectively and efficiently through technologically savvy and customer-driven methods of eligibility determination, enrollment, and retention.[49]

At the federal level, it is imperative that Congress continues to support and incentivize state efforts to modernize benefit systems. The Affordable Care Act provides enhanced federal funding to modernize benefit systems through 2015. State human services directors have called for extending that funding to give them more time to complete the challenging task of overhauling systems.

States should also be given the option to enroll eligible adults in Medicaid based on information the individual has already provided when applying for SNAP benefits; the existing option to do this for children, set to expire in September 2014, should be made permanent. A recent review by the Government Accountability Office found that this option has produced substantial administrative savings, while increasing the number of children with health insurance.[50]

OPENING DOORS FOR TOMORROW'S BREADWINNERS AND CAREGIVERS

As Anthony Carnevale and Nicole Smith explain in their chapter for this report, a college degree or other postsecondary education in well-paying fields can make a tremendous difference in the lives of women and their children.

Women have made considerable progress in education over the past five decades. Today, some 38 percent of women between the ages of 25 and 34 have a four-year college degree or higher, compared to 31 percent of men.[51] Yet that still leaves most young women without a four-year degree. And only 14 percent of low-income women in this age range have a four-year degree.[52] We need to ensure that college is affordable for young women and men and that they have the preparation and support they need to enter and complete college.

It is also important to remember that the gender gap in wages is partly driven by a gender gap in occupations, which exists even after taking educational requirements into account. Two-thirds of women work in just 5 percent of occupational

Investing in the future for her sons, Jessica McGowan is working toward her degree at Virginia College School of Business and Health in Chattanooga, Tennessee. She also works a part-time job.
{BARBARA KINNEY}

categories.[53] And, with the exception of teaching and nursing, the jobs in these categories are among the lowest-paying in our economy.

Women are particularly underrepresented in well-paying "STEM" occupations— science, technology, engineering, and math—as well as many occupations that provide good jobs without requiring a college education. For instance, neither the male-dominated occupation of truck driver nor the female-dominated occupation of child care worker requires more than short-term, on-the-job training. But the typical heavy truck driver earns $18.37 an hour while the typical child care worker earns only $9.38 an hour.[54]

> Two-thirds of women work in just 5 percent of occupational categories. And, with the exception of teaching and nursing, the jobs in these categories are among the lowest-paying in our economy.

One important step is to make sure young women have the information and advice they need to make smart education and career decisions. While students can get information on a school's ranking on particular subject areas, teachers, or campus life, little public information is available on average student debt or starting salaries for students graduating from various programs. This type of information is critical for all students, but especially for lower-income students who can ill afford a misstep with the limited dollars they have to spend on higher education or training.

The Obama administration's efforts to produce a college scorecard have promise, but only when information on earnings, particularly at the program level, become available. Bipartisan legislation such as the Student Right to Know Before You Go Act proposed by Sens. Marco Rubio (R-FL) and Ron Wyden (D-OR) could speed implementation of these initiatives, helping to connect women on the brink with the information they need to make informed decisions about careers.

Finally, we need to enforce existing equal pay and equal opportunity laws. There is evidence that discrimination is one factor contributing to the gender gap in STEM fields. A 2012 study showed that science faculty at research universities rated male applicants higher than identical female applicants and offered male applicants higher starting salaries as well as more career mentoring.[55]

The vigorous enforcement of Title IX in school sports has dramatically increased the participation of women and girls in school sports activities. The National Women's Law Center recommends that the U.S. Department of Education's Office for Civil Rights strengthen the enforcement of Title IX by conducting compliance reviews of schools to ensure that women and girls have equal access to STEM fields and classes.

All federal science agencies should conduct similar reviews for their grantee institutions. Similarly, the Office of Vocational Education could publish a proactive roadmap on how educational institutions can recruit and retain students in nontraditional gender fields. Educational institutions could hold regular trainings for teachers and administrators about Title IX, address factors that could discourage girls and women such as harassment and lack of mentorship, and work to make campuses more welcoming for female teachers in STEM fields to increase the number of role models for women and girls interested in entering these sectors.[56]

WHEN BREADWINNING IS CAREGIVING:
A FAIRER DEAL FOR CARE WORKERS AND DOMESTIC WORKERS

About 4.5 million people are paid care workers; these jobs include child care workers, nursing aides, personal and home care aides, and home health aides.[57] About 89 percent of these paid care workers are women. And nearly half are black, Hispanic, or Asian.[58]

The good news for women interested in these fields is that the jobs are plentiful and growing rapidly. According to projections by the Bureau of Labor Statistics, the number of jobs in child care and adult care will grow by more than 1 million between 2010 and 2020. In percentage terms, two adult care occupations—personal care aide and home health aide—are currently the two fastest-growing occupations in the United States, with both needing 70 percent more workers by 2020.[59]

But the bad news is that these workers are paid much less than workers on average, and too few of them receive health, retirement, and other benefits. The typical wage for a child care worker in 2012 was only $9.38 an hour ($19,510 annually); for a home health aide, it was $10 an hour.[60] Nearly one out of every three adult

Sabrina Jenkins of Goose Creek, South Carolina, meets with occupational therapist Tania McElveen. Sabrina has rheumatoid arthritis and has been receiving care to restore movement—even simple exercises are painful. {CALLIE SHELL}

and child care workers is uninsured, and roughly three-quarters do not have employer-provided retirement benefits.[61]

The workers who care for our children, parents, and grandparents, often women on the brink, deserve a better deal. Policies discussed in this chapter including raising the minimum wage, increasing access to benefits, and expanding educational opportunities are essential parts of that deal.

But we also need to reform the very structure of these jobs. Along these lines, Caring Across Generations, a campaign formed in 2011, has developed a policy agenda focused on both improving the quality of the care provided by adult care workers and ensuring that these jobs come with basic rights and a career ladder for workers.[62] An important step forward came in September 2013 when the Obama administration finalized a rule that will end the exclusion of nearly 2 million home care workers from minimum wage and overtime protections starting in January 2015.[63] While the rule will improve the basic economic security of many home care workers, there is still much more work to do to help the women who care for our aging and disabled family members to push back from the brink.

The 30 occupations projected to add the most new jobs by 2020: Most already have female majorities, but few pay above median wages

Occupation

All occupations

High-growth occupations in which 60 percent or more of jobs are currently held by women

Medical secretaries

Licensed practical and licensed vocational nurses

Child care workers

Medical assistants

Receptionists and information clerks

Teacher assistants

Registered nurses

Bookkeeping, accounting, and auditing clerks

Nursing aides, orderlies, and attendants

Home health aides

Personal care aides

Office clerks, general

Elementary school teachers, except special education

Cashiers

Waiters and waitresses

First-line supervisors of office and administrative support workers

Customer service representatives

Combined food preparation and serving workers, including fast food

Accountants and auditors

High-growth occupations in which less than 60 percent of jobs are currently held by women

Retail salespersons

Postsecondary teachers

Physicians and surgeons

Janitors and cleaners, except maids and housekeeping cleaners

Sales representatives, wholesale and manufacturing, except technical and scientific products

Laborers and freight, stock, and material movers, hand

Security guards

Heavy and tractor-trailer truck drivers

Landscaping and groundskeeping workers

Construction laborers

Carpenters

Sources: Bureau of Labor Statistics, Employment Projections Program and Table 11 in Bureau of Labor Statistics, Household Data Annual Averages.

This table lists the 30 occupations that the Bureau of Labor Statistics projects will add the most jobs during the current decade, sorted by the share of jobs in each occupation currently held by women. For example, BLS projects that there will between 706,800 more people working as home health aides in 2020 than in 2010. The home health aide occupation is currently dominated by women, who account for 87.6 percent of workers, and pays only 61 percent of the overall median wage for all occupations. Women currently hold more than 60 percent of the jobs in 19 of the top 30 high-growth jobs. Only 5 of the top 15 growth jobs pay wages above the overall median. But only 6 of the disproportionately female jobs listed here typically pay wages that are above the overall median wage.

Percentage of jobs in occupation currently held by women	Number of jobs (in thousands)		New jobs (in thousands) projected to be created between 2010–2020		Median annual wage in 2010	Median annual wage for occupation as percentage of median annual wage for all occupations ($33,840 in 2010)
	2010: actual	2020: projected	Number	Percent increase		
47.0%	143,068.2	163,537.1	20,468.9	14.3	$33,840	100%
95.3%	508.7	718.9	210.2	41.3	30,530	90%
94.2%	752.3	920.8	168.5	22.4	40,380	119%
94.1%	1,282.3	1,544.3	262.0	20.4	19,300	57%
93.8%	527.6	690.4	162.9	30.9	28,860	85%
91.5%	1,048.5	1,297.0	248.5	23.7	25,240	75%
91.1%	1,288.3	1,479.3	191.1	14.8	23,220	69%
90.6%	2,737.4	3,449.3	711.9	26.0	64,690	191% *
89.1%	1,898.3	2,157.4	259.0	13.6	34,030	101%
87.9%	1,505.3	1,807.2	302.0	20.1	24,010	71%
87.6%	1,017.7	1,723.9	706.3	69.4	20,560	61%
84.7%	861.0	1,468.0	607.0	70.5	19,640	58%
83.4%	2,950.7	3,440.2	489.5	16.6	26,610	79%
81.4%	1,476.5	1,725.3	248.8	16.8	51,660	153%
71.8%	3,362.6	3,612.8	250.2	7.4	18,500	55%
71.2%	2,260.3	2,456.2	195.9	8.7	18,330	54%
68.5%	1,424.4	1,627.8	203.4	14.3	47,460	140%
67.8%	2,187.3	2,525.6	338.4	15.5	30,460	90%
64.9%	2,682.1	3,080.1	398.0	14.8	17,950	53%
60.9%	1,216.9	1,407.6	190.7	15.7	61,690	182%
50.2%	4,261.6	4,968.4	706.8	16.6	20,670	61%
48.2%	1,756.0	2,061.7	305.7	17.4	45,690	135%
34.3%	691.0	859.3	168.3	24.4	111,570	330%
29.7%	2,310.4	2,556.8	246.4	10.7	22,210	66%
27.0%	1,430.0	1,653.4	223.4	15.6	52,440	155%
18.7%	2,068.2	2,387.3	319.1	15.4	23,460	69%
18.5%	1,035.7	1,230.7	195.0	18.8	23,920	71%
5.4%	1,604.8	1,934.9	330.1	20.6	37,770	112%
5.1%	1,151.5	1,392.3	240.8	20.9	23,400	69%
2.9%	998.8	1,211.2	212.4	21.3	29,280	87%
1.6%	1,001.7	1,197.6	196.0	19.6	39,530	117%

Because federal and state governments play a major role in financing care services through programs such as Medicaid, they could play a major role in improving compensation of the workers who provide these services. The government already plays such a role in certain male-dominated sectors such as the construction of highways and other public works. The Davis-Bacon Act effectively requires companies and employers working on federally funded infrastructure work to pay decent wages to their workers. It's time to apply a similar standard to ensure that public funds are being used to create living-wage jobs in the female-dominated care sectors.

Home care or domestic workers—workers in private households who provide care, housekeeping, or various other services—are among the most vulnerable of all care workers. While the new rule on extending minimum wage and overtime laws to domestic workers is a step forward, these workers are often excluded from other basic labor standards that apply to the vast majority of the workforce.

A growing number of states have adopted or are considering Domestic Worker Bill of Rights laws. These laws would ensure that domestic workers have basic employment protections, such as an eight-hour day, overtime protections, and paid time off. These laws would also extend other protections specific to the unique circumstances of domestic work, such as a right to a minimum number of hours of uninterrupted sleep under adequate conditions.

New York approved Domestic Worker Bill of Rights legislation in 2010, and California and Hawaii approved legislation in 2013. In addition to state-level initiatives like this, we need a nationwide Domestic Worker Bill of Rights, as Ai-jen Poo calls for in this report. Basic labor standards such as these are a win-win—when domestic workers are better off, the people they care for are better off.

ENSURING EQUAL PAY

Many of the solutions discussed in this chapter would help close the wage gap,

FIGURE 4

Female-dominated professions are lower paid across skill levels

$408
$553
$600
$752

Median earnings of full-time workers in low-skill occupations

Median earnings of full-time workers in medium-skill occupations

■ Mostly female: 75 percent or more
■ Mostly male: 75 percent or more

Source: Institute for Women's Policy Research

by helping women balance their roles as breadwinners and caregivers, improving the quality of low-wage work, better enforcing current equal opportunity laws, and providing better pathways into nontraditional, higher-paying fields. But even when controlling for education, experience, occupational choice, and time out of the labor market, there is still an unexplainable gap between men's and women's wages.[64] We need equal pay.

Ensuring equal pay for women has enormous public support: Our poll found that 90 percent of women on the brink and 73 percent of respondents overall strongly favored addressing the gender wage gap as a way to increase women's wages.

Enacting the Paycheck Fairness Act addresses the wage gap factors unexplained by occupation, industry, labor force experience, or education. And it would bring us one step closer to ensuring that women can bring home a paycheck equal to that of their male counterparts.

The bill would strengthen the Equal Pay Act in several important ways, including:

• Requiring employers to show that wage disparities between men and women performing the same work have a business justification and are not gender related

The gender wage gap in action		Median weekly earnings, 2012		Workers (in thousands)			
		Male	**Female**	**Male**	**Female**	**Percent of workers with education beyond HS**	**Typical/required education**
Male dominated	Driver/sales workers and truck drivers	$736	$537	2433	101	31%	HS, Short-term OJT
	Grounds maintenance workers	$452		766	29	25%	LT HS, Short-term OJT
	Construction laborers	$609		913	24	24%	LT HS, Short-term OJT
	Security guards	$537	$501	603	138	54%	HS, Short-term OJT
Female dominated	Nursing, psychiatric, and home health aides	$508	$445	173	1285	44%	Post secondary non degree award
	Personal and home care aides	$465	$412	99	450	44%	LT HS, Short-term OJT
	Secretaries and administrative assistants	$803	$665	105	2146	65%	HS, Short-term OJT
	Bookkeeping, accounting, and auditing clerks	$740	$672	102	755	64%	HS, Short-term OJT

Source: Table 39 in Bureau of Labor Statistics, 2013 Employment and Earnings Online, Annual Average Household Data, February 13, 2013.

HS = High school
LT HS = Less than high school
OJT = On-the-job training

Ensuring equal pay for women has enormous public support: Our poll found that 90 percent of women on the brink and 73 percent of respondents overall *strongly* favored addressing the gender wage gap as a way to increase women's wages.

- Banning employer retaliation against workers who ask about their employers' wage practices or share information about their own wages, both of which help women understand what they are making relative to their colleagues

- Creating a grant program to provide salary negotiation training for women and girls

- Improving remedies for equal pay violations to deter employers from discriminating in the first place

- Strengthening the capacity of the relevant enforcement agencies to prevent gender discrimination and to enforce the law by authorizing additional training, research, education, and data collection[65]

CONCLUSION

At the beginning of this chapter, we posed the question: How do we put women and their families at the center of our public policymaking? Answering this question requires us to acknowledge that today, two-thirds of U.S. mothers are primary or co-breadwinners, but that too many of our public policies are stuck back in 1964, when most families had a woman at home to be the full-time caregiver.

It's time to enact 21st-century policies that help 21st-century women manage their care responsibilities and bolster their potential as breadwinners. Doing so would provide greater opportunities for women to join the workforce and help close the persistent gender wage gap—helping millions of families join the middle class and contributing to long-term economic growth for the nation.

Putting women at the center of our policymaking means enacting paid sick days legislation so that people like Elose don't have to choose between their health and their job. It means expanding affordable, quality pre-K and child care so that more families like Jennifer's can get back on their feet. It means modernizing our policies to provide access to paid family leave so that people don't have to choose between taking a few weeks to welcome a newborn child or earning enough income to provide economic security for their new family. And it means boosting wages for breadwinners through an increase in the minimum wage, modernizing public work supports, giving future college students better information about educational investments, and providing tools for pay equity.

These solutions would help millions of working women achieve financial security. At the same time, the solutions deliver long-term economic benefits and help strengthen our economy.

There are 42 million Eloses and Jennifers—women on the brink—and another 28 million children who depend on them. There is clear evidence that the public solutions outlined in this chapter would help millions of women and families push back and in the process enhance U.S. economic growth and competitiveness.

It's not a question of if we know how to do it. It's a question of whether or not we have the political will to get it done.

THINK ABOUT THIS

The United States is the only industrialized nation in the world without paid sick leave.

ENDNOTES

1   Center for American Progress analysis of the Center for Economic and Policy Research Extracts of the 2012 Current Population Survey Outgoing Rotation Group Files, available at http://ceprdata.org/cps-uniform-data-extracts/cps-outgoing-rotation-group/.

2   Francine Blau and Lawrence Kahn, "Female Labor Supply: Why Is the U.S. Falling Behind?" (Cambridge, MA: National Bureau of Economic Research, 2013).

3   Economists have estimated that the value of unpaid household production in the United States, including unpaid care and housework, is equal to roughly 30 percent of GDP. See Joseph E. Stiglitz and others, "Report by the Commission on the Measurement of Economic Performance and Social Progress" (Paris: Commission on the Measurement of Economic Performance and Social Progress, 2008), available at http://www.stiglitz-sen-fitoussi.fr/documents/rapport_anglais.pdf. And AARP has estimated that the economic value of unpaid family caregiving just for adults with limitations in daily activities amounted to about $450 billion in 2009. See Lynn Feinberg and others, "Valuing the Invaluable: 2011 Update—The Growing Contributions and Costs of Family Caregiving" (Washington: AARP Public Policy Institute, 2011).

4   Rose M. Kreider and Diana B. Elliott, "Historical Changes in Stay-at-Home Mothers: 1969 to 2009" (U.S. Census Bureau, 2010), available at http://www.census.gov/population/www/socdemo/ASA2010_Kreider_Elliott.pdf.

5   For pregnancy disability leave, a doctor needs to certify that the mother is disabled and incapable of doing her regular and customary work because of pregnancy. Typically, the covered disability period is four weeks before the expected delivery date and up to six weeks after the actual delivery. See State of California Employment Development Department, "FAQs—Pregnancy," available at http://www.edd.ca.gov/disability/FAQ_DI_Pregnancy.htm.

6   Bureau of Labor Statistics, *National Compensation Survey: Employee Benefits in the United States, March 2013* (U.S. Department of Labor, issued September 2013), Civilian Worker Table 32, available at http://www.bls.gov/ncs/ebs/benefits/2013/ebbl0052.pdf.

7   National Partnership for Women & Families, "Fact Sheet: The Case for a National Family and Medical Leave Insurance Program (The FAMILY Act)" (2013), available at http://www.nationalpartnership.org/research-library/work-family/paid-leave/family-act-fact-sheet.pdf.

8   For a thorough review of research on this point, see Heather Boushey and Sarah Jane Glynn, "The Effects of Paid Family and Medical Leave on Employment Stability and Economy Security" (Washington: Center for American Progress, 2012).

9   Linda Houser and Thomas Vartanian, "Pay Matters: The Positive Economic Impacts of Paid Family Leave for Families, Businesses and the Public" (New Brunswick, NJ: Rutgers Center for Women and Work, 2012).

10 Bureau of Labor Statistics, *National Compensation Survey: Employee Benefits in the United States, March 2013* (U.S. Department of Labor, issued September 2013), Private Worker Table 32, available at http://www.bls.gov/ncs/ebs/benefits/2013/ebbl0052.pdf.

11 Ibid.

12 Our American Story, "Elose's Story About Paid Sick Days," available at http://halfinten.org/stories/eloses-story-about-paid-sick-days/ (last accessed October 2013).

13 Healthy Families Act, H.R. 1286, 113 Cong. 1 sess. (Government Printing Office, 2013); Healthy Families Act, S. 631, 113 Cong. 1 sess. (Government Printing Office, 2013).

14 Joint Economic Committee, *Expanding Access to Paid Sick Leave: The Impact of the Healthy Families Act on America's Workers* (Government Printing Office, 2010).

15 Ibid. The Joint Economic Committee estimates that 6 million food service workers and 1.4 million personal care workers who currently lack paid sick time would gain access to it under the Healthy Families Act.

16 Bureau of the Census, *Current Population Survey, Annual Social and Economic (ASEC) Supplement* (U.S. Department of Commerce, 2012), Table POV8, "Families with Related Children Under 6 by Number of Working Family Members and Family Structure, Below 200 Percent of Poverty," available at http://www.census.gov/hhes/www/cpstables/032013/pov/pov08_200.htm.

17 Ibid.

18 See Sharmila Lawrence and others, "Parent Employment and the Use of Child Care Subsidies" (New York: National Center for Children in Poverty, 2006).

19 U.S. Department of Education, *School Readiness, Fiscal Year 2014 Request*, page C-8, available at http://www2.ed.gov/about/overview/budget/budget14/justifications/c-schoolreadiness.pdf. For links to leading studies and research summaries, see Ounce of Prevention Fund, "Why Investments in Early Childhood Work," available at http://www.ounceofprevention.org/about/why-early-childhood-investments-work.php.

20 Child Care Aware of America, "Parents and the High Cost of Child Care: 2012 Report" (Arlington, VA: Child Care Aware, 2012), available at http://www.naccrra.org/publications/naccrra-publications/2012/8/parents-and-the-high-cost-of-child-care-2012-report.

21 Bureau of the Census, *Who's Minding the Kids? Child Care Arrangements: 2011—Detailed Tables* (U.S. Department of Commerce, 2011), Tables 5 and 6, available at http://www.census.gov/hhes/childcare/data/sipp/2011/tables.html.

22 Ibid. at Table 2A.

23 Our American Story, "Jennifer's Story About CCDBG and Head Start," available at http://halfinten.org/stories/jennifers-story-about-ccdbg-and-head-start/(last accessed October 2013).

24 This is the percentage of children in 2010 who received child care subsidies from all federal sources (Temporary Assistance, Child Care and Development Fund, and Social Services Block Grant) compared to all children with income at or below 85 percent of the median income of the state where they live. See Department of Health and Human Services Administration for Children and Families, *Child Care and Development Fund*, FY 2014 Budget Justification (2013), p. 54, available at https://www.acf.hhs.gov/sites/default/files/olab/sec2c_ccdbg_2014cj.pdf.

25 W.S. Barnett and others, *The State of Preschool 2012: State Preschool Yearbook* (New Brunswick, NJ: National Institute for Early Education Research, 2012), available at http://nieer.org/sites/nieer/files/yearbook2012.pdf.

26 See details of President Obama's Pre-School for All initiative, U.S. Department of Education, "Early Learning: America's Middle Class Promise Begins Early," at http://www.ed.gov/early-learning.

27 See, e.g., NBC News, "Working Americans Turn Down Pay Raise to Avoid 'Cliff Effect,'" May 24, 2013, available at http://www.nbcnews.com/video/rock-center/51996100.

28 See Cynthia Brown and others, "Investing in Our Children: A Plan to Expand Access to Preschool and Child Care" (Washington: Center for American Progress, 2013).

29 Anna Danziger and Shelley Waters Boots, "The Business Case for Flexible Work Arrangements, Workplace Flexibility 2010" (Washington: Georgetown University Law Center and The Urban Institute, 2008).

30 Ibid.

31 See Government of the United Kingdom, "Guide to Flexible Working," available at https://www.gov.uk/flexible-working/overview.

32 Vermont Act 31, An Act Related to Equal Pay, Section 5, signed by Gov. Peter Shumlin on May 14, 2013, available at http://www.leg.state.vt.us/DOCS/2014/ACTS/ACT031.PDF.

33 Specifically, employers would be required to respond to employees' requests for any of the following: 1) the number of hours they are required to work; 2) the times when they are required to work or be on call for work; 3) where they are required to work; and 4) the amount of notification they receive of work schedule assignments.

34 Susan Anderson, director of human resources policy, Confederation of British Industries, quoted in Ariane Hegewisch, "Employers and European Flexible Working Rights," *WorkLife Law*, UC Hastings College of Law (Fall 2005), available at http://www.worklifelaw.org/pubs/european_issue_brief_printversion.pdf.

35 John Schmitt, "The Minimum Wage Is Too Damn Low" (Washington: Center for Economic and Policy Research, 2012).

36 Janelle Jones and Schmitt, "The Minimum Wage Is Not What It Used to Be," CEPR Blog, July 17, 2013, available at http://www.cepr.net/index.php/blogs/cepr-blog/the-minimum-wage-is-not-what-it-used-to-be.

37 David Cooper and Doug Hall, "Raising the Federal Minimum Wage to $10.10 Would Give Working Families, and the Overall Economy, a Much-Needed Boost" (Washington: Economic Policy Institute, 2013).

38 The Henry J. Kaiser Family Foundation, "Health Reform: Implications for Women's Access to Coverage and Care" (2013), available at http://kaiserfamilyfoundation.files.wordpress.com/2012/03/7987-03-health-reform-implications-for-women_s-access-to-coverage-and-care.pdf.

39 Authors' calculation from Bureau of the Census, *Current Population Survey, Annual Social and Economic Supplement, 2012* (U.S. Department of Commerce, 2013).

40 See Sarah Baron, "10 Frequently Asked Questions About Medicaid Expansion," Center for American Progress, April 2, 2013, available at http://www.americanprogress.org/issues/healthcare/news/2013/04/02/58922/10-frequently-asked-questions-about-medicaid-expansion/; John Holahan, Matthew Buettgens, and Stan Dorn, "The Cost of Not Expanding Medicaid" (Washington: Kaiser Family Foundation, 2013), available at http://kff.org/medicaid/report/the-cost-of-not-expanding-medicaid/.

41 Small Business Majority, "Opinion Poll: Small Businesses Support Increasing Minimum Wage" (2013), available at http://www.smallbusinessmajority.org/small-business-research/downloads/042413-minimum-wage-poll-report.pdf.

42 U.S. Department of Labor, "Minimum Wage Laws in the States—January 1, 2013," available at: http://www.dol.gov/whd/minwage/america.htm.

43 Marc Lifsher, "California Legislature Approves Raising Minimum Wage to $10," *Los Angeles Times*, September 12, 2013, available at http://www.latimes.com/business/la-fi-minimum-wage-20130913,0,1527959.story.

44 *Fair Minimum Wage Act of 2013*, H.R. 1010, 113 Cong., 1 sess. (Government Printing Office, 2013).

45 Bureau of Labor Statistics, *Characteristics of Minimum Wage Workers: 2012* (U.S. Department of Labor, 2013).

46 Chuck Marr, Jimmy Charite, and Chye-Ching Huang, "Earned Income Tax Credit Promotes Work, Encourages Children's Success at School, Research Finds" (Washington: Center on Budget and Policy Priorities, 2013).

47 For more information see WE Connect's website, available at http://www.weconnect.net/.

48 Scott Cody and others, "Simplification of Health and Social Services Enrollment and Eligibility: Lessons for California from Interviews in Four States" (Washington: Mathematica Policy Research, 2010), p. 12.

49 Urban Institute, "Work Support Strategies: Streamlining Access, Strengthening Families," available at http://www.urban.org/worksupport/.

50 Government Accountability Office, "Medicaid and CHIP: Considerations for Express Lane Eligibility," GAO-13-178R, Report to the Chairman, Committee on Finance, United States Senate, December 2012.

51 Authors' calculations from Bureau of the Census, *Educational Attainment in the United States: 2012—Detailed Tables* (U.S. Department of Commerce, 2013), Table 1, available at http://www.census.gov/hhes/socdemo/education/data/cps/2012/tables.html.

52 Authors' calculation from Bureau of the Census, *Current Population Survey, Annual Social and Economic Supplement, 2012* (U.S. Department of Commerce, 2013).

53 Women and Workforce Investment for Nontraditional Jobs Act, H.R. 951, 113 Cong., 1 sess. (Government Printing Office, 2013).

54 Wages estimates are from Bureau of Labor Statistics, *May 2012 National Occupational Employment and Wages Estimates* (U.S. Department of Labor, 2013), available at http://www.bls.gov/oes/current/oes_nat.htm. In 2012, about 94 percent of child care workers were women—roughly the percentage of truck drivers who were men. Bureau of Labor Statistics, *Household Data, Annual Averages: Employed Persons by Detailed Occupation, Sex, Race, and Hispanic or Latino Ethnicity* (Department of Labor, 2013), available at http://www.bls.gov/cps/cpsaat11.pdf.

55 National Women's Law Center citing Corinne A. Moss-Racusin and others, "Science Faculty's Subtle Gender Biases Favor Male Students," *Proceedings of the National Academy of Sciences*, 109 (41) (2012), available at http://www.pnas.org/content/early/2012/09/14/1211286109.full.pdf.

56 National Women's Law Center, "The Next Generation of Title IX: STEM—Science, Technology, Engineering, and Math" (Washington: National Women's Law Center, 2012), available at http://www.nwlc.org/sites/default/files/pdfs/nwlcstem_titleixfactsheet.pdf.

57 Ibid.

58 Authors' calculations from ibid.

59 Bureau of Labor Statistics, *The 30 Occupations with the Fastest Projected Employment Growth, 2010–20* (U.S. Department of Labor, 2012), available at www.bls.gov/news.release/ecopro.t07.htm.

60 Bureau of Labor Statistics, *Occupational Employment and Wages—May 2012* (U.S. Department of Labor, 2013), available at http://www.bls.gov/news.release/ocwage.htm.

61 See Candace Howes, Carrie Leana, and Kristin Smith, "Paid Care Work." In Nancy Folbre, ed., *For Love and Money: Care Provision in the United States* (New York: Russell Sage Foundation, 2012); and Shawn Fremstad, "Maintaining and Improving Social Security for Direct Care Workers" (Washington: Center for Economic and Policy Research, 2011).

62 Caring Across Generations, "About Us," available at http://www.caringacross.org/about-us/.

63 U.S. Department of Labor, "We Count on Home Care: For Workers," available at http://www.dol.gov/whd/homecare/workers.htm.

64 Heather Boushey, "Strengthening the Middle Class: Ensuring Equal Pay for Women," Testimony before the U.S. Senate Committee on Health, Education, Labor, and Pensions, March 11, 2010, available at http://www.americanprogressaction.org/wp-content/uploads/issues/2010/03/pdf/Boushey_testimony.pdf.

65 Paycheck Fairness Act, S. 84, 113 Cong. 1 sess. (Government Printing Office, 2013).

We Have Blown a Huge Hole in Our Safety Net

By PETER EDELMAN, professor of law, Georgetown Law Center, and faculty director, Georgetown Center on Poverty, Inequality, and Public Policy. His most recent book is **So Rich, So Poor: Why It's So Hard to End Poverty in America**. *He has served in all three branches of the federal government.*

In our rich nation, one-third of American citizens —106 million people—have incomes below twice the poverty line, which is just $46,000 for a family of four. Why? And why are they disproportionately women, children, and people of color?

Look back to the early 1970s, when America seemed to be heading in the right direction. We had cut poverty almost in half, to the low rate of 11.1 percent. Of course, the hot economy helped, as did programs from the War on Poverty and changes from the civil rights movement, which resulted in large employment gains for African Americans.

What happened later was mostly unforeseeable. Globalization and new technology started destroying the industrial jobs that had built the middle class. Unions began to lose members. The minimum wage stagnated. Family structures changed, creating a much larger cohort of single mothers coping in the job market by themselves. Urban school systems declined in quality. The concentration of poverty in inner-city areas—already a problem in the 1960s—got far worse. Immigration—especially illegal immigration—flooded the labor market with people willing to work for low wages. The ugly politics of race continued, especially in relation to welfare and crime; drug laws and racialized law enforcement targeted African American and Latino men for incarceration. And

as the number of people who fell into poverty grew and grew, inequality widened spectacularly, with the fruits of economic growth going to those at the very top.

But in spite of what conservative politicians and commentators say, the problem is not that the poor prefer to depend on public benefits rather than go to work. Neither is it an undue use of public benefits. These shopworn accusations persist, but they were false from the start.

The truth is that 68 percent of children who are poor live in families in which someone does have a job.[1] But often, these jobs pay so little that they don't lift families out of poverty, or they leave these families living on the brink. Yes, there are other pressing problems: public education, law enforcement policy, a decent safety net, concentrated poverty, and more. But the fundamental problem with regard to poverty and economic insecurity today is the flood of extremely low-wage work that keeps families stuck on the lower rungs.

Half of the jobs in the country pay less than $34,000 per year. A quarter of them pay less than the federal poverty level for a family of four, which is approximately $23,000 per year. While money has poured into the upper reaches of our economy, wages in the lower half are basically stagnant, having increased by a mere 7 percent over the past 40 years—just one-fifth of a percent per year. The people who hold these low-wage jobs are disproportionately women, especially women with children. It's no wonder that the poverty rate for children who live with single mothers is well over 40 percent and that four out of five families headed by a single mother live on the financial brink.

Public benefits definitely help. A family with a minimum-wage job holder and two children gets about $5,500 from the earned income tax credit and another $1,800 from the child tax credit—nearly a 50 percent increase in income. But we need to do much more, and increasing wages remains at the top of the list. President Barack Obama's proposal to raise the minimum wage to $9 an hour and index it to inflation would help,[2] and Congressman George Miller's proposal to increase it to $10.10 would help even more.[3] The Medicaid expansion in the Affordable Care Act is phenomenally important. Increased investments in child care, housing assistance, and help with postsecondary education would all raise incomes too. These policies free up money for families to spend in their local economies.

The space allotted for this essay does not permit a detailed discussion of education, crime policy, and initiatives focused on concentrated poverty, so I will focus on only one more issue: deep poverty— the 20 million people who, according to the Census, have incomes below half of the poverty line, which is below approximately $9,500 per year for a family of three.

Since 1996, we have blown a huge hole in our safety net with the demise of welfare. The federal "reform" enacted that year led to the virtual disappearance of welfare in about half the states. Before then, 68 percent of families with children received income assistance. Now the number is just 27 percent. It is true that the welfare system needed reform, but it is now clearer than ever that the welfare reform of 1996 has trapped millions of women and children not just in poverty but also often in deep poverty— and they cannot get out. Six million people—again, disproportionately women and children—have an income comprised only of food stamps. That is an income of little more than $6,000 per year for a family of three, or just one-third of the income level considered "poverty."

The large class of people living on the brink is traceable to our economic malaise and the power that some politicians wield in Washington and many states. But our most glaring public policy error is what we have done to the safety net for the most vulnerable women and children in our nation. And our most glaring omission is our failure to address the proliferation of poorly paid jobs that leave working families struggling. We have a lot of work to do.

ENDNOTES

1 Calculated from U.S. Census Bureau, "Current Population Survey (CPS): 2012 Poverty Table of Contents, Table POV13. Related Children by Number of Working Family Members and Family Structure," available at http://www.census.gov/hhes/www/cpstables/032013/pov/toc.htm (last accessed September 2013).

2 The White House, "Fact Sheet: The President's Plan to Reward Work by Raising the Minimum Wage," Press release, February 13, 2013, available at http://www.whitehouse.gov/the-press-office/2013/02/13/fact-sheet-president-s-plan-reward-work-raising-minimum-wage.

3 Democrats, Committee on Education and the Workforce, U.S. House of Representatives, "The Fair Minimum Wage Act (H.R. 1010)," available at http://democrats.edworkforce.house.gov/issue/fair-minimum-wage-act (last accessed September 2013).

The Circle of Protection: Balancing the Budget Does Not Require Burdening the Poor

By LEITH ANDERSON, president of the National Association of Evangelicals and former senior pastor of Wooddale Church in Eden Prairie, Minnesota. He is a signatory of the Circle of Protection, a religious advocacy group focused on protecting programs for the poor.

In the time of the Old Testament, Ruth came to Bethlehem as a foreigner from a strange land and a poor widow. Her story is of a life transformed. Ruth became not just a wife and a mother, but also a leader of her people and the great-grand-mother of Israel's King David. Her story became the eighth book of the Bible, and the New Testament lists her as one of the foremothers of Jesus Christ. For 3,000 years, millions of parents around the world have named their daughters after this once-obscure woman. How did all that happen? Believe it or not, it all started with a government-assistance program!

The biblically mandated program that transformed Ruth from powerless to powerful was an Old Testament practice called "gleaning." The law required farmers not to harvest the corners of their fields, to leave behind crops missed by the first harvest, and not to collect some grapes in their vineyards. The poor, orphans, and immigrants were then invited to gather or "glean" the leftovers to provide for their own families. It was more than charity; it was the law.

Ruth was one of the law's beneficiaries. In Bethlehem, this poor immigrant woman from Moab gleaned the fields of a man named Boaz. She eventually married Boaz and began one of the most famous family dynasties in history.

We evangelical Christians take the Bible seriously, so what does Ruth's story teach us? It teaches us to protect and provide for modern-day Ruths—poor women and others who need help. Even without a government mandate, our churches have established ministries to provide housing, food, preschool education and day care, job placement, medical clinics, and much more for the poor in our communities.

But we also recognize that voluntary help isn't enough. Just as in biblical times, we have government-mandated programs that help the poor and nearly poor in our country. But recently, budget considerations have put these programs in jeopardy.

That is why the National Association of Evangelicals has partnered with a broad array of other religious organizations in a program called "The Circle of Protection" to assure continued help for our population's most vulnerable people. More than 65 heads of denominations, relief and development agencies, and other Christian organizations have joined hands and voices in this coalition. We are forming a Circle of Protection around programs that meet the essential needs of hungry and poor people at home and abroad.

Those of us in the Circle are always in favor of fiscal restraint and the elimination of government budget deficits, but we also insist that budget cuts are not made at the expense of those who need help, most of whom are women, children, and the elderly. Balancing the budget does not require burdening the poor.

In all of the current budget debates, the focus has been on the needs of middle-class Americans. That's legitimate; a strong middle class forms the economic backbone of our country. But little has been said about the tens of millions of poor Americans. If they are discussed, the conversation turns too often to blaming them, dismissing them, slashing programs that help them, and generally pushing them out of sight and out of mind. This is wrong.

We know it's wrong because of the Bible's hundreds of commands to care for the widows, the orphans, the strangers, the marginalized, and the needy. That is why we need what we would call a "moral budget" that protects those whom Jesus called "the least of these." That is, first and foremost, a moral mandate from God to respect those who are created in his image.

But this isn't just about morality; it is a matter of economic pragmatism. Programs that feed the hungry, educate the underemployed, prepare preschoolers, and preserve the family unit are good for everyone. They provide ladders out of poverty and into the middle class. Government-supported job training and work assistance programs help poor people work their way up, ultimately strengthening the U.S. economy by lessening the need for other types of federal aid—a way to reduce the nation's debt. These are not drains on our wealth. They are investments in our nation's greatest source of wealth—its people. It is important to reduce deficits, yes—but in ways that do not increase poverty or inequality.

Since the poor and vulnerable do not have the financial resources or organizational clout to influence government budgets, we will continue to use our influence on their behalf. At the same time, we must do our part to help them outside of government as individuals, churches, and nongovernmental organizations.

Let us all make sure we keep the gate to the American Dream of life, liberty, and the pursuit of happiness open for everyone. It's not just the right thing; it's the smart thing. Just ask Ruth.

From VISTA Corps to Shriver Corps: Providing Solutions for 50 Years

By SHIRLEY SAGAWA, presidential appointee and advisor in the first Bush and Clinton administrations, who has been called "the founding mother of the modern service movement." She was instrumental in the drafting and passage of legislation creating AmeriCorps and the Corporation for National and Community Service.

In 2012, Rosa Carty, a single mom and Army veteran who served her country during the Afghanistan War, was planning a law enforcement career when a car struck her, injuring her badly. As Rosa describes it, "I felt like I was in the prime of my life. Then, all of a sudden, my plans were stripped away from me." During her lengthy recovery, she was unable to find employment that would support her daughter and get her the ongoing medical help she needed. She spent months unsuccessfully seeking help from government and community agencies, but she kept hitting brick wall after brick wall. "There was a lot of misinformation out there, and I was literally nothing more than a case number," she says.

Then Rosa discovered LIFT, an anti-poverty organization where she found not brick walls, but solutions. At LIFT, AmeriCorps members and volunteers teamed up to help her develop an action plan, then find and connect her to the resources she needed. Their efforts paid off. She was able to stabilize her housing situation and find a job.

As Rosa's story shows, national service volunteers can directly help struggling women get on the path to self-sufficiency. Of course, this isn't a new idea.

National service as a strategy to address poverty dates back to 1964, when Sargent Shriver created the domestic Peace Corps equivalent called Volunteers in Service to America, or VISTA, for President Lyndon B. Johnson's War on Poverty. VISTA became part of AmeriCorps when that national volunteer service network was created in 1993.

AmeriCorps members, supported in part through the federal Corporation for National and Community Service, receive modest living allowances and education scholarships in exchange for one or two years of full-time service.[1]

LIFT has made use of AmeriCorps members in its own innovative service-delivery model, which pairs clients like Rosa with these highly trained volunteers who help them identify and achieve their goals: getting a decent job and providing their families with safe homes, quality education for their kids, and economic stability and security. Rosa Carty says that at LIFT, she was a person with a name, not just a number, and that is what differentiates it from other service providers.

Kirsten Lodal—who was a college student when she co-founded LIFT in 1998—says LIFT's culture

Air Force veteran Kristy Richardson relies on public transportation to travel to and from work and the Veterans Administration Hospital in Pittsburgh, Pennsylvania, where she is being treated for PTSD. Even in the face of trauma, Kristy maintains a good attitude and wants to succeed. {MELISSA FARLOW}

of service is based on respect and collaboration. AmeriCorps members and other LIFT volunteers provide direct personal contact and connections—not only helping thousands of clients get hooked up to resources they need now, but also providing the support network, the confidence, and the skills they will need to manage tough times in the future, and to ultimately give back to others through service.

"AmeriCorps members serve because they want to make a difference for a year or two," says Lodal. "But their experience inspires a lifelong commitment to ending poverty." For example, Rosa Carty was inspired to pay it forward herself, returning to LIFT to lead the program that teams AmeriCorps volunteers with veterans like her, and connecting them to life solutions.

For 50 years, this national service model has worked. Today, there are many AmeriCorps programs helping people who are struggling to find the help they need. Here are just a few of those programs:

- **The National Anti-Hunger and Opportunity Corps** engages VISTA volunteers to fight hunger and improve nutrition, primarily by increasing participation in the Supplemental Nutrition Assistance Program, or SNAP—formerly known as food stamps—and by helping anti-hunger community organizations increase their capacity to provide comprehensive benefit assistance and outreach to low-income constituents.

- **VetCorps** in Washington state engages AmeriCorps members to provide support, resources,

and information to help veterans in college navigate the G.I. Bill and university financial aid offices, and also access other federal, state, or local veterans benefits.

- **Minnesota Opportunity Corps Employment Navigators** are AmeriCorps members who use research-based instruction and tools to help clients navigate through employment and post-secondary education and become self-sufficient.

These and so many other programs demonstrate what Sargent Shriver knew 50 years ago. National service members don't just bring savvy and skills plus caring and commitment to their work; they also offer a critical advantage over many traditionally staffed government programs because AmeriCorps members and the volunteers they recruit don't have to keep a constant eye on the clock. They can take the time clients need to get their problems solved.

So today, with many millions of women and families living on or over the brink of poverty, we have a new opportunity. The national service model could present a scalable way to increase opportunity for millions of families.

To this end, Corporation for National and Community Service CEO Wendy Spencer has agreed to deploy VISTAs around the country in a new **Shriver Corps**. They will develop tools connecting eligible low-income families with the educational opportunities, job training, and access to public benefits that can help them get on firm economic footing—and then train community volunteers how to use these tools. By pairing the Shriver

Corps' low-cost, high-impact human capital with computer technology we have today, we can help states easily and efficiently identify and connect struggling women and their families to available sources of assistance—providing more efficient access instead of brick walls.

Unfortunately, even though Congress authorized a large expansion of AmeriCorps in 2009, funding has actually declined in recent years, causing many programs to close. Fully funding Ameri-Corps, particularly VISTA and the Opportunity Corps authorized under the Edward M. Kennedy Serve America Act, would enable programs such as LIFT to grow. In addition, states could use federal Temporary Assistance for Needy Families, or TANF, block-grant funds to support AmeriCorps positions that assist TANF recipients; one of the goals of the law is to "end the dependence of needy parents on government benefits by promoting job preparation, work and marriage."

In this way, a national system of AmeriCorps members leading, training, and working with volunteers—all using shared computer technology to connect clients with programs and opportunities—could provide a scalable solution to supply the human resources needed to help every low-income family find a way out of poverty. Fifty years after the War on Poverty was launched, we can do this.

ENDNOTE

1 AmeriCorps service may also be part time, with benefits prorated.

AMI VITALE

ALLIE WINANS • Missoula, Montana

Allie Winans is the mother of two daughters, and her husband, Frank, is a truck driver for Missoula Septic Services. Both of their daughters suffer from severe disabilities, and Allie is their 24-hour caretaker.

Forced to file for bankruptcy due to health care costs and medical-bill debt, the family struggles to stay afloat financially and emotionally. "We are in survival mode," Allie said. But they remain focused on getting through each day as a team. Allie also relies on Women's Opportunity and Resource Development, Inc. of Missoula for support and as a connection to resources to help her and her family.

A Hand Up, Not a Handout

By C.L. "BUTCH" OTTER, governor of Idaho

Similar to many states, Idaho has spent much of the past five years weathering the Great Recession and its challenges, from job losses to home foreclosures to budget shortfalls. Such dire challenges, however, can often bring change, and these recent changes in our economic landscape have opened the door to a great opportunity.

In 2010, Idaho became one of nine states partnering with the Urban Institute and the Ford Foundation in the Work Support Strategies project, a focused effort to transform the landscape of health and human services—and specifically the delivery of those services to low-income working families—by sharing innovative ideas, identifying best practices, and collaborating on solutions. Idaho's goal is to approach "welfare" from a new perspective: not as a handout, but rather as a strategic hand up.

There is broad consensus in our state that government services should be aimed not at growing entitlement programs but rather at helping families enter and succeed in the workforce. This isn't a new idea. As Thomas Jefferson once said, "If we can but prevent the government from wasting the labors of the people under the pretense of taking care of them, they must become happy."

Through the Work Support Strategies project, the Idaho Department of Health and Welfare has joined with community partners, policymakers, officials in other states, and the Urban Institute to identify gaps in the services available to low-income working Idahoans and reduce the impediments to receiving those services for which they are eligible. We have specifically focused on improving delivery of Supplemental Nutrition Assistance Program, or SNAP, benefits—formerly known as food stamps—Medicaid, child care subsidies, and our temporary cash program to the working poor, while streamlining administration and reducing our own operating costs.

For instance, we have introduced technological innovations such as a cloud-based phone system for statewide universal case management. Now when someone calls to apply for or recertify benefits, any eligibility decision maker anywhere in Idaho can take the phone call and complete the interview. In addition, our new case management system auto-loads verified information, triggering eligibility immediately. We have also enhanced our verification process into one easy-to-use, on-demand tool for those who make eligibility decisions. That increases the accuracy of decision making, while decreasing costly interactions with applicants.

Idaho is also on the cutting edge of what we call "business process re-engineering" to simplify cumbersome agency processes and reduce red tape. One example is our integrated application and interview process, which puts the person in direct and immediate contact with an eligibility decision maker, eliminating the need to fill out our typical eight-page paper application. We are also reducing application-processing time by using telephonic signatures, eliminating the delay caused by moving forms through the mail. One result of all this: Idaho now consistently approves SNAP applications in less than two days on average.

A big focus of our Work Support Strategies project has involved integrating the various programs for low-income families. States have to deal with multiple federal programs administered through multiple federal agencies, each with competing policies, budgets, and reporting requirements. Idaho has spent the past two years integrating our SNAP; Medicaid; Temporary Assistance for Needy Families, or TANF; and child care programs as much as possible. To do this, our state rules on poverty levels, income calculations, verification standards, and reporting requirements have been changed across all programs.

So now with federal waiver requests, integrated application and recertification processes, and new case-management disciplines, Idaho has created a holistic, family-centric approach to service design and delivery.

Improving the Idaho Child Care Program has been another one of our goals. For breadwinners in families living near or below the poverty level—particularly single-parent families—finding and paying for child care is very often a big roadblock to finding and maintaining stable employment. We have redesigned our subsidy calculations to provide a flat rate per child, thereby creating stable, reliable subsidies for both parents and child care providers. We also have changed policies to ensure access for students receiving child care assistance while in school, but not at the expense of low-income working families.

Idaho's commitment to enabling low-income families to enter and stay in the workforce has meant investing in innovative solutions such as these. Yes, acquiring the right technology is critical. But technology is not the driver for innovation; it is only a facilitator. Real change and effective governance come from policy and eligibility innovation, simplified business redesigns with reduced paperwork, integrated verification systems, and improved communication. Now our Welfare Division, which serves one in three Idahoans over the course of a year, operates with one of the lowest-cost and most effective program administrations in the country. Outcomes such as these are proof that government can operate effectively at lower costs and with better results.

We believe that providing cost-effective administration is a responsibility of government. So, too, is providing key supports such as health coverage, food and nutrition assistance, and child care. We also believe that the path to self-sufficiency cannot be found in welfare programs alone but must include integrated and supportive services that help families get into and stay in the workforce, take advantage of new opportunities unfolding as the economy improves, and pave their own path out of poverty and into the mainstream of Idaho's economy. That's not just good for our families but also for our state.

A hand up, not a handout. Idaho's spirit of self-determination and independence is based on this principle, and we value the partnerships we've gained with the Ford Foundation, the Urban Institute, and community and state leaders who are helping us put this spirit into practice.

On the Brink with a Disabled Child

By KATIE BENTLEY of Covington, Kentucky, who testified before Congress about Supplemental Security Income, or SSI, benefits for low-income disabled children. She is on the board of The Arc of the United States, an organization advocating for the intellectually and developmentally disabled.

Will is my 10-year-old son, and he is my hero. He fuels my passion to make the future better for disabled kids and their families. He has taught me everything I know about courage and commitment.

Will seemed fine as a baby, but as he grew, it became clear that something was very wrong. He was unable to talk, take a drink, or feed himself, and the doctors thought that he had autism. Then, when he was 3, he collapsed with a massive seizure. I held him for terrifying minutes as his body banged against me, afraid he would never breathe again.

An MRI revealed brain lesions, the cause of what became frequent, violent electrical storms in his head. The diagnosis: A severe seizure disorder causing memory loss, sensory integration disorder, and developmental and intellectual disability in just about every area of his life.

He went downhill. The more seizures he had, the more he fell behind—struggling every day with feeding himself, walking, and communicating. During the day, he would learn how to do or say something; at night, seizures wiped out the information. He had to learn over and over again, and he did.

My husband William and I both had jobs and medical insurance. He is a diesel mechanic, and I operated a state-certified child care facility. But I was missing too much work because of ferrying Will to therapists and doctor appointments, emergency room visits, and long nights filled with seizures. I closed my business and took a much lower-paying job with flexible hours so I could care for him.

Eventually, Will's anxiety and need for constant care became so great that he was unable to cope. The nurses at his day care said he would lie listless and cry all day long. He would get sick and not eat for days, causing more seizures. Finally, I quit my job to care for my son full time.

William and I had always promised ourselves we would do all of this on our own. But we had to pay $1,000 a month not covered by insurance for Will's anti-seizure medications, and we found we could barely afford the fuel to drive him to frequent appointments for speech, physical, and occupational therapy, not to mention constant visits to physicians on his medical team, including a developmental pediatrician, immunologist, psychologist, allergist, and others—and the co-pays for all those sessions. We were on the brink and needed help.

We turned to Social Security Insurance for low-income children with disabilities. We held our breath, as Social Security turns down almost 60 percent of all applications for this benefit.[1] Months later, Will was awarded SSI. That meant he also qualified for Medicaid coverage to supplement our own policy, alleviating the burden of so many huge co-pays for professionals and medication. And we were now able to purchase the specialized education supplies, therapy equipment, and feeding items we couldn't afford before. Every three years, SSI requalifies him for the benefit by examining his medical records and our income level.

Today, Will is much improved. He has breakthrough seizures, but for the first time, they are mostly under control. He is reading at a third-grade level. Slowly but surely, he is learning how to swim. He has become a great activist for kids with disabilities, and he got a Kentucky State Advocacy Award for helping pass a law protecting children from "restraint and seclusion"[2] in public school—a practice of which Will was a victim. We believe his preschool teacher punished him because he couldn't learn like the other kids, and we found out only after he learned how to talk and told us.

In 2011, Will and I attended a hearing held by the House Ways and Means Subcommittee on Human Resources. I listened as "experts" shared their belief that families of children with severe disabilities are getting rich from SSI government aid. Rich? I told them of our struggles to get and keep what Will needed. I told them that Will wouldn't be where he is today if we hadn't had access to these resources. I talked about my expectations that he will contribute to his community and not be the burden the experts believe these children become as adults. As a matter of fact, I now work part time helping other children with disabilities learn how to do just that: not be afraid to go out and be an active part of their world.

Right before that trip, when he was almost 7, Will picked up a book and read for the first time. I burst into tears. After that, he'd say before reading, "Mommy, are you gonna cry?" My son—my hero—has a big heart. With all of his setbacks, he never quits. And that's the greatest lesson he ever taught me.

ENDNOTES

1 Social Security Administration, "Table V.C2.—Disabled Child Claims: Disposition of Applications for SSI Disability Benefits by Year of Filing and Level of Decision." In "Annual Report of the Supplemental Security Income Program" (2012), available at http://www.ssa.gov/OACT/ssir/SSI12/ssi2012.pdf.

2 U.S. Department of Education, "Restraint and Seclusion," available at http://www2.ed.gov/policy/seclusion/index.html (last accessed September 2013).

Workers at La Cocina's commercial kitchen in San Francisco, California, learn culinary skills and gain experience to start their own businesses. {BARBARA RIES}

What If Employers Put Women at the Center of Their Workplace Policies?

When Businesses Design Workplaces that Support their Employees,
Both the Businesses and the Employees Benefit

By Ellen Galinsky, James T. Bond, and
Eve Tahmincioglu, Families and Work Institute

(!) STUNNING FACT

Forty-two percent of low-income women experience
high levels of stress compared with 22 percent of men.

It's early in the morning in communities all across the United States and people are heading to work. They fill the highways, streets, and sidewalks as they stream into their workplaces. There are nearly 29 million low-income workers in our nation, living in families whose annual incomes fall below 200 percent of the federal poverty level,[1] or less than $36,966 a year for a single mother with two children.[2] Moreover, the median or typical annual income of a low-income family is about $17,000.[3]

To the outside world, these employees may look like everyone else, but the challenges they face are quite different from middle- and higher-income employees.

In this chapter, we provide a snapshot of the low-income workforce and share the stories of several low-income, employed women. Through their experiences, we are able to highlight the distinct challenges they face and what can help them prosper.

Using nationally representative data, we identify the characteristics of jobs and workplaces that improve employee well-being and benefit employers as well and provide examples of companies successfully putting these practices into action.

Finally, we provide a list of questions for employers that we call a "Thrive Index." The index enables employers to identify company policies and best practices that promote the success of these workers, creating a thriving workplace for employee and employer alike.

EDUCATING YOURSELF INTO THE MIDDLE CLASS —THE STORY OF STACEY JONES

Consider Stacey Jones from Denver.[4] At 47 years old, she has a good, steady job as a receptionist for an investment firm. But her life wasn't always like this. At 20, she was a single mother doing everything she could to stay in technical school. During her nearly two years at the now-defunct United College of Business, she was temporarily put on academic probation because of two major challenges she faced—she wasn't prepared to be a student, lacking time management skills and research experience, and she was dispirited by the poor child care choices she had. Because she didn't know of any assistance to help her pay for child care, she left her newborn with a neighbor. "I hated leaving him there," she said. "He was there for 10 months."

Looking back, she felt she had no other choice. "Going to school was the only way for me to eventually get out of the cycle of poverty."

After she finished school that year, graduating with a certificate in business administration, she got a low-wage job. But when she couldn't afford to have her son immunized, she quit, choosing welfare over work because, at that time, she could get her son's health care covered on welfare. She hated this solution. "It was really a safety net," she said. "I never really wanted to live on it." But making $15,000 a year and unable to afford many necessities, she felt it was her only option.

Soon Stacey found another job as a coordinating counselor at a religious social service organization. While her employer covered her personal health insurance, her son remained uninsured. And daily transportation—getting her son to and from child care and herself to and from work—was a nightmare, involving a total of six buses a day. "After two years of doing that, my life wasn't changing," she said. "I didn't want to do it anymore."

At the social service agency, Stacey had a supervisor who pushed her to further her education and consider going to college. "I decided that I *wanted* to go back to school," she said. "I resigned from my job, got welfare, and started college."

During that time, she got married and moved from California to Colorado. When she married, her finances improved somewhat thanks to two incomes supporting one household. "We stayed married 15 years," Stacey said. "I worked really hard to get a career for myself and get an education. I studied mental health and counseling."

Mental health is a subject Stacey understands. Life was very stressful for her, and in order to cope, she made what she calls some unhealthy lifestyle choices. While she had a long-term relationship, she now realizes all of her relationships back then were heavily influenced by financial necessity. She also used alcohol and marijuana to self-medicate and had several unplanned, unwanted pregnancies. "My mental health suffered. I was depressed. I didn't know it at the time," she explained.

But she kept moving forward.

In May 2013, Stacey graduated from college with a Bachelor of Science degree in mental health and counseling from Metropolitan State University of Denver.

It took her 20 years to reach this milestone.

"I don't know if it helped me climb the corporate ladder, but it's changed my life. I do use the skills I learned at school at my job now," she said.

"Just the exposure to educated people changes your life. My goal is applying to graduate school now. I will!"

Stacey is no longer on the brink.

"I know how to make healthy choices in regard to relationships with men and people in general. I do not self-medicate any longer, and I have tools and skills that I can use at any time," she said, adding that she now makes about $50,000 a year and is not receiving any public assistance.

She said: "I *was* a low-income employee—it was in the past!"

PUSHING BACK FROM THE BRINK IS MUCH MORE THAN AN INDIVIDUAL JOURNEY—AN EFFECTIVE WORKPLACE MATTERS

We tend to assume that low-wage employees such as Stacey, who manage to over-come difficult circumstances, improve their long-term financial stability, and move into the middle class, have greater willpower and discipline—that they work harder than others. That's the American myth—the pull-ourselves-up-by-our-bootstraps story. But that's not the whole story. While individual effort matters, this is also a story about the social supports available to these low-income employees.

Here again, the story is more complex than we may think. "Social supports" tend to be seen as helpful parents, encouraging teachers, and perhaps social service providers and the assistance they offer. All of these matter over the course of a lifetime, but so does where someone works and with whom they work.

A person's workplace can make a big difference to her or his well-being and suc-cess in life. Using the National Study of the Changing Workforce, or NSCW—a nationally representative study of the U.S. workforce—Families and Work Insti-tute has been able to identify various characteristics of workplaces that—based on strong research evidence—benefit employees and employers alike. These char-acteristics form the core of an Effective Workplace.

For employers, the benefits include having employees who are more likely to be satisfied with and engaged in their jobs, less likely to have family issues that negatively affect their productivity, and more likely to remain with their organiza-tion. The benefits for employees include a greater likelihood of better physical and mental health and fewer work problems that spill over into their home lives.

Chapter findings

The workplace findings in this chapter primarily come from the National Study of the Changing Workforce, or NSCW, unless otherwise referenced. This ongoing research program of Families and Work Institute peri-odically surveys nationally representative samples of employed people in the United States using random-digit-dial telephone interviews.

These findings are drawn from the 2008 NSCW survey and look only at wage and salaried employees in the U.S. workforce (sample size=2,769). The response rate is 54.6 percent and the maximum sampling error for the total sample is approximately +/- 1 percent.

Sabrina Jenkins of Goose Creek, South Carolina, sorts through paperwork and catches up on phone calls at Charleston County Housing and Redevelopment Authority, or CCHRA, which provides workplace flexibility so that she can attend to her recent health care needs. {CALLIE SHELL}

Families and Work Institute's seven characteristics of Effective Workplaces:
- Adequate benefits
- Job autonomy
- Learning opportunities and challenges
- Supervisor support for job success
- Supervisor support for meeting personal and family needs
- Culture of respect and trust
- Workplace flexibility

It is important to note that the characteristics of Effective Workplaces are linked to positive outcomes for all employees—both men and women, be they low, middle, or high income.[5]

These characteristics mattered a great deal in Stacey's journey. Finishing college has been pivotal, and it was Stacey's supervisor who, many years before, convinced her of the value of a college degree. Her supervisor also gave her the time to pursue her education. This workplace flexibility has made it possible for Stacey to manage on a day-to-day basis. In fact, she began her work at the Denver investment firm in a job-sharing arrangement, working 20 hours per week. Eventually, she was able to move to full time.

During her journey, Stacey had some supervisors who weren't as supportive. She recalled one supervisor who resisted giving her time to attend her son's parent-teacher conferences and others who didn't understand why being low income made her life different from theirs. One supervisor couldn't fathom why she couldn't afford to fix her car. She said it was clear from the way he looked at her that he couldn't relate at all.

Fortunately, at the Denver investment firm where Stacey now works, there are stated values about respecting each individual's insights and expertise. Stacey pointed to the firm's "culture lunches" as promoting an Effective Workplace. These lunches allow employees to learn about the diversity of their co-workers' backgrounds in order to promote a culture of greater mutual respect and support.

LOW-INCOME WOMEN ARE THE BACKBONE OF OUR ECONOMY—AND OF THEIR FAMILIES

The jobs that Stacey held as she moved out of poverty are crucial to our economy. To understand the significance of these jobs, one has only to think, "What if?" What if women in lower-wage jobs didn't go to work for a day? Who would handle reception at companies? Who would wait tables? Who would answer calls at call centers, or provide administrative support and cleaning services in offices? Who would work the checkout counters in stores or be the nursing aides in hospitals? Who would provide home health care for the elderly or care for and teach our youngest children?

From research scientists to brain surgeons, lawmakers to CEOs, entrepreneurs to executives, and from small business owners to all those who earn middle and higher incomes—all of these people depend on the low-wage workforce to provide the services and products they need to do their own jobs. And women are disproportionately represented in these low-paying, support jobs. They are the backbone of our economy.

Families and Work Institute's NSCW[6] finds that low-income employees are more likely than middle- and higher-income employees not only to be women, but also to be younger, less well educated, single, and more likely to have children.

A snapshot of the low-income workforce

The average low-wage employee is:[7]

- **Younger**—63 percent are under 34 years old versus 14 percent of the high-income workforce.

- **Female**—55 percent are female versus 46 percent of the high-income workforce.

- **Less well educated**—Only 36 percent have any postsecondary education, and only 9 percent have a college or higher degree, compared to 82 percent of the high-income workforce—though low-income employees are more likely to be currently enrolled in school or training (28 percent versus 19 percent).

- **Less likely to be married or living with a partner**—36 percent are married or living with a partner compared with 87 percent of the high-income workforce.

- **More likely to have children**—51 percent have children under 18 versus 33 percent of the high-income workforce, and 18 percent have children under 3 compared to 5 percent of the high-income workforce.

Here she fits the statistics, too. According to the NSCW,[8] only 14 percent of all low-income employed women have husbands or partners who are employed full time (versus 77 percent of high-income employed women). Moreover, 26 percent of low-income men who have full-time jobs work in industries where they are likely to experience frequent layoffs or reductions in hours when work is slow; consequently, their income contributions are variable.

Among the 62 percent of low-income employed women with families (that is, they have a spouse/partner and/or children who live with them), 85 percent contribute 50 percent or more of family income and 69 percent contribute 100 percent, according to the NSCW.

Clearly these women are the backbones not just of the economy but also of their families.

THE NEED FOR FLEXIBILITY—
THE STORIES OF KATIE DAVIS AND SOFIA LOPEZ

Katie Davis is 40 years old, lives on her own, and is currently underemployed.[9] For three years, she had a good job with a defense contractor where she managed

FIGURE 1

Personal/family lives of low-income employed women

- **19%** Single, no children, and living with parents
- **19%** Single, no children, and living on own
- **33%** Single mother
- **10%** Husband/partner not employed
- **14%** Husband/partner full time (35+hrs/wk)
- **5%** Husband/partner part time (<35hrs/wk)

Source: Families and Work Institute, "2008 National Study of the Changing Workforce."

workflow software, but in March 2012, she was laid off. She has worked temporary positions ever since. She is representative of the 38 percent of women in the low-wage workforce who are single and have no children; half of these women live with their parents and half live on their own.

Katie is not alone in being underemployed. Low-income employees work fewer hours than high-income employees—41 percent work part time in their main jobs compared with only 9 percent of high-income employees. In addition, they are less likely to work regular daytime hours (56 percent versus 81 percent of high-income employees) and more likely to work on Saturdays and Sundays (38 percent versus 18 percent of high-income employees).[10]

Not surprisingly, 44 percent of the low-income workforce would like to work more paid hours. In contrast, only 6 percent of the high-income workforce want more paid hours.[11]

So what stands in the way of working more? Here, low-income men and women differ dramatically. In the NSCW, men and women were asked why they work fewer hours than they wish. Low-income men were far more likely than the women surveyed to say they can't find a job that offers more paid hours (46 percent versus 22 percent), while low-income women were more likely to say that they can't get the flexibility they need to manage work, personal, and family responsibilities (21 percent versus 1 percent).

Flexibility is very important for Sofia Lopez.[12] She is a part-time student working toward her bachelor's degree; her ultimate goal is to help domestic violence victims. She also works part time as a security officer at a hotel and spa. Her hours are from 7 a.m. until 3 p.m., two to three days a week. She then goes to school from 4 p.m. until 8 p.m. or sometimes until 10 p.m.

Twenty-one percent of low-income women said they work fewer hours than they'd like because they can't get the flexibility they need to manage work, personal, and family responsibilities, as many as said they can't find a job with more hours.

"I have had a 23-cent-per-hour pay raise in four years," Sofia explained. "My monthly rent has gone up $150 since I moved in four years ago. I get paid, and three days later I'm broke. I have my elderly dad that lives with me and I take care of him."

Adding to her stress and responsibilities, Sofia's father has diabetes and her daughter has health problems. "My youngest daughter had surgery a while back. It was bad for her. I had to take time off. They really gave me a hard time about taking time for her surgery and her aftercare."

Sofia feels that more workplace flexibility would make all of the difference in her ability to be productive. "If there was flexibility—if the employer didn't frown upon you and make you feel you're wrong for taking care of your family—there wouldn't be so much stress in the workplace."

Indeed, the majority of low-income women teetering on the economic brink believe they would benefit from employers who provided paid time off to deal with their own illnesses or those of family members. According to polling conducted for *The Shriver Report* by Greenberg Quinlan Rosner Research and TargetPoint Consulting, 90 percent of women in this group feel 10 days of paid sick leave would be "very useful," compared with 78 percent in the general population. This is higher than the 86 percent of women on the brink who felt an increase in pay and benefits would be "very useful."

In the NSCW, employees were asked how important various job characteristics would be in deciding to take a new job. Overall, 55 percent of low-income employed mothers surveyed said it would be "extremely important" to "have the flexibility I need to manage my work and personal or family life." Another 42 percent of working mothers (for a total of 97 percent) said it would be "very important," while only 3 percent said "somewhat important." No one surveyed said it was "not important."[13]

A Certified Nursing Assistant, or CNA, license from a technical school can help low-income women qualify for a higher-paying job. Caitlin Bell, pictured here, works as a CNA in Chattanooga, Tennessee. { BARBARA KINNEY }

THE NEED FOR CHILD CARE—THE STORY OF LUCIA HERRERA

Lucia Herrera is a 30-year-old mother of three children, with a preschooler in a Head Start program and 2-year-old twins.[14] She works four days a week from 8 a.m. to 4 p.m. as a family support worker at a New York City charity. This requires her to make home visits to families in the South Bronx to help them with their problems. She lives with her fiancé, but with a salary of only $28,000 a year, making ends meet has been tough.

"My fiancé just started working recently," Lucia said. "He couldn't find a job for a long while, and everything was on my shoulders. Now things are finally looking up for him."

One of Lucia's biggest expenditures is child care. She has the twins in a private center that costs $300 a week. Because her job entails helping low-income families receive publicly funded supports, such as food and clothing, she understands how to navigate the complex legal requirements for receiving child care assistance. Even so, it was a battle for her to get the subsidy she was entitled to for her own children.

"After a lot of fighting and arguing, I finally received a subsidy to help me pay for day care," she said. "I was wrongfully denied the benefit. It started one week ago. I got fortunate! I have an amazing day care provider who is fully aware of my circumstances. She's been working with me."

The impact of this seven-month battle is that Lucia owes a lot of money to her child care provider. Among all low-income employed women with children, the cost of child care is problematic. According to the National Study of the Changing Workforce, one-third (34 percent) of those surveyed say that it is "very difficult" to pay for child care. The inability to afford child care is also a major reason low-income women are unable to increase their hours. It is a catch-22 when working more hours to earn more money may not, in fact, cover the cost of the additional child care needed to take on more hours.[15]

IT'S NO WONDER LOW-INCOME EMPLOYEES EXPERIENCE HIGH LEVELS OF STRESS

Given the findings about the kinds of lives that low-income employees lead, how are they faring? The answer: not nearly as well as middle- and high-income employees, as Table 1 reveals. According to the National Study of the Changing Workforce,[16] low-income employees are more likely to have:

• **Poorer health:** Despite their generally younger age, 27 percent of the low-income workforce report poor or fair health versus only 15 percent of the high-income workforce.

• **Higher stress:** More than three times as many low-income employees experience high levels of stress (38 percent) as high-income employees (12 percent). Only 14 percent of low-income employees have low levels of stress.

Only 14 percent of low-income employees have low levels of stress.

- **More depression:** In response to questions from a widely used standardized screening scale for depression used by the NSCW, 23 percent of low-income employees exhibit two of the three indicators of depression, compared with 10 percent of high-income employees.

- **Poorer mental health overall:** According to a general measure of mental health, 40 percent of low-income employees rank in the poor category, more than twice the percentage of high-income employees (17 percent).

TABLE 1

Health and well-being of employees at different income levels

Outcomes	Income group			Sig.
	Low income	Middle income	High income	
Health in general	*(n=601)*	*(n=1,480)*	*(n=566)*	
Poor	3%	2%	1%	
Fair	24%	20%	14%	***
Good	43%	49%	52%	
Excellent	29%	29%	33%	
Level of stress	*(n=600)*	*(n=1,482)*	*(n=567)*	
Low	14%	26%	33%	
Moderate	49%	53%	55%	***
High	38%	21%	12%	
Sleep problems	*(n=545)*	*(n=1,294)*	*(n=497)*	
Few or none	21%	27%	29%	
Some	41%	45%	49%	***
Many	38%	28%	22%	
Depression	*(n=599)*	*(n=1,474)*	*(n=565)*	
No indication	55%	65%	77%	
One indication	22%	19%	13%	***
Two indications	23%	16%	10%	
Overall mental health	*(n=601)*	*(n=1,474)*	*(n=565)*	
Poor	40%	23%	17%	
Fair	44%	52%	51%	***
Good	17%	25%	32%	

n=sample size

Source: Families and Work Institute, "2008 National Study of the Changing Workforce."
Statistical significance: *** = p < .001; ns = not statistically significant.

LOW-INCOME WOMEN LEAD PARTICULARLY STRESSFUL LIVES

Part-time security guard and student Sofia Lopez began to see her problems pile up.[17] Her elderly father's diabetes required eye surgeries, while her daughter's surgery required substantial aftercare. The excessive demands that this family care placed upon her limited time and financial resources, as well as pressures at work to act as though none of this was happening, began to make Sofia feel sick, leading to her own trips to the doctor.

"The stress had become so overwhelming recently that the doctor thought I had a mild stroke," she explained. "They did a lot of testing and in the end decided it was an anxiety attack."

Similarly, Lucia Herrera—the mother of three whose job entails making home visits to families in the Bronx—is experiencing the negative impact of mounting pressures at home and at work.

"My stress level is very high," she said. "I have to go to therapy to help me handle stuff."[18]

Stress is more of a problem for low-income women than men: 42 percent of low-income women experience high levels of stress compared with 22 percent of men.[19] And stress can initiate a vicious cycle. Because Sofia Lopez's doctor suspected she had a mild stroke, she had to take time off from her job as a hotel security guard because the doctor wouldn't allow her to go back to work. When she returned to work, they had changed her shift to 3 p.m. to 11 p.m., affecting her ability to continue to go to school.

She explained her dilemma to her manager, saying that she wanted to better herself and stay in school, but to no avail.

"My manager said, 'It must be nice for other people to better themselves, but this is a job. Either you do it or not!'"[20]

Like many others, Sofia is also caught in another catch-22. She is 49 years old and worries that time is passing her by. Her ultimate goal is to help victims of domestic violence, but she believes that to achieve her goal and gain financial stability, she has to stay in college. Yet if she stays in school, she worries she will lose the very job on which her current economic survival depends.

DOES IT HAVE TO BE THIS WAY?

Sofia was so passionate about trying to stay in school that she went to talk to her boss's boss—a risk that could have easily backfired. She made her case to the director of the hotel, explaining she'd been there for several years and had done a good job.

His initial response wasn't encouraging. According to Sofia, he said the hotel reserved the right to change her hours whenever they felt it was necessary.

But soon after, there was hope. Sofia recalled their conversation.

"Then he said, 'But we should be able to figure out an alternative that meets our needs and allows you to meet your obligations.'" Within two hours, her supervisor had called her back. "He's supposed to talk to me to see about giving me my old schedule back."[21]

As is the case for all of the women highlighted, the workplace clearly can cause problems, or it can be part of the solution. Over the past two decades, Families and Work Institute has used data from its ongoing National Study of the Changing Workforce to identify the characteristics of jobs and workplaces that are most strongly linked to positive outcomes. But the outcomes aren't just a benefit to employees such as Sofia, Stacey, Katie, and Lucia. These outcomes benefit employers as well. And while some of these characteristics, such as fringe benefits, involve expenditures, most do not.[22]

Families and Work Institute's seven characteristics of Effective Workplaces

- Adequate benefits
- Job autonomy
- Learning opportunities and challenges
- Supervisor support for job success
- Supervisor support for meeting personal and family needs
- Culture of respect and trust
- Workplace flexibility

HOW EFFECTIVE WORKPLACES CAN BENEFIT EVERYONE[23]

Fostering workplace improvement is not typically on the public agenda when it comes to helping low-income women achieve upward mobility and financial stability. But in an Effective Workplace, everyone wins—both the employee and the employer.

Table 2 summarizes all of the statistically significant relationships we found between our indicators of Effective Workplaces and

Binita "Bini" Pradhan starts the day on her computer at 6 every morning, managing her small business, "Bini's Kitchen." When she is cooking, she says the day-to-day burdens of single motherhood seem to go away. {BARBARA RIES}

various outcomes of interest to both employers and employees. All of the relationships were positive, and most reached statistical significance.

When low-income employees work in more Effective Workplaces, they and their employers benefit in the following important ways:

• Employees are more satisfied with their jobs.

• They are more engaged and thus working harder to help their employers succeed.

• They are less likely to have problems at home that negatively affect their performance on the job, and vice versa.

• They are more committed to remaining with their employers.

• They are in better physical and mental health.[24]

When we compare the impact of Effective Workplaces on low-income women and men, the findings are quite similar for both, though somewhat more positive for women than men. It is also important to note that findings are similarly positive across the board for all employees, regardless of gender or economic status.[25]

Most of the characteristics of Effective Workplaces simply require different ways of behaving, not financial outlays. And taken together, they can yield meaningful results that improve the lives of employees as well as the fortunes of their employers. The only characteristic with unavoidable costs to employers is fringe benefits. However, even the cost of better fringe benefits may be more than offset by the benefits of having more engaged and productive employees as well as lower rates of employee turnover, as some well-known employers have discovered.

Costco is one such example. The national retailer covers almost all of its employees and contributes substantially to their health insurance and retirement plans; it has a much lower turnover rate and has higher sales with fewer employees by comparison with other retailers.[26]

TABLE 2

Characteristics of an Effective Workplace predicting outcomes for low-income employees (*n* = 600 +/-)

Characteristics of an Effective Workplace predicting outcomes	Outcomes of most interest to employers				Outcomes of most interest to employees		
	Higher job engagement	Less negative home-to-job spillover	Greater likelihood of remaining with employer	Greater job satisfaction	Less negative job-to-home spillover	Better physical health	Better mental health
Adequate fringe benefits	•		•				
Job autonomy	•	•	•	•	•		•
Learning opportunities and challenges	•		•	•	•		•
Supervisor support for job success	•	•	•	•	•	•	•
Supervisor support for meeting personal and family needs	•	•	•	•	•		•
Culture of respect	•	•	•	•	•		•
Overall workplace flexibility	•	•	•	•	•	•	•
Workplace effectiveness	•	•	•	•	•	•	•

n = sample size

Source: Families and Work Institute, "2008 National Study of the Changing Workforce." Bullets represent positive outcomes significant at p<.01 or higher (i.e., the finding would occur by chance less than 1 in 100).

Efforts to foster Effective Workplaces should not just be on the public agenda—they should drive it. As our brief case histories of four women clearly demonstrate, access to health care, learning opportunities, supervisor support, and flexible work arrangements—key aspects of Effective Workplaces—can create the conditions necessary for good health, educational achievement, job advancement, upward mobility, and generally better outcomes for employees, employers, and society.

WHEN WORK WORKS—A VEHICLE
FOR TURNING RESEARCH INTO ACTION

Since 2003, Families and Work Institute, or FWI, has been turning its research on Effective Workplaces into action through a project called When Work Works, initially funded by the Alfred P. Sloan Foundation and now in partnership with the largest human resources association in the United States, the Society for Human Resource Management, or SHRM. Today, When Work Works collaborates with communities through SHRM chapters and state councils, and it is scheduled to be present in all 50 states by the end of 2014.[27]

The purpose of the project is to effect change through two primary methods: educational and media outreach about workplace flexibility and effectiveness, and the creation and maintenance of the Alfred P. Sloan Awards for Excellence in Workplace Effectiveness and Flexibility.[28]

There has been considerable progress in making workplace effectiveness and flexibility a critical business issue. The Sloan Awards program began in 2005 with 55 applicants and in 2013 had 536 applicants—an 875 percent increase over eight years—with a total of 4,810 applicant worksites.

The Sloan Award application begins with a rigorous process for employers; a senior representative of each organization at the applying worksite must detail its range of flexibility options and cultural support for flexibility. If the applicant organization qualifies by ranking among the top 20 percent of employers nationwide—based on FWI's ongoing nationally representative study of organizations[29]—a random sample of its employees is asked to fill out a parallel survey. This provides information on whether or not the employees actually have access to an Effective Workplace, based on FWI's seven criteria. Two-thirds of the winning score is based on the employees' responses.[30]

EXAMPLES OF EFFECTIVE WORKPLACES IN ACTION

Although low-income employees generally have less access to Effective Workplaces than more advantaged employees, there are workplaces all over the country—including winners of the Sloan Awards—that show it is not only possible to improve workplaces for all employees, but that it benefits employers to do so.

"The first thing you see with working moms making that transition from public assistance," explained Kevin Schnieders, CEO of Educational Data Systems, Inc., a workforce development consulting company in Dearborn, Michigan, "is they often have less stability in their lives, leading to a host of issues impacting their work." Schnieders's company employs about 400 people, and nearly 20 percent are women making less than $37,000.[31]

Schnieders believes low-income women who are trying to pull themselves out of poverty sometimes need a bit of extra help, pointing to tardiness and absenteeism related to child care problems or child custody issues, for example. In those cases, he said, "we sit down with them, listen, and understand how we can impact it in a positive way, instead of punitive."

Every employer, he continued, "has a limit where they reach their understanding because of financial issues, but we try to stretch that as much as we can." They do it, he added, because it's the right thing to do and because the end result is a loyal, hardworking employee.

Educational Data Systems is one of the Sloan Award winners embodying many of the seven characteristics we find foster an Effective Workplace. In this chapter, we include many of our present and past winners that employ a significant number of low-income workers, or hourly employees, and are considered by their own employees as great employers.

ADEQUATE BENEFITS

In the National Study of the Changing Workforce, or NSCW, employees are asked whether they have the following benefits:
• Personal health insurance available through my main job
• Personal health insurance paid partly or entirely by employer
• Family health insurance coverage available through my main job
• Family health insurance paid partly or entirely by my employer
• Employer makes contribution to pension/retirement plan

Only 32 percent of low-income employees—women and men alike—have high levels of benefits, compared with 69 percent of high-income employees, according to the NSCW.[32]

Employees at 1-800 CONTACTS, based in Draper, Utah, have access to low-cost medical plans, as well as subsidized meals, emergency financial assistance, and financial training workshops, programs that are especially helpful to low-income employees.[33]

The firm, which employs 830 workers, also provides lots of flexibility within its organization, even to call center employees who typically aren't able to work from home or have much control over their schedules. The company offers more than 200 shifts to call center employees who work onsite, and for those whose jobs can be done remotely, the firm equips them with at-home workstations.

Veterans receive extra flexibility and are allowed to work part time as they transition back into civilian life. The families of military members are given extra flexibility on a case-by-case basis and offered up to six weeks of personal leave upon request.

Leaders at the company are convinced all these measures have had a positive impact on productivity and health insurance renewal rates. 1-800 CONTACTS rarely has to advertise open job positions—80 percent of applicants come from employee referrals.[34]

JOB AUTONOMY

Employees in the NSCW are also asked how strongly they agree with having the following in their job:
• I have the freedom to decide what I do on my job.
• It is my own responsibility to decide how my job gets done.
• I have a lot of say about what happens on my job.

Only 13 percent of low-income employees have high levels of job autonomy compared with 20 percent of high-income employees.[35]

LEARNING OPPORTUNITIES AND CHALLENGES

Employees in the NSCW are asked how strongly they agree, or whether they have access, to the following on their job:
• My job requires that I keep learning new things.
• My job requires that I be creative.

• I get to do different things on my job.
• I have the opportunity on my job to develop my own special abilities.
• My employer offers training/education opportunities.
• My employer pays for job-related training/education off the job.

As has been the pattern thus far, low-income employees have fewer opportunities for learning and challenge in their jobs: 19 percent of low-income employees have many learning opportunities compared with 31 percent of high-income employees.[36]

Skylla, an engineering firm in Humble, Texas, with 175 employees, offers tuition assistance for employees wishing to continue their professional development. It also sends its employees to certification trainings.[37]

The firm leaders have also offered to cover relocation expenses to low-income families attempting to move, and they accept special flexibility requests for low-wage employees. Offering such programs to those employees in need clearly hasn't hurt the bottom line. Skylla has enjoyed consecutive growth year after year, as well as below-average attrition rates for the industry.[38]

SUPERVISOR OR MANAGER SUPPORT FOR JOB SUCCESS

Employees in the NSCW are asked how strongly they agree with having the following in their job:
• My supervisor or manager keeps me informed of the things I need to know to do my job well.
• My supervisor or manager has expectations of my performance on the job that are realistic.
• My supervisor or manager recognizes when I do a good job.
• My supervisor or manager is supportive when I have a work problem.

There is no statistically significant difference among low-income, middle-income, and high-income employees in the extent to which their supervisors support them succeeding on the job: 43 percent report that they have very supportive supervisors. Perhaps surprisingly, low-income women have higher levels of support for job success than low-income men (47 percent versus 37 percent). The reasons for this disparity are not clear but worth additional investigation.[39]

Educational Data Systems provides training and tuition assistance for all its employees,[40] but there are times when a person's history may mean they need some extra coaching.

"We don't consciously say, 'We need to train this person more because they're low income,'" said Educational Data Systems CEO Kevin Schnieders, but he pointed out this group often lacks the skills needed to succeed, such as communication skills or the ability to work well in teams.

One employee who came to his company after living on welfare was put into a managerial position about a year and a half ago and ended up struggling in the job. The company embedded a manager in her office for three months, and she got one-on-one management training, Schnieders noted.

"Did we do that because she was a low-income mom? No. But we knew where she came from. There's got to be a level of understanding."

"She's doing great work," he added.

SUPERVISOR OR MANAGER SUPPORT FOR PERSONAL OR FAMILY NEEDS

Employees in the NSCW are asked how strongly they agree with having the following in their job:
• My supervisor or manager is fair and doesn't show favoritism in responding to employees' personal or family needs.
• My supervisor or manager is responsive when I have family or personal business to take care of.
• My supervisor or manager is understanding when I talk about personal or family issues that affect my work.
• I feel comfortable bringing up personal or family issues with my supervisor or manager.
• My supervisor or manager really cares about the impact of work on my personal and family life.

Similarly, there is no statistically significant difference among employees of different income levels when it comes to whether their supervisors provide support when personal and family needs arise—and no difference between low-income men and women.

One might expect one gender to experience more bias, but that is not the case here. Employees, however, are much less likely to report that their supervisors are supportive when they have personal and family issues (27 percent report a high level of support) than supportive of their succeeding on the job (43 percent report high level of support).[41]

The leaders at insurance and benefit provider Unum in Chattanooga, Tennessee, with 2,528 employees, realize some employees may need a bit more economic assistance than others. The needs of low-wage employees are met through child care subsidies, lower-cost cell-phone plans and laptops, a ride-share program, and the opportunity to work remotely to save on commuting costs.[42]

All employees have a performance and development plan that gives them access to a wide range of internal training programs and other developmental opportunities. Unum management knows that the route to an engaged workforce is ensuring their personal and professional well-being. That's why they work hard to support their employees' success.[43]

CULTURE OF RESPECT AND TRUST

Employees are asked in the NSCW how strongly they agree with having the following in their job:
• I can be myself on my job.
• My managers seek information and new ideas from employees.
• On my job I sometimes have to do things that go against my conscience.
• I can trust what our managers say.
• My managers deal honestly and ethically with employees and clients.
• I feel a part of the group of people I work with.

Low-income employees are just as likely (25 percent) as middle- and high-income employees to experience a high level of respect and trust on the job.

Innovative Care Management, or ICM, is a woman-owned health care management company with 53 employees located in Milwaukie, Oregon, that promotes a culture of respect both for patients and for staff. ICM managers know that their employees can be compassionate advocates for patients only if they themselves are treated compassionately.

Dee Saint Franc, 23, laughs with a colleague at Foster Forward in Providence, Rhode Island. Before the organization hired her full time, she served as a volunteer on its youth panel. A former foster child herself, Dee is happy with her position and the supportive, respectful relationships she has with her co-workers. {BARBARA RIES}

To help employees negotiate work and personal needs, ICM takes advantage of technology to provide a telecommuting model, with many staff only in the office once a month, customer service staff able to work from home 60 percent of the time, and a majority of staff opting for four-day workweeks.

The four-day workweek has been particularly helpful in preventing burnout among nursing staff on the frontlines whose patients and families struggle with chronic or catastrophic health conditions. Treating employees with dignity and respect, and continuously reviewing processes and available technology to find efficiencies, works well for this company. Retention is high: 60 percent of employees have been at ICM for five or more years and 38 percent have been at ICM for 10 or more years.[44]

Low-income women also have less access to high levels of workplace flexibility than low-income men (15 percent versus 23 percent).

OVERALL WORKPLACE FLEXIBILITY

Employees are asked in the NSCW whether they have access to the following at their job:
• Receives paid vacation days and paid holidays
• Allowed at least five paid days per year for personal illness and five days per year to care for a sick child without losing pay, using vacation days, or having to make up an excuse
• Allowed to choose own starting and quitting times within some range of hours and to temporarily change starting and quitting times on short notice when special needs arise
• Allowed to work part of regular paid hours at home
• Could arrange to work part time, if currently full time, or full time, if currently part time, in current position
• Has work schedule flexibility needed to manage personal and family responsibilities and has a work schedule or shift that meets needs
• High overall control in scheduling work hours
• Has no difficulty taking time off during a workday to take care of personal/family matters
• No less likely to get ahead in jobs/careers if employee asks for time off or schedule changes to meet personal/family needs
• Less often required to work paid/unpaid extra hours with little or no notice

Low-income employees have far less access to flexibility than middle- and high-income employees. Only 18 percent of low-income employees have high levels of access. By comparison, 37 percent of high-income employees do. Low-income women also have less access to high levels of workplace flexibility than low-income men (15 percent versus 23 percent). This finding is particularly problematic since women need it most, given the numbers who are single mothers and/or largely responsible for the financial well-being of their families.[45]

"When someone has a baby or family life issue we say, 'How can we make this work? You are valued,'" explained Jennifer A. Hearne, director of employee success at Northwest Lineman College based in Meridian, Idaho, a power-line operator training company that employs 80 people, about 30 percent of whom are considered low income. Leadership, she added, "encourages women and everyone to find creative solutions to get the work done without causing an undue family burden."[46]

Lower-income women hold essential positions at the company, including everything from receptionists to payroll clerks to administrative support. "If you can't accommodate them, you won't retain those individuals in your workforce and that leaves a big gap," she said, adding that turnover is a high expense they want to avoid.

In addition, many of the women who started in entry-level jobs at Northwest Lineman, including quite a few low-income working mothers, went on to climb the ladder at the company, Hearne pointed out.

Annie King, vice president of strategic operations at the firm, started out as a receptionist more than a decade ago and had two children under 4 years old at the time. The executive said: "It was important to me that I be there for my children—they are the most important thing in my life. Yet bringing home a paycheck was also important to our family."[47]

King isn't an anomaly. When it comes to a paycheck, 70 percent of low-income women with an employed partner reported their families could not get by without both paychecks, according to polling conducted for *The Shriver Report*. That compared with 47 percent in the general population who feel the same.

Despite work-life challenges, King was able to keep working because her managers let her set up a crib in the office if she ever needed to bring her 11-month-old son to work with her. She could also stay home with the children if they were sick.

"I have never felt that I needed to sacrifice my career to be a mom or sacrifice being a mom to have a career," she maintains. "And for that, Northwest Lineman College will forever have my unwavering commitment."

THE THRIVE INDEX:
Company policies to promote the success of low-wage women workers

Center for Poverty Research and Graduate School of Management, University of California, Davis[48]

What is the Thrive Index? It is a list of questions developed exclusively for *The Shriver Report* by researchers at UC Davis, based on a review of the extensive social science and management literature on the challenges faced by low-wage working women. Its purpose is to identify company policies and best practices that promote the success of these workers, creating a thriving workplace for employee and employer alike.

Our review covered quantitative, survey-based studies of workers; qualitative case studies of specific firms and industries; and many variations in between. Unlike many previous lists of family- or woman-friendly companies, this index is based on the specific challenges faced by women workers at the bottom of the economic ladder—workers who stay out of poverty only when factors in their own lives, their families, and their workplaces come together in a positive way.

For the identified challenges these women face, we developed questions corresponding to company policies that can most directly affect workers' likelihood of successfully navigating these difficulties, continuing as productive members of the workforce, and enhancing outcomes for themselves, their families, and their employers. Whether you're a manager or an HR director, a CEO or a small business owner, the goal is to answer "yes" to as many of the following questions as possible.

Adequate wages and benefits
- ✓ Are part-time workers paid the same (per hour, including benefits) as full-time workers performing the same or similar tasks?
- ✓ Are most part-time workers guaranteed a minimum number of hours per week? If not, are there ways they could be?
- ✓ Are workers who remain on the job for a specified period of time eligible for a pay increase?

- ✓ Are workers who remain on the job for a specified period of time eligible for paid sick leave for themselves or to care for a family member?
- ✓ When job-skill demands or responsibilities increase, are wages adjusted upward?
- ✓ Are workers paid for their entire scheduled shift, even if business is slow?
- ✓ Are hourly wages higher for nonstandard shifts, such as nights or weekends?

Opportunities for learning and upward mobility

✓ Do low-wage workers have opportunities for on-the-job or cross-task training or outside educational opportunities that can lead to upward mobility?

✓ Can schedules accommodate workers' pursuit of educational opportunities?

✓ When skill demands or job responsibilities increase, is training provided for newly assigned tasks?

✓ Can workers cross-train in different areas to increase their flexibility and value to the company (recognizing that outsourcing of some functional areas or other factors may prohibit this)?

✓ Are there opportunities for upward mobility within the company that do not require geographic relocation?

Support for personal and family needs

✓ Can worker breaks be scheduled to accommodate the need for phone calls at pre-specified times for working caregivers?

✓ Are occasional calls for urgent matters allowable? Can children or caregivers call an employee at work when necessary?

✓ Are workers who remain on the job for a specified period of time eligible during their regular work hours to care for their health or a family member's without losing pay (e.g., able to leave for an hour or two for a trip to the doctor)?

✓ Can personal time be taken in small increments of an hour or two (for doctor's appointments, parent-teacher conferences, educational opportunities, etc.)?

✓ Do you offer paid or unpaid maternity or paternity leave for workers? Is the length of this leave negotiable?

Work scheduling, predictability, and flexibility

✓ Is there a systematic way for workers to communicate their preferences for hours and schedules? If not, could some such system be implemented?

✓ Does the shift/hours scheduling system take account of workers' constraints and preferences?

✓ Are work schedules announced more than a day or two in advance? Can workers trade shifts with colleagues when time conflicts develop (allow "shift-swapping")?

✓ If workers are asked to stay beyond the end of scheduled shifts to finish assignments or for administrative procedures, are they given advance notice of when this may be required?

✓ Does the measured workload take into account the quality or difficulty of tasks along with simpler measures of the number of customers, clients, or patients?

Autonomy, respect, and trust

✓ Are workers protected from "no-fault" absence or tardiness policies (ones that lead to disciplinary actions or dismissal, even for excused absences)?

✓ Are workers allowed or encouraged to contribute ideas to better organize or improve their work teams or work areas?

✓ Can workers occasionally make personal phone calls?

CONCLUSION: A CALL TO BUSINESS TO ADAPT TO MODERN WORKERS' CIRCUMSTANCES AND HELP THEM TO THRIVE

We know low-income women are the backbone of our economy and of their families. We also know the challenges these women face are often quite different from those facing middle- and higher-income workers. These women on the brink are more likely to be younger, less well educated, without a partner, and raising kids.

What they need—and what our economy needs—are supportive, flexible, Effective Workplaces, which benefit the employee, the employer, and our nation as a whole.

It is more than an individual journey for these women. Our country faces a turning point, as we acknowledge the changes that must take place to ensure the American Dream is possible for all Americans. From fundamental changes to our educational system that promote skills as well as content knowledge to jobs that provide equitable pay, from two-generational approaches to affordable child care, we must find ways to support the low-wage women who support our economy.

And to do that, we must have Effective Workplaces.

The benefits of implementing the characteristics of an Effective Workplace are numerous for both employees and employers. Employees are more likely to be satisfied with and engaged in their jobs, which increases productivity and benefits employers. They are more likely to stay with their company or organization, which is clearly a win for employers as well. And they are less likely to be burdened with family issues that can reduce their productivity at work. Finally, employees are more likely to be healthy, with fewer work problems that spill over into their home lives. Providing an Effective Workplace makes good business sense.

But what about the cost of creating more Effective Workplaces? We know from our firsthand work with employers, and from the many examples we've studied and provided in this chapter, that the benefits of providing a more Effective Workplace outweigh the costs, most of which are negligible.

Effective management is what's required. This may be a challenge for some employers, but there are solutions. In Families and Work Institute's "2014 Guide to Bold New Ideas for Making Work Work," co-published with the Society for Human Resource Management, we identified organizations in all sectors of the economy that have succeeded in creating good jobs for those at lower levels in the employment pyramid. These employers have created jobs that result in more positive outcomes for their organizations and for their employees. The jobs develop human capital, promote quality of life, and contribute to bottom-line performance.

These are the kinds of jobs our economy and our society need as we continue to adjust to a new era of global competition. We need to move away from talking about low-income women simply getting *a job*, to talking about *good jobs*, in Effective Workplaces. This is an important first step in addressing our evolving economy's needs.

Low-wage women and their employers stand to benefit as much or perhaps even more than others from these efforts. We hope that those who employ and manage low-income workers will view this chapter as a call to action, complete with practical steps to improve workplace effectiveness and in turn both employee well-being *and* business outcomes.

THINK ABOUT THIS

Most of the characteristics of Effective Workplaces benefiting low-wage women simply require different ways of behaving, not financial outlays.

REFERENCES FOR THRIVE INDEX

Appelbaum, Eileen, P. Berg, A. Frost, and G. Preuss. 2002. "The Effects of Work Restructuring on Low-Wage, Low-Skill Workers in U.S. Hospitals." New York: Russell Sage Foundation.

Batt, Rosemary, V. Doellgast, and H. Kwon. 2005. "U.S. Call Center Industry Report 2004 National Benchmarking Report Strategy, HR Practices & Performance." Cornell University Working Paper.

Berg, Peter, and Ann C. Frost. "Dignity at Work for Low Wage, Low Skill Service Workers." *Relations Industrielles/Industrial Relations* 60 (4) (2005): 657–682.

Bernhardt, Annette. 1999. "The Future of Low-Wage Jobs: Case Studies in the Retail Industry." Columbia University Institute on Education and the Economy, Working Paper 10.

Bernhardt, Annette, L. Dresser, and E. Hatton. 2003. "The Coffee Pot Wars: Unions and Firm Restructuring in the Hotel Industry." In E. Appelbaum, A. Bernhardt, and R. Murnane, eds., *Low-Wage America: How employers are reshaping opportunity in the workplace*. New York: Russell Sage Foundation.

Bond, J.T., and E. Galinsky. 2012. "Low-Income Employees in the United States." New York: Families and Work Institute.

Bond, J.T., and E. Galinsky. 2012. "What Difference do Job Characteristics Make to Low-income Employees?" New York: Families and Work Institute.

Bond, J.T., E. Tahmincioglu, and E. Galinsky. 2012. "Not Just 'Jobs' . . . 'Good Jobs': The Low-Income Workforce Challenge." New York: Families and Work Institute.

Bornstein, Stephanie. 2012. "Work, Family, and Discrimination at the Bottom of the Ladder." *Georgetown Journal on Poverty & Law Policy*, Vol. 19.

Carre, Françoise, Chris Tilly, and Diana Denham. 2010. "Explaining Variation in the Quality of US Retail Jobs." New York: Russell Sage Foundation.

Gautié, Jérôme, and John Schmitt, eds. 2010. *Low-Wage Work in the Wealthy World*. New York: Russell Sage Foundation.

Gornick, Janet C., and Marcia Meyers. 2005. *Families That Work: Policies for Reconciling Parenthood and Employment*. New York: Russell Sage Foundation.

Heymann, J., and others. 2002. "Work-Family Issues and Low-Income Families." New York: Ford Foundation.

Lambert, Susan J., Anna Haley-Lock, and Julia R. Henly. 2012. "Schedule Flexibility in Hourly Jobs: Unanticipated Consequences and Promising Directions." *Community, Work & Family* 15 (3): 293–315.

Presser, Harriet B. 1995. "Job, Family, and Gender: Determinants of Nonstandard Work Schedules Among Employed Americans in 1991." *Demography* 32 (4): 577–598. JSTOR. Web. May 19, 2013.

Ton, Zeynep. 2009. "The Effect of Labor on Profitability: The Role of Quality." Harvard Business School Working Paper.

Ton, Zeynep. 2012. "Why 'Good Jobs' Are Good for Retailers." *Harvard Business Review* 90 (1-2): 124–131, 154.

Williams, Joan C. 2006. "One Sick Child Away from Being Fired: When 'Opting Out' is Not an Option." University of California, Hastings: The Center for WorkLife Law.

Williams, Joan C., and Penelope Huang. 2011. "Improving Work-Life Fit in Hourly Jobs: An underutilized cost-cutting strategy in a globalized world." University of California, Hastings: The Center for WorkLife Law.

ENDNOTES

1   Estimate based on analysis of public-use data from the March 2012 Social and Economic Supplement to the Current Population Survey conducted by the U.S. Census Bureau.

2   U.S. Census Bureau, *Poverty Thresholds for 2012 by Size of Family and Number of Related Children Under 18 Years* (2012), available at http://www.taxpolicycenter.org/taxfacts/Content/PDF/poverty_thresholds.pdf.

3   Low-income employees are defined as those living in families below 200 percent of the federal poverty threshold (approximately the bottom quintile or bottom 20 percent); middle-income are defined as those living between 200 percent to 650 percent of poverty; and high-income are defined as those living at 650 percent or more of poverty (approximately the top quintile or top 20 percent). The median annual incomes of families in the three groups, stated in 2013 dollars, are approximately: $16,900 low income; $67,700 middle income; $152,300 high income.

4   Stacey Jones, interview with Eve Tahmincioglu of Families and Work Institute, on July 22, 2013, and on September 5, 2013. The name of the interviewee has been changed to protect her identity and the identity of others referenced in her story.

5   Ibid.

6   The National Study of the Changing Workforce, or NSCW, is an ongoing research program of Families and Work Institute that periodically surveys nationally representative samples of employed people in the United States using random-digit-dial telephone interviews. Unless otherwise noted, the research findings presented in this chapter are drawn from the 2008 NSCW survey and look only at wage and salaried employees in the U.S. workforce (sample size=2,769). The maximum sampling error for the total sample is approximately +/- 1 percent.

7   Ibid.

8   Families and Work Institute, "2008 National Study of the Changing Workforce."

9   Katie Davis, interview with Eve Tahmincioglu of Families and Work Institute, July 23, 2013. The name of the interviewee has been changed to protect her identity and the identity of others referenced in her story.

10   Families and Work Institute, "2008 National Study of the Changing Workforce."

11   Ibid.

12   Sofia Lopez, interview with Eve Tahmincioglu of Families and Work Institute, July 19, 2013. The name of the interviewee has been changed to protect her identity and the identity of others referenced in her story.

13   Families and Work Institute, "2008 National Study of the Changing Workforce."

14   Lucia Herrera, interview with Eve Tahmincioglu of Families and Work Institute, July 23, 2013. The name of the interviewee has been changed to protect her identity and the identity of others referenced in her story.

15   Families and Work Institute, "2008 National Study of the Changing Workforce."

16   Ibid.

17   Sofia Lopez interview with Eve Tahmincioglu of Families and Work Institute, July 19, 2013. The name of the interviewee has been changed to protect her identity and the identity of others referenced in her story.

18   Lucia Herrera interview with Eve Tahmincioglu of Families and Work Institute, on July 23, 2013. The name of the interviewee has been changed to protect her identity and the identity of others referenced in her story.

19   Families and Work Institute, "2008 National Study of the Changing Workforce."

20 Sofia Lopez, interview with Eve Tahmincioglu of Families and Work Institute, July 19, 2013. The name of the interviewee has been changed to protect her identity and the identity of others referenced in her story.

21 Ibid.

22 Families and Work Institute, "2008 National Study of the Changing Workforce."

23 The concept of "workplace effectiveness" evolved from our efforts to identify characteristics of jobs and workplaces most strongly associated with positive outcomes for employers and employees using data from the 1997, 2002, and 2008 National Study of the Changing Workforce surveys. Fuller discussion of what makes for an effective workplace can be found in the following publications: J.T. Bond, E. Galinsky, and E.J. Hill, "When Work Works: Flexibility, a Critical Ingredient in Creating an Effective Workplace" (New York: Families and Work Institute, 2004); J.T. Bond and E. Galinsky, "How Can Employers Increase the Productivity and Retention of Entry-Level, Hourly Employees?" (New York: Families and Work Institute, 2006); J.T. Bond and E. Galinsky, "What Difference Do Job Characteristics Make to Low-Income Employees?" (New York: Families and Work Institute, 2012). These and other reports are available at Families and Work Institute's website.

24 Ibid.

25 Bond and Galinsky, "What Difference Do Job Characteristics Make to Low-Income Employees?"

26 J. Heymann with M. Barrera, *Profit at the Bottom of the Economic Ladder: Creating Value by Investing in Your Workforce* (Boston: Harvard Business Press, 2010); W.F. Cascio, "The Economic Impact of Employee Behaviors on Organizational Performance." In E. E. Lawler III and J. O'Toole, eds., *America at Work: Choices and Challenges* (New York: Palgrave Macmillan, 2006), pp. 241–256.

27 E. Galinsky, K. Matos, and K. Sakai-O'Neill, "Workplace Flexibility: A Model of Change," *Community, Work & Family* 16 (3) (2013): 285–306. The When Work Works project website also describes the project and results in detail.

28 Ibid.

29 The National Study of Employers periodically surveys nationally representative samples of employers in the United States. Findings from the most recent survey are published in K. Matos and E. Galinsky, "2012 National Study of Employers" (New York: Families and Work Institute, 2012).

30 Galinsky, Matos, and Sakai-O'Neill, "Workplace Flexibility: A Model of Change."

31 Kevin Schnieders, CEO of Educational Data Systems Inc., interview with Eve Tahmincioglu of Families and Work Institute, September 10, 2013, Dearborn, Michigan.

32 Families and Work Institute, "2008 National Study of the Changing Workforce."

33 Families and Work Institute and the Society for Human Resource Management, "2014 Guide to Bold New Ideas for Making Work Work" (New York: Families and Work Institute and SHRM).

34 Ibid.

35 Families and Work Institute, "2008 National Study of the Changing Workforce."

36 Ibid.

37 Families and Work Institute and the Society for Human Resource Management, "2013 Guide to Bold New Ideas for Making Work Work" (New York: Families and Work Institute and SHRM).

38 Ibid.

39 Families and Work Institute, "2008 National Study of the Changing Workforce."

40 Families and Work Institute and the Society for Human Resource Management, "2014 Guide to Bold New Ideas for Making Work Work."

41 Families and Work Institute, "2008 National Study of the Changing Workforce."

42 Families and Work Institute and the Society for Human Resource Management, "2013 Guide to Bold New Ideas for Making Work Work."

43 Ibid.

44 Families and Work Institute and the Society for Human Resource Management, "2014 Guide to Bold New Ideas for Making Work Work."

45 Families and Work Institute, "2008 National Study of the Changing Workforce."

46 Jennifer A. Hearne, director of employee success at Northwest Lineman College, Meridian, Idaho, interview with Eve Tahmincioglu of Families and Work Institute, September 13, 2013.

47 Anne King, email to Eve Tahmincioglu of Families and Work Institute, September 13, 2013.

48 The Center for Poverty Research at UC Davis is partially funded by the U.S. Department of Health and Human Services, Office of the Assistant Secretary for Planning and Evaluation. The views expressed here do not necessarily reflect the policies of the Department of Health and Human Services.

Smart Business: Reviving the American Dream

By HOWARD SCHULTZ, chairman, president, and CEO of Starbucks, who says his goal has been to serve a great cup of coffee and build a company with a conscience.

My mother was always a strong woman and a fierce believer in the American Dream. She taught me that if I worked hard, I could achieve anything I set my heart on. But I also learned firsthand that sometimes, despite our best efforts, survival itself becomes the challenge. I experienced that harsh reality growing up in New York.

I was 7 years old when I walked into our small apartment in a Brooklyn public housing project and was surprised to find my father stretched out on the couch. It was winter, and he had slipped on the ice and broken his leg and hip. He was a driver for a diaper delivery service, and when he couldn't work, they fired him. We immediately had more bills but no more paychecks—not to mention no health care coverage, no workers' compensation, no severance, and no insurance. What's more, my mother was pregnant. Unrelenting stress weighed on my parents as they struggled to care for their kids.

The memory of that experience impelled me years later to build the kind of company my dad never had a chance to work for—a company that values its employees and shows them respect. It is why, after I became head of Starbucks Coffee Company in the late 1980s, we began offering some key benefits not just to our full-time partners—which is what we call our employees—but also to our part-timers who work as few as 20 hours per week. For more than two decades, these benefits have enhanced and even saved the lives of countless Starbucks partners, more than 60 percent of whom are women working full time or part time in our stores.[1]

Back in the 1980s, few part-time workers had access to health care coverage, and in fact, soaring health care costs had forced many corporations to cut benefits for all employees.[2] But instead of looking at health coverage as an extravagant expense, I saw it as a core strategy: Treat people like family, and they'll be loyal and give you their all. I was right.

Our partners' stories speak volumes. Take Kara Reuter, a 35-year-old barista who became a store manager in Auburn, Washington. In 2013, she underwent a double mastectomy in her battle against breast cancer. Her hospital bill for the surgery alone hit $117,000—a mind-boggling amount that could have plunged her family of three into economic peril. But with her health insurance from Starbucks, Kara only had to pay $1,000. The relief she received from this "financial and emotional safety net"—as she described her coverage—allowed her to focus on her recovery and her family.

Later, in the early 1990s, we became one of the first corporations to give both full-time and part-time employees a stake in the financial success of the company in the form of Starbucks equity. We call it "Bean Stock," and it has made a big difference in many lives.[3]

Maritza Aubourg, for instance, began working as a barista in New York City when she was 24 years old. She initially used her Bean Stock to help pay for her associate's degree. In 2006, after rising to store manager, this wife and mother of two cashed in $50,000 worth of her accumulated Bean Stock for a down payment on a four-bedroom house. The child of a single mother, Maritza became the first homeowner in her family. "I wanted something better for my own two daughters just like my mom wanted something better for me," she said.

Every year, hundreds of our partners share similar stories.

I have learned that granting hallmark benefits such as health care and company stock is much more than doing the right thing for our people. These are smart business moves and corporate investments that bring huge returns—increased partner loyalty, engagement, productivity, brand value, and ultimately, top- and bottom-line growth.

It goes even further than that. As our country goes through unprecedented social and political pressures and upheaval, these types of employer-provided benefits have become, to my mind, mandatory. That's because the prioritization of partisanship over citizenship in Washington, D.C., is resulting in a historic fracturing of the programs that have long lifted people out of poverty, sustained the middle class, and served as safety nets for those unable to help themselves. The results are evident: high unemployment and reductions in social services for women and families. Our country is experiencing dwindling contributions to charitable organizations and seeing retirement become an elusive goal for many. These are just some of the problems putting millions of Americans—women and single mothers in particular, as this report makes clear—at exceptional risk.

It is clear to me that part of the solution must come from the private sector. Today's companies, with their deep fiscal and intellectual resources, can step in and provide their employees with softer landings when their lives take unfortunate turns, helping ensure that their people have opportunities to achieve their full potential during good times and bad. In addition to staples such as health care, competitive wages, profit sharing, skills training, and educational support, businesses should also find meaningful ways to serve our communities with the same vigor that we serve our customers.

Starbucks is not perfect on this front, but we continue to work on it. In 2013, despite anticipated changes resulting from the nation's new health care law, we have refused to cut benefits for our partners. We are also helping those outside our own corporate family. In response to the country's high unemployment rate, we started Create Jobs for USA with a $5 million seed grant in 2011. This campaign transforms every $5 customer donation into job-creating and job-sustaining financing for America's disadvantaged small businesses and community-development organizations.[4] The goal is to stimulate economic growth in local communities, and the success stories are pouring in.

Cynthia Duprey in recession-devastated Barre, Vermont, is an example. Massive flooding destroyed her house along with her home-based businesses, washing away Cynthia's contribution to the family's income. Jobs in Barre were scarce, and banks were unwilling to lend. But she was able to secure a $40,000 loan from a community-based lender funded in part by Create Jobs for USA. Today, Cynthia's business—Next Chapter Bookstore—is hiring. All told, Create Jobs has raised $15 million, which translates into approximately 5,000 U.S. jobs either saved or created.[5]

In addition, our own partners started the Cup Fund in 1999. Administered by Starbucks and supported with partner contributions and fundraising, it provides a safety net for employees who need help through periods of extreme financial need.[6]

The private sector can also instigate change by doing what we already do within our own organizations: develop great leaders. Our country needs more people working in our communities on the brink, as volunteers or leaders of community-focused organizations with the skills, the knowledge, the confidence, and the ideas to equip citizens—from hourly workers to business owners—with the tools they need to further help themselves.

The Los Angeles Urban League's Business Institute is one example of how trained leaders can benefit underserved communities. Their youth entrepreneurship program teaches business skills to kids ages 11 through 18 to help unlock their entrepreneurial creativity. Program graduates have started companies that employ local residents and funnel earnings back into neighborhood not-for-profit organizations.[7] The institute is one of several youth-leadership initiatives that Starbucks supports. When we provide our communities with the quality of leadership we demand for ourselves, we all win.

My mother was right: The American Dream is not dead. It just needs a lifeline. As business leaders, we have the power and the responsibility to revive the American Dream by giving hard working people such as Cynthia, Maritza, and Kara first and second chances. We cannot be bystanders. We owe it to America to lead our businesses through the lens of humanity with intelligence, creativity, and, above all, compassion.

ENDNOTES

1 CNN Money, "100 Best Companies to Work For: Starbucks," available at http://money.cnn.com/magazines/fortune/best-companies/2013/snapshots/94.html?iid=bc_fl_list (last accessed September 2013).

2 Alain C. Enthoven and Victor R. Fuchs, "Employment-Based Health Insurance: Past Present, and Future," *Health Affairs* 25 (6) (2006): 1538–1547, available at http://content.healthaffairs.org/content/25/6/1538.long.

3 Starbucks, "Your Special Blend: Rewarding Our Partners" (2012), p. 11, available at http://www.starbucks.com/assets/7343fbbdc87845ff9a000ee009707893.pdf.

4 Create Jobs for USA, "Together We're Stronger," available at http://createjobsforusa.org/ (last accessed September 2013).

5 Create Jobs for USA, "How It Works," available at http://createjobsforusa.org/how-it-works (last accessed September 2013).

6 Starbucks, "Your Special Blend," p. 7.

7 Los Angeles Urban League, "Business Institute's Youth Entrepreneurship Program," available at http://www.laul.org/2012-01-13-00-22-23/business-services (last accessed September 2013).

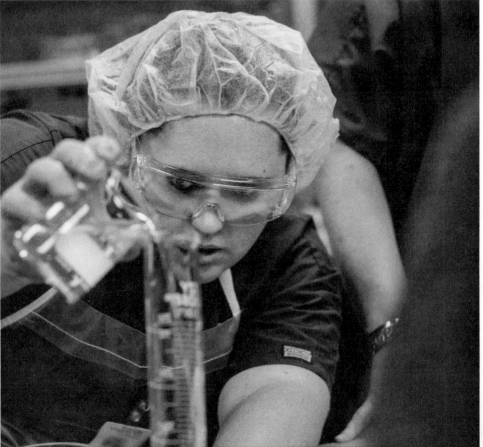

JESSICA McGOWAN • Chattanooga, Tennessee

Jessica is in an unstable relationship with the father of her two sons, and she recently moved back in with her mother. She struggles to make ends meet. She finds herself falling behind on child care and utility payments. But Jessica is planning ahead for her and her sons' futures, taking pharmacy-technician classes at a local college. She recently took a part-time job at Walgreens.

"I feel like a success. My 5-year-old will tell me every day, 'Mommy, you're too old to go to school!', but I tell him that you're never too old."

Empower Women and You Recharge the World

By MUHTAR KENT, chairman of the board and CEO of The Coca-Cola Company. He is also chairman of the International Business Council of the World Economic Forum and the former co-chair of The Consumer Goods Forum.

Our future depends on women. All around the world, women entrepreneurs, women innovators, and women leaders in business, politics, academia, and culture are transforming societies and the global economy. And they will continue to do so.

Why? For starters, women represent the fastest-growing, most dynamic economic force in the world today. Women now control more than $20 trillion in global spending.[1] That means women have an economic impact 50 percent larger than that of the United States and more than twice the size of China and India's economies combined.

In the United States alone, women-owned businesses account for nearly $3 trillion of the gross domestic product.[2] In fact, if American women were measured as a separate country, they would have the fifth-largest economy in the world!

Of course, women's entrepreneurship extends far beyond our shores. The truth is, it's soaring around the globe. In 2012, more than 125 million women were leading new businesses in 67 countries, with nearly 100 million more women heading up established businesses.[3] And the highest percentages of women business owners are in markets you might not expect.

In Uganda, 36 percent of adult women are entrepreneurs. In Thailand, the number is 21 percent. In Chile, it's 19 percent. Brazil, 15 percent; Mexico, 12 percent; China, 11 percent. And these numbers continue to increase.[4]

We have also seen that when women rise in their communities, the communities themselves rise to new heights of prosperity and health. Over and over, studies have found a direct correlation between women's empowerment and GDP growth, business growth, environmental sustainability, improved human health, and other positive impacts.

So as the world seeks ways to accelerate growth across a global economy that is struggling to emerge from recession, the solution is right in front of us: Empower women, and you recharge the world.

Creating a climate of success for women is smart business—and not just for consumer-products companies. Today, it's smart business for every company and every country.

In the years ahead, women's economic participation and entrepreneurial growth will drive the world's economy. It's no longer a matter of "if" but of "to what heights." All of the exciting growth projections for various countries and regions will hinge on greater empowerment of women.

The upward trajectory has already begun. And yet around the world—and across America—we still see too many roadblocks for women: cultural, educational, political, and financial.

Those of us in business, government, and civil society—what we call the "Golden Triangle"—must work together to knock these barriers down. As we do, we will give more women the chance to access financial resources, move into positions of leadership, and start their own businesses.

When it comes to empowering women, the implications for companies, communities, and countries will be vast and profound. Our overall success will, in large measure, depend on the success of women.

If we all do our part, I am convinced that future historians will one day look back on our time as the dawn of "The Women's Century"—a century that is more open, more hopeful, and more prosperous than any that has come before.

ENDNOTES

1   Michael J. Silverstein and Kate Sayre, "The Female Economy" (2009), available at http://hbr.org/2009/09 the-femaleeconomy/ar/1.

2   Center for Women's Business Research, "The Economic Impact of Women-Owned Businesses In the United States" (2009), available at http://www.nwbc.gov/sites/default/files/ economicimpactstu.pdf.

3   Donna J. Kelley and others, "Global Entrepreneurship Monitor 2012 Women's Report" (Global Entrepreneurship Research Association, 2013), available at http://www.babson.edu/ Academics/centers/blank-center/global-research/gem/ Documents/GEM%202012%20Womens%20Report.pdf.

4   Ibid.

Microfinancing Women: Great Return on Investment

By TORY BURCH, an award-winning fashion designer, philanthropist, and CEO of the Tory Burch Foundation, which provides economic empowerment to women entrepreneurs and their families.

In 1998, Sandra Baquero moved to New York from her native Bogotá, Colombia, with $500, a suitcase, and a dream: to start her own clothing design business.[1]

Over the years, Sandra supported herself by working minimum-wage jobs from McDonald's to a beauty salon, where she learned to speak English. "People like to talk in beauty salons," Sandra explains with a smile, "and I didn't have time to go to school." After getting married and having a baby, she provided home care for an elderly neighbor while taking care of her own daughter. And through it all, she continued to design and sew. Finally, in 2007, she launched Sandra Baquero, a women's wear collection.

The future looked bright. Sandra's designs resonated with customers at pop-up markets and trade shows, and she and her husband qualified to buy a home in New Jersey with no down payment.

Then the economy stalled. Sandra's husband lost his job, and they fell behind on paying the mortgage. Sandra suddenly could not come up with the $2,000 entry fee to participate in trade shows—her family's primary source of income. "The business is my passion, but at the same time

it's our money," she says. Similar to many new women entrepreneurs with little or no credit history, Sandra was unable to get a bank loan to keep her company—and her family—afloat. Her small business was in jeopardy at a time when its success mattered more than ever.

I know what it's like to launch a business from your home because I have done it. It's not easy, but I was very fortunate. I was financially secure and had a supportive network of friends and family who believed in me and were able to invest in my venture. That's not the case for many women, who are early stage entrepreneurs with great ideas and talent but without the resources they need to grow and scale their businesses—such as Sandra.

That's why I launched the Tory Burch Foundation in 2009. We support the economic empowerment of women entrepreneurs and their families in the United States through microfinancing, mentorship, and entrepreneurial education.

I was surprised to learn that it's easier for an entrepreneur in a developing country to get a small loan than it is for women entrepreneurs right here in the United States to get one. The numbers are incredible: The Aspen Institute estimates that only 2 percent of potential U.S. microfinance customers are being served, compared to 17 percent being served in the developing world.

Therefore, one of our goals at the Tory Burch Foundation is to provide greater access to capital for women entrepreneurs in the United States. To that end, we are partnering with Accion, an international microfinance nonprofit, to provide loans to promising women entrepreneurs here. Since its founding, the Tory Burch Foundation has given microloans—typically about $7,000 to $10,000—to more than 100 women in a range of fields from design to skin care to food services. And we see many more businesses that we are eager to support.

Sandra Baquero is one of our loan recipients. With small business loans from Accion and the Tory Burch Foundation, she has been able to reach new customers and build her business. "A loan helped me to grow faster," says Sandra, wearing a denim suit from her collection. "It put my business in a good position."

Sandra used her first loan for $6,000 to participate in three trade shows, where she earned $30,000. As a result, she and her husband were able to get back on track with their mortgage payments and focus on scaling Sandra's business. It continues to grow, generating $135,000 in 2012—more than double her revenues from 2010—providing the family with a level of financial security that was unimaginable to Sandra a few years ago. Her daughter Nicole, now age 9,

takes occasional trips to visit their family in California. "We can pay for that," says Sandra with pride, adding that her daughter "has her own computer and her own iPad," which Nicole plays with when she accompanies her mother to business meetings.

Women such as Sandra are our best investment. They pay back their loans—Sandra repaid hers in half the allotted time—and they invest up to 90 percent of their income in their families and their communities. They are also engines for economic growth and job creation. In fact, small businesses "creat[e] nearly two out of every three new jobs," providing approximately 60 million Americans— about half of the private-sector workforce—with employment. It's also worth noting that women are one of the fastest-growing segments of small business owners in this country.[2]

In the past year, Sandra brought her husband in as a business partner and hired one full-time and two part-time employees. "When I have a big order, I work with two small manufacturers in Queens," she says, noting that her designs are available at six stores across the United States. You can check them out at www.sandrabaquero.com.

It is truly thrilling to see early stage women entrepreneurs take their ventures to the next level, and you don't need to have an M.B.A. or start a foundation to make a difference. You can invest in women entrepreneurs through crowdfunding efforts such as Kiva or Kickstarter or by supporting their businesses directly; you can find many of them at www.etsy.com.

There is another simple but invaluable way that we can help women who are struggling to make a better life for themselves and their families: We can become mentors. Having benefited from the wisdom and insight of many mentors over the years, I understand how important the voice of experience can be. Each one of us can be that voice for those who are finding their way. Sandra Baquero herself is sharing her own experience with women in the Tory Burch Foundation's mentoring and entrepreneurial education programs.

Anyone can be part of these very potent, high-impact solutions. Through microfinancing and mentoring, we can leverage our own resources to help women achieve financial security. Doing so benefits not just these women and their families but also their communities and, by extension, all of us.

ENDNOTES

1   Tory Burch Foundation, "Graduates: TBF Entrepreneurs: Get Inspired," available at http://www.toryburch foundation.org/get-inspired/getinspired-tbf-entrepreneurs-graduates,default,pg.html (last accessed November 2013).

2   Tory Burch, "Empowering Women Through Entrepreneurial Education," HuffPost What Is Working: Small Businesses, April 1, 2013, available at http://www.huffingtonpost.com/tory-burch/empowering-women-through-_b_2957017.html.

Encouraging girls to make well-informed decisions about the future can help them grow into self-reliant, independent women. {BARBARA RIES}

Personal Action, Collective Impact

Linking Key Elements of the American Dream—Educational Opportunities,
Financial Stability, and Social Capital—to Improve Women's Lives

By Anne Mosle

STUNNING FACT

Only 12 percent of young girls feel "very confident"
when it comes to making financial decisions.

As a country, we recognize the value of empowering women around the world. We deliberately invest financial, political, and human capital in women and girls across the globe because we know that when women thrive, it creates a radiating and lasting impact across generations and communities.

It is time to apply that same focus here at home. With 42 million women and the 28 million children depending on them living on the economic brink in the United States, continuing business as usual is simply not an option.[1] We must break the intergenerational cycle of poverty and near poverty that plagues our own country. It is a lofty goal, but an essential one. As we have seen the world over, the secret is investing in women.

After all, we know what it takes for families to thrive. A high-quality education, a good job with opportunities for advancement, child care to make work possible, affordable health care, meaningful relationships, and social connections are all key ingredients to success. We also know what can throw any family off track: a lost job, an unintended and unprepared pregnancy, an interrupted education, a medical crisis, or even a broken-down car.

Many struggling, low-wage women workers deftly navigate a complex maze of challenges and confront systems that seem stacked against them. It is their own resilience, fused with optimism and a commitment to the people depending on them, which drives them forward to create a better life. In fact, research by Ascend, a policy program at the Aspen Institute, in 2011 and 2013, as well as by Greenberg Quinlan Rosner Research and TargetPoint Consulting for *The Shriver Report*, demonstrates that despite facing myriad challenges, women on the brink show remarkable resilience.

What if women were at the heart of our efforts to retool our economy and ensure everyone has a shot at the American Dream?

These qualities of resilience and optimism are invaluable and undervalued; recognizing and developing the abilities of low-wage women workers may be the best investment we can make for our economy—and the best investment women can make for their families and themselves.

So how do we get there? We start by listening to the experts—the women and girls struggling for solid financial footing. While a swirl of public debates call on women to pull themselves and their families up by their bootstraps or to juggle it all, the voices of low-income women are seldom included in these conversations. Ascend at the Aspen Institute was created to serve as a national hub for breakthrough ideas and collaborations that move women and children toward educational success and economic security. Listening to and lifting up the voices of parents—especially women—and their children has been an essential element of Ascend's work from the start.

In 2011, Ascend commissioned an ongoing bipartisan focus group research project, Voices for Two-Generation Success. This series focuses on low-income parents and children across race and ethnicity, and it was designed to tap their ideas and include their voices in the public discussion about new policy approaches for women on the brink. The project, conducted in six cities around the country by leading national experts Celinda Lake of Lake Research Partners and Bob Carpenter of Chesapeake

Beach Consulting, offers insights into the gaps between the data that describe women's lives and their day-to-day realities.

In preparation for *The Shriver Report*, Ascend also conducted a series of focus groups with questions designed to offer guidance for the development of Life Education, a curriculum to arm young people, particularly girls, with the information they need to make smart financial and personal decisions (see Appendix A, p. 360, for full methodology). Building upon previous public opinion research in conjunction with the focus groups, this chapter takes a closer look at the lives of mothers living on the brink, as well as middle and high school teens. Throughout this chapter, their voices and perspectives bring to life the challenges and opportunities raised in *The Shriver Report*.

Previous chapters describe the pervasive economic split over the past 50 years—between the increasing number of women who experience wealth and economic power, and the increasing number who have greater responsibility for their families' well-being but lack the resources to achieve financial security. Why hasn't the power of some translated into investment in the potential of all? Why does the pay gap persist? Why aren't workers recognized as caregivers, with paid leave for illness and family responsibilities? Why do national policies woefully underinvest in adequate early care and education for our children? These issues affect all Americans, but for women on the lower rungs of the income ladder, they translate into more severe economic hardship and undercut our nation's economic productivity.

Building from the proven success of investing in women and girls worldwide and directly addressing women living on the brink in this country is a generational game changer.

As women at the top of the ladder contemplate how to exert their own power, it is important that they also hold themselves accountable for creating concrete pathways and policies that tap into all women's economic potential. "Lifting as we climb," a motto adopted by African American women in the early 1900s in their quest for civil rights and women's rights, still rings true today.

In today's economy, there are no sidelines; to thrive, our nation will need to develop every worker's potential. What if women were at the heart of our efforts to retool our economy and ensure everyone has a shot at the American Dream? What if our solutions focused on pathways for women and their children together, two generations at a time? How can we link key elements of the American Dream—educational opportunities, financial stability, and social capital—to improve women's lives?

The answers to these questions could produce bold new approaches to adapting both public policies and our workplaces to the realities—and resilience—of low-wage working women. Most important, they could even change how women see themselves. If we build from the proven success of investing in women and girls worldwide and deal directly with the high number of women and children living on the brink in this country, this courageous and enterprising proposition presents a generational game changer for all.

LEARNING FROM WHAT WOMEN ON THE FINANCIAL BRINK ALREADY KNOW

We know from listening to the voices of women and girls living on the brink that they are on shaky financial footing; they can plummet, or they can soar. Last summer, Voices for Two-Generation Success engaged a diverse group of low-income mothers and teens in a series of frank conversations commissioned by Ascend at the Aspen Institute, in conjunction with *The Shriver Report*. We wanted to know what information and resources moms felt they were missing and how they managed the challenges of the recession. We wanted to know what students wished to learn in high school. We wanted to know what moms expected from themselves and their communities, what they wished they had known when they were in school, and what they would most like their kids to know. And we asked them all how they defined success—and what they thought it would take to achieve it.

> *"I think my challenge is more just to be financially stable in the long run, be able for her to go to college. That's kind of like my challenge now. Even though she is 6, it's good to think about it now just because you never know what's going to happen in the future."*
>
> — Asian American mother, mixed income, Chicago (see Appendix A)

From Denver to Chicago to Richmond, low-income women—both single and married—told us in their own words about their

A central theme emerged from both sets of conversations— an overwhelming desire of the women and girls to be confident, self-reliant, and independent.

Women and girls living on the brink of financial instability can either plummet or soar. Investing in them could be the game changer that breaks the cycle of generational poverty. {BARBARA KINNEY}

aspirations, anxieties, relationships, regrets, goals, and expectations as they work every day to create better lives for their families and themselves. The young people, ages 12 to 18, told us about their hopes and challenges, as well as about their relationships with their parents, their friends, and their communities. They told us of their dreams and how they thought they would get there.

A central theme emerged from both sets of conversations—an overwhelming desire of the women and girls to be confident, self-reliant, and independent. Mothers said they are driven to help their children to be happy and to pursue whatever career they want. They said they understand that education is essential, but so are connections and confidence. And while both women and girls highlighted time and money as challenges, the participants didn't blame anyone for their financial situations; rather, they mostly cited themselves as the biggest barriers to their own success. As a woman in Denver said, "To take the steps and get help and ... to choose to go in the right direction or not is up to me."[2]

Building on these conversations, and Ascend's years of prior research, we have developed three bold ideas that capitalize on women's strength and leverage our collective ability to put women and their families firmly onto a path of financial stability:

• Two-generation strategies
• The economic potential of social capital
• 21st-century Life Education

PROPELLING WOMEN AND FAMILIES FORWARD: TWO GENERATIONS AT A TIME

"I go through the daily rituals of life and I have a smile on my face all the time, and everything is great, but deep inside I am just like, 'Oh my God, I need to find some balance.' When I get home from work, I kid you not, I work myself into a darn panic attack because I know when I walk through that door, it is game on."

—White mother, low income, Richmond

This report describes in depth the changing demographics and new economic reality of 21st-century America. But one statistic bears repeating: In the United States, approximately 70 percent of people in single-mother families are low-income.[3]

Clearly, developing the assets of low-income women is key to addressing our nation's financial insecurity. Too often, fragmented programs and policies that are intended to help struggling women *and* their children instead address their needs separately. This leaves either the child or the mother behind, dimming each family member's chance for success. We need a two-generation approach that builds economic security for children and their mothers together.

The core elements of two-generation strategies are **education**—both early childhood and postsecondary education—and **economic supports combined with financial education**. The return on investment of early childhood education for at-risk children is significant over a lifetime.[4]

At the same time, education that includes skill development linked to high-demand jobs with opportunities for advancement is critical for the parents who support those children.[5]

The mothers we talked to were unified in their belief that education—from early childhood on through college—is essential to their child's success: "If our kids don't go to college," one Richmond mother said, "they really don't have any hope."[6]

The two-generation approach bolsters the education of both parent and child simultaneously. It fosters mutual motivation through quality early learning facilities and a safe and productive environment for children of time-strapped mothers, increasing the likelihood that the moms can further their own education.

In fact, research suggests that children serve as a motivating factor for adults, particularly mothers, and that parents will often do for their children what they won't or can't do for themselves.[7] That's where two-generation strategies are transforming lives.

DOUBLE-IMPACT APPROACHES

Two-generation approaches build upon the international evidence of the power of investing in women as a strategy to improve the economic stability of a family.[8] These approaches are dynamic, crossing sectors and aligning funding to improve results and build on that "mutual motivation moment," when both mothers and their children are learning together. We heard about the power of mutual motivation from a Hispanic mom in Denver who told us, "As I am working towards my dream, it teaches [my children] something that leads them to a better future."[9]

How does a mother view success for her children? "In school, great jobs, athletics, no debt, get a house, not too many struggles, scholarships so school is paid for, and just for them to be proud of, you know, me and what I have done for them, and for them to be proud of themselves and what they are achieving, and no kids too soon."

—African American mother, moderate income, Chicago

Two-generation approaches are simple in theory, but require collaboration from public, nonprofit, and private sectors to become the norm. In a time-strapped and often stressful environment, the balancing act for mothers can be extremely challenging; they need both encouragement and supports to pursue their own education. "It can help them to see you doing something, working hard to do something," a Chicago mother shared. "It could take time away from you doing things with them, but it always shows them that if you are putting your mind towards something, you can do it regardless of what it is."[10]

TWO-GENERATION PROGRAMS IN ACTION: LIFE-CHANGING RESULTS

From Los Angeles to Boston, Alaska Native villages to the Mississippi Delta, policymakers and program leaders are working to integrate services for mothers and their children, sparked by the desire both to achieve better results and to use resources efficiently.

Endicott College in Beverly, Massachusetts, is one institution putting two-generation approaches into practice. Their Keys to Degrees program for single parents—mostly mothers—and their children has connected more than a dozen four-year institutions around the nation to develop on-campus housing and educational support programs for single parents and their kids. The result at Endicott is a 100 percent graduation rate in the program.[11]

Keys to Degrees was developed by Endicott College President Dr. Richard Wylie based on some key premises: If a child is in high-quality, early education, but a mother lacks the educational opportunities needed for a well-paying job, then the family will continue to struggle, and the child will not have access to the resources and stability to thrive. Similarly, if a mother has opportunities to build skills for high-demand jobs, but a child lacks access to high-quality child care and early education, both will struggle to advance.[12]

Other programs are also breaking down traditional "siloed" approaches and providing opportunities for and meeting the needs of mothers and their children together. Shandrell, a single mother in St. Paul, Minnesota, is completing her bachelor's degree in design. At the same time, her young daughter goes to a high-quality early childhood education center just blocks from her mother's college campus and in the same building where the family lives.

Shandrell and her daughter are enrolled in the Jeremiah Program, which began in the Twin Cities in 1998 and is designed to provide housing for single mothers to support their pursuit of postsecondary education while ensuring their children are successfully prepared for kindergarten.[13]

But the Jeremiah Program does so much more: It prepares young moms with the skills they will need to navigate their roles as both caregivers and breadwinners for their family.

Jeremiah moms are assigned Life Skills coaches to help them set and meet goals related to physical and emotional health, respectful relationships, and career development. At the same time, the program's enterprising "Jeremiah Works!" initiative connects mothers and community volunteers to develop employment contacts and job-training opportunities.

In addition to developing two new sites in North Dakota and Texas over the past year, the Jeremiah Program has spurred other sites, such as the Glen at St. Joseph, an Ohio-based housing and education program for single mothers and their children.[14]

These two-generation approaches are anchored in research that demonstrates the strong connection between a mother's education and her child's success in school. The national mean reading and math scores for children entering kindergarten for the first time in the 2010-11 school year increased according to the parents' level of educational attainment.[15]

The return on investment goes beyond family stability: For every 100 graduates of the Jeremiah Program, society received net benefits of about $16 million.

The potential for lasting change for families in each of these models is increasingly evident. In fact, 53 percent of Jeremiah women graduate with an associate's degree and 47 percent graduate with a bachelor's degree. The average wage of a 2012 graduate was $19.35 per hour, and 95 percent of Jeremiah children pass their kindergarten readiness test. A recent study showed that the return on investment goes beyond family stability: For every 100 graduates of the Jeremiah Program, society received net benefits of about $16 million.[16]

In Tulsa, Oklahoma, mothers have jump-started careers in health information technology and nursing through the Community Action Project of Tulsa County, or CAP Tulsa, a trusted community organization that runs a network of high-performing Head Start and Early Head Start sites throughout the city.[17]

CAP Tulsa realized early on that if their children were to succeed, working with their parents was essential, and as a result Career*Advance*® was created: Parents, most of them mothers, whose children are enrolled in early learning programs are eligible for training at the local technology and community colleges.[18] Through Career*Advance*®, they attend classes as a group, with other parents, and with guidance from career coaches, who counsel the parents as they juggle work, parenting responsibilities, and school. With key supports such as transportation funding, and uniforms provided by the program, the parents are poised for living-wage jobs in the growing health sector of Tulsa.

Sisters Madie and Aubrey Winans pretend they are superheroes after swimming in a river near Missoula, Montana. {AMI VITALE}

Mothers in Career*Advance*® say they are more involved with their children's learning as a result of their own participation in postsecondary education. This mutual motivation suggests that the benefits of two-generation programs may be greater than the sum of their separate programmatic parts.[19]

TWO GENERATIONS, ONE FUTURE: A NATIONAL MOVEMENT

A two-generation lens is increasingly being applied to improve the lives of women and their children beyond individual programs. Federal and state governments are beginning to recognize the approach as both effective and cost efficient; programs like these offer a double-bottom-line win—better long-term return on the money as well as better results for moms and their children.

Several Promise Neighborhood sites, for example, funded by the U.S. Department of Education to develop a cradle-to-career education pipeline, have adopted Ascend's two-generation approach, including Washington, D.C.; Buffalo, New York; and Langley Park in Maryland. The Washington, D.C., Promise Neighborhood Initiative, or DCPNI, built on Ascend's two-generation framework to develop their "5 Promises for 2 Generations" approach and successful implementation proposal. Within the DCPNI program is the "Parent Pathways" plan, whose goal is to connect mothers with education and economic supports, such as financial counseling.[20]

The state of Colorado is embedding this two-generation vision throughout its Department of Human Services, linking opportunities for Colorado children to the services their parents receive. As part of its two-generation lens, the state is piloting children's savings accounts, or CSAs, which allow kids to start saving for college and simultaneously build the financial capability of their parents, with matched investment from the state and private institutions. For children enrolled in Colorado child care sites, the state is building a new pipeline of stability for families: At age 18, the savings in CSAs can be used to finance higher education, start a small business, or buy a home.[21]

Moving forward, there are ways to apply this lens to long-standing policies and programs such as Head Start, which is a ripe and ready springboard for both young children and their mothers, as well as to new initiatives such as the Department of Education's Race to the Top Early Learning Challenge, a competition for states to raise the quality of early learning programs.

To spur more of these innovations in the nonprofit, public, and private sectors, Ascend at the Aspen Institute launched the $1 million Aspen Institute Ascend Fund, which will provide financial support and expand a national learning network to fuel a new movement of leaders and initiatives creating opportunity for low-income children and their parents together.

Opportunity becomes a family tradition when we design programs and policies with the whole family's educational and economic future in mind and help them access the social networks needed to make it in life.

SOCIAL CAPITAL—THE SECRET SAUCE FOR UPWARD ECONOMIC MOBILITY

Trusted relationships—between friends, families, institutions, companies, and services—are the networks that form the connective tissue of our lives. This is the "social capital" that helps us maintain stability and achieve success. From caring for a sick child to getting a ride to an appointment, we often rely on others for help.

But these networks of trusted relationships can do much more than just help out in a pinch. They are critical accelerators to upward economic mobility. Increasingly, researchers are finding links that point to social capital as a core element of an intergenerational cycle of opportunity.

A recent study of income mobility in the United States conducted by researchers at Harvard University and the University of California, Berkeley, found a strong correlation between a region's level of social capital and the intergenerational mobility of its residents. In areas with more useful or robust community connections—in low-income neighborhoods that also included a mix of middle-income residents, or where higher numbers of residents were active in a faith community—children were significantly more likely to join the middle class as adults.[22]

Rutgers management professor Nancy DiTomaso has also captured how vital these connections and networks are for people seeking jobs. In recent research interviews, DiTomaso found that "all but a handful [of interviewees] used the help of family and friends to find 70 percent of the jobs they held over their lifetimes; they all used personal networks and insider information if it was available to them."[23]

THE QUIET BUT INCREASING POWER OF SOCIAL CAPITAL AND NETWORKS

Social capital is crucial, yet largely taken for granted by those who have it. Many of us use social capital every day and do not even realize it, such as when we carpool our kids to soccer practice or recommend a colleague for a new job. The relationships and networks each of us have can make a major difference in our lives, helping to determine what school to attend, what jobs to apply for, or even how to access a high-quality child care center. Social capital can mean the difference between, among other things, a well-paying and lower-wage job.

Social capital has existed for centuries in communities across race, ethnicity, and class—manifesting in barn raises, church socials, and block parties. In recent years, social media has radically opened new channels to grow and tap new communities, and innovative tools are rapidly developing that are critical to building relationships and sharing key information that will amplify women's and girls' access to fast-moving information and opportunities. Platforms such as Facebook and LinkedIn are helping to amplify growing networks, but even more exciting are some of the new social networks such as Girls Who Code and the global Girl Effect's Girl Hub, which lift up the voice and potential of the next generation of women.

Geographically, we live in a time of ever-increasing distance from our closest networks, our families: An estimated 73 percent of Americans don't live in the community where they were born. Time and trust have replaced geography as new determinants of a sense of community.

Participants in our recent focus groups told us that when they needed help, they turned to their family—including moms, grandmothers, husbands, boyfriends, their child's father, partners, daughters, aunts, and cousins—and to their friends, including colleagues from work. If these support networks—or "lifelines," as some moms called them—were augmented, it was more likely to be from their faith community or a familiar community organization. Women said they turned to these networks for guidance, resources, and "to vent."

> When asked to explain her desire for more professional networking, a Denver woman said, "My friends are from the hood. It would be different if I met people who knew higher people, who knew higher people, to help you get into a different lifestyle."
>
> — Latina mother, low income, Denver

We also saw the range of ways that these support networks—both formal and informal—help families get through their daily lives. There is the need for informal support, like when, as the mom in Denver told us, "I am having a bad day and need help with the kids." And there is the need for day-to-day logistical support, particularly around transportation and children, like the Asian American mom in Chicago who said, "They will help me pick up and drop off."[24]

Some mothers spoke of very distinct and organized networks. "I have my family, my friends, my church, my neighbors, my sorority, my social club, and my religious club. And I [said] it in that order because that's how I would [reach out]," says one mother.[25]

But many women rely on a narrow yet deep set of relationships based on trust. "One of my support systems is the YMCA," says a woman from Chicago. "They pick my daughter up from school and take her until 6 o'clock, and then my neighbor [who] works there and lives next door to me, she will take my daughter and keep her until I get off work."[26]

No matter what the configuration of the network, however, most low-income women told us they feel as if they are on their own, while wishing for a better set of contacts to find good jobs and manage school.

For low-income women and their children, the untapped potential of social capital is enormous. Dr. Mario Small, dean of the Division of Social Sciences at the University of Chicago, has highlighted the value of bonding social capital (connections within the peer group) and bridging social capital (connections outside the peer group) for single mothers in urban areas.

"If I'm a low-income parent and I'm trying to figure out how to get my kid into college, finding those networks that have that information is a valuable kind of social capital," says Dr. Small. "It's very different from the support found in social networks or the desire to attain the goals that you have set for yourself in light of the norms of those around you with similar desires."[27]

SOCIAL CAPITAL IN ACTION

How do we build and strengthen trusted networks into moving women toward educational success and economic security? Where we live and who we know is fast becoming an increasingly influential predictor of economic mobility.

The path to making healthy and smart decisions starts with gaining self-confidence. Here, Amira Siegal teaches a class about self-esteem in Tacoma, Washington. {BARBARA KINNEY}

Organizations such as the Family Independence Initiative, or FII, are revolutionizing what it means to build social capital for the purpose of financial stability and generational upward mobility. In cities such as Oakland, Boston, and New Orleans, FII focuses on the assets of families, putting them "in the driver's seat of their own change" by developing tools that empower families to improve their social and financial well-being.[28] FII sites develop credit-building lending circles, through which people who may not have access to bank credit or prefer to borrow from people they know and trust can get together to form a group loan.[29] Families work among themselves and within their communities to help build economic stepping-stones for each other.

At the Boston-based Crittenton Women's Union Mobility Mentoring™ Centers, women are guided through individualized plans for financial stability and provided community resource connections. Staff members with special expertise in career management, financial literacy, higher education, and other skills help low-income families set and attain individualized goals that will help them achieve economic independence. At Mobility Mentoring™ Centers, individuals receive free assessments, one-on-one counseling, and referrals to community resources such as housing placements that will help them and their families get ahead.[30]

In South Florida, a region that reflects our country's demographic profile of the future, an innovation is emerging at Miami Dade College, where nearly 70 percent of students are low income.[31]

Under the leadership of Dr. Eduardo Padrón, the college—the largest four-year institution in the United States—has developed an innovative partnership with the county human services agency, which is placing a staff member at Miami Dade College to help students determine their eligibility for benefits such as the earned income tax credit or child care assistance. This unique community college-human services partnership is a cutting-edge model for communities and institutions across the nation and allows students, many of them low-income and first-genera-tion postsecondary students, to focus on what matters most—finishing school.

These enterprising community-focused programs show how social capital can build trust, strengthen networks, and inform women, men, and families to create their own community of success.

ADVICE TO AND FROM THE NEXT GENERATION: DESIGNING 21ST-CENTURY LIFE EDUCATION

Emerging from our work on two-generation strategies and social capital develop-ment is our third bold idea: 21st-century Life Education—a core set of new skills every girl should have as she goes out into the world and builds her future. These solutions provide clear insights into the skills and lessons our daughters will need to prepare for their multifaceted roles in life. In fact, both our daughters and sons share a future where roles, responsibilities, and opportunities are being swiftly rede-fined, from the ways we raise our families to how we grow a strong economy for all.

Decades ago, girls were taught home economics in school; cooking, sewing, and managing the grocery shopping were activities for which women were expected to be prepared. Today's Life Education is a 21st-century twist on this idea, and ensures that girls—across race, ethnicity, geography, and class—are equipped to meet the challenges they will confront as they navigate their roles as both breadwinners and caregivers for their families. These are the must-have skills that will give young women the tools to be their own power source in life.

The world has changed dramatically and quickly, from generation to generation. Girls today need different tools—and guidance that reflects rapidly changing technology—to get on a successful path to modern womanhood. With an eye toward developing this "Life Skills" class for the 21st century, Ascend looked at opportunities for two-generation approaches and social capital to create a core set of lessons that can guide young women. Just as important, we asked diverse, mixed-income teens to design a class that would teach them what *they* thought they needed to know and what they wanted to learn. We also asked them to imagine the one application, or app, they wish they had on their smartphones or tablets to give them the information or knowledge they needed to be successful in their day-to-day lives.

> Both our daughters and sons share a future where roles, responsibilities, and opportunities are being swiftly redefined, from the ways we raise our families to how we grow a strong economy for all.

What emerged was an emphasis on financial literacy—how to buy a car, secure a mortgage, save for college, or budget for basic expenses—combined with concerns about emotional well-being, self-confidence, and healthy relationships. Postsecondary education was universally recognized as a critical goal, yet they were anxious about how they would pay for it. With the Great Recession of 2008's effect upon their parents' finances still fresh in their memories, the young people we spoke to wondered whether the burden of student debt would similarly weigh them down.

Their voices, together with a growing field of two-generation research and a panoply of inspiring national and community-based programs, give us the blueprint for a new Life Education course. Whether formalized into a curriculum or embraced as a framework, our educators, parents, school systems, community programs, and even governments can learn from these conversations. To prepare the next generation for fulfilling and successful lives, we must listen to what our teens tell us they need to know and develop up-to-date tools and programs that answer their call—and inform our own ways of thinking.

THE NEW 'NEED TO KNOW'

Women's social, political, and financial opportunities have improved dramatically over the past 50 years. In 1967, only 27 percent of mothers were breadwinners or co-breadwinners, but recent data show that in 2010, women were co- or primary breadwinners in two-thirds of American families.

And yet young women coming of age in the new millennium face many complex choices for which there is no clear game plan. So what does a 21st-century roadmap for stability and opportunity look like? To help girls accelerate the gains they are making in the classroom, financial literacy and emotional development support are key. They have emerged as critical components of a modern girl's education along-side leadership training, and science, technology, engineering, and mathematics, or STEM, courses. Today's Life Education is what girls need to confidently navigate a social terrain where they will constantly assess trade-offs about school, jobs, finances, career, family, marriage, and children.

Many programs and policies have already embraced teaching girls these Life Education lessons. Some focus on financial literacy skills, such as Girls Inc., which provides courses on saving and budgeting for girls in high school and middle school. Others, such as Girls on the Run, help teenagers develop self-esteem and healthy habits through group activities and mentoring. Programs that integrate two-generation approaches and social capital development—such as the Jeremiah Program and the Glen at St. Joseph—are also integrating behavioral classes, such as the habits of healthy relationships and ways to self-regulate and maintain calm in a crisis. Momentum for these kinds of courses is building partly because girls understand that their world will be different from their mothers' and that they will need to augment their mothers' advice with these skills.

We asked adolescent girls and boys from low-income families what their dreams for the future look like:

"I would be unstoppable. I would just keep going on with what I want to do and how I am going to do it and when I am going to do it."

"I hope to be the person that gets written down for like records. I want to be a great person."

PUSHING BACK: EDUCATION, NETWORKS, AND SELF-ESTEEM

The adolescents Ascend spoke to were acutely aware that they needed to be equipped to meet the demands of a world where college is mandatory but marriage is not. Their professional ambitions are limitless; their relationship goals focus on finding a partner who will respect them.

Growing up in a deep recession has colored their perspectives; they acknowledge the vitality of trusted relationships and networks. "For a year, my dad and I were homeless," one girl shared in Denver, "and our family friends from a really long time ago, they let us use their basement as our house for an entire year and endless thanks goes to them. I can't even begin to describe how lucky we were."[32]

Their responses generally underscored a sophistication mixed with deep anxiety: They know college is essential for a better life, but the costs are daunting. As one girl in Denver lamented, "I am going out of state to college and it's just going to be a struggle. I got a decent scholarship, but I don't know, because my sister is going next year and then [our] parents are divorced. Money is just a struggle."[33]

Girls also expressed a real drive for self-reliance, but a worrying conviction that they are their own greatest liabilities. "I am positive about my future, but you know, there is always still that fear in the back of my mind that I am just going to fail," one girl shared. "You know everybody has that. Especially once you graduate."[34]

Mothers thought self-reliance and independence would equip their daughters for success in the world and even inoculate them from future struggles. As a Chicago mother put it, "Be smart, strong, independent, and not naïve."[35] Both mothers and girls valued respect in their relationships. The sentiment from a Richmond mom was underscored in our conversations with teen girls: "If it's not healthy, if it's hindering, it doesn't need to be a relationship."[36]

21ST-CENTURY LIFE EDUCATION: MAPPING NEW ROADS TO SUCCESS

From their advice, responses, and thoughts, four powerful ways emerged to prepare young girls and boys to create a life of stability and security.

The daunting challenges of growing up can be faced more easily if we equip girls with the skills necessary to thrive. {BARBARA KINNEY}

1. Develop confidence, self-reliance, and healthy relationships
What if your anxieties about the future disappeared? "I would be unstoppable."[37]

What they told us they need

Voices for Two-Generation Success found that girls identify confidence and self-reliance as core values. Being independent is important; surviving on one's own is an aspirational goal. Respect in relationships is also a clear, if sometimes elusive, goal of our focus group participants. Both boys and girls cite respect, honesty, trust, and communication as elements that must be present in a healthy relationship.

The mothers we talked to are actively teaching their sons to respect women and advising their daughters to respect themselves. As one Richmond mom said, "If people don't respect you, you are going to get walked all over."[38]

Girls believe that they are in control of their own futures and that they are the key to their own success. The best advice they say they have received is variations on a similar theme: Believe in yourself, never give up, and be true to yourself.

The app they designed for themselves

"A mirror so that the person using it would have to type in positive things about themselves either physically or mentally each day, something they like about themselves. You set it to tell you something positive about yourself in timed intervals or when you feel bad about yourself. It would make the person using it provide a self-esteem boost coming from themselves."[39]

Solutions to tap

Confidence is clearly a skill girls told us they want and need to persist against daunting challenges. Innovative programs are integrating confidence-boosting activities into their approaches. As mentioned earlier, through Girls on the Run, a nonprofit program with chapters across the country, girls in elementary and middle school participate in afterschool running groups that integrate team-building and life coaching.[40] The mission of the organization, which started in 1996, is to "inspire girls to be joyful, healthy, and confident using a fun, experience-based curriculum which creatively integrates running."

Conversations to better understand how to have healthy relationships—with oneself and with others—are also at the heart of Start Strong, a partnership between Futures Without Violence and the Robert Wood Johnson Foundation.[41] The program operates in 11 communities across the country, teaching girls and boys in middle school about healthy relationships in order to stop dating violence and abuse before it starts.

Elsewhere, two-generation programs that include lessons on confidence building, such as Eveline's Sunshine Cottage in Amarillo, Texas—where young mothers live together with their children and participate in parenting groups and self-esteem workshops—have seen their moms flourish.[42] In Oregon, The National Critten-ton Foundation spearheads a national empowerment program for young women who have experienced significant trauma and abuse to "thrive, build skills, break destructive cycles, and become powerful agents of personal and social change."[43] Within the support of the foundation, many of these women have testified every-where from the halls of Congress to their local city council meeting to push for better mental health and economic policies.

2. Get as much education as you can

"Because nowadays you need really a college education to have a steady job that could support you."[44]

What they told us they need

Young people believe education is essential for success. The more you have, the better your chances are of succeeding. College is a key goal. While they are aware of family members who have jobs or careers without having gone to college, they also know that *not* having a college degree is a barrier to achieving their dreams.

Girls and boys are optimistic about their futures, yet they all share a common worry: successfully managing the academic and financial demands of college. They are acutely aware of how expensive a college education is and how student loans can lead to high debt. As policymakers debate the necessity of liberal arts educa-tion versus more skill- and industry-specific education, teens shared their observa-tions about classmates who are tracked for college and those who clearly are not. Anxious about the need to watch their wallets and balance their time, teens wanted tools to help them manage both. They know that to get into college, they will have to do well in high school—and to finish college, they need a plan to pay for it.

The app they designed for themselves

"A timekeeper based on activities, services, and projects that is also an elec-tronic logbook based on income and expenses. It could help with keeping track of finances and making sure you're on task time-wise. It would give you key information about your financial strengths and weaknesses and how you can improve spending money and time."[45]

Solutions to tap

Making sure girls understand what it takes to go beyond high school and the impact that postsecondary education will have on their earnings potential is central to Life Ed. We can learn from the success of organizations such as the American Association of University Women, or AAUW, a 130-year-old national grassroots organization that has been empowering young women to succeed through a range of programs, including campus leadership trainings and STEM initiatives. AAUW has developed courses that encourage more girls to pursue science and technology careers, such as Tech Trek and Tech Savvy. These courses aim to break down stereotypes surrounding these traditionally male-dominated fields and teach girls that intellectual skills grow over time, regardless of gender.[46]

Other programs use technology to connect directly to girls' aspirations, such as Career Girls, an organization dedicated to providing young girls of all income levels and ethnic backgrounds with the academic tools and support they need to achieve their professional aspirations. The program does this by providing "real-world" context for a teenager's academic studies, specifically through videotaped interviews with positive female role models and a comprehensive collection of easy-to-follow educational resources, all available on the organization's website.

Young single mothers will need even more support, and we have seen in the two-generation programs we have studied that this type of educational support yields benefits for mother and child. For young single mothers in their teens and early 20s, the Higher Education Alliance of Advocates for Students with Children—which grew out of Endicott College's Keys to Degrees program—is a two-generation organization that helps young parents stay in school by promoting supportive housing and early childhood education on college campuses around the country.[47] These kinds of advocacy organizations are vital to helping young people manage the complexity of college, whether they are struggling to support a family and earn a degree, or simply trying to pay for each semester as they progress through school.

3. Seek mentors and tap networks

"My field hockey coach is amazing; I don't know what I would do without her. I definitely look up to my coach 24/7." [48]

Mecca Owens, 16, poses for a portrait in Chicago, Illinois. {BARBARA KINNEY}

What they told us they need

The younger and older girls and boys describe narrow support networks consisting of friends, parents, or siblings, and an occasional friend's parent. Teachers and guidance counselors are essential anchors for young people, and some return to former teachers for advice and support as they get older. As girls increase their participation in sports, coaches also emerge as a critical source of motivation and encouragement. Girls and boys recognize that cultivating trusted relationships— with teachers, coaches, and even community leaders—means having an ear to listen and a shoulder to lean on.

The app they designed for themselves

"An app where you could tell it your problems; it can be anonymous. People can comment on it and not sugarcoat anything but just give you the best advice for that situation. You would use it whenever you have an issue where you can't really talk to anyone about it. It could help you get through issues and problems whenever you get stuck."[49]

Solutions to tap

Research has shown the powerful impact that mentors can have on young people, particularly when those mentors help their mentee to effectively cope with difficulties and express optimism and confidence about their lives.[50]

The nonprofit Urban Alliance applies this lesson, providing urban young adults with mentors and resources to build their potential through professional careers and higher education. Since 1996, Urban Alliance has served more than 1,200 youth in a year-round internship program, partnering with more than 100 local businesses, and it has developed a curriculum that has been shared with more than 15,000 youth through workshops in the community. The curriculum covers business etiquette and issues, including résumé writing, phone skills, and conflict resolution.[51]

Programs that introduce young women to leaders can provide teenage girls with needed mentors for their educational success and emotional well-being—and jump-start their networks and budding social capital.

The Links, Incorporated, is a women's volunteer service organization committed to enriching, sustaining, and ensuring the cultural and economic survival of African Americans. With more than 270 chapters, it sponsors a range of programs that systemically provide support for economic mobility.[52] One program encourages members to work with community college students to provide them with mentoring, academic coaching, and other services needed so that they can transfer to one of the historically black colleges and universities to earn a bachelor's degree.

The founders of Girls Write Now, or GWN, developed a creative writing tutorial program featuring prominent journalists and professionals as volunteers for at-risk high school girls in public schools throughout New York City.[53] With academic support, mentoring, and writing lessons, "100% of GWN's seniors graduate and move on to college—bringing with them portfolios, awards, scholarships, new skills, and a sense of confidence."[54]

4. Become market and money savvy

"Saving up. Every time you say you want to go to the movies, you can take that money that you were going to spend and put it in the bank."[55]

What they told us they need

Teenagers have spent their adolescence watching their parents—single, married, or in the midst of divorce—struggling with the impact and fallout of the Great Recession. They know how easy it is to find oneself on the precipice of financial instability, and they are determined to build security for themselves and their families.

But those paths lack clear maps: Teenage girls say they are anxious about their ability to make smart financial decisions and need better guidance on how to save, borrow, and negotiate more strategically. They are afraid of mistakes and ending up in debt. While meeting the financial challenge of college without going into debt is one reason why financial literacy and a deeper understanding of money management surfaced loud and clear, girls also voiced a desire to learn how to handle money so that they can be on their own, pay for groceries, buy a car, and be able to budget as an adult. Girls also noted the need to choose and prepare for careers that offered good pay and advancement opportunities.

The app they designed for themselves

"This app would let you decide on a job and tell you what that job would pay you so you can then determine how much you would need for bills, like monthly rent and groceries. It would help you understand how much money you would need to live and the cost of things you need for living. It would teach you what you needed for your future."[56]

Solutions to tap

Better understanding of how to save and manage debt is essential knowledge for girls, but so too is the confidence to control one's own money and, someday, others' money as corporate leaders or small business owners.

The Girl Scout Research Institute conducted a nationwide survey of girls ages 8 to 17 in 2012 and found that only 12 percent of young girls feel "very confident" when it comes to making financial decisions. The Girl Scouts has strategies, including a Financial Literacy Badge and curriculum, to help girls develop money management skills for themselves and others. Its decades-old Girl Scout Cookie Program, the largest girl-led business in the world, now includes business ethics lessons, goal setting, and people skills courses.[57] Encouraging girls to develop entrepreneurial drive, the Girl Scouts also teaches "group money-earning" strategies, including developing car wash and pet-sitting businesses, and has an online video series for girls called "It's Your Business—Run It!"

There are other innovations to build on for financial lessons in a Life Ed curriculum: For instance, at Girls Inc., the "Economic Literacy" curriculum includes dynamic workshops such as "She's on the Money!" and "Equal Earners, Savvy Spenders," which arm young girls with vital financial skills early, such as saving, market investing, and entrepreneurship.[58] And Jump$tart, a national advocacy organization that trains teachers how to teach smart money habits to students from kindergarten through high school, hosts conferences on such important issues as identity theft and debt management.[59]

As we have seen in programs that focus on the whole family—such as FUEL Education,[60] which promotes savings circles and accounts to help high school students and their families to prepare for college and emergencies—a better understanding of finances, budgets, and how to use existing economic supports to meet their family's needs is essential if a young person is going to push back from the brink.

Life Ed can be the link to building a stronger future. As we listen to young women, we also understand more clearly the possibilities and the potential pitfalls of positioning the next generation to thrive. The app ideas that teenagers brainstormed are not simply smart tools for smartphones—they represent the needs of a generation of young people who are not being equipped with the tools, ideas, and practical information to help them navigate the challenges and choices presented to them in the modern world.

THE PATH FORWARD—TWO GENERATIONS AT A TIME

Women are poised to set a course for the next 50 years where women and men are truly equal and both are thriving. As women's financial and educational stability for themselves and their families increases, we will move the nation toward greater success and security. Many women have made extraordinary progress over the past 50 years and have attained power their grandmothers, or even some mothers, could hardly have imagined. Men, too, increasingly recognize that women's progress has had a positive impact on their lives as well.

Yet to truly make equality and security a reality in all women's lives, we must be bold. Two-generation approaches and social capital building offer a new mind-set and tools for our educational institutions, nonprofits, and government agencies to ensure the next generation has a strong shot at the American Dream—and that their mothers do well, too. At the same time, practical Life Ed skills and advice—integrated in our schools, our faith communities, even our homes—can help teen-age girls and boys become the emotionally and financially stable contributors our country needs.

Yet we also need the public and political will to push for these changes and invest-ments, be they public or private. We cannot underestimate the power of both indi-vidual and collective action to bring these ideas to life in our own communities. As we move from words to action, let us be energized by Shirley Chisholm's words: "You don't make progress by standing on the sidelines, whimpering and complain-ing. You make progress by implementing ideas."

We have the ideas, and now is the time to get to work, to ensure all women and their families have a fair shot at the American Dream.

Graduation day for the REACH Plus class at Washington Women's Employment and Education, or WWEE, in Tacoma, Washington. {BARBARA KINNEY}

Moving toward economic stability and beyond

We asked women in Voices for Two-Generation Success, "What does a society that fully supports equality and success for all women look like?" They envisioned a "better future and outlook"; "happy community, less violence, more support to one another"; "women would be more united and successful in life"; and "unity, growth, stability."[61]

To realize that vision, women and men must step up, but more importantly, push back—with all their resources—to enable all women to tap their potential power.

How to push back

Take a look at our five suggestions for steps any individual can take to help move the nation toward greater equality and economic security for all. Collectively, we have the power to transform women's lives.

1 Claim your political power

Women make up the majority of American voters. Their political participation has defined the outcomes of many elections from mayor to president. Women will have two major electoral opportunities to leverage their political power in the next two years. In 2014, 36 states will choose their governors, and 33 Senate seats will be up for election as well as thousands of additional openings from the state legislature to the school board. And in 2016, the nation will choose a new president.

All of these elections create an opportunity for women voters to gain commitments from our political leaders to finish the undone work, including: expanding family and medical leave; ensuring high-quality early care and education for all children; and eliminating the wage gap so that these policies become an everyday reality for all women and their families. Voting is one of the simplest yet most powerful ways to create local as well as national impact.

2 Leverage your economic contributions

Women are dominant players in the workforce and as consumers. They have the collective ability to send powerful messages to the private sector on issues ranging from workforce policies to advancement opportunities. Women can learn from examples such as the group of girls in Pennsylvania who organized a challenge—dubbed a "girlcott," to Abercrombie & Fitch in the mid-2000s to take shirts with derogatory language off the shelves—and won.[62]

Leveraging pocketbook power can be just as effective as voting power in improving women's economic lives. Remember, women make 73 percent of consumer purchasing decisions.[63]

3 Tap women at the top

Women at the top of the economic ladder have an opportunity to invest their talent, voice, and money in the potential of low-income women. Women Moving Millions, an innovative women's philanthropic movement, is changing the landscape of possibilities for women through their powerful multimillion-dollar collective gifts, just as women's foundations across the country continue to grow women donors from all backgrounds to give back and make a difference with their treasure, talent, and time.[64]

Business leaders and employers have the ability to build cultures and policies that support low-income families' employment and family success. In doing so, they are creating ladders of opportunity for women and girls.

4 Engage men as allies

Men are our partners and are traversing the same shifting landscape when it comes to work, money, parenting, and relationships. Their participation and perspective in these discussions will help us to map a path toward opportunity and security. These issues aren't just women's issues—they are everyone's issues.

5 Share your mistakes and wisdom with the next generation

Girls have told us what they need. You can give it to them by actively mentoring the girls in your family, community, Sunday school classroom, or office. Women can share their challenges and what they would do differently. Both girls and boys want to learn about college, finances, healthy relationships, and self-respect, so share your lessons learned from life and work and help ensure that both knowledge and economic security pass from one generation to the next.

THINK ABOUT THIS

We need a two-generation approach that builds economic security
for children and their mothers together.

APPENDIX A: VOICES FOR TWO-GENERATION SUCCESS

METHODOLOGY

Lake Research Partners and Chesapeake Beach Consulting conducted 10 focus groups with single and married mothers across races, separated by income levels, as well as with boys and girls of mixed racial backgrounds between the ages of 12 to 14 and 16 to 18. Participants in the mothers' groups were recruited to reflect a mix of educational attainment, employment status, and marital status. Participants in the children's groups were recruited to reflect a racial mix as well as a mix of family backgrounds (single and married parents, non-college educated, currently enrolled, and college educated).

June 17, 2013—Chicago, Illinois

• Boys, ages 16 to 18

• Moderate-income white mothers, ages 35 to 50 (between 200 percent and 400 percent of the federal poverty level, or FPL)

• Mixed-income Asian American mothers, ages 35 to 50

• Moderate-income African American mothers, under 35 (between 200 percent and 400 percent of the FPL)

June 20, 2013—Denver, Colorado

• Boys, ages 12 to 14

• Girls, ages 16 to 18

• Low-income Latina mothers, under 35 (below 200 percent of the FPL)

<u>June 24, 2013—Richmond, Virginia</u>

• Girls, ages 12 to 14

• Low-income white mothers, under 35 (below 200 percent of the FPL)

• Low-income African American mothers, ages 35 to 50 (below 200 percent of the FPL)

The findings in the report use the terms "mothers," "single parents," and "parents" to refer to participants in the parents' groups and "teens," "teenagers," and "preteens" to refer to participants in the boys' and girls' groups.

ENDNOTES

1 U.S. Census Bureau, Current Population Survey: Poverty (U.S. Department of Commerce, 2012), available at http://www.census.gov/hhes/www/cpstables/032013/pov/pov01_200.htm.

2 Lake Research Partners and Chesapeake Beach Consulting, "Voices for Two-Generation Success: Seeking Stable Futures" (2013), available at http://www.insidehighered.com/sites/default/server_files/files/Ascend%20Lake%20Research%20Voices%20for%20Two-Generation%20Success.pdf.

3 Mark Mather, "U.S. Children in Single-Mother Families" (Washington: Population Reference Bureau, 2010), available at www.prb.org/pdf10/single-motherfamilies.pdf.

4 See "The Heckman Equation" details and materials available at http://www.heckmanequation.org. See also Rob Grunewald and Arthur J. Rolnick, "Early Childhood Development: Economic Development with a High Public Return" (Minneapolis: Federal Reserve Bank of Minneapolis, 2003), available at http.//www.minneapolisfed.org/publications_papers/pub_display.cfm?id=3832.

5 Tom Hertz, "Understanding Mobility in America" (Washington: Center for American Progress, 2006), available at http://www.americanprogress.org/kf/hertz_mobility_analysis.pdf.

6 Lake Research Partners and Chesapeake Beach Consulting, "Voices for Two-Generation Success: Seeking Stable Futures."

7 Teresa Eckrich Sommer and others, "Early Childhood Education centers and Mothers' Postsecondary Attainment: A New Conceptual Framework for a Dual-Generation Education Intervention" (New York: Teachers College Record, 2012); Sara Goldrick-Rab, Julie Minikel-Lacocque, and Peter Kinsley, "Managing to Make It: The College Trajectories of Traditional-Age Students with Children," Working Paper 1 (University of Wisconsin-Madison, 2011).

8 See, for example, Sandra Lawson, "Women Hold Up Half the Sky," Global Economics Paper No. 164 (Goldman Sachs Economic Research, 2008), available at http://www.goldmansachs.com/our-thinking/focus-on/investing-in-women/bios-pdfs/women-half-sky-pdf.pdf.

9 Lake Research Partners and Chesapeake Beach Consulting, "Voices for Two-Generation Success: Seeking Stable Futures."

10 Ibid.

11 Ascend at the Aspen Institute, "Two Generations, One Future" (2012), available at http://ascend.aspeninstitute.org/resources/two-generations-one-future.

12 See, for example, Katherine Magnuson, "The Effect of Increases in Welfare Mothers' Education on Their Young Children's Academic and Behavioral Outcomes," Discussion Paper 1274-03 (University of Wisconsin, Institute for Research on Poverty Discussion Paper, 2003).

13 Ascend at the Aspen Institute, "Two Generations, One Future."

14 See The Glen at St. Joseph, available at http://www.glenatstjoseph.org/.

15 Gail M. Mulligan, Sarah Hastedt, and Jill Carlivati, "First-Time Kindergartners in 2010–11: First Findings from the Kindergarten Rounds of the Early Childhood Longitudinal Study, Kindergarten Class of 2010–11 (ECLS-L:2011)" (Washington: National Center for Education Statistics, 2012), available at http://nces.ed.gov/pubsearch/pubsinfo.asp?pubid=2012049.

16 Jeremiah Program, "2012 Annual Report," available at http://www.jeremiahprogram.org/2012-annual-report/.

17 Ascend at the Aspen Institute, "Two Generations, One Future."

18 Robert W. Glover and others, "*CareerAdvance* Implementation Report" (Ray Marshall Center for the Study of Human Resources, University of Texas, Austin, 2011), available at http://ascend.aspeninstitute.org/resources/careeradvance-implementation-report.

19 Personal communication from P. Lindsay Chase Lansdale, professor of human development and social policy, Institute for Policy Research, Northwestern University, January 9, 2012; personal communication from Teresa Eckrich Sommer, senior research scientist/research associate, Institute for Policy Research, Northwestern University, January 9, 2012.

20 See CFED, "Children's Savings Accounts (CSAs)," available at http://cfed.org/programs/csa/.

21 Ibid.

22 See "The Equality of Opportunity Project," available at http://www.equality-of-opportunity.org/.

23 Nancy DiTomaso, *The American Non-Dilemma: Racial Inequality Without Racism* (New York: Russell Sage Foundation, 2012).

24 Lake Research Partners and Chesapeake Beach Consulting, "Voices for Two-Generation Success: Seeking Stable Futures."

25 Ibid.

26 Ibid.

27 Ascend at the Aspen Institute, "Making Family Economic Security a Family Tradition" (2013), available at http://s.bsd.net/ascend/default/page/-/compressed%20-%20fullreport.pdf.

28 See Family Independence Initiative, available at http://ww.fiinet.org.

29 See Family Independence Initiative, "Strategies for Change: Incubate," available at http://www.fii.org/strategy_for_change/incubate.

30 See Crittenton Women's Union, "The Essential Elements of Mobility Mentoring," available at http://www.livework thrive.org/research_and_tools/mobility_mentoring.

31 See Eduardo Padrón, "Helping the Poor Go to Good Colleges," *New York Times* letter to the editor, August 6, 2013, available at http://www.nytimes.com/2013/08/07/opinion/helping-the-poor-go-to-good-colleges.html?_r=0.

32 Lake Research Partners and Chesapeake Beach Consulting, "Voices for Two-Generation Success: Seeking Stable Futures."

33 Ibid.

34 Ibid.

35 Ibid.

36 Ibid.

37 Ibid.

38 Ibid.

39 Ibid.

40 See Girls on the Run, available at http://www.girlsontherun.org/.

41 See Futures Without Violence, available at http://www.futureswithoutviolence.org/.

42 See Eveline's Sunshine Cottage, "Application Process, Past Successes," available at http://www.evelinessunshine cottage.com/#!__application-process--past-successes.

43 See The National Crittenton Foundation, "Who We Are," available at http://www.nationalcrittenton.org/who-we-are/.

44 Lake Research Partners and Chesapeake Beach Consulting, "Voices for Two-Generation Success: Seeking Stable Futures."

45 Ibid.

46 See American Association of University Women, "What We Do: STEM Education," available at http://www.aauw.org/what-we-do/stem-education/.

47 See Higher Education Alliance of Advocates for Students with Children, available at http://www.heaasc.org/.

48 Lake Research Partners and Chesapeake Beach Consulting, "Voices for Two-Generation Success: Seeking Stable Futures."

49 Ibid.

50 Leo B. Hendry and others, "Adolescents' Perceptions of Significant Individuals in Their Lives," *Journal of Adolescence* 15 (3) (1992): 255–270, available at http://www.ncbi.nlm.nih.gov/pubmed/1447412.

51 See Urban Alliance, "Curriculum Outreach," available at http://www.theurbanalliance.org/about/programs/curriculum-outreach.

52 See The Links, Incorporated, available at http://www.linksinc.org/.

53 See Girls Write Now, available at http://www.girlswritenow.org/.

54 See Girls Write Now, "Who We Are: Our Story," available at http://www.girlswritenow.org/who-we-are/our-story/.

55 Lake Research Partners and Chesapeake Beach Consulting, "Voices for Two-Generation Success: Seeking Stable Futures."

56 Ibid.

57 See Girl Scouts, "Financial Literacy," available at http://www.girlscouts.org/gs_central/financial_literacy/.

58 See Girls Inc., available at http://girlsinc.org/.

59 See Jump$tart, "Activities and Initiatives," available at http://www.jumpstart.org/activities-and-initiatives.html.

60 See FUEL Education, "History," available at http://fueleducation.org/history/.

61 Lake Research Partners and Chesapeake Beach Consulting, "Voices for Two-Generation Success: Seeking Stable Futures."

62 See Margaret Farley Steele, "Noticed; Students Protest Provocative T-Shirts," *The New York Times*, November 5, 2005, available at http://query.nytimes.com/gst/fullpage.html?res=9901E0DF1F3EF933A15752C1A9639C8B63.

63 Catalyst, "Catalyst Quick Take: Buying Power" (2013), http://www.catalyst.org/knowledge/buying-power.

64 See Women Moving Millions, "Who We Are: Our Story," available at http://www.womenmovingmillions.org/who-we-are/our-story/.

When Working Women Thrive, Our Nation Thrives

By SHERYL SANDBERG, COO of Facebook and founder of www.LeanIn.org

As I've traveled around the country this past year, I've heard the same message over and over: Women need support.

So many women face serious challenges as they struggle every day to provide for themselves and their families. Too many work standards remain inflexible and unfair and often penalize women. Women are paid less than men for the same work. Some have jobs that offer no time off for illness or to care for a sick child or parent. Many live without regular health care or a safety net.

If women are struggling, our nation struggles. We need to join together to help women who are being pushed to the brink. As community members, employers, and advocates, we must find solutions to help working women help themselves and their families.

We can start with public policy acknowledging that women make up half of the American workforce. It's shocking that of all industrialized nations, the United States is the only one with no paid maternity leave policy. We must fix this immediately. We should also make subsidized leave available to fathers as well as mothers, so that men can take the time to be involved and supportive parents too. In addition, we need to address the high cost of child care, which pushes many women out of the workforce.

Along with improved public policy, we need improved corporate policies. Companies that offer flexible schedules and allow employees to work from remote locations have a competitive advantage in today's labor market. Employers who understand the needs of their workforce and are creative in finding ways to meet those needs are rewarded with more loyal and higher-performing employees.

And perhaps most important, we need to close the wage gap once and for all. The average woman earns only 77 cents for every dollar earned by the average man, and a black woman earns 64 cents[1] and Latinas only 55 cents for every dollar earned by a white, non-Hispanic man.[2] There are many who argue that this wage gap is not real—and it is true that different jobs, career paths, and hours explain part of the gap. But make no mistake: Women get paid less than men for doing the same work. Each company, large and small, should look at its pay practices and fix them where they aren't fair. Every employee should be empowered to negotiate and advocate for himself or herself—including allowing women to ask if they are paid as much as men with the same jobs and get an honest answer from their bosses.

Next, what can individual women do to help those who are living on the brink? We need to make it easier for women to support one another—not just emotionally but also with practical advice. To this end, LeanIn.org offers free tools to create what we call "Lean In Circles"—small peer groups that meet regularly to help members achieve their goals.[3]

Over the past six months, women in all 50 states have started more than 9,000 Lean In Circles. One circle was started by a group of domestic workers in California, who—like so many others—have been denied health care, sick leave, and vacation days. In this circle, they are exploring how to bring about change and gain more benefits for themselves and their children. One of the members told us that her group has helped her gain confidence in her skills and abilities. She said that for the first time, she's looking for a new job—and with all the women in her circle cheering her on, she's not alone anymore.

To solve these challenges, women not only need to support one another; they also need the opportunity to lead. Research suggests that companies with more women in leadership roles have more family-friendly work-life policies, more women in mid-level management, and smaller gender gaps in executive compensation. By adding more female voices at the top levels of companies, institutions, and government, we will extend fairer treatment to all.

Women deserve better—and must demand better—so that the benefits of achieving equality can be felt by all. When women thrive, our nation thrives.

ENDNOTES

1   National Partnership for Women & Families, "African American Women and the Wage Gap" (2013), available at http://go.nationalpartnership.org/site/DocServer/ Wage_Gap_for_African_American_Women_in_20_States. pdf?docID=11702.

2   National Partnership for Women & Families, "Latinas and the Wage Gap" (2013), available at http://go. nationalpartnership.org/site/DocServer/Wage_Gap_for_ Latinas_in_20_States.pdf?docID=11701.

3   Lean In, "Circles," available at http://leanin.org/circles.

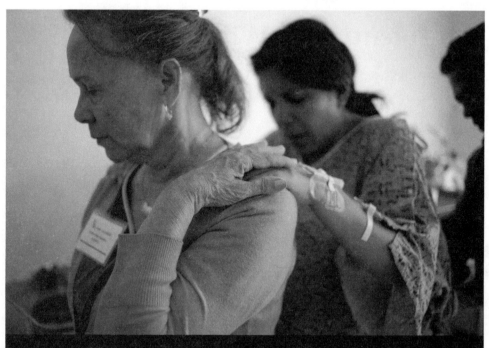

CARMEN RIOS • Greenbrae, California

Carmen Rios has been a birthing coach for 18 years and currently works with the Canal Alliance in Marin County to help Spanish-speaking clients understand proper prenatal and early infant care. Carmen has three grown children and seven grandchildren. Although she lives alone, the family works together to support each other emotionally and financially.

Carmen loves working with women to give them the support they need to raise healthy, happy families. "Maybe one day I will call you and say, 'I won the lottery!'" she said. "But if not, I am a happy camper."

When Women Achieve Their Full Potential, So Will America

By SENATOR KIRSTEN GILLIBRAND (D-NY), whose signature legislative priorities are strengthening the armed services, children's and elders' health care issues, transparency in government, and—above all—rebuilding the U.S. economy. She is married and the mother of two young children.

I have traveled across my state and around the country to speak a simple truth: If we are going to bring the change and growth we need in America, women are the solution. We need more women in office at every level of government—from city councils to city halls to state legislatures to governors' mansions to the halls of Congress in Washington, D.C.

We need more women in government not because women's voices are better than men's but because women's voices are different. We bring a different lens to problem-solving, and that balancing perspective often leads to better results. I have seen for myself that when women are at the table, a broader agenda is discussed—an agenda that looks out for all Americans, particularly those who have no voice.

For example, in 2013, we in the Senate finally started taking on leadership in the military to end the disturbing crisis of military sexual assaults. The Defense Department estimates there were a shocking 26,000 incidents of unwanted sexual contact in 2012, yet only 302 cases even went to trial.[1] It's no coincidence that the ongoing silence on this issue was broken only when a record 20 women U.S. senators spoke out—and when 6 other women of both parties and I made history by serving on the Committee on Armed Services at the same

time, asking the tough questions and demanding change.[2] What we are seeing in the Senate proves what we already know about women: We work very well together. We reach across party lines. We build consensus, we reach compromise, and we know how to get things done.

We also know that women's issues are the nation's issues. And we know that today, with the economy as our biggest problem, women are the untapped solution—not just in elected office but also in every workplace around the United States.

According to *The Economist*'s 2013 "Glass-ceiling index,"[3] a study that ranked countries' efforts to give women the best chance of equal treatment in the workplace, America came in 12th, behind France and Denmark. That's right; the United States didn't even make it into the top 10.

I have been developing a legislative agenda that would empower women to reach their full economic potential, which will help rebuild the middle class and power our economy back to full health. Its points are as follows:

- Since women are often the primary caregivers of infants, children, and elderly parents, we need to make it easier for them to move in and out of the workforce so they can meet those family needs without being punished. That means paid family and medical leave and access to flextime arrangements.

- We must make sure that a new mother knows that quality daycare is available. When a woman can't afford the child care necessary for her to get back to work, how can she keep earning a paycheck for her family? We also need universal pre-kindergarten—not only to give kids a good start but also to allow their mothers to fully engage in their work and help our economy grow.

- At long last, we must eliminate the gender wage gap and increase our minimum wage. It's infuriating that 64 percent of minimum-wage earners are women,[4] and that those with children are trying to make do with pay that puts them $3,000 below the poverty line.

Our nation's need for these family-friendly policies is why I advocate for more women to become activists and make their voices heard. The mission of my Off the Sidelines campaign has been to trumpet the need for all women's voices to be heard. All around this country, I tell women—particularly young women—to get off the sidelines because every single day, decisions are being made that will have a major impact on their lives, and if they do not have a seat at that table, they may not like the outcomes they get. Women—no matter what age, ethnicity, sexual preference, or income—need to get in the game, become leaders in their communities, and press for change on the range of issues that are important to women.

That means more women voting and holding their elected leaders accountable, more women supporting women candidates with the resources they need to win, and yes, more women running for office themselves. Studies show that it takes more convincing to get a woman to run for office than a man[5]—but when women do choose to run, their campaigns are successful at the same rate as men's campaigns.[6]

We have to do better. That requires demanding better from our elected leaders, and to me, that means changing the face of those leaders so that their agendas reflect women's needs. It's time to rewrite the rules and modernize the American workplace for women workers with policies that reflect our values and treat women as men's equals.

This is an emergency because I strongly believe it will only be when every American girl, every American woman, achieves her full potential that America will achieve hers.

ENDNOTES

1 Sexual Assault Prevention and Response Office, *Department of Defense Annual Report on Sexual Assault in the Military* (U.S. Department of Defense, 2013), p. 12, available at http://www.sapr.mil/public/docs/reports/FY12_DoD_SAPRO_Annual_Report_on_Sexual_Assault-VOLUME-ONE.pdf.

2 Luisita Lopez Torregrosa, "Women in Congress Confront the Military on Sexual Assault," *International Herald Tribune*, May 28, 2013, available at http://rendezvous.blogs.nytimes.com/2013/05/28/women-in-congress-confront-the-military-on-sexual-assault/?_r=0.

3 Economist.com, "Daily chart: The glass-ceiling index," Graphic detail, March 7, 2013, available at http://www.economist.com/blogs/graphicdetail/2013/03/daily-chart-3.

4 Center for American Progress analysis of U.S. Bureau of Labor Statistics data and Center for Economic and Policy Research Uniform Extracts of Current Population Survey Outgoing Rotation Group data for 2012.

5 Jennifer L. Lawless and Richard L. Fox, "Girls Just Wanna Not Run" (Washington: American University, 2013), p. 2, available at http://www.american.edu/spa/wpi/upload/Girls-Just-Wanna-Not-Run_Policy-Report.pdf.

6 Political Parity, "Women Candidates and their Campaigns" (2012), available at http://www.politicalparity.org/research-inventory/women-candidates-and-their-campaigns/.

It's Time to
Push Back

Jeannie James lives on the Navajo Nation reservation in Arizona. Window Rock is in the backdrop. She currently works as an administrative assistant for the Department of Social Services. {JAN SONNENMAIR}

Where Do We Go from Here?

By Olivia Morgan and Karen Skelton

Fifty years after President Lyndon B. Johnson called for a War on Poverty and enlisted Sargent Shriver to oversee it, the most important social issue of our day is once again the dire economic straits of millions of Americans. The deep and chronic poverty of a sliver of America in the 1960s has given way to a broader financial insecurity now experienced by a third of the country, mostly women and children. The fragile economic status of millions of American women is the shameful secret of the modern era—yet these women are also our greatest hope for change. That is the focus of this report.

The Shriver Report: A Woman's Nation Pushes Back from the Brink asks—and answers—big questions. Why are so many millions of women financially vulnerable, when so many other women are doing so well? Why are so many millions of women struggling to make ends meet, even though they are proudly working so hard and juggling so much? And why are working women more likely to be poor than working men? What is it about our nation—government, business, family, and even women themselves—that drives women to the financial brink? And what is at stake?

To answer these questions, we examined in detail three major cultural and economic changes over the past 50 years:
• Women work more outside the home, but still earn less than men.
• Women lead more families on their own.
• Women today need higher education, no longer just a high school education, to enter the middle class.

What we found is that Americans themselves are far ahead of government and business in adapting to changes in the nation that affect women and families. For example, people appear to understand that marriage—though it may offer families the best foundation for financial stability—is no longer the status quo for most Americans. Our groundbreaking polling shows that nearly two-thirds of people surveyed want government and society to adapt to the reality of single-parent families and to support them in all their new shapes and variations.

To forge a path forward that recognizes this reality and more, *The Shriver Report* brought together the best and brightest minds and challenged them to collaborate with us to develop fresh thinking around practical solutions. What makes this report unique is the combination of its components—academic research, personal reflections, authentic photojournalism, groundbreaking poll results, frontline workers, and box-office celebrities—all together in the same place, all contributing to a single issue of national importance: women and the economy. In *The Shriver Report*, Davos meets Main Street.

In America, one in three women is living in or near poverty. Forty-two million American women—and the more than 28 million children who depend on them—live on or over the brink of financial crisis. We know these women. They are our sisters, our aunts, and our neighbors. They are our dental hygienists, our restaurant servers, and our receptionists. They are the caretakers of our aging parents and our children. While most of these women on the brink are white, they are every color, creed, and ethnicity. And we should care about their well-being, not only because they make our own lives better, but also because they can make our nation richer and stronger.

The team that built this report produced bold ideas. Taken together, these ideas present a modern social architecture designed to make individuals, businesses, and government stronger, more innovative, and better adapted to the realities of America's hardworking families.

One of the most important approaches of *The Shriver Report* is that the change needed for this nation to modernize its relationship with women begins with women themselves. Women on the brink of poverty may be the key to leading our nation to economic prosperity—and the most important first step may be their recognition of their own importance as providers for themselves and as leading players in our nation's growth. Our poll found that more than 7 in 10 Americans believe women play an essential role in the national economy. Maria Shriver makes the case in her chapter that if we lead with women, we will have a robust nation. If we don't, we won't.

And women are a good bet. Women in our poll, despite their financial hardships, are resilient. An inspiring 79 percent of single mothers in our survey believe their economic situation will improve over the next five years. Eighty-three percent of low-income women making less than $20,000 a year told us, "I believe I have the ability to make significant changes in my life to make my life better."

But girls don't always bet on themselves—or recognize the stakes. With that in mind, we developed Life Education, or **Life Ed**: a call to women and girls to get smart. The schoolyard rhyme lays out the old life order: First comes love, then comes marriage, and only then comes the baby in the baby carriage. Today, the most important lesson we can impress on girls to keep them off the brink is "college before kids." These girls are likely to become their own and their family's most important resource as caregiver and breadwinner, and they need to see themselves that way while they're still young and invest in themselves as future providers. With the clarity of hindsight, women in our poll identified leaving school early and not putting a higher priority on their career and education as the biggest regrets in their lives.

Led by Anne Mosle and Ascend at the Aspen Institute, *The Shriver Report* has developed a blueprint for this new Life Ed curriculum to teach girls how to meet the demands of the modern era. Fifty years ago, they were taught home economics, or Home Ec, because sewing, cooking, and managing the household were understood to be the ways in which they would interact with the economy. Life Ed draws on years of prior research, along with focus groups conducted for this report, to identify knowledge and skills crucial to today's teens: self-esteem, education, mentors and networks, and financial savvy.

With the benefit of experience, 39 percent of the women on the brink polled said they wished they had delayed having kids or had fewer children. Nearly half (47 percent) of single mothers polled said the same—a significant number, and a painful confession. As Ann O'Leary details in her chapter, "Marriage, Motherhood, and Men," it must be a national priority to reduce unintended and unplanned pregnancies. We hope that Life Ed will be one of the tools that teaches future women the critical importance of developing their own skills and knowledge first, before parenthood, so that the "baby carriage" comes when the baby's parents are prepared for parenting and its challenges.

Women can't do it alone. Mothers are breadwinners or co-breadwinners in two-thirds of American families, and their success depends upon a workplace that supports their dual roles. During much of the 20th century, the idea of a "family wage" led many employers to provide greater compensation to male breadwinners than to married mothers and other workers not caring for family members. Today, employers need once again to adapt to support their changed workforce—to lift up the nation's new providers. Ann Stevens, director of the Center for Poverty Research at the University of California, Davis, drew on the expertise of Ellen Galinsky and Families and Work Institute's concept of Effective Workplaces—plus new research conducted for this report—to create an index of workplace policies that are the most significant factors in the well-being of low-wage women workers and the success of their employers. Together, we present a Thrive Index for businesses, a first-of-its-kind compilation of questions for employers to identify and adopt the best workplace policies that most effectively support low-wage women workers.

While a college education is the surest individual path to financial security, our economy also depends on low-skilled workers, as Heather Boushey describes in her chapter on women and the economy. Over the next 20 years, the greatest growth will occur in job sectors that do not require postsecondary education—fully one-third of all U.S. jobs. These low-wage jobs are largely in the care and service industries on which the rest of the economy depends. We need people to fill these jobs, yet we cannot continue to consign tens of millions of women and families to jobs with low pay and few benefits, leaving them teetering on the brink of poverty. So we must also transform our workplaces, so that even the lowest-paying jobs can be balanced with family obligations and educational opportunities, becoming stepping-stones to a brighter future.

The public is well ahead of policymakers on many of these issues. In our poll, the most popular policy changes for both the public and private sector explicitly attempt to accommodate work with family life. Melissa Boteach and Shawn Fremstad's rigorous analysis of public solutions identify many policies that the government should adopt to benefit low-income women and provide a stable economic grounding on which families can build. Ninety percent of Americans, including 88 percent of Republicans, support "ensuring that women get equal pay for equal work in order to raise wages for working women and families," the most popular public-policy proposal tested in our polling. Overwhelming support also exists in this country for paid sick leave, which was identified by low-wage women in our poll as the single most helpful policy their workplaces could adopt.

Women doing it all are often carrying the weight of an entire family as both breadwinner and caregiver. Lists such as this one, written by Crystal Thompson of Chicago, Illinois, are how many busy mothers organize the appointments and responsibilities of a regular week. {BARBARA KINNEY}

But Washington has proven increasingly sclerotic and dysfunctional. We cannot ask millions of women in poverty and on its brink to wait for action from Congress. Inspired by the success of Gov. Butch Otter's program in Idaho and building on Maria Shriver's pioneering work with WE Connect in California, we worked with the Corporation for National and Community Service, or CNCS, VISTA, and LIFT to develop the Shriver Corps, a new pilot national service project dedicated to building pathways to prosperity for low-income women and families by simplifying and modernizing the process by which they access benefits, training, and other services.

Shriver Corps members will develop and implement volunteer-training programs and build local services and partnerships to help families access resources that will put them on sounder economic footing. At the same time, Corps members will design and develop new pilot programs to deploy throughout six target regions across the country. Through this three-year partnership with CNCS, the Shriver Corps will build capacity to lift untold numbers of women and families off the brink of financial insecurity.

Why does this matter? It matters because millions of resilient, hardworking women will strengthen our nation's economy and our children's future. It matters because America wants to be competitive in a global economy, and it has disadvantaged itself by sidelining women. It matters because pervasive insecurity and economic hardship are the single most common American story today.

Millions of women on the brink know more about stretching a budget, not wasting a dime, and investing in what matters than many of the people who make 100 times more money than they do. They are tenacious and entrepreneurial. The American spirit lives through them.

Yet too many of the nation's institutions are still based on assumptions from half a century ago—assumptions that don't respect women's work; don't support their ambition, their careers, and caregiving roles; and don't respond to their occasional and temporary, yet essential, needs.

The Shriver Report reveals this quiet reality: The people who we expect to raise us, care for us, and work to support us are too often left unsupported and uncared for. As more women have joined the paid labor force, a portion of the work they do without pay—cooking, cleaning, and caregiving—has been outsourced to paid caregivers. But perhaps in part because it continues to be seen as "women's work," this work is undervalued. The typical child care worker, for example, makes only about $9.50 an hour.

In the first and second *Shriver* reports, we celebrated women as half the workforce for the first time in our nation's history and as the primary caretakers for an aging population struggling with Alzheimer's and other debilitating diseases that require round-the-clock care. We proclaimed that A Woman's Nation "changes everything." The fact that women are half of all workers and primary caretakers does change everything, but not necessarily for the better. We as a nation have not come to terms with what it actually takes for women working in poorly compensated jobs to meet these demands.

Not only do the extraordinary contributors to this special report distinguish it from any other report of its kind, but—for the first time this year—our report is being amplified through an unprecedented complement of diverse media. To bring emotional counterbalance to our academic research, Maria Shriver brought our work to the iconic documentarian Sheila Nevins at HBO, who agreed to fund a film in conjunction with this report, bringing to life the challenges, hopes, and reality of women living on the brink. At the same time, we are once again partnering with NBC News for a week of special coverage across multiple programs. *Atlantic Monthly* is bringing the report to life by convening thought leaders in Washington, D.C., to discuss the report's findings and implications. Our website, www.ShriverReport.org, brings the report to life as a new digital home for these special *Shriver* reports and a place to publish people reporting from the front lines. Our all-female team of award-winning photojournalists also brings the report to life, having crisscrossed the country to capture images of women living on the brink. Finally, university professors around the country will use the *Shriver Report* as a text to teach a new generation of students and future leaders.

Many American women have grown increasingly powerful. Still, there is much to be done to achieve equality. We cannot hope to provide equal opportunity to rise when a third of our nation struggles for footing on financially shaky ground.

To strengthen the foundation for women, we argue for *A Woman's Nation Reimagined*. In a reimagined nation, political, business, media thought leaders, and women themselves all understand what it means for women to be both driving the economy and caretaking. Collectively, the nation makes adjustments that provide women a solid foundation, so they can push back from the brink and thrive.

Dee Saint Franc and her daughter, Azariah, always keep each other laughing, despite the difficult circumstances keeping them on the brink. {BARBARA RIES}

At the end of this report, we provide a list of 10 things we all can do individually to collectively help our nation push back from the financial brink.

Women have long led transformational change in this country, from the fight to abolish slavery to the fight for women's suffrage, from the push to obtain college degrees to the push against the glass ceiling. Having upended the nation's social structure, we can change the nation's laws around paid sick days, pay equity, and child care. We can change the way businesses accommodate mom bread-winners. And we can change the way girls are educated about their important role as providers.

We can do this. And we must.

Learn more at www.ShriverReport.org.

10 Things
You Can Do

TO POWER A WOMAN'S NATION

1 Get *The Shriver Report: A Woman's Nation Pushes Back from the Brink* at www.Shriver Report.org. Read it, discuss it, implement it, and pass it on.

2 Get smart. Build a stable foundation for your future by putting college before kids. Women with only a high school diploma are three to four times more likely to live on the financial brink than those with a college degree.

3 Invest in yourself. Today's women and girls need to think of themselves as providers in their families, not provided for. Increase your own earning power, learn about savings plans, and be financially savvy.

4 Use your economic power. You can hold businesses accountable with your money. Be an informed and influential consumer by supporting companies that create a more conscious, caring, compassionate workplace for their employees.

5 Engage men as allies. These issues are everyone's issues. Fathers, sons, and brothers are part of the solution, and many are poised to partner.

6 Vote. But don't give your vote away. Make candidates earn it. Vote for women and men who want to modernize the nation's relationship to women and their families. Support laws that can add half a trillion dollars to the national economy by closing the wage gap.

7 Be a 21st-century "boss," even at home. Recognize the power you have to impact women. Provide benefits and workplace supports for your child care providers and people who help you with elder care. Offer sick days, be flexible with schedules, leave good tips for waitresses and room attendants when you travel, and educate yourself and your employees about government programs that can help.

8 Finance women's work. Invest in women entrepreneurs and nonprofit organizations that support, promote, and respect modern American families. See a list of organizations and resources at www.ShriverReport.org.

9 Mentor and motivate girls. Be a Life Ed teacher to the girls in your life. Teach them about the importance of making smart decisions—financial, personal, and educational—that enhance their self-esteem and their career prospects. Foster the mind-set that girls must invest in themselves and that they have the power to succeed.

10 Be an architect of change. We *can* push back from the brink.

Increasing Economic Opportunities for Women: The Right Thing to Do, and the Smart Thing to Do

By HILLARY RODHAM CLINTON, who has served as U.S. secretary of state, senator, and first lady.

I have always believed that women are not victims. We are agents of change, we are drivers of progress, and we are makers of peace. All we need is a fighting chance. That firm faith in the untapped potential of women at home and around the world has been at the heart of my work my entire life—from college and law school, to Arkansas, to the White House, to the Senate, and most recently to the State Department.

Everything I have done and learned in my work over the years has convinced me that improving the rights and the status of women is not simply a matter of human dignity. It is also essential to our security and our prosperity. When we liberate the economic potential of women, we elevate the economic performance of communities, nations, and the world. That's why we put women at the heart of our foreign policy priorities at the State Department.

I was proud to be at the historic 2011 signing of the San Francisco Declaration, when the United States, Canada, Peru, Chile, Mexico, and the rest of the 21 countries in the Asia-Pacific Economic Cooperation forum all made commitments to lower barriers and increase economic opportunities for women. I said then what I said all over the world as secretary of state: This isn't just the morally right thing to do—it is the smart thing to do. No country can achieve its full economic potential when women are left out or left behind.

As information transcends borders and creates opportunities for farmers to do their banking on mobile phones and children in distant villages to learn remotely, I believe that here, at the beginning of the 21st century, we are entering the participation age. This is the age where every individual, regardless of gender or other characteristics, is poised to be a contributing and valued member of the global marketplace.

The increasing numbers of women in the economy and the rising productivity gains from improving the distribution of their talents and skills has undoubtedly helped fuel significant growth everywhere. A rising tide of women in an economy raises the fortunes of families and nations.

Data show that investing in women's employment, health, and education drives better outcomes for entire societies. Economists tell us that when more women participate in the economy, there is a ripple effect: Businesses have more consumers, families both spend and save more, farmers produce and sell more food, education improves, and so does political stability.

We're seeing this all over the world. Latin America and the Caribbean have steadily increased women's participation in the labor market since the 1990s, and now women account for more than half of all workers in the region. The World Bank estimates that extreme poverty in the region has decreased by 30 percent as a result. Furthermore, *The Economist* points out that the increase in employment of women in developed countries during the past decade has added more to global growth than China has—and that's a lot.

But let's focus on the United States. Traveling the globe as secretary of state for four years reaffirmed and deepened my pride in our country and the ideals we represent. But it also challenged me to think about who we are and the values we are supposed to be living here at home, in order for me to effectively represent us abroad. After all, our global leadership for peace and prosperity, for freedom and equality, is not a birthright. It must be earned by every generation.

Some signs are good. A 2011 McKinsey study found that between 1970 and 2009, American women went from holding 37 percent of all jobs to almost 50 percent. In sheer value terms, these women have punched well above their weight. The productivity gains attributable to this increase in women's overall share of the labor market account for approximately one-quarter

of this country's current gross domestic product, or GDP—more than $3.5 trillion, which is more than the GDP of Germany and more than half the GDPs of China and Japan.

Yes, it's true that we now have American women at high levels of business, academia, government—you name it. But as we've seen recently, women still find themselves asking age-old questions about how they can make their way in male-dominated fields and how they can balance the demands of work and family. *The Economist* recently published a "glass-ceiling index," ranking countries based on factors such as opportunities for women in the workplace and equal pay. The United States didn't even make it into the top 10.

That's not the way it's supposed to be. I think of the extraordinary sacrifices my mother made to survive her own difficult childhood, to give me not only life but also opportunity, along with love and inspiration. I'm very proud of my own daughter, and I look at all these young women I've been privileged to work with or know through Chelsea, and it's hard to imagine turning the clock back on them. But in places throughout America large and small, the clock is turning back.

Recent studies have found that, on average, women live shorter lives in the United States than in any other major industrialized country. Think about that for a minute. We are the richest and most powerful country in the world, yet many American women today, especially those with the least education, have a shorter life span than their mothers had.

There is no single explanation for why this is happening. Prescription-drug overdoses, obesity, and smoking are all factors—but there is also intractable poverty and a lack of health insurance. The fact is that for too many American women, the dream of upward mobility and opportunity— the American Dream itself—remains elusive.

So we have work to do. Renewing America's vitality at home and strengthening our leadership abroad will take the energy and talents of *all* our people, women and men. If America is going to lead, we need to empower women here at home to participate fully in our economy and our society. In these tough economic times, no country can afford to perpetuate the barriers facing women in the workforce. The United States needs to make equal pay a reality. We need to extend paid family and medical leave benefits to more workers. We need to encourage more women and girls to pursue careers in math and science.

I'm amazed that too many otherwise-thoughtful people continue to see the fortunes of women and girls as somehow separate from society at large. They nod, they smile, and then they relegate these issues once again to the sidelines. I have seen it over and over again. I have been kidded about it, I have been ribbed, I have been challenged in boardrooms and official offices across the world.

But fighting to give women and girls a fighting chance isn't just a nice thing to do. It isn't some luxury that we only get to when we have time on our hands. This is a core imperative for every human being in every society. If we do not continue the campaign for women's rights and opportunities, the world we want to live in—and the country we all love and cherish—will not be what it should be.

So let's learn from the wisdom of all the mothers and fathers all over the world who teach their daughters that there is no limit on how big they can dream and how much they can achieve.

One sure way to maximize the chance for our country to do even better is to be sure we give girls and women the chance to compete and to demonstrate what they can contribute to us all. We need to invest in *all* our people so they can live up to their own God-given potential. That is how America will lead in the world.[1]

ENDNOTE

1 All points and statements are from various speeches Clinton delivered all over the world from 2011 to 2013 as secretary of state.

Jeannie James hangs laundry with her granddaughter outside of their home in Winslow, Arizona.
{JAN SONNENMAIR}

Failure to Adapt to Changing Families Leaves Women Economically Vulnerable

By Anna Greenberg, David Walker, Alex Lundry, and Alicia Downs

Americans recognize and applaud the growing role of women in our economy. Seventy-one percent of Americans—including an equal number of men and women—describe women's financial contribution to our national economy as essential; an insignificant 4 percent do not believe women play an essential role. Demographic trends prove Americans right in their assessment of women's economic contribution; women now make up nearly half of the employed population, and the majority of all people employed in management and professional occupations are women.[1] And a majority of mothers—especially single mothers—are working mothers. As women continue to outpace men in educational attainment and entry into the fastest-growing occupations, the economic power of women will continue to rise.

Many of these changes have been chronicled in past research by *The Shriver Report*. The research in *A Woman's Nation Changes Everything*, published in 2009, documented in detail the many changes in our economy and our society from the massive influx of women into the American workforce over the past few decades. The country—men and women alike—accepted and even celebrated the rising financial role of women. Domestically, both men and women embraced the growing trend of men taking on household and child care duties, even if the reality of men's contribution to household labor often fell short of the ideal. In that report, we declared, "the battle of the sexes is over."

This report addresses the essential role women play in our economy, but also explores a different kind of change—one the country does not always celebrate but, rather, recognizes the need to respond to: the evolution of the American family and the consequent change in demands on American women. This report makes plain that the failure of government and business to adapt to these changes creates significant and unnecessary financial burdens for many women and diminishes the overall contribution women can make to our economy and our nation.

Currently, more than half of the children born to mothers under age 30 are born to single mothers. A significant proportion of these women are women on the brink, or women just getting by. Other women may have husbands or partners but do not have jobs that give them the flexibility to fulfill both financial and family priorities and do not have the family income to give them the choice of surrendering one income. Other women do not have the education or training to adjust to an evolving, information-age economy. For many of these women, the current economy just does not seem to have a place for people like them. Many believe that no matter how hard they work, they cannot get ahead, even if they make all the right choices.

And yet, paradoxically, their story is not one of victimhood. Despite their many challenges, most financially vulnerable women—blue-collar women, single mothers, low-income women, women of color—say they are optimistic about their economic future and confident in their own ability to make the changes they need to turn their lives around. In policy terms, they are not looking for handouts but for specific accommodations that allow them to fulfill their role as both primary caregiver and primary breadwinner. They see a disconnect between their own ability to move ahead, which is quite high, and the ability of the current economic structure to evolve with the changing family dynamics in this country, which is often frustratingly low in their eyes.

The country itself is willing to adapt. While the nation does not absolve single parents of primary responsibility for their families, a convincing majority of Americans believe women raising children on their own face tremendous challenges and government, employers, and communities should help them out financially. Nearly two-thirds of Americans believe the government should set a goal of helping society adapt to the reality of single-parent families.

Policies in both the public sector and the private sector that explicitly seek to accommodate modern families where women are the primary or significant breadwinner—paid sick leave, flexible hours, pay equity, job security for pregnant women, college assistance for single mothers—find overwhelming support in the country. What is most striking in this age of partisan gridlock is that Democrats and Republicans support these policies with near-equal enthusiasm.

A Woman's Nation Foundation, in partnership with the Center for American Progress and generously supported by the AARP, commissioned a large national survey to explore Americans' attitudes toward women and the economy, marriage, regrets in life that affect financial status, and policies aimed at generating more economic mobility for financially vulnerable women. The poll explored the attitudes of financially vulnerable women, including their job satisfaction, their personal ambition, and their attitudes toward divorce, but also measures of how these women live their lives—whether they have children, their marital status, the level of support they receive from their child's other parent, whether their parents were divorced, things in their lives that create stress, and their goals in life, as well as their regrets.

Working with Republican pollsters Alex Lundry and Alicia Downs of TargetPoint Consulting, the Democratic polling firm Greenberg Quinlan Rosner Research interviewed 3,500 adults across the country to help write a statistical narrative of the women who rarely lead network news stories or dominate celebrity gossip in social network surveys but are an essential part of our nation's fabric and economy.

Polling methodology

Greenberg Quinlan Rosner Research and TargetPoint Consulting, in collaboration with the Center for American Progress and *The Shriver Report*, contacted 3,500 adults by landline and mobile telephone from August 21 to September 11, 2013. Telephone numbers were chosen randomly and in accordance with random-digit-dialing, or RDD, methodology. The survey included oversamples of 250 African American (574 in the total sample) and 250 Hispanic adults (501 in the total sample) to allow for more detailed subgroup analysis. The sample was adjusted to census proportions of sex, race or ethnicity, age, and national region.

The margin of sampling error for adults is plus-or-minus 1.7 points. For smaller subgroups, the margin of error may be higher. Survey results may also be affected by factors such as question wording and the order in which questions were asked. The interviews were conducted in English and Spanish.

A PRAGMATIC PERSPECTIVE ON SINGLE MOTHERS

As stated earlier, more than half of the children born to mothers under the age of 30 are born to single mothers. Dating back to the Moynihan Report in 1965,[2] a great deal of social science research exploring the rise of single-parent households focused on the bad outcomes disproportionately affecting these families. The high number of single mothers among women on the brink in this research further attests to the high financial costs of raising children in a single-parent household. (See Ann O'Leary's chapter, "Marriage, Motherhood, and Men.")

But Americans bring a practical perspective to this issue. Nearly 60 percent of Americans agree that "women raising children on their own face tremendous challenges and government, employers and communities should help them out financially." This more tolerant attitude grows sharply among younger people (77 percent agree). At the same time, a slim majority believe single parents should be held "completely responsible" for the children they bring into this world. All told, 53 percent agree with the statement, "If women have children without being married, they need to take complete financial responsibility for their children." Interestingly, women (56 percent) are somewhat more likely to agree than men (51 percent).

Moreover, the public greatly prefers a government policy of "helping society adapt to the reality of single-parent families" (64 percent) over a goal of "reducing the number of children born to single parents and encouraging two-parent households" (just 51 percent). Among economically vulnerable women—including, not surprisingly, single mothers—this number grows even higher. While not suspending judgment, at least not entirely, the public wants to accommodate the reality of the new American family.

This research did not ask the respondents to assess the morality of single parenthood; rather, it asked respondents to address how to best respond to the reality of the new American family. And their approach is pragmatic. While they do not absolve single mothers of the primary responsibility for their children, they also task the broader society with the obligation of doing what it can to help these mothers and their children succeed.

FIGURE 1

Pragmatic perspective on single mothers

Currently, over half the children who are born to mothers under the age of 30 are born to single mothers. With this in mind, please tell me if you agree or disagree with the following statements.

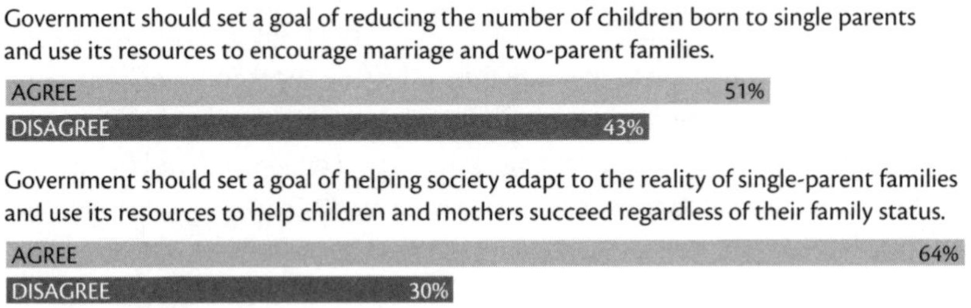

Government should set a goal of reducing the number of children born to single parents and use its resources to encourage marriage and two-parent families.

AGREE	51%
DISAGREE	43%

Government should set a goal of helping society adapt to the reality of single-parent families and use its resources to help children and mothers succeed regardless of their family status.

AGREE	64%
DISAGREE	30%

OUR ECONOMY DOES NOT WORK
FOR ECONOMICALLY VULNERABLE WOMEN

In no small measure because policymakers and businesses have failed to adapt to changes in the American family, the current economy simply does not work for many women in our country. Single-parent households rely on one income. Even for married families, the debate between "stay-at-home moms" and "working moms" is irrelevant, as they do not have the financial flexibility to choose between one or two incomes. But women in these families often do not have flexible work schedules and lack the appropriate education or training to find more accommodating jobs.

In the survey, many of these financially vulnerable women believe—unlike other Americans—that the harder they work, the farther they fall behind. They suffer disproportionate levels of stress, mostly related to bills and expenses. It is not that these women—and economically vulnerable men—do not want to work or succeed. It is that the current economic structure does not afford them the opportunity.

Slightly more than one in four Americans (28 percent) believe the statement "the harder I work, the more I fall behind" accurately describes them. Women are significantly more likely to agree than men (33 percent and 24 percent, respectively), but this sentiment jumps to 48 percent among single mothers and 54 percent among lower-income women.

TABLE 1

Our economy does not work for economically vulnerable women

Please tell me if this statement describes you very well, describes you somewhat well, does not describe you well or does not describe you at all.

(Total well)	The harder I work, the more I fall behind	Even if I made all the right choices in life, I still could not get ahead because the economy doesn't work for people like me
Total	28	42
Noncollege women	36	49
Low-income women	54	60
Women 50–64	34	49
Separated/divorced/widowed women	37	49
Single mothers	48	37
Unemployed men	31	44
Unemployed women	43	56

FIGURE 2

Higher levels of stress

On a scale of 0 to 10, please rate the overall level of stress you are feeling these days. A 10 would mean you feel a lot of stress. A zero would mean you do not feel much stress overall. 5 would be an in-between response. You may choose any number between 0 and 10.

MEN	20%
WOMEN	27%
LOW-INCOME WOMEN	36%
SINGLE MOTHERS	36%

Forty-two percent of Americans agree that the statement "Even if I made all the right choices in life, I could still not get ahead because the economy does not work for people like me" describes them well. Women are more likely to agree than men, but the numbers really take off among lower-income and other financially vulnerable women. The percentages in Figure 2 depict the portion of men/women/low-income women/single mothers who report that they are facing "extreme stress" defined as 8 or higher.

Not surprisingly, economically vulnerable people struggle with more stress than other Americans. In this survey, we asked respondents to rate their levels of stress on a 10-point scale. Overall, 46 percent of Americans rate their level of stress a

Women living on the brink of financial instability suffer from disproportionate levels of stress. {MELISSA FARLOW}

6 or higher. Women overall face more extreme stress (8 or higher) than men. Single moms, particularly those with no partner, are among the most stressed (10), as are lower-income women.

Thirty-six percent of lower-income women suffer extreme stress (8 or higher), compared to 23 percent of the population as a whole and 27 percent of all women.

Economically vulnerable women also differ somewhat in the kinds of stress they face or at least in the scale. The leading stress point for all Americans is bills and expenses (36 percent), which climbs to 44 percent among women earning less than $60,000. The second-leading stressor nationally is "your job," at 24 percent overall. Fourteen percent peg balancing caretaking and career responsibilities as a key source of stress, and 11 percent identify caring for kids.

Balancing career and family and caring for kids loom particularly large, not surprisingly, for single mothers. Forty percent of single moms identify either "balancing caretaking and career responsibilities" (18 percent) or caring for kids (22 percent) as a leading cause of stress in their lives.

TABLE 2
Stressed-out single moms

Causes of stress	Total	Women	Low-income women	Single mothers
Bills and expenses	36	37	44	45
Your job	24	22	14	16
Balancing caretaking and career responsibilities	14	13	11	18
Your family's health	14	16	19	9
Your health	13	14	18	9
Caring for your kids	11	13	16	22
Your relationship with your partner	8	6	5	11
Being alone	4	5	8	4

While notable in scale and scope, few of the challenges facing these women are surprising. What is surprising is that despite these many obstacles, these women are no less optimistic, determined, and satisfied with their lives than other segments of the population. This may seem like a contradiction, but it is not. Although most Americans are optimistic about their own future and generally happy when asked about it in a public opinion survey, these results reveal something deeper about the specific population of vulnerable women.

When we ask these women about things they can control, specifically their own ability to work hard and change their lives, they react with optimism and resilience. However, when we ask about things they cannot control, such as the current economic structure in the country, this optimism fades substantially. This is how the same woman on a survey can state she believes she has what it takes to improve herself (self-directed) while at the same time insist that the economy does not work for people like her (outwardly directed).

ECONOMICALLY VULNERABLE WOMEN REMAIN RESILIENT AND OPTIMISTIC

Americans believe in themselves. Even with the backdrop of the Great Recession and a glacial recovery, they remain generally happy and satisfied with their lives. Americans believe in their own ability to work hard, succeed, and make the changes necessary to improve their lives. This powerful American optimism and resilience runs just as strongly among economically vulnerable women as anyone else. Financial challenges aside, they are generally happy and satisfied with their lives. More important, they also believe they can change their lives. In their resilience, they build informal networks of people to help sustain them, even while formal networks of businesses and governments often fail them.

Nationally, nearly two-thirds (62 percent) of Americans believe their financial situation will get better over the next five years; 23 percent believe it will get much better. Women (59 percent believe it will get better) are only marginally less optimistic than men (65 percent); these numbers hold for noncollege women (58 percent) and lower-income women (62 percent) and increase to 79 percent among single mothers. Women of color are also disproportionately optimistic about the next five years (83 percent among African American women; 74 percent among Hispanic women).

TABLE 3

Personal financial optimism

*Regardless of your financial situation right now, do you believe your financial situation
will get better or get worse over the next five years?*

	Total better	Total worse
Total	62	25
Women	59	25
Single mothers	79	12
White women	52	30
Black women	83	9
Hispanic women	74	12

Nine in 10 Americans describe themselves as "generally happy and satisfied
with their lives." Although the number is somewhat lower, an overwhelming
majority (87 percent) of lower-income women as well as single moms (79 percent)
also describe themselves as happy and satisfied with their lives. Why is it that
financially struggling women on the one hand believe that the harder they work,
the more they fall behind and that the economy does not work for them and, on
the other hand, describe themselves as generally happy and satisfied? They are
more confident in *their own* abilities to change their financial situation compared
to their confidence in what the government or employers can *do for them.*

Even more striking, 87 percent of Americans agree with the statement, "I believe
I have the ability to make significant changes in my life to make my life better."
An inspiring 87 percent of single moms believe the same thing, as do 95 percent of
African American women and 92 percent of Hispanic women. Millennial women
are nearly unanimous in the belief of their own ability to change their lives for the
better (98 percent).

Some of these women believe they have economic resources that other women do
not see in their lives. Economically vulnerable women are significantly more likely
to believe the statement "If I have financial difficulties, I reach out to my friends
and family members" than respondents overall (just 43 percent overall, 46 percent
among noncollege women, 66 percent among lower-income women, 54 percent
among single moms). This is particularly true in communities of color (54 percent
among African American women, 56 percent among Hispanic women). In contrast,
only 36 percent of upper-income women (earning more than $100,000 a year)
believe they can reach out to family and friends if they have financial difficulties.

Kristy Richardson and her husband, Shawn, play with their sons in Pittsburgh, Pennsylvania. {MELISSA FARLOW}

TABLE 4

Personal financial resilience

Now I am going to read you a series of statements. For each one I read, please tell me if this statement describes you very well, describes you somewhat well, does not describe you well or does not describe you at all.

(Total well)	If I have financial difficulties, I reach out to my friends and family members
Total	43
Noncollege women	46
Upper-income women	36
Low-income women	66
African American women	54
Hispanic women	56

These women are survivors. When in trouble financially, they reach out to their informal networks (friends and family), because sometimes more formal networks (business and government) fail them. Despite the huge challenges outlined in this chapter and in the research in this report, these women believe in themselves, their work ethic, and their ability to change—just like other Americans. But they do not necessarily believe—or recognize—the ability of the current economic structure to accommodate people like them. Financially vulnerable women see a divide between their own ambition and ability and the current economic reality they face.

TABLE 5

Financially vulnerable women believe in themselves

Financially vulnerable women believe in themselves . . .
I believe I have the ability to make significant changes in my life to make my life better.

Total (all respondents)	87
Women	87
Low-income women	83
Blue-collar women	86
Nonwhite women	92
Single mothers	87

. . . but do not believe the economy works for people like them
Even if I made all the right choices in life, I still could not get ahead because the economy
doesn't work for people like me.

Total (all respondents)	42
Women	44
Low-income women	60
Blue-collar women	49
Nonwhite women	45

LOOKING BACK: THE REGRETS OF ECONOMICALLY VULNERABLE WOMEN

Few economically vulnerable women are doing what they thought they would do when they were growing up. This is an outcome they share with all Americans (only 33 percent of whom are doing what they thought they would do). Where they part with the rest of the country—and from economically vulnerable men—is their perspective on having children.

The financial burdens of children on one's ambition are disproportionately borne by women. Overall, 15 percent of women identify having children too early as the reason they did not fulfill the ambitions of their youth, compared to only 1 percent of men. Sixteen percent of noncollege women identify having children too early as the reason they did not fulfill the ambitions of their youth, also compared to 1 percent of noncollege men. Not surprisingly, single mothers are the most likely (24 percent) on an open-ended question to identify children as the reason for not doing what they thought they would be doing when they were growing up. The economic consequences of early or unintended pregnancy are profoundly different for men and women.

However, it is critical to recognize that one immediate consequence of an unplanned pregnancy for many economically vulnerable women is a delay—often a lifetime "delay"—in educational attainment. Indeed, a significant number of financially vulnerable women regret having children or at least the timing of the children. Indeed, given the difficulty of sharing such a confession in a phone survey, the number here is probably understated. But the larger regret for financially vulnerable women is, indeed more so than anything else, leaving school early, which distinguishes these women from the rest of the country.

TABLE 6

Variety of regrets

*Thinking specifically in terms of your own life up to this point, please tell me
if you could do it all over again, whether you would do the following*

YES	Total	Noncollege women	Low-income women	Single mothers	Nonwhite women
Made better financial choices	65	68	79	70	77
Put a higher priority on your education and career	58	67	77	68	69
Avoided debt	58	55	56	57	55
Taken better care of your health	54	55	61	52	60
Stayed in school longer	54	65	70	70	65
Gotten out of a bad relationship sooner	41	43	55	76	49
Entered a different profession	40	44	48	51	50
Stayed in your marriage	36	29	19	15	22
Delayed getting married	27	39	52	63	41
Delayed having kids or had fewer kids	21	28	39	47	37
Had children	18	25	30	-	20

Where men and women part ways, particularly among financially vulnerable populations, is on the issue of marriage and divorce.

Interestingly, most divorced women do not regret their decision to end their marriages. Only 28 percent of divorced women wish that they had stayed married, compared to 47 percent of divorced men. Only 19 percent of lower-income women who have been divorced wish they had stayed in their marriage, compared to 53 percent of divorced lower-income men. Lower-income women are also significantly more likely to regret not delaying marriage (52 percent) than lower-income men (33 percent). Seventy-six percent of single mothers wish they had gotten out of bad relationships sooner.

> The challenge seems less about reorienting family life to fit the needs of careers and business and more about changing business models and rules, as well as domestic arrangements, to allow for an evolving family structure.

These women look back on their lives with the clarity of hindsight. Notably, issues of family, pregnancy, early marriage, and divorce certainly play a major role in their current financial vulnerability, specifically in damaging their education and ability to focus on a career. Still, Americans do not necessarily accept this outcome as an inevitable, lifetime consequence of "bad" choices. Americans believe a woman who has a child in her early 20s can still focus on her education and career with a little help—or at least they support policy changes with that explicit goal. As we think through potential public- and private-sector policies that can help economically vulnerable women, the challenge seems less about reorienting family life to fit the needs of careers and business and more about changing business models and rules, as well as domestic arrangements, to allow for an evolving family structure.

WHAT BUSINESSES AND GOVERNMENT CAN DO TO HELP ECONOMICALLY VULNERABLE WOMEN

Both the public sector and the private sector can play an important role in improving the lives of economically vulnerable women—and men—in this country. These are people who have the same drive and ambition as other Americans, the same confidence and belief in their ability to work hard and ultimately succeed.

While a minority of economically vulnerable women ascribes their financial struggles to overt discrimination in the workplace, many business practices discriminate against women in their impact. Overall, 69 percent of the public believe women "have a fair shot at the workplace and have the same opportunities to succeed as men" (74 percent among men, 63 percent among women). Views do not change among noncollege women (65 percent) or women of color (67 percent).

These women, however, argue for changes in policy that remediate de facto discrimination and, more specifically, help them accommodate their jobs with the responsibilities of family life that still disproportionately fall on women. Many need such accommodations to move up the economic ladder, such as a bump in pay or pay equity, additional training, laws protecting the rights of workers who get pregnant, and access to child care. As much as anything, the policy agenda of economically marginalized women emphasizes the ways business and government can accommodate diverse family obligations.

Respondents with full-time or part-time jobs were asked to describe a number of things businesses could do to improve their job as very useful, somewhat useful, not very useful, or not at all useful. Not surprisingly, increasing pay and benefits ranks as the leading response overall. But among lower-income and noncollege women, just as many identify paid sick leave as very useful in their lives. Ninety-six percent of single moms identify paid sick leave as very useful to their lives, compared to 82 percent of all women. These women are also disproportionately interested in on-site child care and flexible work hours.

TABLE 7
What businesses can do
Thinking specifically about your life, after each one I read, please tell if this would be very useful to you, somewhat useful to you, not very useful to you, or not at all useful to you.

(VERY USEFUL)	Total	Total women	Noncollege women	Low-income women	Single mothers
Increase pay and benefits	82	83	82	86	95
Provide up to 10 days a year of paid time off if you are sick or have to take care of a family member who is sick	78	82	84	87	96
Provide workers with paid time off after the birth of a child, to care for a seriously ill family member, or to recover from their own serious illness.	74	78	77	77	95
Provide on-the-job training or financial assistance for additional education outside the job to prepare you for advancement	65	65	65	70	80
Provide clear steps so you know what it takes to advance to higher levels in your organization from where you are now	61	61	59	57	78
Provide opportunities to work from home and more flexible work hours	48	60	58	59	71
Provide on-site child care	38	46	46	44	72

Government policy needs to change as well. As with changes in the business world, economically vulnerable women focus largely on accommodations for families. Pay equity is the leading item, critical for single-mother households. Seventy-two percent of lower-income women strongly favor rights protecting workers who get pregnant. Lower-income women are 18 percentage points more likely to *strongly* favor paid leave for workers who provide care for elderly parents or disabled children and 28 points more likely to strongly favor expanding college opportunities for single moms. Understandably, single moms are much more likely (27 points) to strongly favor expanding access to high-quality, affordable child care.

TABLE 8

What policymakers can do (part 1)

Now I am going to read you some steps the government could take to improve economic security for people in this country. For each one I read, please tell me if you strongly favor this proposal, somewhat favor this proposal, somewhat oppose this proposal, or strongly oppose this proposal.

(STRONGLY FAVOR)	Total	Low-income women	Single mothers
Ensure that women get equal pay for equal work in order to raise wages for working women and families	73	85	91
Protect pregnant women and new mothers so they can't get fired or be demoted when they become pregnant or take maternity leave	67	72	76
Increase the minimum wage to establish a mandatory, national living wage of $10 an hour, or $42,000 per year for a dual-income family of four, and automatically increase the minimum wage to rise with inflation	52	55	52
Establish paid leave for workers who provide care for elderly parents or disabled children who are unable to perform everyday tasks	52	70	76
Expand access to high-quality, affordable child care for working families	50	54	77
Increase the number of low-income single mothers who go to college by providing them with financial assistance and child care	45	73	73
Create a universal 401(k) so that workers who do not have a retirement savings account through their job will have access to an automatic workplace savings account	43	45	70
Eliminate the marriage penalty in our tax system, in which married dual-income couples tend to pay higher tax rates than they would if they had remained single	42	38	22
Consolidate the federal government's social welfare programs—such as welfare, food stamps, rental payment assistance, job training, disability assistance—into a single debit-card account for needy individuals, streamlining the application process and saving money by eliminating bureaucracy	34	29	43

Though still popular, the one policy explicitly geared toward married families notably falls toward the bottom of the list: 42 percent strongly favor (63 percent total favor) eliminating the marriage penalty in our tax system.

Partisan gridlock now grips Washington, as every budget deadline or debt ceiling bill becomes an occasion for government showdown and shutdown. But when it comes to policy ideas for helping economically vulnerable women, the public demonstrates impressive bipartisan consensus. Ninety-five percent of Democrats support pay equity, as do 88 percent of Republicans. Ninety percent of Democrats support protecting the rights of pregnant workers, as do 86 percent of Republicans.

FIGURE 3
What policymakers can do (part 2)

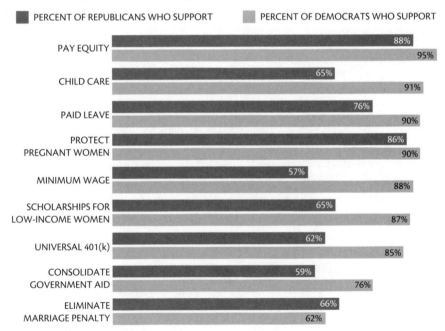

■ PERCENT OF REPUBLICANS WHO SUPPORT	■ PERCENT OF DEMOCRATS WHO SUPPORT

PAY EQUITY — 88% / 95%
CHILD CARE — 65% / 91%
PAID LEAVE — 76% / 90%
PROTECT PREGNANT WOMEN — 86% / 90%
MINIMUM WAGE — 57% / 88%
SCHOLARSHIPS FOR LOW-INCOME WOMEN — 65% / 87%
UNIVERSAL 401(k) — 62% / 85%
CONSOLIDATE GOVERNMENT AID — 59% / 76%
ELIMINATE MARRIAGE PENALTY — 66% / 62%

Julie Kaas, a single mother and preschool teacher, rides her motorcycle down the road to her home in Washington. {BARBARA KINNEY}

CONCLUSION

The country is changing.

We have moved from a dominant model of single-income, two-parent households to dual-income, two-parent households to an increasing number of single-parent, single-income households. These changes have profoundly impacted the broader American economy but also present significant financial challenges for women. Economically vulnerable women themselves recognize and often regret some of the decisions they made that have inhibited their financial potential. Even as women as a whole have captured a growing role in the American economy, this economy has left too many women behind. In the eyes of these women, this outcome is less about overt gender discrimination in the workplace than about the failure to accommodate changing family structures.

Importantly, the country itself recognizes this challenge. While the country does not absolve women—or men, for that matter—of the primary responsibility for raising their own children, a convincing majority of Americans believe government and society have a role to play in helping these new families. Even more convincing, majorities of Democrats and Republicans support a suite of policy changes in both the private sector and the public sector to accommodate these families and give these women the space they need to improve their economic standing.

The changing trends in the American family will continue. The nation has already made the choice to adapt to these changes, as witnessed by the survey results above and the broad embrace of policies to help financially vulnerable women. The question is whether policymakers in the public sector and the private sector will make the same choice. Doing so will ensure that economically vulnerable women have a fair shot to reach their full potential, and in the process strengthen our economy and our country.

ENDNOTES

1   U.S. Bureau of Labor Statistics, *Women in the Labor Force: A Databook* (U.S. Department of Labor, 2013), available at http://www.bls.gov/cps/wlf-databook-2012.pdf.

2   Office of Policy Planning and Research, *The Negro Family: The Case for National Action* (U.S. Department of Labor, 1965).

Acknowledgments

The Shriver Report *exists thanks to the generosity of our Lead Partners: The Ford Foundation, AARP, and Wells Fargo; our Premier Partners: JPMorgan Chase, Marvell Technology Group, California Endowment, Coca-Cola Company; and the generous support of Dawn Arnall, Shawn Byers, Marcy Carsey, Cisco, John and Ann Doerr, Eileen and John Donahoe, Kresge Foundation, Lean-In Foundation, Jillian Manus, Ronald Perelman, SAP, Sherwood Foundation, Verizon, and our many contributors. Without their belief in us,* The Shriver Report *would not be possible.*

FROM MARIA SHRIVER

There is an extraordinary team behind *The Shriver Report* led by the incomparable Karen Skelton. The truth is, there wouldn't even be a *Shriver Report* without her fearlessness, her intelligence, her perseverance, her dedication, her passion, and her leadership. She has been the heart and soul of this project since its inception and she has kept everyone on it motivated, on track, and focused. My name is on the cover but her hand is on every page. We have worked side by side for close to a decade. I respect her, I trust her, and I'm grateful to her for her leadership and her loyal friendship.

As we've worked together on all three *Shriver* reports, I have come to admire and respect Olivia Morgan's immense talents and fierce commitment. She has singlehandedly raised the quality of our report as our managing editor, working with multiple authors on diverse subjects—questioning, digging, revising, reshaping—and all with grace as she looks forward, never behind. She leads us with her passionate commitment to women on the brink, savvy policy analysis, love of original research. Above all that, she's got brick-solid integrity, and she truly represents the best of our woman's nation.

If this were a sports team, Becky Beland would be its most valuable player. She nails every single assignment she's given, from organizing high-profile and hard-to-reach essayists, to writing beautiful prose, to executing a sophisticated, multidimensional, modern national political outreach plan. I have depended on her more than she knows.

This report wouldn't be what it is without Roberta Hollander, my mentor in work and in life, who worked her editorial magic for months on every essay in this report. She has an ear for the real story, and she's brought to the report stories of women and men you cannot find anywhere else in the world. She is a brilliant writer, reporter, and editor, and I rely on her honesty and commitment to maintain our standard of excellence. If I said anything more about her, she would be mad at me, but she is indispensable.

Matthew DiGirolamo has transformed the way we communicate about *The Shriver Report.* He built a team of national professional media experts from scratch, and together they built a modern communications architecture that spanned all media channels and plat-forms. He is the brave (and maybe lucky!) man working with a strong team of women, including media strategists Marissa Moss and Taylor Royle, social media strategist Alli Maloney, and digital strategist Cara Lemieux, the managing editor of our extraordinary new website, ShriverReport.org.

Without Erin Stein, we would not have been funded, pure and simple. Erin's sterling repu-tation and strong belief in the project translated into hundreds of relationships that have made us smarter and more able to expand our reach and impact. As the executive director of A Woman's Nation, she is always thinking of new ways to bring this project to life. We have been friends for two decades. We have worked together for a decade. I trust her com-pletely and I know she is always one step ahead of me and so many others. I am grateful for her steady hand, clear mind, and unwavering friendship.

Dixie Noonan, a young mother and wise attorney, led our efforts to deliver our Shriver Report Classroom Initiative and to create a first-ever Shriver Corps dedicated to connect-ing working families more efficiently with government resources. I'll always be grateful for her multitasking skills and in awe of how she manages her family, work, and volunteer service. I would also like to thank O'Melveny & Myers LLP for lending Dixie to us and for taking *The Shriver Report* on as a pro bono project.

One of the project's greatest assets is the Center for American Progress. I am honored to partner again with CAP and its leader Neera Tanden, and John Podesta before her. CAP's contributions were many, beginning with Neera's commitment and life story, which inspires all aspects of our work. Daniella Gibbs Léger stepped into the role of CAP's lead with patience, strength, confidence, and style. Fierce when she needed to be, bending when that worked better, Daniella has been a masterful manager of a professional staff of art-ists, designers, academics, statisticians, editors, and lawyers. She is largely and almost singlehandedly responsible for our successful cross-country partnership. Our entire team has relied with profound gratitude on Lauren Vicary's experience, professionalism, and commitment—at all hours of the day and night—to producing the best possible work. She is an excellent artist with a red pencil. Melissa Boteach, Katie Wright, John Halpin, and

Debbie Fine all provided invaluable and exceptional contributions from the CAP team, for which I will always be grateful. And to the rest of the CAP teams—the economic and education policy shops, art, editorial, and legal—thank you for all your hard work, even through a government shutdown!

Special thanks to the Dewey Square Group, my go-to consults over the years. They have a team of savvy public affairs gurus, writers, and communications experts who seamlessly extended our capacity across every aspect of the project. I have relied greatly on the dedicated work of Karen Breslau, Tamara Torlakson, Angela Pontes, and the visionary Margaret Lyons.

When we got the idea for this *Shriver Report*, I immediately thought it could make a great documentary. I went to my friend Sheila Nevins at HBO, she agreed, and we are joining forces to executive produce a film that will be an important part of *The Shriver Report*. From the beginning, HBO has been a partner in bringing to life the story we tell in print. Many of the women we quote here are from Chattanooga, Tennessee, and send their children to the Chambliss Center, a 24-hours-a-day child care center. The Chambliss Center serves as a backdrop for the upcoming HBO documentary film by Emmy® Award-winning filmmakers Shari Cookson and Nick Doob. The documentary provides a deeply personal and moving journey through the daily life of Katrina Gilbert, a single mom and certified nursing assistant juggling work, child care, financial challenges, and family responsibilities. Thank you to Nancy Abraham and Sascha Weiss as well for your patience and support. The film is scheduled to debut on HBO in 2014.

The Shriver Report is an initiative of A Woman's Nation, a nonprofit we created to help women and men find a new way forward in our changing world. Special gratitude goes to the board: Erin Stein, Sandy Gleysteen, Donna Lucas, Nancy McFadden, Jan Miller, Nadine Schiff, Julia Paige, Sheryl Lowe, Shannon Marven, Holly Martinez, Babette Campbell; and to our professional staff and lawyers Sandra Lady, Steven Guise, Lawrence Rudolph, Gary Hecker, Maria Giammanco, and Scott Galer.

From the beginning, my friends and former colleagues have generously provided advice, criticism when needed, and steady support, including Karen Baker, Carl Bendix, Tina Frank, John Bridgeland, Matt James, Maya Harris, Yvonne Hunt and her team at Legacy Venture, Nancy LeaMond, Leslie Miller, Laura Nichols, Barbara O'Connor, Amy Rosenberg, Charlotte and George Shultz, and all of my new friends in Silicon Valley who came early on to discuss our report in a meaningful, inspiring evening co-hosted by Jillian Manus and Carl and Leslee Guardino at the home of Sheryl Sandberg and David Goldberg.

This report would not have come to life without the amazing award-winning photographers who traveled across the country to capture beautiful images of families living on the brink. A special thanks to my friend, the phenomenal Barbara Kinney, who brought together this unprecedented female photojournalism team: Melissa Farlow, Melissa Lyttle, Barbara Ries, Callie Shell, Jan Sonnenmair, and Ami Vitale.

Taking the pictures was one thing, and finding the subjects was another challenge altogether. I want to thank everyone who helped along the way to produce our groundbreaking photographs, including hardworking co-workers and classmates of La Cocina and Washington Women's Employment and Education; Jennet Robinson Alterman and Gayle Goldin of the Women's Fund of Rhode Island; Stephenie Lazarus of LIFT Chicago; Naomi Thornton and Jane Guest of Women's Opportunity and Resource Development, Inc.; Janie Allen of Washington Women's Employment and Education; Michele Q. Margittai of Veterans Leadership Program of Western Pennsylvania, Inc.; Geetika Agrawal and Caleb Zigas of La Cocina; Thomas Cody of Leupp, Arizona; and Sean Maloney of Clermont, Florida.

I would also like to thank Phil Acord and Katie Harbison and the entire team at the Chambliss Center for Children in Chattanooga, Tennessee, for their generous assistance in organizing a facility tour and roundtable discussion with working moms and staff that strengthened our thinking and commitment on this project.

We thank our contributing institutional partners for the academic rigor and resources they brought to the project: Ascend at the Aspen Institute; Families and Work Institute; Institute for Women's Policy Research; Next Generation; Michelle R. Clayman Institute for Gender Research at Stanford University; Graduate School of Management and Center for Poverty Research at the University of California at Davis; and the Center on Education and the Workforce at Georgetown University.

We have been emboldened and humbled by the diverse men and women who agreed to advise us along the way. Their reputations and influence expand our impact, reach, and credibility. Thank you to our National Advisory Committee:

Madeleine Albright	Sister Joan Chittister	Bill Frist
Melody Barnes	Blair Christie	Andrea Gibson
John Bouman	Kelly Coffey	Austan Goolsbee
Maria Cardona	Weili Dai	Maya L. Harris
Dr. Maria Carrillo	Geena Davis	Heidi Hartmann
Majora Carter	Barbara Ehrenreich	Ron Haskins
Jean Chatzky	Eve Ensler	Mary Kay Henry

Jessica Herrin	Monica C. Lozano	Sheryl Sandberg
Barbie Izquierdo	Frank Luntz	Anne-Marie Slaughter
Patricia Kempthorne	Jillian Manus	Olympia J. Snowe
Maj. Gen. (Ret.) Mary J. Kight	Todd McCracken	Hilda Solis
	Brian McLaren	Lisa Stevens
Billie Jean King	Pat Mitchell	Melanne Verveer
Wendy Kopp	Susan Molinari	Laysha Ward
Nancy LeaMond	Christiane Northrup	Kerry Washington
Tiffany Dena Loftin	Ai-jen Poo	Sheryl WuDunn
Eva Longoria	Tony Porter	Jacki Zehner

Finally, we are again grateful to our media partners NBC News and The Atlantic. They will bring this report to life in a brand-new way. In so doing, they will expand the realm of this report. They will amplify the voices in it and they will pass it on.

FROM EDITORS OLIVIA MORGAN AND KAREN SKELTON

Producing the *Shriver* reports is a labor of love and learning, an opportunity and a challenge. We are profoundly grateful to have been part of this effort to bring the truth of modern women's lives to the forefront of American discourse. We are fueled both by the extraordinary women we meet and work with along the way and the importance of the work itself, and we carry with us deep appreciation for the stories we hear as well as the responsibility for sharing them.

Our greatest inspiration comes from Maria Shriver. Maria has shaped every aspect of this project. She has rolled up her sleeves, hunkered down with the work, and committed her enormous brainpower to taming, trimming, and transforming our content into a manageable, understandable, meaningful project. She is simply masterful at communicating to a mass audience. She is a gifted convener of people, from the world's top celebrities and elected officials to the nation's most vulnerable workers and families. She demands innovation and creativity of her staff and leads by example. She generates literally hundreds of ideas, like ground balls hit from a prolific batter. The excellence of this project, and its impact on the nation, starts with Maria Shriver. We have been both honored and humbled to work with her.

The Center for American Progress has been generous to this report in every way. Neera Tanden embraced its vision from the beginning and allowed her personal story of growing up on the brink to be published for the first time. Daniella Gibbs Léger has led the effort with dedication, skill, humor, and friendship. Lauren Vicary dove in like the pro she is, with the focus, intelligence, clarity, organization, and grace that define an effective editor. She has been tireless in ensuring every sentence of this report says what it means to say. Partnering with CAP has allowed us to draw on a remarkable team of policy experts, including, in particular, Melissa Boteach, who showed us how to "do it all" with grace. We are enormously grateful as well to John Halpin, Debbie Fine, and the rest of the CAP team—especially Katie Wright, who has been an invaluable help and a delightful colleague, stepping into every breach without hesitation.

One of the joys of producing *The Shriver Report* is the great brains with which we interact. As editors, we are especially grateful for the tremendous authors in this report. All of them contributed more than their chapter content and surpassed the expectations of standard report contributors. Most excitingly, they were open- minded to new ways of presenting information, to developing new content, and to putting our ideas to work beyond the pages of *The Shriver Report*. Anne Mosle and Sarah Haight at the Aspen Institute trusted and grew our idea of developing a blueprint for Life Ed; Ellen Galinsky and her team of Eve Tahmincioglu, Terry Bond, and Ken Matos embraced our Thrive Index and incorporated it into their own work with employers; Nicole Smith and Tony Carnevale took up the idea of mapping education paths. Melissa Boteach and the encyclopedic-minded Shawn Fremstad were resources on every chapter in this report. Ann O'Leary and Heather Boushey continue to expertly guide *Shriver* reports, as we strive to meet the high bar they set as editors of the first report in 2009.

Our essayists breathe life into the portraits we paint through the chapters of *The Shriver Report*. Roberta Hollander works magic from her perch along the Pacific Ocean, where she extracts from an amazing array of writers "their story," bringing brilliant illumination and authentic voices into these reports with integrity and lyricism. Stephanie Coontz worked and reworked her contribution to best lift the report as a whole and guided us beyond her own text. Ann Stevens, Shirley Sagawa, and Marianne Cooper each took a creative leap with our ideas and turned them into cutting-edge contributions, and we know their willingness to do so will add to their impact.

Becky Beland has long been at the heart of the *Shriver* reports, having worked on all three, and in the process has become our backbone. We are forever indebted to her for her competence, patience, willingness to keep coming back, great sense of humor, and ability to keep her finger on the pulse of American style, Millennial culture, and social trends. And thanks to Angela Pontes who assisted Becky and the rest of us with such professionalism and steadiness for her years. Patricia Kempthorne is consistently generous with her time and boundless energy and inspires us with her commitment to supporting working families. Marissa Astor's cool head, wise ways, and unwavering professionalism kept us at our best. Alli Maloney's vision and empathy shine through the ambitious and masterfully managed photography project. Tamara Torlakson was our first staffer and has gracefully managed our advisory committee throughout. Karen Breslau was a lifesaver and a brilliant editor to boot. Dixie Noonan is an all-around powerhouse, whose intellect is matched only by her determination—and ability—to develop worthy ideas into living programs. Her cheerful-while-unyielding commitment ensures the report will have an impact beyond these pages. The crew at A Woman's Nation Foundation, especially Erin Mulcahy Stein and Matthew DiGirolamo (and the entirely inventive, fearless Cara Lemieux), are now lifelong family that keep us grounded, protected, laughing, and supported beyond reasonable explanation and expectation.

Countless colleagues have guided us along the way. For their input throughout the phases of developing this report, we thank Karen Anderson from the Hamilton Project; Michele Jolin from the Center for American Progress; Ron Haskins at the Brookings Institution; Bob Greenstein and his team at the Center on Budget and Policy Priorities; Dr. David Gray at the New America Foundation; Donna Cooper; Shelley Waters Boots; Jodie Levin-Epstein at the Center for Law and Social Policy; Debbie Weinstein at the Coalition on Human Needs; Mark Clapham; George Sheldon, Acting Assistant Secretary for the Administration for Children and Families under the U.S. Department of Health and Human Services; AnnMaura Connolly of City Year; Suzy George at Albright Stonebridge Group; Anmarie Widener of Georgetown University; Kirsten Lodal and Molly Day at LIFT; Heidi Hartmann and the Institute for Women's Policy Research; John Bridgeland of Civic Enterprises; Wendy Spencer and Mary Strasser at the Corporation for National and Community Service; Karen Baker at CaliforniaVolunteers; Walter Dellinger at O'Melveny & Myers LLP; Commissioners Chai Feldblum and Victoria Lipnic of the Equal Employment Opportunity Commission; Vin Weber, Adam Mendelsohn, and Alan Elias at Mercury Public Affairs; Betty Nordwind at the Harriett Buhai Center for Family Law; and Alix Burns of Bay Bridge Strategies.

Finally, we are grateful to our families. David Plouffe and Jeffrey Barbour have been sounding boards, supporters, and devil's advocates. They have been patient and attentive fathers, carrying more than their share of the parenting load when we needed to spend weekends and evenings hunched over laptops or cellphones. Karen thanks her husband for lending this project his experience as an exceptionally gifted public defender of many people living on the brink and her daughters for forgiving occasional absences from soccer and water polo and for promising to share our work on their social media. Olivia thanks her 8-year-old son for telling his 4-year-old sister, "When you grow up, why don't you be president of the United States? And I will be your chief of staff," so that she could do this work confident that a reimagined nation is entirely within our grasp.

FROM DANIELLA GIBBS LÉGER AND LAUREN VICARY AT THE CENTER FOR AMERICAN PROGRESS

We would like to thank Maria Shriver and CAP president Neera Tanden for their leadership and vision on this project. We are fortunate to have such strong women leading this effort and our institution. Thank you also to CAP founder John Podesta, who was Maria's CAP partner in the first book and who continues to help guide us, and to Tom Perriello and Carmel Martin for their leadership and support in our endeavor. Large thanks also go to Maria's entire team, led by Karen Skelton and Olivia Morgan, for their hard work and dedication to making this effort the best it can possibly be. Roberta Hollander, Dixie Noonan, Becky Beland, Matthew DiGirolamo, and the rest of their team have all been true professionals and a pleasure to work with.

We couldn't have done this project without the assistance of the great people at CAP. Tremendous thanks must go to Melissa Boteach, our policy lead, and the Poverty to Prosperity Program at CAP. In addition to being a chapter co-author, Melissa has been a steady and calm presence throughout this entire process, from the very first meetings on content, through her maternity leave, and right to the very end. Right along with her, Katie Wright supplied valuable insight and knowledge and a willingness to jump in on any task. Thanks as well to Donna Cooper, who started off this journey with us, and to Shawn Fremstad, without whom we would not have been able to get across the finish line.

Thanks go to our Economic Policy team contributors, led by chapter author Heather Boushey, as well as Sarah Jane Glynn, Jane Farrell, and Olenka Mitukiewicz. And we would have been lost without the input and guidance of our fantastic Education teams. Our thanks to David Bergeron, Melissa Lazarín, Katie Hamm, Rob Hanna, Tiffany Miller, and Elizabeth Baylor for all of their help.

Of course, the book didn't just manifest itself out of thin air. For that, major kudos must go to CAP's fantastic Art and Editorial teams. Thanks to Art Director Pete Morelewicz and Senior Designer Chester Hawkins for their hard work and long hours pulling this together, Lauren Allen for her ongoing creative help, and Jan Diehm and Alissa Scheller for providing valuable direction early on. The entire process was aided daily by David Hudson's editing skills and invaluable support, in conjunction with the rest of CAP's outstanding Editorial team, including Carl Chancellor, Meghan Miller, Jason Mogavero, Anne Paisley, and Eliot Sasaki. Many thanks go to John Halpin for his tireless work on our poll. We are grateful for his expertise and his time.

Thanks also to Debbie Fine, Norma Espinosa, and Joe Smolskis for their time and effort spent keeping the project on track and to Bridget Petruczok and Winnie Stachelberg for advising us on and helping set up countless outreach meetings. And a big shout out to all the others at CAP who helped and assisted along the way, including—but not limited to—Joy Moses, Andrea Purse, Marlene Cooper Vasilic, Madeline Meth, Lindsay Hamilton, Sarah Baron, Sasha Post, Jocelyn Frye, Buffy Wicks, Sally Steenland, and Emily Baxter.

A special thanks to Jamal Hagler, and Sophia Kerby before him, for the very important support you provided to each and every one of us.

Daniella would like to thank Lauren for a list of things too long to mention. Her leadership and vision, not to mention her keen editing skills and friendship, made this project what it is, and for that she is grateful.

Lauren would also like to thank Daniella, not only for her knowledge and management that deftly guided us all, but also for her friendship, grace, sense of humor, and ridiculous ability to keep track of every last piece of the puzzle.

Finally, this would not have been possible without the support of our families, particularly our spouses, Matthew Léger and Nathan Wakefield. You endured long nights and weekends alone, as well as occasionally stressed, short-tempered, and harried versions of us. Your love and encouragement gets us through, always.

FROM INDIVIDUAL CHAPTER AUTHORS

Heather Boushey

The author would like to thank Daniella Gibbs Léger, Melissa Boteach, and Lauren Vicary for their tremendous legwork in guiding, editing, and shaping this chapter. Many thanks go to Jane Farrell and Alexandra Mitukiewicz for their invaluable research assistance. The author would also like to thank Donna Cooper, Shawn Fremstad, Sarah Jane Glynn, Jamal Hagler, Heidi Hartmann, David Hudson, Judith Warner, Katie Wright, and the rest of the CAP team for their support and assistance. Finally, the author thanks Maria Shriver and her team, particularly Olivia Morgan and Karen Skelton, for their hard work and dedication to this report and to improving the lives of America's working women.

Ann O'Leary

The author would like to thank Maria Shriver for her continued work on behalf of women—particularly those who have limited time, resources, or power to act on their own behalf—and for always enthusiastically including her on the team. Thank you to

Olivia Morgan, Dixie Noonan, and Karen Skelton for their patience and good graces in shepherding this chapter to the end. The author also thanks Dixie, Rey Fuentes, Sarah Jo Szambelan, and Hong Van Pham for critical research support in development of this chapter. Finally, the author thanks Sarah Jane Glynn for reaching out to offer her research support and final edits as the author worked to balance her own work-family demands in order to complete this project.

Anthony Carnevale and Nicole Smith

The authors would like to express their gratitude to the individuals and organizations that have made this chapter possible. First, the authors thank the Bill and Melinda Gates Foundation, Lumina Foundation, and the Joyce Foundation for their support of our research over the past few years. In particular, they are grateful for the support of Daniel Greenstein and Elise Miller from the Gates Foundation; Jamie Merisotis and Holly Zanville from Lumina Foundation; and Matthew Muench and Whitney Smith from the Joyce Foundation. The authors are honored to be partners in their mission of promoting postsecondary access and completion for all Americans. The authors would also like to thank Artem Gulish for providing superb research assistance; our in-house designer, Ana Castanon; and the editor, Karen Breslau, for their patience and hard work in completing this report. Special thanks to our colleagues at the Center for American Progress, for their strategic guidance throughout the process. Specifically, we would like to thank David Bergeron, Katie Hamm, Elizabeth Baylor, Melissa Lazarin, Rob Hanna, Tiffany Miller, Katie Wright, Melissa Boteach, and Becky Beland.

Melissa Boteach and Shawn Fremstad

The authors would like to thank Katie Wright for her in-depth research assistance and keen analysis; The Kresge Foundation for their support; Heather Boushey, Sarah Glynn, and Jane Farrell for their guidance and expertise; the Shriver Team for their collaboration; the Center for American Progress's economic and education policy teams for their feedback; Daniella Gibbs Léger for her mentorship and management throughout the process; and Lauren Vicary for making all of us look better through great editing.

Ellen Galinsky

The authors would like to thank Eve Tahmincioglu for conducting insightful interviews for this chapter and for reviewing and revising the Sloan Award winner case studies; Kelly Sakai O'Neill for reviewing hundreds of Sloan Award winners and selecting the profiles for inclusion in this chapter; Ken Matos for his wise statistic advice; Lauren Vicary and Alissa Scheller for their keen editing and design work; and finally, Olivia Morgan for her leadership every step of the way in framing this chapter and helping us turn this vision into a chapter that we all hope will improve business solutions that benefit low-income women and their families.

Anne Mosle

The author would like to thank Celinda Lake, Jonathan Voss, and Alysia Snell of Lake Partners Research and Bob Carpenter of Chesapeake Beach Consulting for their research expertise and commitment to lifting the voices of low-income mothers and children; Sarah Haight and Andrea Camp for their invaluable assistance with research and editing and for their passion for building women's economic security; and Olivia Morgan for her feedback and guidance.

ESSAYISTS FOR *THE SHRIVER REPORT:*
A WOMAN'S NATION PUSHES BACK FROM THE BRINK

We would also like to thank the awe-inspiring essayists who contributed authentic stories from their personal experiences in life. Their essays distinguish this report from any other of its kind. We are grateful and humbled by their words both in print and online:

Leith Anderson	Barbara Ehrenreich	Eduardo Padrón
Sunshine Maria Anderson	Catherine Emmanuelle	Gloria Perez
Katie Bentley	Jennifer Garner	Wendy Pollack
Gordon Berlin	Kirsten Gillibrand	Ai-jen Poo
Angela Glover Blackwell	Carol Gilligan	Tony Porter
Sonya Borrero	Maya Harris	Betsy Price
John Bouman	Nadine Burke Harris	Selena Rezvani
Tory Burch	Ron Haskins	Shirley Sagawa
Sister Joan Chittister	LeBron James	Sheryl Sandberg
Hillary Rodham Clinton	Muhtar Kent	Howard Schultz
Stephanie Coontz	Almeta Keys	Kathleen Sebelius
Marianne Cooper	Beyoncé Knowles-Carter	Anne-Marie Slaughter
Cara Cortez	Eva Longoria	Jada Pinkett Smith
Arne Duncan	Ron Manderscheid	Lidia Soto-Harmon
Peter Edelman	Danielle Moodie-Mills	
Kathryn Edin	C.L. "Butch" Otter	

About the Contributors

Maria Shriver is a mother of four, a Peabody and Emmy Award-winning journalist and producer, a six-time *New York Times* best-selling author, and an NBC News Special Anchor covering the shifting roles, emerging power and evolving needs of women in modern life. Since 2009, Shriver has produced a groundbreaking series of *Shriver* reports that chronicle and explore seismic shifts in the American culture and society affecting women today. Shriver was California's first lady from 2003 to 2010 and, during that time, she spearheaded what became the nation's premier forum for women, The Women's Conference. Shriver's work is driven by her belief that all of us have the ability to be what she calls Architects of Change—people who see a problem in their own life or the community around them, then step out of their comfort zone and do what it takes to create the solution.

Neera Tanden is the President of the Center for American Progress. Tanden previously was senior advisor for health reform at the Department of Health and Human Services, advising Secretary Sebelius and working on President Obama's health reform team to develop and pass the Affordable Care Act. Prior to that, Tanden was the Director of Domestic Policy for the Obama-Biden campaign, managing all domestic policy proposals. She had served as Policy Director for the Hillary Clinton presidential campaign and Associate Director for Domestic Policy and Senior Advisor to the First Lady in the Clinton administration. She received her bachelor of science from UCLA and her law degree from Yale Law School.

Karen Skelton is the President of Skelton Strategies and has been CEO and Editor-in-Chief to all three *Shriver* reports. Skelton is an award-winning political strategist, lawyer, and author who has managed some of the most complex projects in the nation for presidents, vice presidents, governors, CEOs, foundations, moms, and families. After graduating with a master's degree from Harvard's Kennedy School of Government and a J.D. from U.C. Berkeley Law School, Skelton spent about a decade in Washington, D.C., working in the Clinton/Gore administration, and another decade managing a national public affairs firm, building it from scratch into a multimillion-dollar business. For seven years she was the Co-Executive Producer of Maria Shriver's The Women's Conference. Skelton serves on the Advisory Committee of the Public Policy Institute of California and on the boards of UC Berkeley's Institute of Governmental Studies and the Anthony M. Kennedy Federal Judicial Learning Center.

Olivia Morgan has been at the creative edge of government, public policy, and political communications throughout her career. This is the second *Shriver Report* on which she has served as Managing Editor. She is President of a politicultural communications firm, OM Strategies. Morgan previously launched and grew a bicoastal, multimillion-dollar communications and public affairs consulting practice, where she managed projects designed to shape public policy debates and aid the development of nonprofit organizations. Morgan served as the Director of Federal Relations for California under Gov. Gray Davis and has been a spokesperson for elected leaders at national and state levels. Morgan is honored to serve on the President's Committee on the Arts and the Humanities, on the board of the New England Center for Children, and on the National Leadership Council of Polaris Project's Vision 2020.

Daniella Gibbs Léger is the Senior Vice President for American Values & New Communities at the Center for American Progress, where her work focuses on the intersection of politics, race, demographic change, religion, and values. Prior to CAP, Gibbs Léger served as a Special Assistant to the President and Director of Message Events in the Obama administration. Gibbs Léger was previously the Vice President for Communications at CAP, where she specialized in domestic and economic policy, as well as overall communications strategy. She has also been the Deputy Director of Communications at the Democratic National Committee, where she began as Communications Director for the Women's Vote Center, and was a Regional Media Director during the 2004 presidential cycle. Prior to that, Gibbs Léger was with the National Newspaper Publishers Association and Sony Music. She holds a degree in government and a minor in sociology from the University of Virginia.

Lauren Vicary is the Vice President for Editorial at the Center for American Progress, where she manages the editorial, art, and video teams. A veteran political journalist and editor, Vicary has launched numerous properties for several news organizations, including Bloomberg's politics and elections websites, and Political Capital newsletter and blog. She was an editor at PoliticsDaily.com as well as the Political Editor at NBCNews.com, where she launched their politics and elections websites. Vicary began her tenure in Washington, D.C., at the Associated Press, where she spent nearly a decade in various roles including Reporter, Assignment Manager, Editor, and Lead Political Producer, and was instrumental in the launch of the AP's digital operations in Washington. Vicary was also a reporter for various affiliates and a program director at both PBS and Time-Life Video and Television. Vicary holds a B.A. in English from the University of Pennsylvania.

CHAPTER CONTRIBUTORS

James T. Bond is the Senior Research Advisor for Families and Work Institute, or FWI. He also served as the Institute's Vice President for Research from 1992 through 2010. He continues to be involved in the Institute's work-life research program, which includes the ongoing National Study of the Changing Workforce, or NSCW, and National Study of Employers, or NSE. The NSCW periodically surveys nationally representative samples of employees, while the NSE surveys representative samples of employers. Over the years, Bond has authored or co-authored many FWI publications, most of which are described on the Institute's website—www.familiesandwork.org.

Melissa Boteach is Director of Half in Ten and the Poverty to Prosperity Program at American Progress, where she coordinates "Half in Ten: The Campaign to Cut Poverty in Half in Ten Years." Boteach previously worked as a senior policy associate and the poverty campaign coordinator at the Jewish Council for Public Affairs, or JCPA, where she represented the JCPA to Congress, the administration, and in coalition on issues related to poverty, the federal budget, hunger, housing, and health care. As poverty campaign coordinator, Boteach also spearheaded JCPA's national antipoverty campaign. A Harry S. Truman and George J. Mitchell Scholar, Boteach earned a master's degree in public policy from The George Washington University with a concentration in budget and public finance, as well as a master's degree in equality studies from University College Dublin. She also graduated summa cum laude from the University of Maryland with degrees in government and Spanish.

Heather Boushey is a Senior Fellow and Executive Director of the Washington Center for Equitable Growth at the Center for American Progress. Her research focuses on U.S. employment, social policy, and family economic well-being. She co-edited *The Shriver Report: A Woman's Nation Changes Everything* in 2009 and was a lead author of "Bridging the Gaps," a 10-state study about how low- and moderate-income working families are left out of work-support programs. Her research has been published in academic journals and has been covered widely in the media, including regular appearances on *PBS NewsHour* and in *The New York Times*, where she was called one of the "most vibrant voices in the field." She also spearheaded a successful campaign to save the U.S. Census Bureau's Survey of Income and Program Participation from devastating budget cuts. Prior to coming to CAP, Boushey held economist positions with the Joint Economic Committee of the U.S. Congress, the Center for Economic and Policy Research, and the Economic Policy Institute, where she was a co-author of their flagship publication, *The State of Working America 2002/3*. She received her Ph.D. in economics from the New School for Social Research and her B.A. from Hampshire College.

Dr. Anthony Carnevale currently serves as Director of the Georgetown University Center on Education and the Workforce. Between 1996 and 2006, Carnevale served as Vice President for Public Leadership at the Educational Testing Service, or ETS. While at ETS, he was appointed by President George W. Bush to serve on the White House Commission on Technology and Adult Education. Before joining ETS, he was Director of Human Resource and Employment Studies at the Committee for Economic Development, or CED, the nation's oldest business-sponsored policy research organization. While at CED, he was appointed by President Bill Clinton to chair the National Commission on Employment Policy. Carnevale founded and was president of the Institute for Workplace Learning, or IWL, from 1983 to 1993. Prior to founding IWL, he served as Director of Political and Government Affairs for the American Federation of State, County, and Municipal Employees, or AFSCME, the largest union in the AFL-CIO. Before joining AFSCME, he was a senior staff member in both houses of Congress. Carnevale was appointed as the Majority Staff Director on the Public Financing Subcommittee of the House Committee on Government Operations and served on the Senate Committee on Budget. He also served as Senior Economist for the Senate Democratic Policy Committee.

Shawn Fremstad is an attorney and consultant in Washington, D.C. After graduating from the University of Minnesota Law School, he worked as a legal services attorney representing low-income people in legal matters involving family law, housing, benefits, and other civil issues. His work also included policy advocacy on behalf of the Minnesota Coalition on Battered Women and work as a member of the Minnesota Supreme Court Commission on Child Support Rules, where he represented low-income mothers who were owed child support. Fremstad worked for six years at the Center on Budget and Policy Priorities, where he was a Senior Policy Analyst and Deputy Director of the Welfare Reform and Income Support Division. Since 2007, he has been affiliated with the Center for Economic and Policy Research, where he directed the Bridging the Gaps Project and is currently a Senior Research Associate. In his role as a consultant and policy advisor, he has written reports and conducted research for a number of national, nonprofit organizations, including CAP, the National Academy of Social Insurance, Demos, the National Council of La Raza, and the National Skills Coalition.

Ellen Galinsky is President and Co-Founder of Families and Work Institute, or FWI. She helped establish the field of work and family life while she was at Bank Street College of Education, where she was on the faculty for 25 years. Her more than 45 books and reports include the best-selling *Mind in the Making: The Seven Essential Life Skills Every Child Needs*; *Ask The Children*; the now-classic *The Six Stages of Parenthood*; and the highly acclaimed *Workflex: The Essential Guide to Effective and Flexible Workplaces*. She has published more than 125 articles in academic journals, books, and magazines. At FWI, Galinsky co-directs the National Study of the Changing Workforce, the most comprehensive nationally representative study of the U.S. workforce. She also co-directs When Work Works, a project on workplace flexibility and effectiveness that was first funded by the Alfred P. Sloan Foundation. When Work Works launched the Sloan Awards and conducted the National Study of Employers, a nationally representative study that has tracked trends in employment benefits, policies, and practices since 1998. A leading authority on work-family issues, Galinsky was a presenter at the 2000 White House Conference on Teenagers and the 1997 White House Conference on Child Care. She was a planner and participant at the March 2010 White House Forum on Workplace Flexibility. She served as the elected President of the National Association for the Education of Young Children, the largest professional group of early childhood educators.

Anne Mosle is a Vice President at the Aspen Institute and Executive Director of Ascend. In these roles, she is an advisor to the senior leadership of the Aspen Institute and directs the vision and strategic goals of Ascend, a policy program of the Institute. Ascend serves as the national hub for breakthrough ideas and multisector collaborations that move children and their parents toward educational success and economic security. The Aspen Institute's mission is to foster leadership based on enduring values and to provide a non-partisan venue for dealing with critical issues. Prior to the Aspen Institute, Mosle served as a Vice President and officer of the W.K. Kellogg Foundation, where she developed the Family Economic Security and Civic Engagement portfolios and oversaw the launch of the Mission-Driven Investing program. Prior to the W.K. Kellogg Foundation, Mosle served as the President of the Washington Area Women's Foundation. Earlier in her career, Mosle was a member of the leadership team at the Center for Policy Alternatives. She serves on the Advisory Committee of the Oxford University Said School of Business.

Ann O'Leary is the Director of the Children and Families Program at Next Generation. Her work includes spearheading "Too Small to Fail"—Next Generation's joint initiative with the Clinton Foundation to help parents and businesses take meaningful actions to improve the health and well-being of children younger than age 5—developing a national research portfolio, and leading policy activities in California. O'Leary also serves as a Senior Fellow at the Center for American Progress, where she writes about work-family policies. She previously served as a lecturer in health law at University of California, Berkeley, School of Law; as Executive Director of the Berkeley Center on Health, Economic & Family Security; as a Deputy City Attorney for the city of San Francisco; and as Legislative Director to Sen. Hillary Rodham Clinton (D-NY). She also led the children and family policy team on the White House Domestic Policy Council under President Bill Clinton. O'Leary is a member of the board for KQED, Northern California's public news provider, and the East Bay Community Law Center, a legal aid clinic for low-income community members. She earned a bachelor's degree from Mount Holyoke College, a master's in education policy from Stanford University, and a law degree from the University of California, Berkeley, School of Law.

Dr. Nicole Smith is a Research Professor and Senior Economist at the Georgetown University Center on Education and the Workforce, where she leads the Center's econometric and methodological work. Smith has developed a framework for restructuring long-term occupational and educational projections. She is part of a team of economists working on a project to map, forecast, and monitor human capital development and career pathways. Smith was born in Trinidad and Tobago and graduated with honors from the University of the West Indies, or UWI, St. Augustine campus, with a double major in economics and mathematics. She was the recipient of the Sir Arthur Lewis Memorial Prize for outstanding research at the master's level at the UWI and was a co-recipient of the 2007 Arrow Prize for Junior Economists for educational mobility research. She received her Ph.D. in economics from American University in Washington, D.C. Prior to joining the Center, Smith was a faculty member in economics at Gettysburg College in Pennsylvania and at the University of the West Indies, St. Augustine campus. Her current research is on the role of cognitive and noncognitive competencies in shaping workforce outcomes and intergenerational education mobility.

Eve Tahmincioglu is the Director of Communications at Families and Work Institute and an award-winning labor columnist. She is the voice behind the popular CareerDiva.net blog and the author of *From the Sandbox to the Corner Office: Lessons Learned on the Journey to the Top.* As a columnist and business reporter for NBC-News.com, she was named top online business columnist in 2009 by the Society of American Business Editors and Writers, was awarded a Jesse H. Neal National Business Journalism Award in 2005 for team small business coverage for *BusinessWeek,* and earned a fellowship with the Economics Institute for Journalists in 1995. In addition, *CareerBuilder* and CNN named her one of the top 10 career/workplace tweeters on Twitter, and *CareerBuilder* and Forbes named CareerDiva.net one of the top blogs in the country. She has more than 20 years of experience as a business reporter working as a staffer for *Women's Wear Daily,* United Press International, and the *St. Petersburg Times.* She was also a longtime contributor to *The New York Times, BusinessWeek,* and *Workforce Management.*

Join the
Conversation

www.shriverreport.org